AT THE BOUNDARIES OF LAW

AT THE BOUNDARIES OF LAW

FEMINISM AND LEGAL THEORY

Edited by
MARTHA ALBERTSON FINEMAN
and
NANCY SWEET THOMADSEN

Routledge □ New York London

Published in 1991 by

Routledge
An imprint of Routledge, Chapman and Hall, Inc.
29 West 35 Street
New York, NY 10001

Published in Great Britain by

Routledge
11 New Fetter Lane
London EC4P 4EE

Printed in the United States of America

Library of Congress Cataloging-in-Publication Data

At the boundaries of law : feminism and legal theory / edited by
Martha Albertson Fineman and Nancy Sweet Thomadsen.
p. cm.
"Papers . . . selected from a larger group presented over a four-year period [1985–1989] at sessions of the Feminism and Legal Theory Conference at the University of Wisconsin"—Introd.
Includes bibliographical references (p.
ISBN 0-415-90305-X. — ISBN 0-415-90306-8 (pbk.)
1. Women—Legal status, laws, etc.—Congresses. 2. Women—Social conditions—Congresses. 3. Feminism—Congresses. I. Fineman, Martha. II. Thomadsen, Nancy Sweet, 1950– . III. Feminism and Legal Theory Conference (1985–1989 : University of Wisconsin)
K644.A55 1985
346.01'34—dc20 90-8743
[342.6134]

British Library Cataloguing in Publication Data

At the boundaries of the law : feminism and legal theory.
1. Great Britain, Society, Role of women, Legal aspects.
I. Fineman, Martha A. 1943– II. Thomadsen, Nancy Sweet, 1950–
344.102878

ISBN 0-415-90305-X
ISBN 0-415-90306-8 pbk.

Dedication

From Martha: To the memory of my Mother, the promise of my daughters and the joy of my granddaughter.

From Nancy: To my parents, Arthur and Shirley Sweet and to Larry, Raph, Jordie T. and Kevin P.

Acknowledgments

I would like to thank the governing board of the Institute For Legal Studies for their continued financial support for the Feminism and Legal Theory Conference which produced these (and other) wonderful papers. I particularly want to thank Dorothy L. Davis for her patience and supportive assistance as the Institute's Administrative Assistant and Cathy Meschievitz, Associate Director, without whom no Conference budget could have been formed. Margo A. O'Brien Hokanson and Sherry Lund also provided essential assistance. David M. Trubek as Director of the Institute consistently supplied needed encouragement and helpful criticism of the feminist legal theory project from its beginning. My student, Anne MacArthur, provided invaluable assistance and essential support in running several of the conferences as did Belinda Bennett the year she was my graduate student.

M.A.F.—Madison, 1990

Contents

Introduction

Martha Albertson Fineman

This book is the product of an increased interest in feminist scholarship as it relates to legal issues. Law is an area relatively untouched by the post-modern currents that have washed through other disciplines, but now appears to be caught within tides of critical methodologies and conclusions that threaten its very roots. This collection of papers was selected from a larger group presented over a four year period at sessions of the Feminism and Legal Theory Conference at the University of Wisconsin. They reveal that feminist legal theory represents both a subject and a methodology that are still in the process of being born. There are no "right" paths, clearly defined. This scholarship, however, can be described as sharing the objective of raising questions about women's relationships to law and legal institutions.

Theory and Practice

Given the newness of the inquiry, many practitioners of feminist legal theory are more comfortable describing their work as an example of feminist "methodology" rather than an exposition of "theory." Some in fact believe that method *is* theory in its most (and perhaps only) relevant form.

In my opinion, the real distinction between feminist approaches to theory (legal and otherwise) and the more traditional varieties of legal theory is a belief in the desirability of the concrete. Such an emphasis also has had rather honorable nonfeminist adherents. For example, Robert Merton coined the term "theory of the middle range" to describe work that mediated between "stories" and "grand" theory. He described such

---

This Introduction is based on a presentation made at the University of Florida in 1989. It will be published in the Florida Law Review in 1990.

scholarship as being better than mere storytelling or mindless empiricism as well as superior to vague references to the relationships between ill-defined abstractions (Merton, 1967, p. 68).

Feminist scholarship, in nonlaw areas at least, has tended to focus on specifics (Weedon, 1987, p. 11). Feminist legal scholarship, however, recently seems to be drifting toward abstract grand theory presentations. Carol Smart has warned that feminist legal theorists are in danger of creating in their writing the impression that it is possible to identify from among the various feminist legal theories that are in competition one specific form of feminist jurisprudence that will represent the "superior" (or true) version. She labels this totalizing tendency, evident in the work of many of the most well-known North American legal feminists, as the construction of a "scientific feminism," and she is explicitly critical of such grand theorizing (Smart, 1988, p. 71). The papers presented here avoid such theorizing and are connected with the material and concrete.

Grand theorizing represents the creation of a new form of positivism in a search for universal truths discoverable and ascertainable within the confines of the methodology of critical legal analysis. Middle range theory, by contrast, mediates between the material circumstances of women's lives and the grand realizations that law is gendered, that law is a manifestation of power, that law is detrimental to women. These realizations have previously been hidden or ignored in considerations of those laws that regulate women's lives. As the articles in this collection illustrate, such inequities in the legal treatment of women are best exposed by referencing and emphasizing the circumstances of their lives.

One cannot help but be aware of the difficulty of trying to do work using middle range feminist methodology within the confines of legal theory, however. Not only is there the pull toward grand theory that operates to categorize less grand scholarship as "nontheoretical," but I fear that feminist sensibilities become lost or absorbed into the morass of legal concepts and words. I, for one, am a legal scholar who has lost faith. Feminism, it seems, has not and, perhaps, cannot transform the law. Rather, the law, when it becomes the battleground, threatens to transform feminism. This is true I believe because of the obvious pull and power of the law as a "dominant discourse"—one which is self-contained (though incomplete and imperfect), self-congratulatory (though not introspective nor self-reflective) and self-fulfilling (though not inevitable nor infallible).

In order to even have a chance to be incorporated into and considered compatible with legal theory, feminist thought must adapt, even if it does not totally conform, to the words and concepts of legal discourse. Feminism may enter as the challenger, but the tools inevitably employed are those of the androphile master. And, the character of the tools determines to a large extent the shape and design of the resulting construction. It seems to me, therefore, that the task of feminists concerned with the law and legal institutions must be to create and explicate feminist methods and theories that explicitly challenge and compete with the existing totalizing nature of grand legal theory. Such a feminist strategy would set its middle range theory in opposition to law—outside of law. That is the task that has also defined the creation of this collection.

Feminist Methodologies

In these articles, there are several characteristics that in various permutations and combinations provide examples for the construction of feminist legal analyses that challenge existing legal theory and paradigms. First, feminist methodology is often critical. The critical stance is gained from adopting an explicitly woman-focused perspective, a perspective informed by women's experiences. I personally believe that anything labeled feminist theory can *not* be "gender-neutral" and will often be explicitly critical of that paradigm as having historically excluded women's perspectives from legal thought. "Gender-sensitive" feminism, however, should not be viewed as lacking legitimacy because of an inappropriate bias. Rather, it is premised on the need to expose and correct *existing* bias. "Gender-sensitive" feminism seeks to correct the imbalance and unfairness in the legal system resulting from the implementation of perspectives excluding attention to the circumstances of women's gendered lives, even on issues that intimately affect those lives.

There is a tendency in traditional legal scholarship to view the status quo as unbiased or neutral. This is the logical place for feminist analysis to begin—as an explicit challenge to the notion of bias, as contrasted with the concepts of perspective and position. Feminist legal theory can demonstrate that what *is* is *not* neutral. What *is* is as "biased" as that which challenges it, and what *is* is certainly no more "correct" than that which challenges it, and there can be no refuge in the status quo. Law has developed over time in the context of theories and institutions which are controlled by men and reflect their concerns. Historically, law has been a "public" arena and its focus has been on public concerns. Traditionally, women belonged to the "private" recesses of society, in families, in relationships controlled and defined by men, in silence.

A second characteristic of much of feminist work is that it uses a methodology that critically evaluates not only outcomes but the fundamental concepts, values and assumptions embedded in legal thought (MacKinnon, 1982, pp. 239–40). Results or outcomes in cases decided under existing legal doctrines are not irrelevant to this inquiry, but criticizing them is only a starting point. Too many legal scholars end their inquiry with a critique of results and recommendations for "tinkering"-type reforms without considering how the very conceptual structure of legal thought condemns such reforms to merely replicating injustices (Fineman, 1986). When, as is so often the case, the basic tenets of legal ideology are at odds with women's gendered lives, reforms based on those same tenets will do little more than the original rules to validate and accommodate women's experiences.

From this perspective, feminism is a political theory concerned with issues of power. It challenges the conceptual bases of the status quo by assessing the ways that power controls the production of values and standards against which specific results and rules are measured. Law represents both a discourse and a process of power. Norms created by and enshrined in law are manifestations of power relationships. These norms are coercively applied and justified in part by the perception that they are "neutral" and "objective." An appreciation of this fact has led many feminist scholars to focus on the legislative and political processes in the construction of law rather than on what judges are doing. It has also led many feminists to concentrate on social and cultural perceptions and manifestations of law and legality at least as much as on formal legal doctrinal developments.

Implicit in the assertion that feminism must be a politically rather than a legally focused method or theory is a belief about law and social change that assumes the relative powerlessness of law to transform society as compared to other ideological institutions of social constitution within our culture. Law can reflect social change, even facilitate it, but can seldom if ever initiate it. No matter what the formal legal articulation, implementation of legal rules will track and reflect the dominant conceptualizations and conclusions of the majority culture. Thus, while law can be used to highlight the social and political aspects it reflects, it is more a mirror than a catalyst when it comes to effecting enduring social change.

A third characteristic of much of feminist legal methodology is that the vision it propounds or employs seeks to present alternatives to the existing order. This may be, of course, a natural outgrowth of other characteristics of feminist legal thought, particularly when it is critical and political. I place it as separate, however, because an independent goal of much of feminist work is to present oppositional values. It is often at its core radically nonassimilationist, resistant to mere inclusion in dominant social institutions as the solution to the problems in women's gendered lives. In fact, the larger social value of feminist methodology may lie in its ability to make explicit oppositional stances vis-à-vis the existing culture. The objective of feminism has to be to transform society, and it can do so only by persistently challenging dominant values and defiantly not assimilating into the status quo. The point of making women's experiences and perspective a central factor in developing social theory is to change "things," not to merely change women's perspective or their position vis-à-vis existing power relationships. To many feminist scholars, therefore, assimilation is failure, while opposition is essential for a feminist methodology applied to law.

One other characteristic of much of feminist legal theory is that it is evolutionary in nature. It does not represent doctrine carved in stone or even printed in statute books. Feminist methodology at its best represents a contribution to a series of ongoing debates and discussions which take as a given that "truth" changes over time as circumstances change and that gains and losses, along with wisdom recorded, are not immutable but part of an evolving story. Feminist legal theory referencing women's lives, then, must define and undertake the "tasks of the moment." As the tasks of the future cannot yet be defined, any particular piece of feminist legal scholarship is only a step in the long journey feminist legal scholars have begun.

Within feminist legal thought and, indeed, within the articles included in this collection, there is explicit contest and criticism as well as implicit disagreement about the wisdom of pragmatic uses of law, the effectiveness of law as an instrument of social change and, most broadly, the importance of law as a focus for feminist study. Some feminist scholarship reveals antagonist, even violent disagreement with other feminist works. Disagreements aside, however, it seems clear to me that feminist legal theory has lessons for all of society, not just for women or legal scholars. Ultimately, it is the members of our audience that will judge the effectiveness of our individual and collective voices.

Conclusion

Feminist concerns are, and must continue to be, the subject of discourses located outside of law. Law as a dominant rhetorical system has established concepts that limit and contain feminist criticisms. Feminist theory must develop free of the restraints imposed by legalized concepts of equality and neutrality or it will be defined by them. Law is too crude an instrument to be employed for the development of theory that is anchored in an appreciation of differences in the social and symbolic position of women and men in our culture. Law can be and should be the *object* of feminist inquiry, but to position law and law reform as the *objective* of such theorizing is to risk having incompletely developed feminist innovations distorted and appropriated by the historically institutionalized and inextractable dictates of the "Law."

The scholarship presented here is critical, is political, is part of ongoing debates and is concerned with methods and processes that comprise law. It is typical of the very best feminist legal scholarship in that it is about law in its broadest form, as a manifestation of power in society, and, for the most part, it recognizes that there is no division between law and power. Many of the articles recognize that law is not only found in courts and cases, in legislatures and statutes, but also in implementing institutions such as the professions of social work and law enforcement. Others reflect the fact that law is found in discourse and language used in everyday life reflecting understandings about "Law." It is evident in the beliefs and assumptions we hold about the world in which we live and in the norms and values we cherish.

I hope that the reader enjoys the excursion to the boundaries of law undertaken in this volume. A few are sure to be disturbed by some of the work presented, others, hopefully, will be inspired. Feminist legal theory has begun to expand the boundaries, redefine the borders of the law.

Madison, 1990

I

Perspectives from the Personal

Feminists assume that experiences of certain sorts facilitate genuine theoretical insights and that recreation of such experiences are legitimate contributions to legal discourse. Not only can the right "stories" provoke insights into the nature of law, they do so with a richness that eludes traditional presentations by summary or succinct arguments. Just as an appropriate picture may be "worth a thousand words," so too the representations of personal experience can be worth an indefinite number of conventionally relevant abstract-theoretic arguments.

In affirming the connection between the personal and more theoretical discussions, feminist authors acknowledge the relevance of experience, social position, and perspective to the development of theories of law. All scholars approach their subject from some particular point in the social universe and from that perspective; no "unbiased" points of view exist. In feminist scholarship, explication of the position from which the scholarship emanates is a significant part of the methodology.

In Kathleen Lahey's "Reasonable Women and the Law," for example, the author uses descriptions of encounters between women and the law to reveal how the normative notion of "reasonable" behavior functions as a justification for dismissing the voices of persons judged not to conform. This presents a particular dilemma for feminist practitioners of law. On the one hand, women lawyers and judges, as well as clients, must exemplify "reasonableness" in order to be taken seriously. At the same time, women who exemplify the accepted norms of reasonable behavior serve as standards against which non-conforming women are judged deficient. They are thus often unwittingly complicit in the victimization of "unreasonable" women. There are deep psychic costs of adopting an alien persona in order to conform to accepted societal standards.

Patricia Williams's personal struggle to come to terms with her family history, particularly in relation to her great-great grandmother's experience as a slave woman, leads with startling directness to insight into the legal saga of "surrogate" mother Mary Beth Whitehead. Williams's stories, although very different from those presented by Lahey, echoes many of the same general themes: the experience of wrestling with feelings of self-betrayal in choosing to enter the legal profession, recognition of the deep effect the perceptions of others have on one's own sense of being, sensitivity to the process of making distinctions between those persons who "count" and those who don't, as well as an appreciation of the vast categories of things about which we dare not speak.

From a different perspective, unacknowledged barriers to speech in the courtroom is the focus of Lucie White's paper. Her story is based on her experience representing a woman from whom reimbursement for an alleged welfare "overpayment" had been demanded. The author uses this to show how, although guaranteed the formal right to a hearing, persons in socially subordinate positions often find their ability to speak and be heard undercut by their vulnerability to retaliation, by their lack of skill in the dominant mode of courtroom discourse, and by the externally legally imposed constraints of "relevancy." The emphasis of this paper is on barriers to the speech of women who are legal clients, but the pressure on practitioners of law to endorse strategies which are likely to be effective, rather than ones which genuinely reflect their understanding of the case, is also illustrated.

1

Reasonable Women and the Law

Kathleen A. Lahey

I

Women's struggle for access to the legal process has been many things: It has been a strategy for improving the distribution of social goods between women and men; it has been a goal in its own right; it has been a method of defending women against the worst oppressions of women; it is a way to construct the "public" (in patriarchal terms) for women, and on terms that women can tolerate. Over the last one hundred and fifty years, a lot has been thought, said, and written about these faces of women's struggles in law, and an impressive body of feminist jurisprudence is now being constructed out of this discourse.

There is another aspect of this struggle, an aspect that is not as easy to think, talk, or write about: the strategies that men and male sympathizers have used to keep women from succeeding in their struggles have affected the women who engage in them. These strategies—men's strategies—have also affected our beliefs about the ways that women should be.

On one level, this is merely a statement of the all too obvious. One of the greatest accomplishments of feminist legal scholarship has been to identify the ideological content of masculist legal theory, of legal reasoning, and indeed, of reasoning itself. To point out that this ideological content actually affects the real and lived lives of women is merely to demonstrate that ideas become real through ideology and that reality affects ideology. This is nothing new.

On another level, however, women who involve themselves with power processes live within the shadow of ideologies that are compatible with the acquisition and exercise of power. Thus it would not be surprising

---

Reprinted with permission of the author.

to find that women who are involved in power processes are themselves influenced by the very forces they think they are combatting. And to the extent that this influence is effective, those women (all of us) must be blind to it, or think that it is minimal, or think that it is something they can control, or think that it is not relevant to what they are trying to do.

In other words, this second level of women's struggle has to do with the ways in which women who are involved in using the legal process to improve the status of women embody or become complicit in the very values, processes, ideologies, and structures against which they are struggling.

This embodiment, complicity, goes by many names. Some women think of it as a survival technique under conditions of male supremacy. Other women describe it as the "gatekeeper price." Others talk in terms of cooptation or assimilation. All of these labels are accurate. Women do have to survive, especially when they live under conditions of male supremacy. Women do have to pay a price to the gatekeeper who—male or female—enforces ideologies that perpetuate male supremacy. These forces do coopt, because power is powerful. Many women do become assimilated to existing power structures, because in assimilation lies safety, a sense of accomplishment, a source of enhanced self esteem. And women who do not have to struggle for bare survival, but who have some racial or class or other privileges, are also motivated by their particular wants: they want to feel safe, they want to feel a sense of accomplishment in their living and working, they want to enjoy enhanced self esteem. All of this seems to be entirely natural.

But this essay is not just about women's embodiment of oppression, of complicity. It is also about the steps we might all take toward liberating ourselves from our own personal and political histories as we work within law for the liberation of women as a sex class. The first step toward changing women's relationships to structures of sex-gender oppression is to identify the ways we, women working in law, embody many of the forces we are trying to change. The second step might be to imagine ways of talking about this embodiment, this complicity, that show respect and compassion for women's realities at the same time that we do not deny them. This is a difficult balance to achieve; without compassion and respect, naming our own complicities can all too easily slide into nihilism, trashing, the search for "political correctness," knowing better, betrayal, or moralism. Ways of addressing our complicities must avoid those reactions.

The third step, and by far the most difficult one, I think, is to imagine how women can work with each other despite our varying commitments to respect, compassion, responsibility for the quality of our interactions, and honesty, and despite our varying abilities to refrain from nihilism, trashing, the search for "political correctness," denial, betrayal, or moralizing. Talking about internalized oppression, complicity, might in fact be easier than actually working together to change the conditions of women's existence, because the process of rejecting personal complicity may well uncover the personal damage that has made that complicity inevitable. This culture damages women, and damaged people have even more reason to hold tightly to their own survival techniques. In this third step, then, women need to create healing processes within and alongside their own liberatory processes.

I do not claim to have any special insight into any of these three steps, beyond being able to say that I think we need to take them, are taking them. My contribution to taking these steps is to begin by talking about the concept of "reasonableness" in legal discourse from my vantage point as a "white" lesbian survivor of various kinds of abuse. "Reasonableness" is perhaps one of the most central fixtures of north american legal culture, and it is used to silence women who try to speak in law, often before they even get to open their mouths. It is my contention that various kinds of abuse—racism, sexism, classism, heterosexism, able-ism, as well as physical, sexual, and emotional abuse—condition and shape people in ways that often make it easy to label them "unreasonable," and hence not entitled to the same respect, compassion, and legal protections that others enjoy.

The method of this essay is experiential. I first think through some of my own senses of difference and how that has affected my consciousness. I then quote at length Kobina Sekyi's story of Kwesi, an alienated British-trained African barrister. The rest of the essay is made up of other stories of women whose lives have been profoundly affected by their encounters with "reasonableness" in law. Not surprisingly, these are stories of abuse. I try to tell them with respect and compassion because I think these are the people we have to have respect for before we can begin to understand the relationship between reasonableness and law.

II

I am five years old, maybe nearly six. I am strong, fast, usually sort of funny. I feel myself somewhat damaged, but the important thing is that I do feel myself. Damaged in my being, I have only a few memories. I treasure one memory in particular, both for the simple reason that I have it and because of what it is.

When I have this memory, it is more like looking at a picture than like having sensations. I remember having the picture of what I am about to tell you in my eyes, and I remember this picture going from my eyes to my mind, where it is stored and can be called up at will for me to look at inside my head, talk about. But the memory is empty in a curious way, an emptiness of knowing that it is I who have this memory, I who made this memory, but that I am walled off from myself within myself because I can remember the seeing of what I am about to tell you without remembering the I who was seeing it.

> This distinction is crucial:
>
> It is the difference
between
remembering being
and
remembering pictures
of being.

If you can imagine that distinction, then you can understand what this emptiness is. You can also understand why remembering is so important even when I cannot remember being the child who has done the remembering, can remember only as pictures what others might actually remember.

I try once more to remember that moment: I remember seeing through the eyes that made these pictures that I call a memory; I remember that I must have had legs to stand on, to see this thing that became this memory; I remember that I must have felt the air with my skin—the air was probably hot, this is a summer story—when I saw this thing that became this memory; I remember that my face must have felt hot when I realized what I must have realized when I saw this thing that has become this memory; I remember that I felt sort of invisible at that moment; I remember that I felt sort of neat inside myself for feeling what I was feeling at that moment; I remember that I felt sure that this was something I would not be able to talk to anyone about for a long, long time, if ever. It is difficult to keep my present sense of how I feel in my being out of my memory, if any, of how I felt while I saw what has become this memory. As best I can reconstruct it, this is how I felt then: seeing, standing, possibly hot, maybe a bit embarrassed, sort of invisible, neat, certain that I would not be able to tell anyone. And quite possibly totally fascinated, because I think I knew that I was seeing part of my life.

I am five years old, maybe nearly six. I am strong, fast, usually sort of funny. I feel myself somewhat damaged. I am standing at the side of an enormous hole, a huge excavation that will become the basement of our new house. It is a bright blue summer day, there is no breeze, but there is some edge to the air because it is not quite hot. It is very bright, there are not many other buildings because this is a new neighborhood, not even a neighborhood yet: it is just a field with some houses here and there, and this huge excavation that will become the basement of a house.

I am five years old, maybe nearly six. I am strong, fast, usually sort of funny. I feel myself somewhat damaged. There I am at the side of this huge excavation, not big enough to climb down in it, knowing that if I were to try to do it (and I do not seriously think about trying to do it, that thought does not actually crystallize in my mind), I would get into trouble, never mind with who, I just know it the way I knew a lot of things.

I am five years old, maybe nearly six. I am strong, fast, usually sort of funny. I feel myself somewhat damaged. I am at the side of this huge excavation, not big enough to climb down into it, knowing that if I were to try to do it, I could do it, that it would be fun, but that I am not to try to do that. Not now, anyway. And I watch a big girl, a bigger girl than I, a strong, fast, and totally serious girl, climb nonchalantly down into this huge excavation, taking her time, completely absorbed, having a good time. And I can only watch.

I know that the fascination I felt when I watched this big girl, this bigger girl, nonchalantly climb down into this huge excavation and seriously poke around in what was to become the basement of our new house was due not only to the fact that this girl was doing this, but was also due to the fact that I had only recently, in meeting her, found out what it felt like to be in love with/totally fascinated by/completely and dopily and uncontrollably infatuated with another girl: a bigger girl, it is true, but a girl nonetheless. And I felt myself to be somewhat damaged.

So this is the memory, the remembering that I cannot remember the feeling of, but can remember the image of, the picture of: I am standing at the edge of this huge excavation, this enormous hole, my future basement, on a bright blue and somewhat hard-edged day, my entire body suffused with the thrill of seeing this girl that I loved absolutely with my entire and whole being, completely fascinated by her nonchalance and her climbing down there, poking around with a stick, I think, not paying any attention to me at all, ignoring me, even, knowing that it was totally out of the question for me even to think about climbing down there too or trying to talk to her, loving being able simply to see her do all of that, wondering why I felt the way I did about her, loving the look of her very beautiful and quite serious face, her shiny dark hair, her energy, her nonchalance, her climbing, my loving her. And knowing that I remember that I felt sure this was something I would not be able to talk to anyone about for a long, long time, if ever.

So there I was: captured in that moment of knowledge that something had happened to me, something that had to do with the fact that watching this particular girl climb down into that huge excavation on that particular bright blue and hard-edged day touched my sense of what it is that makes life so wonderful. It was, as they say, a moment of self-recognition. It was also and at the same time: a moment of celebration; a moment of despair; a moment that I still cannot remember actually feeling, although it is obvious that I must have felt a lot right then; a moment in which I learned, if I had not known before then, what conscious silence felt like, what not-being-able-to-name-something felt like, what not being able to do or be what I wanted to do or be felt like, and what being infatuated with girls felt like.

The end of this story of remembering is not nearly as important as the actual memory itself.

> I never did tell anyone.
>
> The girl and I became next door neighbors.
>
> I loved her for ten or twenty years, I forget exactly which.
>
> I even forgot which of the two sisters who lived together next door was the one that I loved. (I think it might have been the one who was three or four years older than me.)
>
> I forget when it was that I actually stopped loving her.
>
> If it is the sister that I think it was, she now lives in the same small town my own sister lives in on the other side of this continent. This is unremarkable to me now.
>
> My own sister reported to me recently that shortly after the time that this thing I remember took place, I became hysterical, cried and cried one evening, was unconsolable, crying because I said that I would never have any children.
>
> I never did have any children from my own body, but I do have two daughters from my heart.

III

What does any of this have to do with complicity? with reasonable women in the law? with women's possibilities for political action?

I can only say what I, as an adult remembering myself at that moment of self-recognition, have learned from that remembering—and from that not-feeling: I have learned that central to my identity in ways that go beyond the socially-ascribed meaning of the word *lesbian* is my woman focus. I have learned that if I think of myself as a woman who is as indifferent to other women as are women who are not so centrally woman-identified, I get out of touch with what I am really thinking, really feeling, when I interact with other women. I have learned that I have been aware of this since I was at least five or six years old, and that I must have learned to act as if I were not this way at the very moment that I knew this about myself. I have learned that I have been totally silenced about the way I feel about women for a major portion of my life; even though I formally crystallized the thought that women could be lesbian, and that I might be lesbian myself, when I was around fifteen years old, my entire life has been a continuous coming out to the recognition of how powerful this identification has always been for me. I have learned that it is better to not tell, to not identify, to not bother other women with the details of my feelings for women, to distance myself from other women as a way to protect myself from their reactions to my feelings about women, to avoid intimacy as a method of self-protection, to separate my lesbianness from my politics, to always try to seem to be reasonable.

These are the lessons of denial. These are also the lessons of silence, of complicity, of self-imposed separation from others.

> Not that other women are actually endangered by my attentions. I am not usually attracted to women who are not attracted to me at some level; indeed, one of the ways I know whether a woman is at all woman-centered is by whether she seems to be at all attracted to me. Few straight women actually are.
>
> But women who are attracted to me—even on a friendly level—who do not want me, themselves, or other people to suspect them of being anything but heterosexually identified, usually stay well away from me. This destroys on a deep level many possibilities for creating our own meanings of "reasonable," for working together.

IV

Kobina Sekyi published "a psychological study of a type of present-day [1930] young Gold Coastian who has been educated partly in the English manner" as "Extracts from 'The Anglo-Fanti' " in Nancy Cunard's *Negro: An Anthology* (Paris: Hours Press, 1934). The problem he struggles to name and make real is "Europeanization," a process by which colonized people are rendered intolerable to themselves at the same time that their mannerisms do not make them tolerable enough to their colonizers to bring the condition of colonization to an end. Here are extracts from his story of Kwesi, a young Fanti. Kobina Sekyi wrote this after returning from England, where he was educated as a barrister:

"There exists a sperm of snobbishness in the character of our young friend; it is involved in Europeanisation as it exists in spheres of influence, and shows itself clearly in the feeling of superiority exhibited by the boy in European clothes, or the boy whose parents are educated in the European sense. This feeling is supported by the meek acceptance of the situation which characterises the boy in national costume or the boy whose parents are illiterate. The burden of bad precedent and illegitimate prestige established under the aegis of the early missionaries is too much for the boys on either side. . . .

"The sperm of snobbishness develops. Strange conceptions of behaviour proper to Europeans and their satellites are gathered from the many books on European life put forth in Europe by European authors. Kwesi and his companions are convinced that European life is the ideal. Clubs are therefore formed with the avowed object of cultivating the accomplishments of the perfect European gentleman. The acquisition of fluency in speaking English is sought by means of debating societies and daily conversations in English. Boys who have passed through the Low School and are signalising their completed education by discarding the national costume give "breakfasts" at which etiquette as prescribed in books such as *Don't,* and *Rules and Manners of Good Society,* is *de rigueur.*

[Kobina Seyki then tells how Kwesi travels to England to study a profession. The narrative then focuses on his life in England.]

"It does not take him long to find out he is regarded as a savage even by the starving unemployed who ask him for alms. Amusing questions are often put to him as to whether he wore clothes before he came to England; whether it was safe for white men to go to his country since their climate was unsuitable to civilised people; whether wild animals wandered at large in the streets of his native town. He concludes that the people of the class to which his landlady belongs are, to say the least, poorly informed as to the peoples of other countries, especially of those parts known as 'The Colonies.' On the whole he is much disappointed with England as he has seen it by the time he is six months in England. His countrymen resident in London hear of him. Those of his own age or thereabouts call on him and he calls on them. He complains of his disillusionment; but some laugh and say he is not the only one disappointed, and others tell him he has not yet seen anything of England. . . . At the educational establishments he notices that there is no better information possessed by his fellow-students respecting 'natives' in 'The Colonies' than is possessed by those less educated; the only difference is that the better educated people ask questions that are less rude.

"For the next three years at least Kwesi is engaged in qualifying himself for his professional career. He possesses no mean ability for study, therefore his professional course has no terrors for him; he knows he will finish in time. But the professional is such a small part of the more general training in all sorts of other pursuits and accomplishments which he receives during his sojourn in England. . . . In matters outside his professional course he is self-taught. The groundwork of these by-studies is the belief in the superiority of things European to things non-European, a belief he brought with him to England. It is true that his old ideas of European superiority have been much disturbed since he began to see England with his own eyes; but his friends, even those who have been similarly disillusioned have begun to accept certain disconcerting matters as incidental to civilisation, and, instead of arguing from the unpleasantness of such incidents to the inherent unwholesomeness of that to which they are incidental, they conclude somewhat perversely that whoever cannot explain away such unpleasantness is not civilised. This view, moreover, is much strengthened by the remarks let fall by certain friends belonging to classes reckoned as high, who, speaking from their very insular standpoint, by reason of their pardonable and exclusive appreciation of things English as against things non-English, and of things European as against things non-European, have given Kwesi and his friends to understand that those incidents of civilised life at first sight undesirable to those visiting Europe from Africa and Asia, are hallmarks of refinement.

[Kwesi acquires the class biases of the English upper classes; he feels patronized by white women, who act as though they are "conferring a favour" on Black men; Kwesi returns to Africa and sees himself through the eyes of his neighbors at the same time that he sees his neighbors through his own Europeanized eyes.]

"Since his return Kwesi . . . feels that . . . he must exercise a great deal of diplomacy. In his own family circle his undisguised partiality for the Fanti mode of doing everything is causing some uneasiness. . . . On the point of the national mode of clothing, therefore, the family have had to intimate to him their views: that no one will take any serious objection to his wearing such garb within the privacy of the family circle itself, if he is so whimsical as to prefer that mode of clothing: that if he seeks to go out in the national costume, such a thing may conceivably be permitted *at night:* that he ought not to forget that nobody before him has ever done such a thing as he evidently proposes to do, a course of conduct which, if he persists in it, will assuredly attach to himself the imputation of lunacy, and to them that of incapacity to control one of their children. . . . He disconcerts them by retorting . . . that if now it is proposed to keep him literally an Anglo-Fanti, Fanti as to his internals and English as to his externals, and such a conjunction pleases them, who are responsible for his having lived up to this time to become such a double person, then he will fall in with their wishes.

[Kwesi struggles against the hegemony of Europeanization; he refuses to marry; his family worries that he is secretly married to a white woman in England; he finally marries a Europeanized Fanti woman in an English wedding ceremony; he refuses to participate with her in Europeanized social activities; she divorces him through local custom; he finally comes to understand the causes of Europeanization and of his own tragedy; he has a nervous breakdown, becomes ill, and dies. He leaves one last wish:]

"[I]f at any time any other member of the family, trained in England, on coming back, preferred to live as a Fanti man who had merely been trained in England, instead of living as a [B]lack Englishman who understood Fanti, they should leave such a one to live his own life as long as he was not undutiful; they should not seek to constrain him to live an artificial life; for the Fanti man's life was at least as good as the Englishman's life, and the mere accident of scientific development in the invention of machinery was not sufficient in itself to give any nation ground for calling itself civilised."

V

In her book on the moral development of women, *In a Different Voice,* Carol Gilligan reports on the differential impact that legal education has had on the ways that Hilary, a female lawyer, and Alex, a male lawyer, think about the rationalist ethic of justice and the particularized ethic of care.

Before going to law school, Alex apparently existed in an intellectual world of ethical conformity, formal rationality, and instrumentalized ideas of justice which involved logical hierarchies of moral values and insensitivity to the existence of differences. It was in law school, Carol Gilligan reports, that Alex apparently began to discover "the reality of differences" and "the contextual nature of morality and truth" as he realized that "you don't really know everything" and "you don't ever know that there is any absolute. I don't think that you ever know that there is an absolute right. What you do know is that you have to come down one way or the other. You have got to make a decision."

Carol Gilligan interprets Hilary's moral development as running in the opposite direction of Alex's. Describing Hilary as starting with an ethic of care and sensitivity to personal interdependences, she concludes that Hilary had "matured" morally when she decided to not help an opposing lawyer win a case for a client for whom Hilary felt some personal concern. Carol Gilligan concluded that Hilary made this decision out of a sense of self-preservation: she acted in conformity to the rules of professional ethics in order to protect her status as a lawyer.

Carol Gilligan decided that this was a "growth" experience for Hilary because she modified her ethic of care—which is based on an injunction against engaging in behavior that hurts other people—to include the principle that she is not obliged to honor such a principle when it would cause harm to herself: she says that Hilary discovers that there is "no way not to hurt" in some situations. As Carol Gilligan concludes, Hilary matured morally by recognizing that "both integrity and care must be included in a morality that can encompass the dilemmas of love and work that arise in adult life."

Carol Gilligan reads Hilary and Alex's stories as moving toward mature moralities that both struggle to integrate the "complementary ethics of care and justice at the level of the individual." Because Carol Gilligan's overall project is to demonstrate the gender links between these two opposing ethical grounds, she then argues that just as both Hilary and Alex integrate two distinct ethics—despite divergent starting points—in the course of becoming adults, men and women move toward "a greater convergence in judgment." She stops short of finding a complete synthesis, however, and does recognize "the dual contexts of justice and care," which means that one's "judgment depends on the way in which the problem is framed." Carol Gilligan's personal resolution of the tension between the ethics of justice and care, then, is to treat them as being dialectically interactive. In this dialectic, the absence of sensitivity to one of the two opposing ethics generates a "lack" which then transforms the dominant ethic.

This resolution ignores the disparities in power that usually travel with such a "lack." I found myself musing on Hilary's reasons for acting in an adversarial fashion toward a woman for whom she felt some concern. Many lawyers—among them committed feminist lawyers and other radical lawyers—do not hesitate to tell their adversaries how to win a case that is supposedly being conducted in an adversarial fashion, despite what the rules of practice or canons of ethics may have to say about such conduct. Such occasions are rare, but do occur, as when a feminist lawyer is required by her employer to foreclose on a single woman's house.

I have tentatively decided that Hilary did not necessarily act *against* her own personal sense of ethics as care when she chose to act as she did—she may well have been coerced into acting in conformity with a distasteful set of rules (such as "do not sell out your own client") because of the realities of her dependence on her employer, her perceived need to keep her license to practice law as a condition of her own survival, or her sense of her own powerlessness to change the rules of the game she has, for many reasons, chosen to play. Compared with the quality of Alex's abandonment of a sense of the logical hierarchy of values as a result of what he learned in law school, Hilary's maturing judgment, which is said to converge with Alex's, looks more like a sensible and realistic compromise with extensively organized systems of domination. This does not, to me, seem to be particularly empowering.

Alex's "maturity," however, does look like empowerment. As most law teachers can appreciate, Alex's newfound ability to shift from one ethical paradigm to another, without moral qualms and as the strategy of the case dictates, is the essence of "thinking like a lawyer." Thus Alex emerges as a moral degenerate whose "ethic of care" is largely instrumental—yet Carol Gilligan concludes that he is morally more mature.

Increasingly, feminists are learning that Hilary's decision to cut herself off from her feelings about her adversary's plight is a way to "take care" of herself. And indeed it is. But look at what such self care involves, and look at the professional and personal contexts in which there are no other ways to take care of oneself. And think about who is ultimately empowered when those are women's choices.

VI

Compare the saga of Julia Girvin. (Julia Girvin is a pseudonym.) Julia Girvin is a labor activist and organizer from atlantic Canada who was admitted to a Canadian law school on alternative criteria. The members of her selection committee were particularly impressed by her published writing, organizing, and political abilities.

Applying her life skills to law school examinations, Julia Girvin failed all but one of her courses in first year. She was allowed on petition to repeat first year, whereupon she failed all of her first year courses the second time through. She was then dismissed from law school. This story has something of a happy ending: Julia Girvin, her life skills honed to near perfection by now, filed a law suit against the then dean of the law school. The suit was settled in her favor. Where had Julia Girvin gone wrong? Julia Girvin had refused (some still say she was unable) to adopt the ungrounded and cynical mode of analysis ("thinking like a lawyer") called for in law school examinations, in which the student is expected to pick through a fact situation, test it for affinity to one or another area of legal doctrine, conjure up "arguments" designed to convince the teacher that one can argue either side of the case with equal facility and conviction, draw in "policy" considerations that have to be balanced off against literalist doctrinal outcomes, and produce a persuasive and qualified result.

In her law school examinations, Julia Girvin chose to apply her life skills by discussing why the participants in these hypothetical transactions were on the verge of (or enmeshed in, or appealing) a law suit, what they ought to do in order to avoid getting involved in (or finishing, or appealing) a law suit, and how to reconcile their differences without compromising them in a way that violated their personal values. In short,

Julia Girvin refused to act as if the participants in these hypotheticals were forced to solve their problems within the legal process.

On the level of morality, Julia Girvin rejected a definition of moral "maturity" which required her to substitute a "converged" ethical base for her own highly contextual and realistic approach. Julia Girvin was not convinced that, in Alex's words, "you have to come down one way or another. You have got to make a decision." She simply refused to view the adversarial legal process as the best or the only way to resolve disputes.

Nor did Julia Girvin feel so intimidated by the canons of ethics—or so convinced that admission to the practice of law was crucial to her survival—that she decided that the principles of personal "integrity" obliged her, as they did Hilary, to adopt an alien mode of thinking purely for survival purposes. With a strong sense of her own identity as an organizer, Julia Girvin was not interested in exhibiting the relativistic adversarial skills of certifiable lawyers, even at the "cost" of never being certified as a lawyer. And in the end, she refused to recognize the legal professions' monopoly claim on dispute resolution, although she had skillfully used the legal process to get her perspective taken seriously.

VII

Linda Watt and Maureen Marshall were initially employed as clerical workers by the regional municipality of Niagara, Ontario. In the late 1970s, they both obtained positions as laborers. Although they were assigned to different work crews, they did work together frequently.

Before becoming a laborer, Linda Watt had already been labelled "difficult." Her "difficulty" might be traced back to her involvement in a disciplinary matter relating to a strike; soon after that matter was resolved (in her favor) she was suspended twice and then voluntarily transferred to the Roads Department under threat of termination. Years later, the personnel director for the municipality described her discipline record as the worst one he had ever seen. Her supervisor considered her work to be "totally unacceptable." He described her as "an immature spoiled child" who reacted strongly to any kind of discipline and whose work performance was so unsatisfactory that he did not feel he could trust her with any task. In performance evaluations, she had been accused of being habitually late, absent from work for various periods of time, and absent from her work station. Her attitude was described as negative and intimidating.

When Linda Watt moved to the Roads Department, she was first a temporary worker, and was later made permanent. Her first supervisor was not very enthusiastic about her work. During the first few months of her probationary period, he issued a reprimand for punctuality; that was the only occurrence of that kind while he remained her supervisor, and a later work report noted some overall improvement in her work performance. There was some suggestion that Linda Watt had not been able to do some heavy work, or had said she could not do it; that incident was said to have negatively affected her co-workers' attitudes toward her. She was also apparently involved in a relationship with a married co-worker. Her first supervisor later claimed that he would not have offered her permanent employment because he had not been impressed by her work, but said that he had made her permanent because he simply "did what he was told."

Her second supervisor was a different matter. His name was Alex Wales, and he was described variously as a "stern disciplinarian," "tough," "of the old school," and a "real barker." Alex Wales claimed that as an old friend of Linda Watt's father, he felt friendly toward her at the beginning, but that she was "quite unresponsive," "hostile," and "very unlike the only other female laborer in the roads crew, Maureen Marshall."

According to Linda Watt, Alex Wales personally made so many abusive and sexist comments (both to her and generally) that the working atmosphere became intolerable. When he transferred her to another road crew, allegedly for disciplinary reasons, she filed a complaint under the Ontario Human Rights Code for sexual harassment and disparate treatment. The written reasons given by John McCamus, the hearing officer (and then dean of Osgoode Hall Law School) for dismissing her complaint contain a trilogy of viewpoints on this abuse, and offer some insight into what is considered to be reasonable female behavior under such conditions.

"*I do not want . . . women working in my yard*" Alex Wales apparently told Linda Watt "I do not want or approve of women working in my yard." Alex Wales flatly denied making that statement at all, although he had openly conceded that he did not think that this sort of work was suitable for women: "I didn't think actually that women were ever put on this earth to do the work of men. That was my, just my way of being brought up." He had also said that this might not be as true of women "from one of the foreign countries where they are brought up on the farm and everything else, consequently their muscles develop, their leg muscles develop, they become where they are stronger than men."

John McCamus, the hearing officer, found that Linda Watt's version of this comment was "distorted" because she left off one bit of that statement; according to her original complaint, Alex Watt allegedly said: "I have bent over backwards for Maureen and you even though I do not want . . . women working in my yard." Thus John McCamus found that she lacked credibility. He did find that Alex Wales had made the statement, but decided that it was "essentially innocuous" when considered in its entirety. It was not evidence of prejudice, because Alex Wales had actually conceded that he was prejudiced. Nor was it evidence that Alex Wales had acted on admitted prejudices: "it is a strong statement to the contrary." He then decided that the transfer had not been motivated by sex discrimination, but merely by concerns over Linda Watt's work attitudes: "[T]he evident feistiness of the complainant's attitude and her apparently cavalier attitude to such matters as safety rules is something which would be especially troubling to a zealous supervisor such as Mr. Wales." And he found confirmation in Maureen Marshall: "The absence of similar treatment being meted out to Ms. Marshall is of some relevance."

Linda Watt "had lost all her femininity" Linda Watt said that Alex Wales had told her that she had "lost all her femininity" working in the yard. In her complaint, Linda Watt had said that this statement had "shocked" her. Alex Wales claimed that he had merely complained to Linda Watt that her "language was disgraceful and that she had 'detracted from her femininity' with her language in the yard." John McCamus agreed that "the language used by workers was quite crude and obscene as a general matter. There was a good deal of abuse, good-natured or otherwise, meted out in conversation." John McCamus pointed to evidence that Linda Watt also used crude language: she had "a notorious tongue," and she had conceded that she regularly used profane language.

John McCamus concluded that correcting Linda Watt for her language in such a situation would ordinarily constitute a double standard: if foul language on such a work site was considered to be acceptable for men, it should also be acceptable for women. He also understood that such a double standard was sexist and violated Linda Watt's civil liberties: "Mr. Wales's views, however naturally they may have come to him as a result of his cultural environment, are virtually a caricature of the sorts of attitudes which led to the social injustice which the Code attempts to remedy."

Nonetheless, John McCamus ruled that such a sexist comment and such a double standard did not in this case violate her civil liberties or constitute sexual harassment because "the holding of such a view, surely, is not a very startling phenomenon." He felt that Alex Wales was merely communicating to Linda Watt "mere personal distaste" for her crude language. Therefore it was not a statement that would "reasonably 'shock' a person in the complainant's position."

The "dead animal" comment A third incident is described in John McCamus' opinion: "At approximately 8:15 one morning, a small group, including at least the complainant, Ms. Marshall and Mr. Brown, were sitting at a picnic table in the yard awaiting work orders. There was a very unpleasant odor in the yard as someone had apparently left a dead animal in one of the trucks. The complainant asked what the cause of the aroma was and Mr. Brady, who was nearby, is alleged by the complainant to have come over to her and pulled apart her legs, insinuating that she was the source of the unpleasant odor. It was Mr. Brady's evidence that although he did make a remark in general terms about the odor, he did not touch the complainant in the fashion alleged. A good deal of evidence in these proceedings was led on this particular point and I am satisfied that at the very least, Mr. Brady made a remark which specifically referred to the complainant in this context or, more probably, did in some fashion touch the complainant in such a way as to indicate, albeit in a joking manner, that the complainant was the source of the odor."

The "passion pills" comment Another "joke" related to Alex Wales's pillbox. On one occasion, he took a pillbox out of his pocket to take a pill. He showed the pillbox to Linda Watt, pointed to one of the pills, and said: "Watch out for that one, that's a passion pill, if you take it you'll run into the woods and take your pants off." Linda Watt testified that she walked away after that comment. Alex Wales testified that she laughed with him about it.

Linda Watt's complaint was tried as a claim that she was required, as a term or condition of her employment, to work in an "abusive environment." John McCamus realized that perspective was everything in evaluating the evidence, and he felt that he had four perspectives to choose from: the objective viewpoint of a reasonable abuser; the objective viewpoint of a reasonable victim; the subjective viewpoint of a reasonable abuser; and the subjective viewpoint of a reasonable victim. He decided that "the proper perspective is the objective one of the reasonable victim." He felt that such a standard would "protect women from the offensive behaviour that results from the divergence of male and female perceptions of appropriate conduct, but it would not penalize defendants whose victims were unusually sensitive." He agreed with the authors of the comment that judges could protect sensitive victims—unreasonable women—only when those sensitive women clearly notify the offender of their distaste.

This standard of the reasonable victim is intended to "protect the defendant by ensuring that he would not be held liable for conduct not obviously offensive to a reasonable woman unless the victim had clearly communicated her distaste to him."

In this case, it is painfully apparent that Maureen Marshall—unwittingly or not—played the role of the reasonable woman. John McCamus went to a great deal of trouble to explain precisely why none of the incidents complained of (there were many more than just these four) constituted sexual harassment, either in the more commonly understood sense or as features of an abusive environment. But it was not until he could use Maureen Marshall as a standard against which to hold Linda Watt that he seemed to feel really confident about his judgment: "In reaching the conclusions that Mr. Wales did genuinely attempt to [go along with employing women], it is of some interest that his relations with Ms. Marshall appear to have been quite cordial and that he had no complaints about her work whatsoever. Nor did Ms. Marshall offer evidence of verbal or other harassment directed at herself by either Wales or Brady. There appears to be no explanation—other than performance or attitudinal problems of the complainant—as to why Mr. Wales would treat the complainant differently from Ms. Marshall."

Linda Watt's complaint was dismissed because the insults or taunts that were directed at her did not reach a level of offensiveness and frequency that was considered to be "abusive." She did offer detailed testimony on the effects this abuse was having on her, but even here, the reasonable woman, Maureen Marshall, helped show why this testimony did not count either: Ms. Marshall, who had had close personal conversations with Linda Watt during the entire period in question, testified that Linda Watt had been very upset by her recent divorce, as well as by the breakup of her affair with a co-worker. On the basis of this testimony, John McCamus concluded that "her evidence on this question is therefore not sufficiently reliable to find a causal link between her contact with Mr. Wales and whatever emotional distress she may have endured during this period."

VIII

Gayle Bezaire was beaten, sexually assaulted, and abandoned when she was a child. She was eventually committed to a refuge for adolescent girls. When she was seventeen, she became pregnant, refused to have an abortion, and got married. She became a battered wife when she became pregnant with her second child. Within a few years of the birth of her second child, she came out as a lesbian, laid charges for criminal assault against her husband, for which he was convicted, and left him. He apparently was not an easy man to leave; he attempted to maintain control over his wife and his children despite their separation, went to jail rather than pay child support (he actually spent forty days in jail rather than pay support arrears), and ingratiated himself with his wife's family and friends in order to deprive her of their support and to turn those who meant the most to her against her. Once when she had moved to the other side of Canada to start a new life, he and his mother flew into town, removed the children from the front yard of their house, and tried to rush them off to the airport before their mother knew that they were gone. Gayle Bezaire was able to get the police to retrieve the children, who were crying and screaming in the back seat of the car with their grandmother.

Gayle Bezaire's lesbianism was especially infuriating to her husband. Neither of them had filed for divorce for some five years after they first separated, but her husband did finally file in 1979—on the grounds of his wife's 'homosexuality.' Gayle Bezaire counter-petitioned on the grounds of cruelty, but the judge dismissed her petition and granted the husband's because he decided that the evidence of her lesbianism was more fully established than the evidence of his cruelty.

Gayle Bezaire received custody of her two children, but it was conditional custody. After hearing detailed expert evidence on the impact of lesbianism on parenting, he made two important findings. The first finding was that a parent's homosexuality is "a negative factor" to be considered in deciding custody. The second finding was that homosexuality "in no way is a determining factor, a factor which is so compelling that it, by its very self, would require the removal of the child, or children from the custody of that parent." On the basis of these two findings, he made her custody conditional on not engaging in any homosexual relationship without permission of the court.

At the time Gayle Bezaire received conditional custody, the children were eight and nine years old, and had lived with her continuously for their entire lives. Shortly thereafter, however, her former spouse obtained a reversal of custody in a variation proceeding, prevented her from exercising her visitation rights on all but a few occasions, and began to abuse the children. She appealed to the Ontario Court of Appeal, which refused to return custody to her despite a report from a clinical psychologist who had concluded that the children exhibited strong symptoms of being abused in their father's home. A few months after this last ruling, and while waiting for a hearing on yet another application for a variation, Gayle Bezaire allegedly discovered evidence of further abuse of her children on a rare visit, and took them to live with her in the United States for five years.

The five years underground were not easy ones. Gayle Bezaire had to deal with the possibility of being apprehended, the fact that she did not know any of the women she had to trust to keep her and her children safe, and the fact that she had to begin her life all over again in every community they visited. Some of the women she turned to for help actually ended up testifying against her in subsequent criminal proceedings. (One of those women was a lesbian lawyer who had actually helped Gayle Bezaire and her children while she was underground.)

After five years underground, Gayle Bezaire turned herself in to the Canadian police and was tried before a jury for abduction and harboring. The jury, which consisted of eight women and four men, returned a verdict of guilty. Her Honor Sidney Dymond gave Gayle Bezaire an absolute discharge on the abduction count and a suspended sentence on the harboring counts. She refused to order a custodial term on the grounds of general deterrence: "Does the possibility of jail operate when a parent who is bonded with her child honestly believes that her child is in danger really deter anyone? I do not believe it will. Should there be another parent in these circumstances, jail will not be a deterrent."

Significant in Her Honor's disposition is her refusal to characterize any of the earlier judicial rulings as discriminatory. Even though Gayle Bezaire in fact originally lost custody of her children because she had insisted on her right to live openly as a lesbian, Her Honor found as a matter of fact that those judges had no responsibility for subsequent developments. This part of her ruling resonated with other women's attitudes toward this case. LEAF, a women's litigation and defense fund, did not think that the case had anything to do with Gayle Bezaire's lesbianism, and agreed to fund her defense only with respect to the role that abuse had played in the entire sequence of events. There was considerable dispute in the women's community generally as to whether the case was really about lesbianism, or about child abuse, or about Gayle Bezaire's allegedly "difficult" personality.

Even after the sentencing hearing, Gayle Bezaire's former husband was still calling for her imprisonment. A Toronto newspaper reporter described his reaction to the disposition: "When his mother began complaining to reporters about the sentence, Mr. Bezaire shoved her away and told her to shut up. Pulling his wife toward him by the arm, he said: 'Tell them.' 'There is no abuse at our home,' Sue Bezaire said. 'The only abuse was when I got married (to Gail),' he said. 'I went through 15 years of hell.' His mother interrupted, 'And I did too.' With television cameras rolling, Mr. Bezaire hit his mother on the chest with the back of his hand to silence her so that he could tell the story himself."

And in a sense, George Bezaire (that is his name) did really get the last word: "I've had it with these lesbians," he said. "Where is justice?"

2

On Being the Object of Property

Patricia J. Williams

On Being Invisible

Reflections

For some time I have been writing about my great-great-grandmother. I have considered the significance of her history and that of slavery from a variety of viewpoints on a variety of occasions: in every speech, in every conversation, even in my commercial transactions class. I have talked so much about her that I finally had to ask myself what it was I was looking for in this dogged pursuit of family history. Was I being merely indulgent, looking for roots in the pursuit of some genetic heraldry, seeking the inheritance of being special, different, unique in all that primogeniture hath wrought?

I decided that my search was based in the utility of such a quest, not mere indulgence, but a recapturing of that which had escaped historical scrutiny, which had been overlooked and underseen. I, like so many blacks, have been trying to pin myself down in history, place myself in the stream of time as significant, evolved, present in the past, continuing into the future. To be without documentation is too unsustaining, too spontaneously ahistorical, too dangerously malleable in the hands of those who would rewrite not merely the past but my future as well. So I have been picking through the ruins for my roots.

What I know of my mother's side of the family begins with my great-great-grandmother. Her name was Sophie and she lived in Tennessee. In 1850, she was about twelve years old. I know that she was purchased when she was eleven by a white lawyer named Austin Miller and was immediately impregnated by him. She gave birth to my great-grand-

First published in *Signs: Journal of Women in Culture and Society* (1988) 14.

mother Mary, who was taken away from her to be raised as a house servant.[1] I know nothing more of Sophie (she was, after all, a black single mother—in today's terms—suffering the anonymity of yet another statistical teenage pregnancy). While I don't remember what I was told about Austin Miller before I decided to go to law school, I do remember that just before my first day of class, my mother said, in a voice full of secretive reassurance, "The Millers were lawyers, so you have it in your blood." (P. Williams, 1987a, p. 418)

When my mother told me that I had nothing to fear in law school, that law was "in my blood," she meant it in a very complex sense. First and foremost, she meant it defiantly; she meant that no one should make me feel inferior because someone else's father was a judge. She wanted me to reclaim that part of my heritage from which I had been disinherited, and she wanted me to use it as a source of strength and self-confidence. At the same time, she was asking me to claim a part of myself that was the dispossessor of another part of myself; she was asking me to deny that disenfranchised little black girl of myself that felt powerless, vulnerable and, moreover, rightly felt so.

In somewhat the same vein, Mother was asking me not to look to her as a role model. She was devaluing that part of herself that was not Harvard and refocusing my vision to that part of herself that was hard-edged, proficient, and Western. She hid the lonely, black, defiled-female part of herself and pushed me forward as the projection of a competent self, a cool rather than despairing self, a masculine rather than a feminine self.

I took this secret of my blood into the Harvard milieu with both the pride and the shame with which my mother had passed it along to me. I found myself in the situation described by Marguerite Duras, in her novel *The Lover:* "We're united in a fundamental shame at having to live. It's here we are at the heart of our common fate, the fact that [we] are our mother's children, the children of a candid creature murdered by society. We're on the side of society which has reduced her to despair. Because of what's been done to our mother, so amiable, so trusting, we hate life, we hate ourselves." (Duras, 1985, p. 55)

Reclaiming that from which one has been disinherited is a good thing. Self-possession in the full sense of that expression is the companion to self-knowledge. Yet claiming for myself a heritage the weft of whose genesis is my own disinheritance is a profoundly troubling paradox.

Images

A friend of mine practices law in rural Florida. His office is in Belle Glade, an extremely depressed area where the sugar industry reigns supreme, where blacks live pretty much as they did in slavery times, in dormitories called slave ships. They are penniless and illiterate and have both a high birth rate and a high death rate.

My friend told me about a client of his, a fifteen-year-old young woman pregnant with her third child, who came seeking advice because her mother had advised a hysterectomy—not even a tubal ligation—as a means of birth control. The young woman's mother, in turn, had been advised of the propriety of such a course in her own case by a white doctor some years before. Listening to this, I was reminded of a case I worked on when I was working for the Western Center on Law and Poverty about eight years ago. Ten black Hispanic women had been sterilized by the University of Southern California–Los Angeles County General Medical Center, allegedly without proper consent, and in most instances without even their knowledge. (Madrigal v. Quilligan, 1979) Most of them found out what had been done to them upon inquiry, after a much-publicized news story in which an intern charged that the chief of obstetrics at the hospital pursued a policy of recommending Caesarian delivery and simultaneous sterilization for any pregnant woman with three or more children and who was on welfare. In the course of researching the appeal in that case, I remember learning that one-quarter of all Navajo women of childbearing age—literally all those of childbearing age ever admitted to a hospital—have been sterilized.[2]

As I reflected on all this, I realized that one of the things passed on from slavery, which continues in the oppression of people of color, is a belief structure rooted in a concept of black (or brown, or red) anti-will, the antithetical embodiment of pure will. We live in a society in which the closest equivalent of nobility is the display of unremittingly controlled will-fulness. To be perceived as unremittingly will-less is to be imbued with an almost lethal trait.

Many scholars have explained this phenomenon in terms of total and infantilizing interdependency of dominant and oppressed. (Elkins, 1963; Stampp, 1956; Jordan, 1968) Consider, for example, Mark Tushnet's distinction between slave law's totalistic view of personality and the bourgeois "pure will" theory of personality: "Social relations in slave society rest upon the interaction of owner with slave; the owner, having total dominion over the slave. In contrast, bourgeois social relations rest upon the paradigmatic instance of market relations, the purchase by a capitalist of a worker's labor power; that transaction implicates only a part of the worker's personality. Slave relations are total, engaging the master and slave in exchanges in which each must take account of the entire range of belief, feeling, and interest embodied by the other; bourgeois social relations are partial, requiring only that participants in a market evaluate their general productive characteristics without regard to aspects of personality unrelated to production."[3] (Tushnet, 1981, p. 6)

Although such an analysis is not objectionable in some general sense, the description of master-slave relations as "total" is, to me, quite troubling. Such a choice of words reflects and accepts—at a very subtle level, perhaps—a historical rationalization that whites had to, could do, and did do everything for these simple, above animal subhumans. It is a choice of vocabulary that fails to acknowledge blacks as having needs beyond those that even the most "humane" or "sentimental" white slavemaster could provide.[4] In trying to describe the provisional aspect of slave law, I would choose words that revealed its structure as rooted in a concept of, again, black anti-will, the polar opposite of pure will. I would characterize the treatment of blacks by whites in whites' law as defining blacks as those who had no will. I would characterize that treatment not as total interdependency, but as a relation in which partializing judgments, employing partializing standards of humanity, impose generalized inadequacy on a race: if pure will or total control equal the perfect white person, then impure will and total lack of control equals the perfect black man or woman. Therefore, to define slave law as comprehending a "total" view of personality implicitly accepts that the provision of food, shelter, and clothing (again assuming the very best of circumstances) is the whole requirement of humanity. It assumes also either that psychic care was provided by slave owners (as though a slave or an owned psyche could ever be reconciled with mental health) or that psyche is not a significant part of a whole human.

Market theory indeed focuses attention away from the full range of human potential in its pursuit of a divinely willed, invisible handed economic actor. Master-slave relations, however, focused attention away from the full range of black human potential in a somewhat different way: it pursued a vision of blacks as simple-minded, strong-bodied economic actants.[5] Thus, while blacks had an indisputable generative force in the marketplace; their presence could not be called activity; they had no active role in the market. To say, therefore, that "market relations disregard the peculiarities of individuals, whereas slave relations rest on the mutual recognition of the humanity of master and slave" (Tushnet, 1981, p. 69) (no matter how dialectical or abstracted a definition of humanity one adopts) is to posit an inaccurate equation: if "disregard for the peculiarities of individuals" and "mutual recognition of humanity" are polarized by a "whereas," then somehow regard for peculiarities of individuals must equal recognition of humanity. In the context of slavery this equation mistakes whites' overzealous and oppressive obsession with projected specific peculiarities of blacks for actual holistic regard for the individual. It overlooks the fact that most definitions of humanity require something beyond mere biological sustenance, some healthy measure of autonomy beyond that of which slavery could institutionally or otherwise conceive. Furthermore, it overlooks the fact that both slave and bourgeois systems regarded certain attributes as important and disregarded certain others, and that such regard and disregard can occur in the same glance, like the wearing of horseblinders to focus attention simultaneously toward and away from. The experiential blinders of market actor and slave are focused in different directions, yet the partializing ideologies of each makes the act of not seeing an unconscious, alienating component of seeing. Restoring a unified social vision will, I think, require broader and more scattered resolutions than the simple symmetry of ideological bipolarity.

Thus, it is important to undo whatever words obscure the fact that slave law was at least as fragmenting and fragmented as the bourgeois worldview—in a way that has persisted to this day, cutting across all ideological boundaries. As "pure will" signifies the whole bourgeois personality in the bourgeois worldview, so wisdom, control, and aesthetic beauty signify the whole white personality in slave law. The former and the latter, the slavemaster and the burgermeister, are not so very different when expressed in those terms. The reconciling difference is that in slave law the emphasis is really on the inverse rationale: that irrationality, lack of control, and ugliness signify the whole slave personality. "Total" interdependence is at best a polite way of rationalizing such personality splintering; it creates a bizarre sort of yin-yang from the dross of an oppressive schizophrenia of biblical dimension. I would just call it schizophrenic, with all the baggage that that connotes. That is what sounds right to me. Truly total relationships (as opposed to totalitarianism) call up images of whole people dependent on whole people; an interdependence that is both providing and laissez-faire at the same time. Neither the historical inheritance of slave law nor so-called bourgeois law meets that definition.

None of this, perhaps, is particularly new. Nevertheless, as precedent to anything I do as a lawyer, the greatest challenge is to allow the full truth of partializing social constructions to be felt for their overwhelming reality—reality that otherwise I might rationally try to avoid facing. In my search for roots, I must assume, not just as history but as an ongoing psychological force, that, in the eyes of white culture, irrationality, lack of control, and ugliness signify not just the whole slave personality, not just the whole black personality, but me.

Vision

Reflecting on my roots makes me think again and again of the young woman in Belle Glade, Florida. She told the story of her impending sterilization, according to my friend, while keeping her eyes on the ground at all times. My friend, who is white, asked why she wouldn't look up, speak with him eye to eye. The young woman answered that she didn't like white people seeing inside her.

My friend's story made me think of my own childhood and adolescence: my parents were always telling me to look up at the world; to look straight at people, particularly white people; not to let them stare me down; to hold my ground; to insist on the right to my presence no matter what. They told me that in this culture you have to look people in the eye because that's how you tell them you're their equal. My friend's story also reminded me how very difficult I had found that looking-back to be. What was hardest was not just that white people saw me, as my friend's client put it, but that they looked through me, that they treated me as though I were transparent.

By itself, seeing into me would be to see my substance, my anger, my vulnerability, and my wild raging despair—and that alone is hard enough to show, to share. But to uncover it and to have it devalued by ignorance, to hold it up bravely in the organ of my eyes and to have it greeted by an impassive stare that passes right through all that which is me, an impassive stare that moves on and attaches itself to my left earlobe or to the dust caught in the rusty vertical geysers of my wiry hair or to the breadth of my freckled brown nose—this is deeply humiliating. It re-wounds, relives the early childhood anguish of uncensored seeing, the fullness of vision that is the permanent turning-away point for most blacks.

The cold game of equality-staring makes me feel like a thin sheet of glass: white people see all the worlds beyond me but not me. They come trotting at me with force and speed; they do not see me. I could force my presence, the real me contained in those eyes, upon them, but I would be smashed in the process. If I deflect, if I move out of the way, they will never know I existed.

Marguerite Duras, again in *The Lover,* places the heroine in relation to her family. "Every day we try to kill one another, to kill. Not only do we not talk to one another, we don't even look at one another. When you're being looked at you can't look. To look is to feel curious, to be interested, to lower yourself." (Duras, 1985, p. 54)

To look is also to make myself vulnerable; yet not to look is to neutralize the part of myself which is vulnerable. I look in order to see, and so I must look. Without that directness of vision, I am afraid I will will my own blindness, disinherit my own creativity, and sterilize my own perspective of its embattled, passionate insight.

An ardor

The child

One Saturday afternoon not long ago, I sat among a litter of family photographs telling a South African friend about Marjorie, my godmother and my mother's cousin. She was given away by her light-skinned mother when she was only six. She was given to my grandmother and my great-aunts to be raised among her darker-skinned cousin, for Marjorie was very dark indeed. Her mother left the family to "pass," to marry a white man—Uncle Frederick, we called him with trepidatious presumption yet without his ever knowing of our existence—an heir to a meatpacking fortune. When Uncle Frederick died thirty years later and the fortune was lost, Marjorie's mother rejoined the race, as the royalty of resentful fascination—Lady Bountiful, my sister called her—to regale us with tales of gracious upper-class living.

My friend said that my story reminded him of a case in which a swarthy, crisp-haired child was born, in Durban, to white parents. The Afrikaner government quickly intervened, removed the child from its birth home, and placed it to be raised with a "more suitable," browner family.

When my friend and I had shared these stories, we grew embarrassed somehow, and our conversation trickled away into a discussion of laissez-faire economics and governmental interventionism. Our words became a clear line, a railroad upon which all other ideas and events were tied down and sacrificed.

The market

As a teacher of commercial transactions, one of the things that has always impressed me most about the law of contract is a certain deadening power it exercises by reducing the parties to the passive. It constrains the lively involvement of its signatories by positioning enforcement in such a way that parties find themselves in a passive relationship to a document: it is the contract that governs, that "does" everything, that absorbs all responsibility and deflects all other recourse.

Contract law reduces life to fairy tale. The four corners of the agreement become parent. Performance is the equivalent of obedience to the parent. Obedience is dutifully passive. Passivity is valued as good contract-socialized behavior; activity is caged in retrospective hypotheses about states of mind at the magic moment of contracting. Individuals are judged by the contract unfolding rather than by the actors acting autonomously. Nonperformance is disobedience; disobedience is active; activity becomes evil in contrast to the childlike passivity of contract conformity.

One of the most powerful examples of all this is the case of Mary Beth Whitehead, mother of Sara—of so-called Baby M. Ms. Whitehead became a vividly original actor *after* the creation of her contract with William Stern; unfortunately for her, there can be no greater civil sin. It was in this upside-down context, in the picaresque unboundedness of breachor, that her energetic grief became hysteria and her passionate creativity was funneled, whorled, and reconstructed as highly impermissible. Mary

Beth Whitehead thus emerged as the evil stepsister who deserved nothing.

Some time ago, Charles Reich visited a class of mine.[6] He discussed with my students a proposal for a new form of bargain by which emotional "items"—such as praise, flattery, acting happy or sad—might be contracted for explicitly. One student, not alone in her sentiment, said, "Oh, but then you'll just feel obligated." Only the week before, however (when we were discussing the contract which posited that Ms. Whitehead "will not form or attempt to form a parent–child relationship with any child or children"), this same student had insisted that Ms. Whitehead must give up her child, because she had *said* she would: "She was obligated!" I was confounded by the degree to which what the student took to be self-evident, inalienable gut reactions could be governed by illusions of passive conventionality and form.

It was that incident, moreover, that gave me insight into how Judge Harvey Sorkow, of New Jersey Superior Court, could conclude that the contract that purported to terminate Ms. Whitehead's parental rights was "not illusory."[7] (*In the Matter of Baby "M"*, 1987)

(As background, I should say that I think that, within the framework of contract law itself, the agreement between Ms. Whitehead and Mr. Stern was clearly illusory.[8] On the one hand, Judge Sorkow's opinion said that Ms. Whitehead was seeking to avoid her *obligations*. In other words, giving up her child became an actual obligation. On the other hand, according to the logic of the judge, this was a service contract, not really a sale of a child; therefore delivering the child to the Sterns was an "obligation" for which there was no consideration, for which Mr. Stern was not paying her.)

Judge Sorkow's finding the contract "not illusory" is suggestive not just of the doctrine by that name, but of illusion in general, and delusion, and the righteousness with which social constructions are conceived, acted on, and delivered up into the realm of the real as "right," while all else is devoured from memory as "wrong." From this perspective, the rhetorical tricks by which Sara Whitehead became Melissa Stern seem very like the heavy-worded legalities by which my great-great-grandmother was pacified and parted from her child. In both situations, the real mother had no say, no power; her powerlessness was imposed by state law that made her and her child helpless in relation to the father. My great-great-grandmother's powerlessness came about as the result of a contract to which she was not a party; Mary Beth Whitehead's powerlessness came about as a result of a contract that she signed at a discrete point of time—yet which, over time, enslaved her. The contract-reality in both instances was no less than magic: it was illusion transformed into not-illusion. Furthermore, it masterfully disguised the brutality of enforced arrangements in which these women's autonomy, their flesh and their blood, were locked away in word vaults, without room to reconsider—*ever*.

In the months since Judge Sorkow's opinion, I have reflected on the similarities of fortune between my own social positioning and that of Sara Melissa Stern Whitehead. I have come to realize that an important part of the complex magic that Judge Sorkow wrote into his opinion was a supposition that it is "natural" for people to want children "like" themselves. What this reasoning raised for me was an issue of what, exactly, constituted this "likeness"? (What would have happened, for example, if Ms. Whitehead had turned out to have been the "passed" descendant of my "failed" godmother Marjorie's mother? What if the child she bore had turned out to be recessively and visibly black? Would the sperm of Mr. Stern have been so powerful as to make this child "his" with the exclusivity that Judge Sorkow originally assigned?) What constitutes, moreover, the collective understanding of "un-likeness"?

These questions turn, perhaps, on not-so-subtle images of which mothers should be bearing which children. Is there not something unseemly, in our society, about the spectacle of a white woman mothering a black child? A white woman giving totally to a black child; a black child totally and demandingly dependent for everything, for sustenance itself, from a white woman. The image of a white woman suckling a black child; the image of a black child sucking for its life from the bosom of a white woman. The utter interdependence of such an image; the selflessness, the merging it implies; the giving up of boundary; the encompassing of other within self; the unbounded generosity, the interconnectedness of such an image. Such a picture says that there is no difference; it places the hope of continuous generation, of immortality of the white self in a little black face.

When Judge Sorkow declared that it was only to be expected that parents would want to breed children "like" themselves, he simultaneously created a legal right to the same. With the creation of such a "right," he encased the children conforming to "likeliness" in protective custody, far from whole ranges of taboo. Taboo about touch and smell and intimacy and boundary. Taboo about ardor, possession, license, equivocation, equanimity, indifference, intolerance, rancor, dispossession, innocence, exile, and candor. Taboo about death. Taboos that amount to death. Death and sacredness, the valuing of body, of self, of other, of remains. The handling lovingly in life, as in life; the question of the intimacy versus the dispassion of death.

In effect, these taboos describe boundaries of valuation. Whether something is inside or outside the marketplace of rights has always been a way of valuing it. When a valued object is located outside the market, it is generally understood to be too "priceless" to be accommodated by ordinary exchange relationships; when, in contrast, the prize is located within the marketplace, all objects outside become "valueless." Traditionally, the Mona Lisa and human life have been the sorts of subjects removed from the fungibility of commodification, as "priceless." Thus when black people were bought and sold as slaves, they were placed beyond the bounds of humanity. And thus, in the twistedness of our brave new world, when blacks have been thrust out of the market and it is white children who are bought and sold, black babies have become "worthless" currency to adoption agents—"surplus" in the salvage heaps of Harlem hospitals.

The imagination

"Familiar though his name may be to us, the storyteller in his living immediacy is by no means a present force. He has already become something remote from us and something that is getting even more distant. . . . Less and less frequently do we encounter people with the ability to tell a tale properly. . . . It is as if something that seemed inalienable to us, the securest among our possessions, were taken from us: the ability to exchange experiences." (Benjamin, 1969, p. 83)

My mother's cousin Marjorie was a storyteller. From time to time I would press her to tell me the details of her youth, and she would tell me instead about a child who wandered into a world of polar bears, who was prayed over by polar bears, and in the end eaten. The child's life was not in vain because the polar bears had been made holy by its suffering. The child had been a test, a message from god for polar bears. In the polar bear universe, she would tell me, the primary object of creation was polar bears, and the rest of the living world was fashioned to serve polar bears. The clouds took their shape from polar bears, trees were designed to give shelter and shade to polar bears, and humans were ideally designed to provide polar bears with meat.[9]

The truth, the truth, I would laughingly insist as we sat in her apartment eating canned fruit and heavy roasts, mashed potatoes, pickles and vanilla pudding, cocoa, Sprite, or tea. What about roots and all that, I coaxed. But the voracity of her amnesia would disclaim and disclaim and disclaim; and she would go on telling me about the polar bears until our plates were full of emptiness and I became large in the space which described her emptiness and I gave in to the emptiness of words.

On life and death

Sighing into space

There are moments in my life when I feel as though a part of me is missing. There are days when I feel so invisible that I can't remember what day of the week it is, when I feel so manipulated that I can't remember my own name, when I feel so lost and angry that I can't speak a civil word to the people who love me best. Those are the times when I catch sight of my reflection in store windows and am surprised to see a whole person looking back. Those are the times when my skin becomes gummy as clay and my nose slides around on my face and my eyes drip down to my chin. I have to close my eyes at such times and remember myself, draw an internal picture that is smooth and whole; when all else fails, I reach for a mirror and stare myself down until the features reassemble themselves like lost sheep.

Two years ago, my godmother Marjorie suffered a massive stroke. As she lay dying, I would come to the hospital to give her her meals. My feeding her who had so often fed me became a complex ritual of mirroring and self-assembly. The physical act of holding the spoon to her lips was not only a rite of nurture and of sacrifice, it was the return of a gift. It was a quiet bowing to the passage of time and the doubling back of all things. The quiet woman who listened to my woes about work and school required now that I bend my head down close to her and listen for mouthed word fragments, sentence crumbs. I bent down to give meaning to her silence, her wandering search for words.

She would eat what I brought to the hospital with relish; she would reject what I brought with a turn of her head. I brought fruit and yogurt, ice cream and vegetable juice. Slowly, over time, she stopped swallowing. The mashed potatoes would sit in her mouth like cotton, the pudding would slip to her chin in slow sad streams. When she lost not only her speech but the power to ingest, they put a tube into her nose and down to her stomach, and I lost even that medium by which to communicate. No longer was there the odd but reassuring communion over taste. No longer was there some echo of comfort in being able to nurture one who nurtured me.

This increment of decay was like a little newborn death. With the tube, she stared up at me with imploring eyes, and I tried to guess what it was that she would like. I read to her aimlessly and in desperation. We entertained each other with the strange embarrassed flickering of our eyes. I told her stories to fill the emptiness, the loneliness, of the white-walled hospital room.

I told her stories about who I had become, about how I had grown up to know all about exchange systems, and theories of contract, and monetary fictions. I spun tales about blue-sky laws and promissory estoppel, the wispy-feathered complexity of undue influence and dark-hearted theories of unconscionability. I told her about market norms and gift economy and the thin razor's edge of the bartering ethic. Once upon a time, I rambled, some neighbors of mine included me in their circle of barter. They were in the habit of exchanging eggs and driving lessons, hand-knit sweaters and computer programming, plumbing and calligraphy. I accepted the generosity of their inclusion with gratitude. At first, I felt that, as a lawyer, I was worthless, that I had no barterable skills and nothing to contribute. What I came to realize with time, however, was that my value to the group was not calculated by the physical items I brought to it. These people included me because they wanted me to be part of their circle, they valued my participation apart from the material things I could offer. So I gave of myself to them, and they gave me fruit cakes and dandelion wine and smoked salmon, and in their giving, their goods became provisions. Cradled in this community whose currency was a relational ethic, my stock in myself soared. My value depended on the glorious intangibility, the eloquent invisibility of my just being *part* of the collective; and in direct response I grew spacious and happy and gentle.

My gentle godmother. The fragility of life; the cold mortuary shelf.

Dispassionate deaths

The hospital in which my godmother died is now filled to capacity with AIDS patients. One in sixty-one babies born there, as in New York City generally, is infected with AIDS antibodies. (Lambert 1988) Almost all are black or Hispanic. In the Bronx, the rate is one in forty-three. (Lambert, 1988) In Central Africa, experts estimate that, of children receiving transfusions for malaria-related anemia, "about 1000 may have been infected with the AIDS virus in each of the last five years." (*New York Times,* 1988) In Congo, 5 percent of the entire population is infected. (Brooke, 1988) The *New York Times* reports that "the profile of Congo's population seems to guarantee the continued spread of AIDS." (Brooke, 1988)

In the Congolese city of Pointe Noir, "the annual budget of the sole public health hospital is estimated at about $200,000—roughly the amount of money spent in the United States to care for four AIDS patients." (Brooke 1988)

The week in which my godmother died is littered with bad memories. In my journal, I made note of the following:

Good Friday: Phil Donahue has a special program on AIDS. The segues are:

a. from Martha, who weeps at the prospect of not watching her children grow up
b. to Jim, who is not conscious enough to speak just now, who coughs convulsively, who recognizes no one in his family any more
c. to Hugh who, at 85 pounds, thinks he has five years but whose doctor says he has weeks
d. to an advertisement for denture polish ("If you love your Polident Green/then gimmeeya SMILE!")
e. and then one for a plastic surgery salon on Park Avenue ("The only thing that's expensive is our address")
f. and then one for what's coming up on the five o'clock news (Linda Lovelace, of *Deep Throat* fame, "still recovering from a double mastectomy and complications from silicone injections" is being admitted to a New York hospital for a liver transplant)
g. and finally one for the miracle properties of all-purpose house cleaner ("Mr. Cleeean/is the man/behind the shine/is it wet or is it dry?" I note that Mr. Clean, with his gleaming bald head, puffy musculature and fever-bright eyes, looks like he is undergoing radiation therapy). Now back to our show.
h. "We are back now with Martha," (who is crying harder than before, sobbing uncontrollably, each jerking inhalation a deep unearthly groan). Phil says, "Oh honey, I hope we didn't make it worse for you."

Easter Saturday: Over lunch, I watch another funeral. My office windows overlook a graveyard as crowded and still as a rush-hour freeway. As I savor pizza and milk, I notice that one of the mourners is wearing an outfit featured in the window of Bloomingdale's (59th Street store) only since last weekend. This thread of recognition jolts me, and I am drawn to her in sorrow; the details of my own shopping history flash before my eyes as I reflect upon the sober spree that brought her to the rim of this earthly chasm, her slim suede heels sinking into the soft silt of the graveside.

Resurrection Sunday: John D., the bookkeeper where I used to work, died, hit on the head by a stray but forcefully propelled hockey puck. I cried copiously at his memorial service, only to discover, later that afternoon when I saw a black rimmed photograph, that I had been mourning the wrong person. I had cried because the man I *thought* had died is John D. the office messenger, a bitter unfriendly man who treats me with disdain; once I bought an old electric typewriter from him which never worked. Though he promised nothing, I have harbored deep dislike since then; death by hockey puck is only one of the fates I had imagined for him. I washed clean my guilt with buckets of tears at the news of what I thought was his demise.

The man who did die was small, shy, anonymously sweet-featured and innocent. In some odd way I was relieved; no seriously obligatory mourning to be done here. A quiet impassivity settled over me and I forgot my grief.

Holy communion

A few months after my godmother died, my Great Aunt Jag passed away in Cambridge, at ninety-six the youngest and the last of her siblings, all of whom died at ninety-seven. She collapsed on her way home from the polling place, having gotten in her vote for "yet another Kennedy." Her wake was much like the last family gathering at which I had seen her, two Thanksgivings ago. She was a little hard of hearing then and she stayed on the outer edge of the conversation, brightly, loudly, and randomly asserting enjoyment of her meal. At the wake, cousins, nephews, daughters-in-law, first wives, second husbands, great-grand-nieces gathered round her casket and got acquainted all over again. It was pouring rain outside. The funeral home was dry and warm, faintly spicily clean-smelling; the walls were solid, dark, respectable wood; the floors were cool stone tile. On the door of a room marked "No Admittance" was a sign that reminded workers therein of the reverence with which each body was held by its family and prayed employees handle the remains with similar love and care. Aunt Jag wore yellow chiffon; everyone agreed that laying her out with her glasses on was a nice touch.

Afterward, we all went to Legal Seafoods, her favorite restaurant, and ate many of her favorite foods.

On candor

Me

I have never been able to determine my horoscope with any degree of accuracy. Born at Boston's now-defunct Lying-In Hospital, I am a Virgo, despite a quite poetic soul. Knowledge of the *hour* of my birth, however, would determine not just my sun sign but my moons and all the more intimate specificities of my destiny. Once upon a time, I sent for my birth certificate, which was retrieved from the oblivion of Massachusetts microfiche. Said document revealed that an infant named Patricia Joyce, born of parents named Williams, was delivered into the world "colored." Since no one thought to put down the hour of my birth, I suppose that I will never know my true fate.

In the meantime, I read what text there is of me.

My name, Patricia, means patrician. Patricias are noble, lofty, elite, exclusively educated, and well mannered despite themselves. I was on the cusp of being Pamela, but my parents knew that such a me would require lawns, estates, and hunting dogs too.

I am also a Williams. Of William, whoever he was: an anonymous white man who owned my father's people and from whom some escaped. That rupture is marked by the dark-mooned mystery of utter silence.

Williams is the second most common surname in the United States; Patricia is *the* most common prename among women born in 1951, the year of my birth.

Them

In the law, rights are islands of empowerment. To be un-righted is to be disempowered, and the line between rights and no rights is most often the line between dominators and oppressors. Rights contain images of power, and manipulating those images, either visually or linguistically, is central in the making and maintenance of rights. In principle, therefore, the more dizzyingly diverse the images that are propagated, the more empowered we will be as a society.

In reality, it was a lovely polar bear afternoon. The gentle force of the earth. A wide wilderness of islands. A conspiracy of polar bears lost in timeless forgetting. A gentleness of polar bears, a fruitfulness of polar bears, a silent black-eyed interest of polar bears, a bristled expectancy of polar bears. With the wisdom of innocence, a child threw stones at the polar bears. Hungry, they rose from their nests, inquisitive, dark-souled, patient with foreboding, fearful in tremendous awakening. The instinctual ferocity of the hunter reflected upon the hunted. Then, proud teeth and warrior claws took innocence for wilderness and raging insubstantiality for tender rabbit breath.

In the newspapers the next day, it was reported that two polar bears in the Brooklyn Zoo mauled to death an eleven-year-old boy who had entered their cage to swim in the moat. The police were called and the bears were killed. (Barron, 1987a)

In the public debate that ensued, many levels of meaning emerged. The rhetoric firmly established that the bears were innocent, naturally territorial, unfairly imprisoned, and guilty. The dead child (born into the urban jungle of a black, welfare mother and a Hispanic alcoholic father who had died literally in the gutter only six weeks before) was held to a similarly stern standard. The police were captured, in a widely disseminated photograph, (*New York Post,* 1987, p. 1) shooting helplessly, desperately, into the cage, through three levels of bars, at a pieta of bears;

since this image, conveying much pathos, came nevertheless not in time to save the child, it was generally felt that the bears had died in vain. (Barron, 1987b)

In the egalitarianism of exile, pluralists rose up as of one body, with a call to buy more bears, control juvenile delinquency, eliminate all zoos, and confine future police. (Barron, 1987b)

In the plenary session of the national meeting of the Law and Society Association, the keynote speaker unpacked the whole incident as a veritable laboratory of emergent rights discourse. Just seeing that these complex levels of meaning exist, she exulted, should advance rights discourse significantly. (P. Williams, 1987b)

At the funeral of the child, the presiding priest pronounced the death of Juan Perez not in vain, since he was saved from growing into "a lifetime of crime." Juan's Hispanic-welfare-black-widow-of-an-alcoholic mother decided then and there to sue.

The universe between

How I ended up at Dartmouth College for the summer is too long a story to tell. Anyway, there I was, sharing the town of Hanover, New Hampshire, with about two hundred prepubescent males enrolled in Dartmouth's summer basketball camp, an all-white, very expensive, affirmative action program for the street-deprived.

One fragrant evening, I was walking down East Wheelock Street when I encountered about a hundred of these adolescents, fresh from the courts, wet, lanky, big-footed, with fuzzy yellow crew cuts, loping toward Thayer Hall and food. In platoons of twenty-five or so, they descended upon me, jostling me, smacking me, and pushing me from the sidewalk into the gutter. In a thoughtless instant, I snatched off my brown silk headrag, my flag of African femininity and propriety, my sign of meek and supplicatory place and presentation. I released the armored rage of my short nappy hair (the scalp gleaming bare between the angry wire spikes) and hissed: "Don't I exist for you?! See Me! And deflect, godammit!" (The quaint professionalism of my formal English never allowed the rage in my head to rise so high as to overflow the edges of my text.)

They gave me wide berth. They clearly had no idea, however, that I was talking to them or about them. They skirted me sheepishly, suddenly polite, because they did know, when a crazed black person comes crashing into one's field of vision, that it is impolite to laugh. I stood tall and spoke loudly into their ranks: "I have my rights!" The Dartmouth Summer Basketball Camp raised its collective eyebrows and exhaled, with a certain tested nobility of exhaustion and solidarity.

I pursued my way, manumitted back into silence. I put distance between them and me, gave myself over to polar bear musings. I allowed myself to be watched over by bear spirits. Clean white wind and strong bear smells. The shadowed amnesia; the absence of being; the presence of polar bears. White wilderness of icy meat-eaters heavy with remembrance; leaden with undoing; shaggy with the effort of hunting for silence; frozen in a web of intention and intuition. A lunacy of polar bears. A history of polar bears. A pride of polar bears. A consistency of polar bears. In those meandering pastel polar bear moments, I found cool fragments of white-fur invisibility. Solid, black-gummed, intent, observant. Hungry and patient, impassive and exquisitely timed. The brilliant bursts of exclusive territoriality. A complexity of messages implied in our being.

Notes

1. For a more detailed account of the family history to this point, see Williams (1986, p. 79).
2. This was the testimony of one of the witnesses. It is hard to find official confirmation for this or any other sterilization statistic involving Native American women. Official statistics kept by the U.S. Public Health Service, through the Centers for Disease Control in Atlanta, come from data gathered by the National Hospital Discharge Survey, which covers neither federal hospitals nor penitentiaries. Services to Native American women living on reservations are provided almost exclusively by federal hospitals. In addition, the U.S. Public Health Service breaks down its information into only three categories: "White," "Black," and "Other." Nevertheless, in 1988, the Women of All Red Nations Collective of Minneapolis, Minnesota, distributed a fact sheet entitled "Sterilization Studies of Native American Women," which claimed that as many as 50 percent of all Native American women of childbearing age have been sterilized. According to "Surgical Sterilization Surveillance: Tubal Sterilization and Hysterectomy in Women Ages 15–44, 1979–1980," issued by the Centers for Disease Control in 1983. "In 1980, the tubal sterilization rate for black women . . . was 45 percent greater than that for white women" (7). Furthermore, a study released in 1984 by the Division of Reproductive Health of the Center for Health Promotion and Education (one of the Centers for Disease Control) found that, as of 1982, 48.8 percent of Puerto Rican women between the ages of 15 and 44 had been sterilized.
3. There is danger, in the analysis that follows, of appearing to "pick" on Tushnet. That is not my intention, nor is it to impugn the body of his research, most of which I greatly admire. The choice of this passage for analysis has more to do with the randomness of my reading habits; the fact that he is one of the few legal writers to attempt, in the context of slavery, a juxtaposition of political theory with psychoanalytic theories of personality; and the fact that he is perceived to be of the political left, which simplifies my analysis in terms of its presumption of sympathy, i.e., that the constructions of thought revealed are socially derived and unconscious rather than idiosyncratic and intentional.
4. In another passage, Tushnet observes: "The court thus demonstrated its appreciation of the ties of sentiment that slavery could generate between master and slave and simultaneously denied that those ties were relevant in the law" (67). What is noteworthy

about the reference to "sentiment" is that it assumes that the fact that emotions could grow up between slave and master is itself worth remarking: slightly surprising, slightly commendable for the court to note (i.e., in its "appreciation"), although "simultaneously" with, and presumably in contradistinction to, the court inability to take official cognizance of the fact. Yet, if one really looks at the ties that bound master and slave, one has to flesh out the description of master-slave with the ties of father-son, father-daughter, half-sister, half-brother, uncle, aunt, cousin and a variety of de facto foster relationships. And if one starts to see those ties as more often than not intimate family ties, then the terminology "appreciation of . . . sentiment . . . between master and slave" becomes a horrifying mockery of any true sense of family sentiment, which is utterly, utterly lacking. The court's "appreciation," from this enhanced perspective, sounds blindly cruel, sarcastic at best. And to observe that courts suffused in such "appreciation" could simultaneously deny its legal relevance seems not only a truism; it misses the point entirely.

5. "Actants have a kind of phonemic, rather than a phonetic role: they operate on the level of function, rather than content. That is, an actant may embody itself in a particular character (termed an acteur) or it may reside in the function of more than one character in respect of their common role in the story's underlying 'oppositional' structure. In short, the deep structure of the narrative generates and defines its actants at a level beyond that of the story's surface content" (Hawkes, 1977, p. 89).
6. Charles Reich is author of *The Greening of America* (Reich, 1970) and professor of law at the University of San Francisco Law School.
7. This decision was appealed, and on February 3, 1988, the New Jersey Supreme Court ruled that surrogate contracts were illegal and against public policy. In addition to the contract issue, however, the appellate court decided the custody issue in favor of the Sterns but granted visitation rights to Mary Beth Whitehead.
8. "An illusory promise is an expression cloaked in promissory terms, but which, upon closer examination, reveals that the promisor has committed himself not at all" (Calamari and Perillo, 1987, p. 228).
9. For an analysis of similar stories, see Levins and Lewontin, 1985, p. 66.

3

Subordination, Rhetorical Survival Skills, and Sunday Shoes: Notes on the Hearing of Mrs. G.

Lucie E. White

> The profound political intervention of feminism has been . . . to redefine the very nature of what is deemed political. . . . The literary ramifications of this shift involve the discovery of the rhetorical survival skills of the formerly unvoiced. Lies, secrets, silences, and deflections of all sorts are routes taken by voices or messages not granted full legitimacy in order not to be altogether lost. (Johnson, 1987, pp. 25 and 31)

Mrs. G. is 35 years old, Black, and on her own.[1] She has five girls, ranging in age from four to fourteen. She has never told me anything about their fathers; all I know is that she isn't getting formal child support payments from anyone. She lives on an AFDC grant of just over $300 a month and a small monthly allotment of Food Stamps.[2] She probably gets a little extra money from occasional jobs as a field hand or a maid, but she doesn't share this information with me and I don't ask. She has a very coveted unit of public housing, so she doesn't have to pay rent. She is taking an adult basic education class at the local community action center, which is in the same building as my own office. I often notice her in the classroom as I pass by.

The first thing that struck me about Mrs. G., when she finally came to my office for help one day, was the way she talked. She brought her two oldest daughters with her. She would get very excited when she spoke, breathing hard and waving her hands and straining, like she was searching for the right words to say what was on her mind. Her daughters would circle her, like two young mothers themselves, keeping the air calm as her hands swept through it. I haven't talked with them much, but they strike me as quite self-possessed for their years.

A longer version of this article has been published in the *Buffalo Law Review* (Winter 1990) 38.

At the time I met Mrs. G., I was a legal aid lawyer working in a small community in south central North Carolina. I had grown up in the state, but had been away for ten years, and felt like an outsider when I started working there. I worked out of two small rooms in the back of the local community action center. The building was run-down, but it was a storefront directly across from the Civil War Memorial on the courthouse lawn, so it was easy for poor people to find. There were two of us in the office, myself and a local woman who had spent a few years in Los Angeles, working as a secretary and feeling free, before coming back to the town to care for her aging parents. Her family had lived in the town for generations. Not too long ago they, and most of the other Black families I worked with, had been the property of our adversaries—the local landowners, businessmen, bureaucrats, and lawyers. Everyone seemed to have a strong sense of family, and of history, in the town.

Mrs. G. and two daughters first appeared at our office one Friday morning at about ten, without an appointment. She showed me a letter from the welfare office that said she had received an "overpayment" of AFDC benefits.

When I questioned her about the letter, Mrs. G. told me that a few months before, she had received a cash settlement for injuries she and her oldest daughter had suffered in a minor car accident. After medical bills had been paid and her lawyer had taken his fees, her award came to $592. Before Mrs. G cashed the insurance check, she took it to her AFDC worker to report it and ask if it was all right for her to spend it. With a few exceptions, any "income" she reported would be subtracted, dollar for dollar, from her AFDC stipend. The worker told her that she could spent it however she wanted.

Mrs. G. cashed her check that same afternoon, and took her five girls on what she described to me as a "shopping trip." They bought Kotex, which they were always running short on at the end of the month. They also bought shoes, dresses for school, and some frozen food. Then she made two payments on her furniture bill. After a couple of wonderful days, the money was gone. Two months passed. Mrs. G. received and spent two AFDC checks. Then she got the overpayment notice, asking her to repay to the county an amount equal to her insurance award.

I asked Mrs. G. if she could put together a list of all the things she had bought with the insurance money. If she still had any of the receipts, she should bring them to me. I would look at her case file at the welfare office and see her again in a couple of days.

The case file had a note from the case worker confirming that Mrs. G. had reported the insurance payment when she received it, and showing that the worker did not include the amount in calculating her stipend. The "overpayment" got flagged two months later, when a supervisor, doing a random "quality control" check on her file, discovered the worker's note. Under AFDC law, the insurance award was considered a "lump sum payment." As such, it counted as income for AFDC purposes under the state's regulations; indeed, the county should have cut Mrs. G. off of welfare entirely for almost two months, on the theory that her family could live for that time off of the insurance award. If the county did not now attempt to collect this "overpayment" from Mrs. G., it would be sanctioned for an administrative error.

I met again with Mrs. G. the following Friday. She insisted that she had asked her worker's permission before spending the insurance money. But, she explained, she hadn't meant to do anything wrong. I told her that it looked like it was the county who had made a mistake, and explained that she would probably have to ask for a hearing to get the matter straightened out.

Mrs. G. had been in court a few times, to get child support and to defend against evictions, but she had never been to a welfare hearing. She knew that it was not a good idea to get involved in hearings, however, and she understood why. Fair hearings were a hassle and an embarrassment to the county. A hearing meant pulling an eligibility worker and several managers out of work for a few hours, which—given the chronic under-staffing—was more than a minor inconvenience. It also meant exposing the county's administrative problems to state-level scrutiny. I could tell that Mrs. G. was not entirely comfortable with the idea of a hearing. Yet when she nervously agreed to allow me to file the request, I didn't second-guess her decision.

Mrs. G. brought all five of her girls to my office to prepare for the hearing. I told her that I saw two stories we could tell. The first was the story she had told me. It was the "estoppel" story, the story of the wrong advice she had gotten from her worker about spending the insurance check. The second story was one that I had come up with from reading the law.

The state had laid the groundwork for this story when it opted for the "life necessities" waiver to the lump sum rule that was permitted by federal regulations. If a client could show that she[3] had spent the sum to avert a crisis situation, then it would be considered "unavailable" as income, and her AFDC benefits would not be suspended. I didn't like this second story very much, and I wasn't sure that Mrs. G. would want to go along with it. How could I ask Mrs. G. to distinguish "life necessities" from mere luxuries, when she was keeping five children alive on $300 a month, and when she was given no voice in the calculus that had determined her "needs"?

Yet I felt that the necessities story might work at the hearing, while by telling the "estoppel" story, we risked uniting the county and state against us. According to legal aid's welfare specialist in the state capital, state officials didn't like the lump sum rule. It made more paperwork for the counties. And, by knocking families off the federally financed AFDC program, the rule increased the pressure on state and county-funded relief programs. But the only way the state could get around the rule without being subject to federal sanctions was through the necessities exception. Behind the scenes, state officials were saying to our welfare specialist that they intended to interpret the exception broadly. In addition to this inside information that state officials would prefer the necessities tale, I knew from experience that they would feel comfortable with the role that story gave to Mrs. G. It would place her on her knees, asking for pity as she described how hard she was struggling to make ends meet.

The estoppel story would be entirely different. In it, Mrs. G. would be pointing a finger, turning the county itself into the object of scrutiny. She would accuse welfare officials of wrong, and claim that they had caused her injury. She would demand that the county bend its own rules, absorb the overpayment out of its own funds, and run the risk of sanction from the state for its error.

As I thought about the choices, I felt myself in a bind. The estoppel story would feel good in the telling, but at the likely cost of losing the hearing, and provoking the county's ire. The hearing officer—though charged to be neutral—would surely identify with the county in this challenge to the government's power to evade the costs of its own mistakes. The necessities story would force Mrs. G. to grovel, but it would give both county and state what they wanted to hear—another "yes sir" welfare recipient.

This bind was familiar to me as a poverty lawyer. I felt it most strongly in disability hearings, when I would counsel clients to describe themselves as totally helpless in order to convince the court that they met the statutory definition of disability. But I had faced it in AFDC work as well, when I taught women to present themselves as abandoned, depleted of resources, and encumbered by children, to qualify for relief. I taught them to say yes to the degrading terms of "income security", as it was called—invasions of sexual privacy, disruptions of kin-ties, the forced choice of one sibling's welfare over another's. According to the Court, of course, poor women were free to say no to welfare if they weren't pleased with its terms.

What story should we tell at the hearing, I wondered out loud. Without appearing to comprehend my dilemma, Mrs. G. suggested that we tell both.

I then asked for the list she had promised to make, of all the things she had bought with the insurance money. Kotex, I thought, would speak for itself, but why, I asked, had she needed to get the girls new clothes and new shoes? She explained that the girls' old shoes were pretty much torn up, so bad that the other kids would make fun of them at school. Could she bring in the old shoes? She said she could.

We rehearsed her testimony, first about her conversation with her worker about the insurance award, and then about the Kotex and the shoes. Maybe the hearing wouldn't be too bad for Mrs. G., especially if I could help her see it all as strategy, rather than the kind of talking she could do with people she could trust.

The hearing itself was in a small conference room at the welfare office. Mrs. G. arrived with her two oldest daughters and five boxes of shoes. We took our seats across the table from the AFDC director. The hearing officer set up a portable tape recorder and got out his bible. Mrs. G.'s AFDC worker, a Black woman about her age, entered through a side door and took a seat next to her boss. The hearing officer turned on the recorder, read his obligatory opening remarks, and asked all the witnesses to rise and repeat before god that they intended to tell the truth. Mrs. G. and her worker complied.

The officer then turned the matter over to me. I gave a brief account of the background events, and then began to question Mrs. G. First I asked her about the insurance proceeds. She explained how she had received an insurance check of about six hundred dollars following a car accident in which she and her oldest daughter had been slightly injured. She said that the insurance company had already paid their medical bills and the lawyer; the last six hundred dollars was for her and her daughter, to spend however she wanted. I asked her if she had shown the check to her AFDC worker before she cashed it. She stammered. I repeated the question. She said she may have taken the check to the welfare office before she cashed it, but she couldn't remember for sure. She didn't know if she had gotten a chance to talk to anyone about it. Her worker was always real busy.

Armed with the worker's own sketchy notation of the conversation in the case file, I began to cross-examine my client, coaxing her memory about the event we had discussed so many times before. I asked if she remembered her worker telling her anything about how she could spend the money. Mrs. G. seemed to be getting more uncomfortable. It was quite a predicament for her, after all. If she "remembered" what her worker had told her, would her story expose mismanagement in the welfare office, or merely scapegoat another Black woman, who was not too much better off than herself?

When she repeated that she couldn't remember, I decided to leave the estoppel story for the moment. Maybe I could think of a way to return to it later. I moved on to the life necessities issue. I asked Mrs. G. to recount, as best she could, exactly how she had spent the insurance money. She showed me the receipts she had kept for the furniture payments, and I put them into evidence. She explained that she was buying a couple of big mattresses for the kids, and a new kitchen table. She said she had also bought some food—some frozen meat, and several boxes of Kotex for all the girls. The others in the room shifted uneasily in their chairs. Then she said she had also bought her daughters some clothes and some shoes. She had the cash register receipt for the purchase.

Choosing my words carefully, I asked why she had needed to buy the new shoes. She looked at me for a moment with an expression that I couldn't read. Then she stated, quite emphatically, that they were Sunday shoes that she had bought with the money. The girls already had everyday shoes to wear to school, but she had wanted them to have nice shoes for church too. She said no more than two or three sentences, but her voice sounded different—stronger, more composed—than I had known from her before. When she finished speaking the room was silent, except for the incessant hum of the tape machine on the table and the fluorescent lights overhead. In that moment, I felt the boundaries of our "conspiracy" shift. Suddenly I was on the outside, with the folks on the other side of the table—the welfare director and the hearing officer. The only person I could not locate in this new alignment was Mrs. G.'s welfare worker.

I didn't ask Mrs. G. to pull out the children's old shoes, as we'd rehearsed. Nor did I make my "life necessities" argument. My lawyer's language couldn't add anything to what she had said. They would have to figure out for themselves why buying Sunday shoes for her children—and saying it—was indeed a "life necessity" for this woman. After the hearing, Mrs. G. seemed elated. She asked me how she had done at the hearing, and I told her that I thought she was great. I warned her, though, that we could never be sure, in this game, who was winning, or even what side anyone was on.

We lost the hearing, and immediately petitioned for review by the chief hearing officer. I wasn't sure of the theory we'd argue, but I wanted to keep the case open until I figured out what we could do.

Three days after the appeal was filed, the county welfare director called me unexpectedly, to tell me that the county had decided to withdraw its overpayment claim against Mrs. G. He explained that on a careful review of its own records, the county had decided that it wouldn't be "fair" to make Mrs. G. pay the money back. I said I was relieved to hear that they had decided, finally, to come to a sensible result in the case. I was sorry they hadn't done so earlier. I then said something about how confusing the lump sum rule was, and how Mrs. G.'s worker had checked with her supervisor before telling Mrs. G. it was all right to spend the insurance money. I said I was sure that the screw up was not anyone's fault. He mumbled a bureaucratic pleasantry and we hung up.

When I told Mrs. G that she had won, she said she had just wanted to "do the right thing," and that she hoped they understood that she'd never meant to do anything wrong. I repeated that they were the ones who had made the mistake. Though I wasn't sure exactly what was going on inside the welfare office, at least this crisis was over.

This essay is a reading of the story of Mrs. G. It is centered on the "fair hearing," the legal frame within which her actions took place. What kind of space did this hearing give to Mrs. G. in which to speak? What use did she make of it, and how did its conventions and its context limit what she could say? Finally, "what kind of hearing" might enable Mrs. G.—a person subordinated as a speaker and a citizen by her gender, race, and class identity—to participate with greater dignity in social decision making about her needs?

According to *Goldberg v. Kelly,* (1970), the landmark Supreme Court case that read the Federal Constitution to guarantee hearing rights to welfare recipients, the right to a hearing is an expression of the "Nation's basic commitment . . . to foster the dignity and well-being of all persons within its borders." There is no doubt that *Goldberg* was a significant strategic victory for the poor. But the reality of Mrs. G.'s hearing was much more complex than the Court's rhetoric would suggest. It was intimidating, humiliating, frustrating—silencing. But at the same time it allowed her, for a moment, to speak out. If Mrs. G.'s hearing realized the *Goldberg* Court's vision of participation, it was only in a deeply ambiguous way.

The disjuncture between the liberal vision of due process and the complex experiences of women like Mrs. G.—poor women, women of color, single women with children—at fair hearings is a sign of the deep structures of subordination that underwrite our legal culture. The vision of the hearing as an occasion for participation, dignity, and fairness assumes that speakers all come to it with fundamentally equal power as social persons and fundamentally similar presumptive capacities for speech. Yet subordinating ideologies such as race and gender, and the realities of political, economic, and cultural domination that those ideologies sustain, undermine the liberal goals of hearing procedures.

Mrs. G. had a hearing in which all of the rituals of due process set out in *Goldberg v. Kelly* were scrupulously observed. No formal doctrines were invoked to prohibit her from speaking, or to dismiss or second-guess what she said. And yet Mrs. G. did not find her voice welcomed at that hearing. A pattern of social, economic, and cultural forces underwrote the procedural formalities of her hearing, repressing and devaluing her voice. And the law—by its principled indifference to Mrs. G.'s lived experience—condoned and even supported those forces.

Thus, Mrs. G.'s experience at the hearing stands as a critique of the legal norms and social realities that compel some speakers, in order to participate, to silence themselves. Yet at the same time, the hearing also shows a woman finding the momentary power to reject the legal norms and rename the social realities that compelled her silence. Before we can interpret the hearing, however, we must look more closely at the constraints under which she spoke.

A Survey of the Landscape of Mrs. G.'s Hearing: The Forces Urging Silence

Out of the complex social context of Mrs. G.'s hearing, three forces stand out as obstacles to her participation. All of them are linked, sometimes subtly, to her social identity as poor, Black, and female. First, she did not feel that she could risk speaking her mind freely to welfare officials. Second, even if she could find the courage to speak out at the hearing, her words were not likely to be credited as legitimate testimony, because of the language she had learned to speak as a poor woman of color, and because of the kind of person that racist and gendered imagery portrayed her to be. And finally, because she had no voice in the political process that set the substantive terms of her welfare eligibility, (*Thornburg v. Gingles,* 1986)[4] the issues that she was constrained to talk about bore little relation to her own questions about the meaning and fairness of the state's action.

Intimidation: The Hierarchy of Caste

Perhaps Mrs. G.'s strongest feelings as she approached the hearing were fear and intimidation. The people she had to face at the hearing were the same ones who would decide if she would get welfare and Food Stamps in the future. From her standpoint, they were also the ones who could take her children away, if they wanted to, or make it hard for her to stay in her apartment or find the occasional jobs she needed to make ends meet.

The ground of her fear was very deep. It reflected the long history of violence toward her people in that county, and the daily reminders that the history was not over. But her fear also responded to her real present-day relationship to the welfare office. First of all, a convergence of factors—the lack of child care, training, and, most importantly, jobs, especially safe, stable, decent-paying jobs—made her dependent on the county, the welfare office, the housing authority, to survive. And she knew that the rules of welfare would give the county plenty of ways to make her life hard if she became known as a troublemaker.

Thus, her fear reflected the racial caste system that still structured social relations in the community, and the more particular structures of welfare doctrine that gave the dominant caste, the white power structure—she called it simply "the Man"—a potent modern-day weapon for keeping her quiet. The caste system has been treated at length in historical and anthropological literature. (Davis, 1941; Dollard, 1937, p. 245)[5] Mrs. G.'s story suggests that, in spite of the sweeping changes that the Civil Rights era brought in social norms and legal structures, this system has not changed much for people like her in the half-century between the 1930s and the 1980s.

Her fear also reflected her sense that her welfare "entitlements" offered her no real security. The function of welfare to control the poor has been well studied. (Piven and Cloward, 1971; Bell, 1965) Recent changes in the structure of welfare law, changes made in the 1970s and 1980s and justified on the basis of cutting costs, have made it a stronger weapon of social control. These changes have made welfare eligibility much more bureaucratized, much more rule-bound than it had previously been. Initially, welfare advocates supported the formalization of eligibility rules as a way to extend benefits to Blacks and other groups who were excluded in the earlier regime of unfettered local discretion. But by the early 1980s, the formalization of eligibility rules was serving a very different political agenda. In the 1980s legalistic eligibility requirements were imposed to reduce welfare expenditures. In addition to providing new reasons for denying welfare to otherwise eligible clients, new procedural requirements made welfare programs too complex and burdensome for many poor people to negotiate. (Lipsky, 1984, p.3)

In Mrs. G's experience, these highly formalized rules have a more important function than the wholesale exclusion of people from the rolls. They also keep people in fear. First of all, "churning," the occasional, arbitrary termination of large numbers of people for technical reasons, has the effect of keeping all recipients uncertain about whether their next check will come. And the technical rules, although they appear very rigid, actually conceal countless enclaves of discretion, hidden places for harassing clients who get out of line, and obscuring the human agency behind that harassment (Frug, 1984; Ferguson, 1984; Fraser, 1987).

Mrs. G. believed that "going to legal aid" or "asking for a hearing" were the best ways to make sure that this discretion would be used against her.

Thus, Mrs. G.'s experience of fear about confronting the welfare office was engendered by concrete legal and social arrangements. From her perspective, these structures subverted the formal protections of the hearing process, and posed a barrier to her speech. Had Mrs. G. not found her way to a lawyer, that barrier might have excluded her from the hearing process altogether: it would certainly have been safer for her simply to stay away. (Gwaltney, 1981, p. 31)[6] But even *with* a lawyer to protect her, Mrs. G.'s deep fear of retaliation was not completely put to rest. She did not need to be a legal scholar to understand that the law was largely impotent— or indifferent— to the subtle texture of retaliation in the welfare office. Her only real protection lay in the self-negating verbal strategies that she had learned so well— speaking female, crafting her words like a mirror (Gwaltney, 1981, p.44)[7] to reflect what she sensed the Other—"the Man"— wanted her to say.

Self-Doubt: The Ideology of Welfare Fraud

A second local force, the imagery of welfare fraud, posed a further barrier to Mrs. G.'s speaking frankly and with dignity at the hearing. While her social and economic marginality made her reluctant to speak at all, the mythology of welfare fraud would undermine her credibility if she sought to be heard. This imagery predisposed the hearing officer to distrust Mrs. G., and led her to second-guess the integrity of her own actions. Furthermore, overbroad measures to control fraud deterred her from voicing any challenge to welfare officials.

"Welfare fraud" has long been one of the dominant themes expressing the ambivalence, indeed aversion, within modern political culture, to welfare. "Fraud" connotes an idea— a negative image of the "typical welfare recipient." (Pear, 1983)[8]. At the same time, it justifies an elaborate regime for monitoring eligibility determinations and restricting the welfare rolls ("Providing Effective Representation in Welfare Fraud Cases" 1981, p.53)[9]. In periods of constriction of welfare benefits, as in the last decade, the government has typically flooded the media with stories about the extent of the fraud problem, as it enacted overextensive programs of fraud control.

Given the inadequacy of AFDC benefit levels and the dollar for dollar reduction of benefits when a recipient reports work (Wickes, 1985),[10] many welfare recipients must add other income to their welfare stipends when they can. Furthermore, program rules are so complex and terminations so frequent and so arbitrary that few recipients know how much they should be receiving, or why. In these circumstances, recipients typically feel themselves vulnerable to fraud charges. A finding of fraud means suspension from some benefit programs and a very real threat of jail. Thus, "fraud" is a very concrete threat that adds to the more diffuse fear of the welfare office that recipients like Mrs. G. feel. This threat overwhelmed her at one point in the story, when, distrusting her own lawyer's assurance, she contracted with the fraud investigator to give back the overpayment. But even when her fear of fraud did not silence her entirely, it counselled her to keep a "low profile" before the welfare office, asking few questions and making few demands.

Furthermore the obsession with fraud, in the media and in the eligibility process itself, places a stigma on all welfare recipients. It leads some to forego welfare altogether. (Physicians' Task Force on Hunger in America, 1986) And the popular mythology about welfare recipients—embodied in the Black, jewel-bedecked, Cadillac-driving welfare queen—conveys a negative stereotype to the broader public. This image—superficially moralistic, but fundamentally racist and sexist—encourages others to dissociate themselves from the political interests of welfare recipients.

For a woman like Mrs. G., who does not have the option to forego welfare, fraud control becomes a constant message that she is not a person worthy of trust. Rather, fraud imagery dictates that she will try at every moment to cheat the system, to lie. This image resonates with the ancient stereotype of woman as liar, as well as other negative images of poor women of color. With these deeply negative images evoked, she begins to doubt her own decisions and her own words. Thus, the fraud policy—so defensible on its face—is one of the structures that exacts silence, or self-defeating speech, from Mrs. G.—in the welfare office and at the hearing. When she is told so clearly, so incessantly, that she is expected to lie, her way of affirming her own dignity is to assume her own guilt, explaining that "I didn't *mean* to do anything wrong."

Passivity: The Logic of Bureaucracy

A third local force that obstructed Mrs. G.'s full participation in the hearing is the bureaucratic structure of social welfare policy, and indeed, of the legal-political institutions that create it. This force entered the hearing through the questions that the advocate put to Mrs. G. The lawyer taught Mrs. G. to conform her words to the elements of the "lump sum" rule, the "life necessities" exception, and estoppel. Unlike the other two forces—which sought to silence Mrs. G. entirely or to undermine the value of her speech—this third force dictated the shape that Mrs. G. had to give to her story—its basic plot and its motivating themes—if she was to be heard.

Mrs. G.'s persistent feeling about being on welfare was, in her words, that she was "boxed in." None of the formal rules of the welfare set up boundaries to protect her against churning or retaliation. Yet those rules confined her: they reduced her need to a mathematical formula for assistance. In all of her dealings with the welfare system—whether she was filling out forms at the welfare office, answering questions at a hearing, or casting her vote for those with the power to write the rules—Mrs. G. felt boxed in.

This bureaucratization of welfare was the third force that silenced Mrs. G. As public regulation of social life has expanded in complex societies, more and more activities have been made compatible with bureaucratic logic. That is, modes of acting—intuitions or customs—have been "legalized," or reformulated as systems of explicit rules, and values have been translated into a uniform currency—or "monetized." Bureaucracy has been a means for both centralized resource allocation and uniform policy implementation across large, diverse populations. But these apparent "efficiencies" of bureaucracy carry a significant hidden cost; many social critics argue that the process of bureaucratization has gotten "out of control" in the regulatory state. Although they use different language, these critics share the sense that the expanding bureaucratization of modern life threatens to destroy the face to face networks and practices that we rely on, as human actors, to make sense of our social experience. (Habermas, 1983; Habermas, 1985, pp. 210–11; Fraser, 1989, p. 291). Some of these critics make the stronger argument that in capitalist or patriarchal societies, bureaucracy becomes a specific vehicle of gender and class subordination.

Mrs. G. and her children are among the most vulnerable to this "pathology" of over-bureaucratization. Because they are stranded by the economy, they must depend directly on the state for their subsistence. To manage the task of maintaining them, the welfare bureaucracy constitutes the terms of their lives in a form, a currency, that it can process. It equates Mrs. G.'s need with the sum of the stipends the state is willing to pay her.[11] It then contains her anger and her pain by locating those feelings as symptoms, within a de-politicized "self" that psychiatric technologies are developed to manage.

Mrs. G. has no role in negotiating the meaning of either her psychiatrically-defined pathologies or her bureaucratically-constructed "needs." She is excluded on principle from the therapeutic discourse: it is the experts who had the prerogative to say how her psyche and culture are defective. (L. Gordon, 1988a)[12] Her status in the conversation about welfare policy is more problematic, however. According to the theory of representative democracy, she *should* feel herself a participant in the process that creates welfare policy. When she confronts the "lump sum rule" at her fair hearing, she should know that her vote gave her at least a *virtual* hand creating that rule. Yet that "knowledge" is not part of her experience.

First of all, racism has kept her community from voting for much of its history. But Mrs. G.'s exclusion from the formulation of welfare policy has a deeper source as well. The public discussion of welfare—even among those who *have* access to the debate—has itself been framed by a bureaucratic logic. Its broad outlines reinforce deeply rooted moral judgments about the poor, but its details are left to experts—economists and managers—to design. The discourse has become one of costs and incentives, of crisis containment and systems management, rather than a search among citizens for the social meanings of their interdependent needs. In this discourse, welfare is defined as a technical problem, rather than an ethical and political challenge to the entire community. In this discussion, Mrs. G.—the primary *target* of welfare policy—is not regarded as a speaking being. The talk she might do—plain, angry, personal, . . . uncertain—is not accepted as sensible speech. Rather, she occupies the familiar female position. She is the Object who is shaped by those with the authority to speak, to reflect the internal logic of their own systems of power.

Feminist scholars are beginning to expose the concrete ways that a welfare policy that is generated in this bureaucratized discussion has reflected and sustained women's subordination. Mothers' pensions, and their federalization in the Social Security Act, gave some poor women, generally women from elite social groups, a small measure of economic power to escape patriarchal households if they so chose. Yet at the same time the Social Security Act systematically reinforced the male-headed nuclear family. All of the New Deal welfare programs were infused with incentives to encourage this family pattern at the expense of egalitarian or woman-centered alternatives. (Abramovitz, 1988; L. Gordon, 1988a, pp. 108–15; Pearce, 1986, pp. 29–46) Furthermore, the AFDC program was unique among New Deal welfare programs in requiring claimants to open up their sexual lives to the scrutiny and control of welfare workers. In order to participate in AFDC, Mrs. G. had no choice but to conform her life to these conditions.

At the fair hearing, it was Mrs. G's *voice,* rather than her behavior, which was compelled to assent to the bureaucratized—and arguably also gendered—logic of welfare. The law of evidence—doctrines of relevancy and materiality—commanded her to keep her speech within the categories that the legislative/administrative process had generated. Even though the technicalities of evidence law did not apply to her case, the hearing officer would only attend to the narrow issues that the AFDC regulations charged him to decide. Was Mrs. G.'s insurance award covered under the "lump sum" rule? Did Mrs. G.'s expenditures meet the administrative criteria of "life necessities?" Were the features of estoppel present in the case, and should the doctrine apply? Discrete responses to those questions—that was the measure of "participation" that this hearing gave to Mrs. G. She best not "fight the questions" (Menkel-Meadow, 1985) if she wanted her voice to be heard at all. Rather, she had to speak her need as an accounting of how she had spent a few hundred dollars. Within these constraints, her speech might be worth that sum if she won; it would have no other consequence.

The Route Taken: Evasive Maneuvers or a Woman's Voice?

If we measure Mrs. G.'s hearing against the norms of procedural formality, it appears to conform. The hearing appears to admit every person to speak on equal terms. Yet within the local landscape of her hearing, Mrs. G.'s voice is constrained by forces that procedural doctrine will neither acknowledge nor oppose. Each of these forces attaches a specific social cost to her gender and race identity. The caste system implements race and gender ideology in social arrangements. The "fraud issue" revives misogynist and racist stereotypes that had been forced at least partly underground by the social movements of the 1960s and 1970s. And the welfare system responds to gender and race-based injustice in the economy by constructing the poor as Woman—as an object of social control. Given the power amassed behind these forces, we might predict that they should win the contest with Mrs. G. for her voice.

Yet to detect these forces, we have read the story through a structuralist lens, which shows only the stark dichotomy of subordination and social control. (L. Gordon, 1986) It is ironic that this lens, which works so well to expose the contours of Mrs. G.'s silence, also leaves her—as a woman actively negotiating the terrain in which she found herself—entirely out of focus. If we re-center our reading on Mrs. G., as a woman shaping events, unpredictably, to realize her own meanings, we can no longer say with certainty what the outcome will be. We cannot tell who prevailed at the hearing, or where the power momentarily came to rest. Rather, what we see is a sequence of moves, a set of questions. Why did Mrs. G. depart from the script she had rehearsed for the hearing, to speak about Sunday shoes? And why did the county finally abandon its claim to cut her stipend?

Why Did Mrs. G. Depart from her Script at the Hearing?

The lawyer had scripted Mrs. G. as a victim. That was the only strategy for the hearing that the lawyer, within the constraints of her own social position, could imagine for Mrs. G. She had warned her client to play the victim if she wanted to win. Mrs. G. learned her lines. She came to the hearing well-rehearsed in the lawyer's strategy. But in the hearing, she did not play. When she was cued to perform, without any signal to her lawyer, she abandoned their script. For a moment she stepped out of the role of the supplicant. She ignored the doctrinal pigeonholes that would fragment the sense of her voice. She put aside all that the lawyer told her the audience wanted to hear. Instead, when asked about "life necessities," she explained that she had used her money to meet *her own* needs. She had bought her children Sunday shoes.

Mrs. G.'s talk about Sunday shoes spoke in several different ways about what she needed to live her life. On the most literal level, she was making a statement about religion, and its importance in her life. For subordinated communities, physical necessities do not meet the minimum requirements for a human life. Rather, subordinated groups must create cultural practices through which they can elaborate an autonomous, oppositional culture and consciousness. Without shared rituals for sustaining their survival and motivating their resistance, subordinated groups run the risk of total domination—of losing the *will* to use their human powers to subvert their oppressor's control over them. Religion, spirituality, the social institution of the Black Church, has been one such self-affirming cultural practice for the communities of African-American slaves, and remains central to the expression of Black identity and group consciousness today. By naming Sunday shoes as a life necessity, Mrs. G. was speaking to the importance of this cultural practice in her life, a truth that the system's categories did not comprehend.

At the same time that Mrs. G.'s statement affirmed the church, it condemned the welfare system. By rejecting the welfare's definition of life necessities, she asserted her need to have a say about *the criteria* for identifying her needs. Her statement was a demand for meaningful participation in the political conversations in which her needs are contested and defined. In the present welfare system, poor women—the objects of welfare—are structurally excluded from that conversation. When Mrs. G. insisted on her need to say for herself what her "life necessities" might be, she expanded, for a moment, the accepted boundaries of that conversation.

Mrs. G.'s statement also spoke to a third dimension of her "life necessity." When Mrs. G. talked about buying Sunday shoes, she defied the rules of legal rhetoric—the rule of relevancy, the rule against "rambling," the unwritten rule that told her to speak like a victim if she wanted to win. Had Mrs. G. spoken the language that was proper for her in the setting, her relevant, logical, submissive responses to their questions might have been comprehended. But, by dutifully speaking the language of an institution from which subordinated groups have historically been excluded, and in which Mrs. G. felt herself to have no stake, her voice would have repeated, and legitimated, the very social and cultural patterns and priorities that kept her down. Had she been a *respectful* participant in the legal ritual, Mrs. G. would have articulated someone else's need, or pleasure, rather than her own.

Mrs. G. did not boycott the hearing altogether. Rather, in her moment of misbehavior, she may have been standing her ground within it. Although she appeared, at first, to be deferring to the system's categories and rules, when she finally spoke, she animated them with her own experience. She stretched the category of "life necessity" to express her own values, and turned it around to critique the welfare's systemic disregard of her own point of view. By talking about Sunday shoes, she claimed, for one fragile moment, what was perhaps her most basic "life necessity." She claimed a position of equality in the speech community—an equal power to take part in the *making* of language—of the categories and institutions and norms of her community—as she spoke through that language about her needs.

When Mrs. G. claimed this power, she affirmed the feminist insight that the dominant languages do *not* construct a closed system, from which there can be no escape. (Jardine, 1985) Although dominant groups may control the *social institutions* that regulate these languages, those groups cannot control the *capacity* of subordinated peoples to speak. Thus, women have evaded complete domination through their *practice* of speaking, like Mrs. G. spoke at her hearing, from their own intuitions and their own experience. Feminist writers have drawn three figures—play, archaeology, and poetry—to describe this emancipatory language practice. (Yaeger, 1988, p. 18; Daly, 1979, p. 24; de Lauretis, 1984; Lorde, 1984a, pp. 37–38)[13]

When Mrs. G. construed "life necessities" to include Sunday shoes, she turned the hearing into a place where she could talk, on a par with the experts, about her "needs." For a moment she defied the rigid official meaning of necessity, and refused to leave nameless the values and passions that gave sense to her life. Adrienne Rich describes the process:

> For many women, the commonest words are having to be sifted through, rejected, laid aside for a long time, or turned to the light for new colors and flashes of meaning: power, love, control, violence, political,

> personal, private, friendship, community, sexual, work, pain, pleasure, self, integrity. . . . When we become acutely, disturbingly aware of the language we are using and that is using us, we begin to grasp a material resource that women have never before collectively attempted to repossess. . . . (Rich, 1979a, p. 247)

Mrs. G. might want to add "participation" and "need" to the poet's list.

The story of Mrs. G. tells us that the hearing officer ruled against Mrs. G., and then the county welfare department decided to drop the case, restoring her full stipend. But the text does not say how the men across the table experienced the hearing, or why the county eventually gave in. Did Mrs. G.'s paradoxical "strategy" disarm her audience? Did she draw a response from her audience that was different—more compelling—than the pity that her lawyer had wanted to play upon? Did her presentation of herself as an independent, church-going woman, who would exercise her own judgment, and was willing to say what she needed—did these qualities make the men fear her, respect her, regard her for a moment as a person, rather than a case? Did they feel a moment of anger—about the ultimately powerless roles that they were assigned to play in the bureaucracy that regulated all of their lives? Were these men moved, by the hearing, to snatch her case from the computer and subject it to their own human judgment?

We do not know why the county decided to drop Mrs. G.'s case. What we do know, however, is that the outcome of Mrs. G.'s hearing—regardless of what we take it to mean—did not change the terms on which Mrs. G. and others like her must live out their lives. Even if Mrs. G. felt a moment of power—of personhood—at the hearing, and even if the welfare officials in the audience responded to her voice, that moment did not reverse the systematic forces that subordinate her. She remained a Black, single mother on welfare—poor, dependent, despised. The landscape which shaped her life continued to constrict her expression. Mrs. G.'s unruly participation at her fair hearing was *itself* political action. Yet substantial change in Mrs. G.'s life chances will come only as that landscape itself is transformed through further action, that is guided by a collective inquiry into our differing experiences, mutual responsibilities, and common aspirations.

Notes

1. This story is based upon my work as a legal aid lawyer in North Carolina from 1982 to 1986. Certain details have been changed to avoid compromising client confidentiality.

2. Aid to Families with Dependent Children, 42 U.S.C. 601 *et seq.*
3. I use "she" because virtually all of my clients who received AFDC benefits were single mothers. Although single fathers with custody of their children are technically eligible to receive AFDC, they account for an insubstantial percentage of the recipient pool: in my four years of welfare advocacy, I did not encounter any single fathers on AFDC.
4. A class action by Black voters in North Carolina in which the court found that "the legacy of official discrimination in voting matters, education, housing, employment, and health services; and the persistence of campaign appeals to racial prejudice acted . . . to impair the ability of geographically insular and politically cohesive groups of black voters to participate equally in the political process." 106 S.Ct. 2752, 2757 (1986).
5. These works explain how the sanctions of lynching and starvation were systematically used to control Blacks, by punishing them for transgression.
6. In John Gwaltney's ethnographic study of working class Blacks, *Drylongso,* Ms. Ruth Shays gives expression to this choice, familiar to all subordinated peoples. After stating that things have not changed much since slavery, Ms. Shays explains that "our foreparents had sense enough not to spill their in-guts to whitefolkes. . . . They just kept everything to themselves."
7. A Black working class man states the same theme to anthropologist John Gwaltney when he explains that "[w]hite people want black people to do whatever white people want them to do at that time. They just don't want black people to have a mind of their own, or anyway, they want to be sure that we don't show it. . . . You simply cannot be honest with white people."
8. The article reports how President Reagan used an anecdote of a Chicago "welfare queen" which grossly exaggerated the facts of the case to justify his policy "cracking down" on welfare fraud, and on welfare eligibility in general.
9. The article states that, "[P]oor people often suffer unduly when they are suspected of welfare fraud. . . . All too often, welfare recipients faced with such threats [of termination and/or criminal prosecution] agree to leave the public assistance rolls, even though they remain eligible for assistance. In other instances, recipients sign agreements to repay all benefits claimed to have been received improperly, without a prior determination that funds were in fact wrongfully received.")
10. In 1984 the combined level of AFDC and Food Stamp payments was on average, only about 67 percent of the federal poverty level. For a complete breakdown, see Wickes (1985).
11. In the AFDC program, the states are given almost unchecked discretion to set "need standards" for AFDC families that are based on their own fiscal concerns rather than their best estimates of actual costs of subsistence expenses. See "State Cost of Living Measures and AFDC Payments," 1987. The states are then free to set their AFDC *payment* levels substantially below their own need estimate. See *Jefferson v. Hackey,* (1972).
12. For a historical perspective on the recurring literature that would define Mrs. G.'s personal experience of poverty as a psychiatric or cultural problem, see L. Gordon (1988).
13. The figure of play connotes an exuberant, unruly approach toward conventions of discourse which disarms an oppressive language-system, reanimating it with women's experiences. Patricia Yaeger (1988) elaborates:

    [P]layfulness and word play are very much at issue in the woman writer's reinvention of her culture. . . . [P]lay itself is a form of aesthetic activity in which

> . . . what has been burdensome becomes—at least momentarily—weightless, transformable, transformative. As women play with old texts, the burden of the tradition is lightened and shifted; it has the potential for being remade.

The figure of archaeology refers to the collective searching of private memories and the shared past to uncover the suppressed meanings that are latent in familiar words. Mary Daly (1979, p. 24) invokes archaeology when she describes how, in her writing, she searches for the hidden powers of words:

> Often I unmask deceptive words by dividing them and employing alternate meanings for prefixes. I also unmask their hidden reversals, often by using less known or "obsolete" meanings. . . . Sometimes I simply invite the reader to listen to words in a different way. When I play with words I do this attentively, deeply, paying attention to etymology, to varied dimensions of meaning, to deep background meanings and subliminal associations.

The third figure that guides this emancipatory language practice is poetry—coaxing the language just beyond its systemic boundaries, toward images and understandings that both expand, and challenge, its rule. Used in this sense, poetry is closely connected to consciousness raising—the feminist method in which women, through their *practice* of talking together about their own experience, create the common language which makes that talking possible. See T. de Lauretis, *Alice Doesn't: Feminism, Semiotics, Cinema* (1984) (defining consciousness raising as "the collective articulation of one's experience of sexuality and gender . . . [which] has produced, and continues to elaborate, a radically new mode of understanding the subject's relation to social-historical reality. Consciousness raising is the original critical instrument that women developed toward such understanding, the analysis of social reality and its critical revision.") Consciousness raising places new demands on the language because, through it, women grope to share feelings that have previously gone unnamed. When those feelings find words, poetry is produced. As Audre Lorde expresses the matter in her essay, "Poetry is Not a Luxury":

> We can train ourselves to respect our feelings and to transpose them into a language so they can be shared. And where that language does not yet exist, it is our poetry which helps to fashion it. See Lorde (1984a).

II

The Construction of Body in Law

Once the Cartesian conception of humans as subjective immaterial souls inhabiting, but essentially independent of, physical bodies is rejected, the question of defining the characteristics of bodies becomes inseparable from that of defining persons. So, too, is the power *to define bodies the* power *to determine persons. Appreciation for the power of language and of the significance of the symbolic in the task of definition of women's bodies in law permeate these papers, as does a corresponding scepticism of the existence of pre-socially "natural" human behavior.*

The papers in this section critique standard representations of women's embodied selves. Judith Grbich and Kristin Bumiller are explicitly concerned with how legal institutions "protect" only those women who conform to male expectations and interpretations of "Woman." Grbich focuses on the practice of awarding compensation for physical disfigurement. Bumiller describes a rape trial.

Both papers are attentive to how the female "victim" finds herself the inevitable object of scrutiny, her fate as legal claimant dependent on her presentation of herself as conforming to male-defined standards. Like Lucie White in the preceding section, both authors emphasize how legal constraints suppress expression of women's perceptions and experiences. Women realize they must alter their realities to succeed in the legal arena, where they can claim redress only by being drawn as caricatures in power scenarios constructed by the male legal system. They affirm these constructions, and such affirmation, in turn, serves to further reinforce male-defined conceptions of "woman," however alien to women's self perceptions.

Judith Grbich insists that women's voices must determine the meaning of practices in which women engage. Claudia Card's discussion serves as an example of such self-definition. Card echoes Grbich's complaint that women's experience is currently interpreted as simulated male experience, the female body portrayed as a simulated male body. As Card notes, the classification of lesbian love-making as sexual *activity, in spite of the fact that neither reproduction nor reproductive organs are involved, is incomprehensible unless such love making is seen as simulated heterosexual behavior. Rather than accept a definition of their identities and practices grounded in the oppressive institution of sexuality, Card urges lesbians to define their selves and relationships in ways that they can stand behind as genuine expressions of character.*

4

The Body in Legal Theory

Judith E. Grbich

Introduction

Women have always been incredulous about the naturalness of power but their experience has been defined as ignorance by professional communities whose beliefs have been established as foundations of knowledge. Feminist jurisprudence has begun to question these professional communities about the naturalness of legal power and the foundational character of beliefs about law (MacKinnon, 1982, 1983). This paper will address some issues raised by feminist work upon the theory of the subject (Coward and Ellis, 1977), it will investigate the place of subjectivity within disciplinary constructions of meaning. It aims to consider the theory of the subject within jurisprudence as a way of articulating the issues which traditional jurisprudence ignores—the positionality of knowers about law, the negotiation of meaning about authority, and the professional academic practices which exclude women's experience from the development of legal theory. It investigates the epistemological status of the body. I prefer to describe this project as one of legal theory rather than jurisprudence as legal theory connotes to me an inquiry into the relation of individual subjects to the question of authority; it could just as well be described as feminist jurisprudence. But the present meaning of jurisprudence seems to present "law" as an existing object waiting to be discovered, while I prefer to understand my project as an inquiry into the practices whereby the beliefs and questions about authority create our understanding of "law."

This paper is a substantially edited version of "The Body in Legal Theory" *Wisconsin Women's Law Journal* (pending). A draft, exploratory version was presented to the Third Annual Feminism and Legal Theory Conference "Women and Intimacy" Madison, Wisconsin (July 27–August 1, 1987).

The theory of the subject questions the origins of knowledge and directs attention to social practices which contain and confine what subjects can know. It places our recognition of what is "natural" as an effect of power—whether the naturalness of femininity or the naturalness of legal institutions. It can provide a link with feminist political struggle, for it seeks to promote women's subjectivity as valid knowledges, their sense of what is just and unjust in present social conditions become the resources for changing our beliefs and knowledge about authority.

Part One of the paper raises questions about frameworks or assumptions regarding legal knowledge (Stewart, 1981; Duncanson, 1982). It assumes that the search for criteria of knowledge, the search for certainty, can only be abandoned when one occupies a position of social power. It assumes that the calls for abandoning epistemology and simply entering the "conversations of mankind" (Rorty, 1980), as a theory of knowing, cannot be heeded while women's experience continues to be constituted as inexpert, unreasonable and merely gossip. Beliefs in the existence of foundations can only be abandoned by those who control entry to the conversations, in which case it is only the form of foundationalism which is being changed, not its existence as social practice. Poststructuralist theory is considered in the context of the present concerns of feminist jurisprudence with the meaning of legal language and the possibilities for female subjects of changing the meanings of words. I argue that problematizing the linguistic categories of thought should be thought of as a question of subjectivity, as expressions of life, rather than as interpretation.

Part Two develops the idea of language practices as sexualized forms of representation, of language as always expressing the imaginary or metaphorical form by which we constitute the "forms of life." Part Two is concerned with developing a feminist theory of law as embodied imagination, as a way of locating the present concrete practices by which we are required to believe that professional, masculine metaphors of "being" are universal. Part Three is an enquiry into practices of constituting women as subjects for male lives; it is an attempt to develop the theory of law as embodied imagination in order to make places for women's imaginings, for women's theories of being which have been excluded by professional practices of the disciplines. Anti-discrimination practices are theorized as part of the postmodern conditions in which women must negotiate the reality of individual mistreatment.

I Frameworks of Knowledge: Ways of Knowing

This part is an investigation of some of the present conditions of writing feminist legal theory. Its aim is to interrogate the current frameworks of knowledge within which the feminist jurisprudential endeavour is placed. Its purpose is to locate those features of professional, academic law-writing which appear to distance the legal theory project from the concerns of current political practice for women. It locates the writer as part of the investigation in order to retain as far as possible the nature of the writing conditions of feminist legal theory. One problem to be investigated is how can I write a legal theory for women (Smith, 1979), that is, an account of the nature of power and authority which is sensitive to the different understandings which women experience about authority, without reproducing the conditions of that authority?

Questions about the nature of understanding in the law discipline link theories of knowledge or epistemologies with present social conditions. Is the way in which we know about a society connected to the way in which it is? Is the way in which we know about law, and jurisprudence, connected to the way in which women can achieve social justice? The commitment to "rights" within liberal political philosophy and liberal legal theory is premised upon a theory of knowledge in which the "objects" of knowledge, the knowledge itself, are understood to be separate from the subject or inquirer.[1] A "right" is taken to be a thing which someone can have and know the qualities of independently of the differing conditions of their lives. The question which a focus upon frameworks of knowledge makes possible is the materiality of "rights talk." Can "rights talk," the expression of rights, be used by oppressed groups to change the concept of what is just and unjust? Can the expression of what is just and unjust alter the practice of oppression and exploitation? An adequate approach to considering the materiality of "rights talk" requires attention to the subject of language, ideology and knowledge—the knower. It also requires changing the epistemological status of the knower to that of an active subject situated in relations within which meaning can be negotiated.

Finding Poststructuralist Epistemology

Poststructuralist theory takes different forms in different disciplines and coheres as "post structuralism," as an "ism," only by a common origin in Saussurian linguistic theory (Weedon, 1987). Saussure theorized language as a structure within which meaning was produced by the differences between the words or signifiers. Structuralism became that theory of meaning in which the networks of differences supported themselves. Poststructuralism was that dissatisfaction with the subject as a "programmed" individual. Poststructuralist theories have differed in the extent to which human activity, subjectivity or consciousness was placed as an account of the active subject but nevertheless they have retained the focus upon the primacy of language and discourse. It is difficult to find an epistemology or theory of knowing within poststructuralism, as the priority retained for language over subjectivity has meant the subject is always theorized as knowing within terms whose meaning is never fixed. Where meaning is always deferred and present justifications of the authenticity of belief by reference to experience must be rejected, epistemological concerns have been transposed into those of hermeneutics or "the conversations of mankind" (Rorty, 1980).[2] However, where meaning can be regarded as temporarily fixed or as contingent upon the time and place of the conversation, certainty can be claimed from experience and knowledgeability posed. This does not imply any return to picture theories; beliefs gain their authenticity as knowledge by inclusion in the conversations which language and power make available. The difference that matters is that exclusions from conversations by use of reason, logic, science, expertise or professionalism can be identified as privileged beliefs, beliefs which would otherwise remain as barriers to those constituted by powerful conversations as irrational, illogical, unscientific, inexpert or simply unknowledgeable.

Structuralist linguistic theory was a resource available for the psychoanalytical theory of Lacan, the political theory of Althusser, Foucault's early archaeologies of knowledge and the deconstruction methodology proposed by Derrida. In each, language as systems of signification is given priority over subjectivity; meaning is always deferred and certainty forever dispersed. Lacan emphasized the primacy of language, a system of symbols or signifiers, in the construction of the individual as subject or self. It is the child's entry into the symbolic universe, via language, that constitutes the child as self or separate from his or her mother (Coward and Ellis, 1977, 93–121). The idea of acquiring a position in consciousness by identification through language with imaginary signifiers was taken up by Althusser in his concept of interpellation (Althusser, 1971, 162). Subject positions are created within discourse and the human person is located within the theoretical structure only so far as he or she may occupy such a position, a position which must always be the site of various intersecting discourses. This Althusserian theorization of the social construction of the human subject has borrowed from Lacan the idea that the individual takes up his or her social position and subjectivity as a person by entering into the discourse of language. The individual is interpellated into the social, in the Althusserian sense of being hailed by the categories of speech and thought; the individual recognizes himself or herself as the person hailed and is thereby constituted as a person.

In *The Birth of the Clinic,* an early archaeology by Foucault of medical knowledge, meaning was that play of signification between words. Foucault was writing a history of the beliefs by speakers that words represented objects of pathological anatomy. Knowledge was a relation between words which was forever being rearranged at another site (Foucault, 1973, p. 90). In *The Archaeology of Knowledge* he stated that he had no wish to exclude or discourage others in their efforts to uncover and free "prediscursive" experiences from the "tyranny of the text," he did not wish to "neutralize discourse, to make it the sign of something else" nor to "pierce through its destiny in order to reach what remains silently anterior to it . . ." (Foucault, 1972, 47). He preferred to "maintain it in its consistency, to make it emerge in its own complexity." In the "Order of Discourse" a commentator upon the text was understood by Foucault to be simply reiterating that meaning which was within a text and always silently beyond (Foucault, 1984, 116). Derrida was writing in opposition to the belief that western thought has been structured in terms of dichotomies or polarities: good vs evil, truth vs error and man vs. women. Derrida's project was to expose the privileging of terms given first place in the preceding list. Meaning was to be located outside these oppositional structures, within the gaps, elsewhere, and at another time. Meaning was difference from the logical differences within the structure of language and deferred. The deconstructive project involved reversing the priorities of oppositional structures and displacing them. Simple reversals of logocentrism would not be enough, one had to tease out the "warring forces of signification within the test itself" by the techniques of displacement, and supplement (Johnson, 1981, p. xiv; Derrida, 1976).

One of the problems which these linguistically oriented forms of post-structuralist theory pose for a feminist writing project in legal theory is the absence of a position for the active, intentional and inquiring subject. It is assumed the individual, the subject, is constituted by the terms of the discourse. As an epistemology there is no space provided for the negotiation of subjectivity, identity, or personhood. In each of these linguistically oriented theories knowing is separated from the knowing subject—it has an existence of its own. It is the referent of the signifiers—the words, and is deferred. In separating knowledge from the consciousness of subjects it appears the subject/object epistemology of the picture theory is resurrected where it had been abandoned. As theories these versions of poststructuralism appear unable to contribute to an effective political practice against oppression primarily because they cannot challenge the dominant meanings which the words are represented as holding. Partial challenges in the form of new meanings introduced by displacement and supplement are unacceptable as a political practice as it is a practice which excludes the majority of oppressed people. They are excluded because they either cannot write or have no resources for a writing or a publication project.

Other versions of poststructuralist theory provide resources capable of grounding a political practice. If subjectivity is given a non-hierarchial place with language/signification, knowledge and meaning can be represented as enhering in the subjectivity of the individual. This means she can claim to hold a justified belief that her experiences of life give to the language a better and more comprehensive meaning than that embedded in the dominant discourse. If *she* cannot claim at least an authenticity to the new meaning of words, at least a temporary fixing of meaning, *she* can have no political practices. We must assume practice is underwritten by communication through word or deed—both can only acquire status as practical activity through language. Poststructuralist theories which have retained a place for subjectivity appear to be more able to ground a particularly feminist legal theory.

In the work of the french philosopher Foucault language and subjectivity are retained in forms which do not presuppose the priority of either. Foucault's work has become controversial as a feminist resource perhaps as a result of his explicit disinterest in feminist politics. It is certainly capable of both feminist and patriarchal readings (Martin, 1982; Butler, 1986a; Kurzweil, 1986; Alcoff, 1988; Diamond and Quinby, 1988). It appears to me that his concept of the subject as an effect of discursive, disciplinary power upon the body is one in which subjectivity is retained in a multiple and non-essentialist form (Foucault, 1982). He uses the concept of body in the tradition of Merleau-Ponty, as a "body subject," which carries the meaning of both the situated physical body and the intentional knowledgeable subject (Merleau-Ponty, 1962, 1963).[3] The body is subjectivity in a post-Cartesian framework; why assume bodies do not encompass thought and intentionality?

In the work of Foucault knowledge emerges as that temporary form of truth constituted by institutions which produce and monitor discourse (Foucault, 1980c, p. 78). Language is the site of struggle and the thing to fight for (Foucault, 1984, p. 110); control of meaning is the victor's prize, but only as an emblem or effect of power. The focus of Foucault's later works (Foucault, 1979, 1980a, 1986a, 1986b) is upon a study of bodies as the effects of power/knowledge. He states "we must attempt to study the myriad of bodies which are constituted as peripheral subjects, as a result of the effects of power" (Foucault, 1980c, p. 98). The subject or individual becomes both the effect of power and the "element of its articulation." In this framework discourses of biological difference, can be theorized as temporal, temporary and as resources. Discourses about female biology and bodily capacities are thereby made available, not for constructing a vision of the true woman or even for repudiating others' visions but as metaphors for knowing which privilege women's historically specific social positions.

In Foucault's framework power is invested in the body (Foucault,

1980c, p. 56; 1979, p. 151). This means that the language which we use to give meaning to our experience of the body is available to structure and constitute women's social experience beyond what is normally understood as matters of biology.[4] If we think of bodies as elements in the articulation of power, in Foucault's sense, we can begin an inquiry into language as expression and the practices of expression. This inquiry would locate male and female bodies as the temporal sites at which meaning about sexuality, labor and identity are constructed. It would have as a goal the mapping of the sexualized forms of representations about power/authority and the ways in which these representations enter the conversations of humanity.

Representation appears always to have had a sexualized form. It appears to be a legacy of the picture theory epistemology that power has become located outside and separate from an embodied subject in the same way that "representation" is commonly understood to reflect the nature of the object, rather than the nature of the subject. The implications of changing inquiry from language about things to language as expressive of subjective life include understanding "representation" as the imaginary or metaphorical form in which we constitute the "forms of life." Representations are imaginary in the sense they are beliefs that meaning pre-exists the communication of representation. That we commonly understand the term representation to be "about" a pre-existing known object and the term imaginary to be "about" the fictional is simply the effect of resources invested in the picture theory epistemology from which representation has traditionally taken its meaning.

Once the move is made to an epistemology in which knowing is an active involvement of the subject in intentional and purposive practice upon the world all representations of what the world "is like" are imaginary or creative, as meaning no longer pre-exists the practices of representation. If language is understood to be expressive of embodied practices of situated experience, work can begin on how these forms of expression constitute our "being" in the world and, particularly, what kinds of social relations are built upon these "theories" of being. We can begin to consider other theories of being.

II Knowing about Law: Law as Embodied Imagination

In a feminist legal theory project inquiry into the sexualized forms of representation would not begin with questions regarding the nature of "law" as a discrete phenomenon (Duncanson, 1988, p. 305). Law cannot be an object, as knowledge is not separate from the inquiring subject, so it would not make sense to inquire into matters of *it's* nature. It would be assumed that mainstream theories of what law "is" are the representations from the male experience of power, representations from positions of empowerment (Duncanson, 1982, p. 11). Considerable work has already been done on the jurisprudential settlement reached for constituting the new class order of the 17th and 18th century English nobility (Duncanson, 1978, 1989a). It has been argued by Duncanson that the "rule of law" and its jurisprudential supports is that theoretical position which enabled a new arrangement of power to be distinguished from the aspirations of the powerful (Duncanson, 1982, p. 8–11; 1984, p. 160; 1988). Law as a "discrete phenomenon" is understood to be a representation from a class position, that of the powerful. Law as an "interpretive concept" (Dworkin, 1986, p. 410) appears to make the legal process available as an authoritative representational form for all players but this account limits representation to those life experiences of persons holding authoritative community positions—the officials of the official order (Duncanson, 1989b). Can the jurisprudential settlements on the autonomy of individuals, underwritten by the development of "legal rights," (Duncanson, 1988, p. 311) be interpreted also as a sexed representation about power, a representation which was drawn from the experience of separateness in male life and which constituted the plight of the female as the atomized relations of capitalism progressed? Feminist political theorizing has drawn our attention to these issues (Young, 1986; Benhabib, 1987).

If we begin to theorize law as language expressive of subjective life, representations of what law "is" become the resources for building feminist legal theory. In each of these expressions about "law" we can inquire into the "forms of life" from which the subjects have taken their theories, assumptions or ontologies of being. "Law" then becomes a theory of embodied imagination, the metaphors of "being" in the world, and the feminist legal theory project becomes the task of engaging with those practices which appear to have excluded women's imaginings of life possibilities from the conversations of "humanity."

These practices would appear to include the professionalized form of legal theory writing and beliefs about the nature of legal reasoning. It is part of the legal theory tradition that we engage with other theorists who have constructed their project as one of the nature of "law" as a discrete phenomenon. Because "law" has been understood to be legal doctrine and other rulings or interpretations of officials, legal theory writing for feminists carries sanctions of irrelevancy or unprofessionalism if departures are made from the representations with which she is engaging. If we want to begin with a conception of "law" as embodied imaginings, so that its sexualized form can be recognized and expanded with the metaphors from female embodiment, part of the writing project must

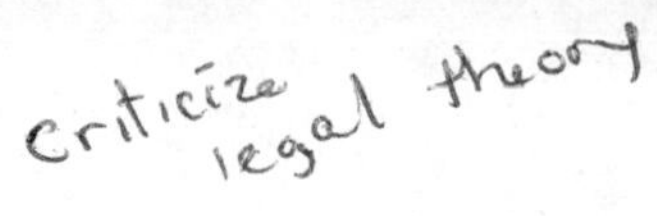

include the mapping of these "sanctions." This is not to paint a picture of a hostile and grudging academic community in which feminist writing projects are ridiculed and publications disproportionately rejected, although such practices are well known already. It is instead to include in the feminist writing project the interrogation of our own assumptions about "law," in order to permit the sexualized representations from women who are not professionally trained in legal writing to enter the conversations upon the experience of authority (Foucault, 1980b; Miller, 1986). This is my original problem of investigating those practices which would permit the writing of an account of power and authority which was sensitive to women's experience of that authority. I simply do not know what such an account would be like, but I suspect it would be unlike present legal theory.[5]

Part of the feminist legal theory project must include inquiry into the ways in which legal reasoning transforms the embodied imaginings from male lives into the "objective" form of doctrine which passes for the "normative." Catherine MacKinnon has shown how abstract rights "authorize the male experience of the world." She argues that "the liberal view that law is society's text, its rational mind, expresses this in a normative mode . . ." (MacKinnon, 1983, p. 658). We have to start "conceiving reason differently" (Taylor, 1987, p. 483), a task which has already constituted the conditions for creativity in feminist social sciences. Criteria of objectivity and neutrality have been already argued as specific practices of displacing the positionality of knowers—whether in the natural sciences, the social sciences or the law tradition. "Objectivity" in legal research is one more writing practice with which the feminist legal theory project has begun to engage. However, to expand inquiry into the practices of positionality to include the legal reasoning of judicial officials appears to present other kinds of problems. If one focuses upon legal decisions as "just" the representations of male lives one nevertheless confirms *that* embodied imagination as the "law" vision. The problem appears to be how can one overcome the "looking glass effect," (Stewart, 1981, p. 118) where the looking glass which is "law" is that embodied imagination with which we appear compelled to engage? The resolution seems to be that the embodied imaginings or looking glass effects can never be overcome, because they remain simply an expression of what might be. To aspire to overcome particular embodied representations because of their partiality or because of a different "embodiment" would be to return to the picture theory world of certainty with its known hazards.

If we begin to conceive of legal reasoning without its "law-ness," that is, not as a privileged representation but as just representation we all become its "officials." We can undertake our research outside the forums of the official. Continuing to heed the relevance of judicial decisions and legal doctrine becomes one writing practice of maintaining "relevancy" and "professionalism" under conditions not of our making, conditions which must remain contested.

III Writing Feminist Legal Theory

The aim of this section is an inquiry into a set of practices which appear to place a woman's subjectivity in a bodily form which she does not experience as "self." The aim is to develop the theory of law as embodied imagination by tracing women's resistance to or denial of the myriad representations within privileged or "policed" discourses upon the nature of women. It is an archeology of finding women's embodied imaginings, their theories of being which have been excluded by the professionalized and masculinized nature of the disciplines. It is a preliminary inquiry which focuses upon disciplinary conversations.

I am assuming that a feminist writing project in legal theory—ultimately an inquiry into the negotiation of the meaning of authority—should include current political practices of women as the resources of the theory, that the theory should attempt to make sense or give meaning to practice, not in a facile, post hoc way but, by incorporating the validity of women's experience into a conversation where those experiences are interpreted as justified beliefs. Individual experience takes the form of knowledge in social practices which provide justifications for the validity of experience (Woolgar, 1988). This place for theory in the development of knowledge—the social forms of understanding—is not new, it is assumed within the practices of any professionalized knowledge. It appears to be new only where the experiences one seeks to bring within a professionalized discipline are outside that discipline. The need to articulate the validity of experience and the practices of justification are the effects of the disciplinary exclusions of closed conversations—whether exclusions on grounds of reason, logic, science, expertise or professionalism.

A feminist legal theory project should aim to trace those practices in which women resist the sexualized representations of male lives. It should be asked in what ways do women's theories of being re-map the forms of human flourishing? Part of this project is to highlight the specific practices of displacing the positionality of knowers, here the forms of legal reasoning and textual mediation and promotion of professional knowledges. The conversations of "mankind" displace women as knowledgeable. The professional, masculine maps of human flourishing must be placed in the legal theory project *as maps,* so that the practices of their resistance can be brought within feminist theorizing in ways which highlight the continuous renegotiation of meaning.

The Order of Simulation and Scenario

The aim of writing feminist legal theory should include the interrogation of current frameworks of knowledge as a form of practice in which resistance can be placed as an embodied imagining. The political agendas of the period have constituted the postmodern conditions of our writing in which models of the real are created without origins or realities. Representations can only simulate the real, they have become imaginary in which each is a negation of the fixity of any sign (Baudrillard, 1988, p. 166). With the deferral of any sense in the real by present conditions of writing, representation has taken on the form of the imaginary and has become a scenario of power, which endlessly repeats its attacks upon the order of the real (Baudrillard, 1988, p. 122).

Laqueur has written of the discontinuities in representations of male and female bodies and questioned the nature of the political agendas underlying representations of bodies and their sexual differences (Laqueur, 1987). His work on the medical and philosophical production of knowledge concerning reproductive biology points to a shift of interpretation of bodies during the early eighteenth century. Laqueur argues that the old model was one of hierarchial ordering, by which he means they were vertically ordered and "according to their degree of metaphysical perfection, their vital heat, along an axis whose telos was male . . ." (1987, p. 3). This homological ordering of bodies changed in the eighteenth century to a new model of incommensurability, in which male and female bodies were regarded as "horizontally ordered, as incommensurable . . ." (Laqueur, 1987 p. 3). The assumptions of homologies was inadequate in light of the new politics and society of the Enlightenment. Fundamental sexual differences between male and female bodies were sought as the political agenda changed. Political theorists such as Hobbes argued that there was no basis in nature for authority of king over people, nor man over woman (Laqueur, 1987, p. 18). As Londa Schiebinger argues "to the mind of the natural-law theorist, an appeal to natural rights could be countered only by proof of natural inequalities" (Schiebinger, 1987, p. 43). Laqueur argues that "the political, economic and cultural transformations of the eighteenth century created the context in which the articulation of radical differences between the sexes became culturally imperative . . . New claims and counterclaims regarding the public and private roles of women were thus contested through questions about the nature of their bodies as distinguished from those of men" (Laqueur, 1987, p. 35).

The feminist legal theory project is set within sexualized representations of a simulated female body. Male and female bodies are represented as the same, as equal, the simulacrum of the other. In the professional discourses of "mankind" the embodied imaginings from male lives constitute male and female experience *as if* they were real, a position which can become true only for the male conversants. Women are now required to simulate another's reality.

In the sex discrimination discourse of Australia and the United Kingdom a male or female who wishes to claim a juridical remedy must begin with an assertion of social commensurability for male and female bodies. The practice of litigation requires proof that the individual has been treated unfavorably in circumstances in which a person of the other sex would not have been so treated. The individual must first specify the circumstances which would be the same, or not materially different, for a person of the other sex. The Australian Federal or Commonwealth legislation, *Sex Discrimination Act 1984* provides a definition of "direct" discrimination, as follows, Section 5:

> 5. (1) For the purposes of this Act, a person (in this sub-section referred to as the "discriminator") discriminates against another person (in this subsection referred to as the "aggrieved person") on the ground of the sex of the aggrieved person, if by reason of—
>
> (a) the sex of the aggrieved person;
> (b) a characteristic that appertains generally to persons of the sex of the aggrieved person; or
> (c) a characteristic that is generally imputed to persons of the sex of the aggrieved person,
>
> the discriminator treats the aggrieved person less favourably than, in circumstances that are the same or not materially different, the discriminator treats or would treat a person of the opposite sex.

Unless the dialogue is constructed in such a way that the individual asserts the sameness of economic and social practices for men and women the claim for a remedy for individual mistreatment cannot begin. It is one of the conditions of litigation that a woman must represent that there can be conditions of social life which are experienced by women the same as they would be experienced by men. She must take part in a representation which contradicts her experience and her imaginings, she is drawn into a scenario of power each time she claims the reality of her mistreatment. She must represent a woman's experience of some aspect of social life *as if* it were male experience and assert the reason of sex as the ground upon which she has been treated less favorably. The *Sex Discrimination Act* does provide another "definition" of discrimination, that of Section 5(2), known as indirect or systematic discrimination, as follows:

> 5. (2) For the purposes of this Act, a person (in this sub-section referred as the "discriminator") discriminates against another person (in this sub-section referred to as the "aggrieved person") on the ground of the sex of the aggrieved person if the discriminator requires the aggrieved person to comply with a requirement or condition—
>
> (a) with which a substantially higher proportion of persons of the opposite sex to the aggrieved person comply or are able to comply;
> (b) which is not reasonable having regard to the circumstances of the case; and
> (c) with which the aggrieved person does not or is not able to comply.

Here she is not required to represent that the conditions of women's lives are experienced by women the same as they would be experienced by men. Here her representations of reality require different simulations. She must represent that the conditions of male lives are those with which she cannot comply by reason of *her* sex, whereas it must appear to her that she is constituted as having an inability by reason of other's power. Her sex alone does not constitute her inability, for the reasonableness of the conditions of male lives can displace this rationale. In these social practices in which the meaning of oppressive conditions is negotiated, she must endlessly negotiate the reality of her unfavourable treatment against a scenario of power constituted by another, a negotiation in which she designates which aspects of her experience mean the required rationale of sex. She must designate a sexuality which is determined by another's logic.

Other juridical practices can also be investigated in this broader context of the simulable body. The judiciary have recently decided that, as a matter of "objective fact," males and females suffer the same amount of distress where the bodily surface or form is injured, the court must assume it is simply a human body in question.[6] The New South Wales Court of Appeal held that "differential approaches to the assessment of cosmetic injury to men and women, as such, should be regarded as inadmissible. Men and women who come to our courts are entitled to the assessment of their damages by judges who approach their functions without preconceived discriminating distinctions. If such distinctions are to be drawn, the only safe ground for them is to be found in evidence, properly proved, in relation to the particular individual before the court." New non-discriminatory standards of judging now require a female to represent that there can be conditions of social life which are experienced by injured women in the same way as they would be experienced by injured men. She is required to express the experiences of a simulated body. Assessment of distress is now to be made solely by "subjective" legal tests, that is, according to the litigant's own assessment or statement of emotional pain and suffering, properly proved.[7] The judiciary has let it be known that as females generally do suffer greater emotional distress in cases of disfigurement they would anticipate that, "in the natural course of things," female litigants would report a heightened experience of pain and suffering. Where she used to constitute the male as normal by her "abnormal" experience of heightened emotionality, she is now required to imagine other women conforming to the male experience of normality and herself as deviant because she cannot simulate this new reality of women.

The questions seem to have changed but for woman who take part in present practices the answers remain the same. A woman is still required to report that amount of emotionality expected of a female body, she is still placed between normality and insanity and her sexuality is "read off" her female body through male eyes. But the answers for males appear to be different. In *Ralevski* v. *Dimovski* the male appellant had initially stated that the facial scarring had not caused his embarrassment. Kirkby, P. commented, as follows ". . . I am inclined to believe that the initial answer did not represent a true indication of the appellant's feelings but a response to perceived norms of a culture which is inclined in some quarters to deny males the luxury of the public admission of concern about their appearance." The injured male, who gives the requisite "subjective" account of little pain and suffering, is nevertheless, by virtue of a stated reliance upon sex discrimination legislation, entitled to the same amounts of monetary compensation as would be awarded to a female.

The new paradigm in which she must imagine women's experiences as the same as men's is part of the process whereby the social activity of humans transforms the material available. The particular woman in current sex discrimination litigation still has to live the present meaning of "woman." If she is denied employment because she is disfigured, or simply not attractive enough, she is required to assert that her female body is the cause of the employer's departure from normal employment practices. The dialogue requires her to assert that employment practices are the same for men and women, that male and female bodies are, alike, not normally judged for aesthetic qualities in the employment decision. Whether she wins or loses, a simulable female body is asserted, whether she wins or loses the judicial "masters" of the court have entered into a dialogue with the employer on the attractiveness of her body and whether the employer's opinions on this had influenced the employment decision. Under the present meaning of "woman" it is always *she* who will be scrutinized and unveiled before a court simply because it is still women who are constituted around male aesthetics and male sexuality. The body of woman now, the feminine body as it is presently understood, is the material upon which the social practices of simulation operate.

Present meanings of "woman" differ as much as women's lives differ. They are diverse and different to each other as they are to men's lives. It is this diverse positionality of women's lives which has been denied by the traditions of western knowledge. Male knowledge as objectivity not only places women as unknowledgeable, it excludes the different representations about power constituted within women's lives. Women are placed in relations in which their labouring skills are devalued in different ways. They may live as the aesthetic objects of another and also seek employment in institutions where female bodies are required to display beauty as well as labor. Women seek maintenance awards from judges who decide that little maintenance is required as an attractive body will soon find another spouse to assist in maintaining a home. Women find an award of compensation for unlawful dismissal at age sixty is diminished because a judge decides her appearance is attractive enough to warrant further employment by some unknown, or "universal," male.

Writing feminist legal theory must include preserving the presence of active and intentional subjects within the remapping of the forms of human flourishing. The focus becomes one of retrieving women's experiences of authority in both senses of being subjected by the traditions of objectivity and rationality and being the subjects of authority, that is, being knowledgeable about relations of power. Women's writing is replete with the experiences of subjection but we are only beginning to claim the resources necessary for communicating women's knowledges of themselves as authorities. The male jurisprudential tradition can then be seen as a professionally constituted and legitimated vision of the male as an authority, as one kind of authorship which underwrites the relations of power.

Notes

1. Ronald Dworkin's work is an example of the epistemological commitments of liberalism. Propositions of law are understood to be interpretive of a single legal history which is the "enterprise in hand." Law becomes that legal history which it is the judges' job to continue into the future; Dworkin argues that this history can and should be treated by its authors "as an object in itself." Dworkin has raised the question "whether liberalism can indeed be traced, as many philosophers have supposed, back into a discrete epistemological base, different from that of other political theories . . ." (Dworkin, 1985, 166).
2. While the phrase is intended by Rorty to cover the conversations of both men and women I have retained the phrase in this article only where a conversation or theoretical position appears to arise from a male standpoint.
3. Simone de Beauvoir also uses the concept of the body "as situation" (de Beauvoir, 1973, p. 38; Butler, 1986b).

4. Marie Ashe's metaphor of birthing provides an example of this kind of endeavor. She draws upon her experience of creating a new life to constitute the theorization of law as labor, uncertainty, division, coherence and promise (Ashe, 1987).
5. I think Pat Williams's writing on the black experience of authority provides such an account. (Williams, 1988)
6. *Ralevski v. Dimovski* N.S.W.L.R. 487 (1986).
7. Kirkby, P. in *Ralevski v. Dimovski,* p. 494.

5

Intimacy and Responsibility: What Lesbians Do

Claudia Card

Character—the willingness to accept responsibility for one's own life—is the source from which self-respect springs. (Joan Didion, 1974)

A paradigm case of taking responsibility for one's sexuality is coming out as a lesbian.
(Joyce Trebilcot, 1984, p. 422)

Coming out as a lesbian, as a paradigm of taking responsibility, can be a major source of self-respect. This paper argues that for this purpose, lesbian relationships are better conceived as relationships of erotic intimacy than as sexual relationships.[1] Understanding coming out as a lesbian as an undertaking of responsibility for erotic intimacy, rather than for sexuality, seems to remove the bases for regarding lesbianism as perverse or even deviant.

The expression "coming out" has an older and a more recent meaning. It is the more recent meaning that I have in mind when I use the expression. In the older sense, a woman "came out" when she first entered into an overtly lesbian relationship, however that may be defined. In the more recent sense of the expression, however, "coming out" is an act of communication, an identification of oneself to one or more others. Asking to whom a woman is "out," is not asking who her lovers are but, rather, to whom has she identified herself as lesbian. Coming out, in this sense, is often done for sheerly political reasons—to make extortion impossible, to make oneself accessible to others like oneself in order that combination for political purposes be possible, and so forth. It might be thought that the more recent sense of "coming out" includes the older one, or at least presupposes it. However, it is not clear that that is so. Perhaps neither sense presupposes the other. Women have entered into overtly lesbian relationships without admitting to themselves that that is what they were doing and certainly without embracing a lesbian identity. And women sometimes have embraced lesbian identities on other grounds than any experience with relationships commonly recognized as overtly lesbian. Some women identify themselves as lesbian celibates. The more recent sense of "coming out" challenges certain common un-

Reprinted with permission of the author.

derstandings of what it is that lesbians do. This exploration of coming out as an act of taking responsibility for one's physically intimate relationships may show why the relationships between the two senses of "coming out" are as unclear as they are.

So far lesbian feminism has had relatively little to do with taking responsibility for institutions structuring reproduction. From the perspective of reproduction, it appears puzzling, even downright perverse, that lesbian relationships have been dealt with in law and psychiatry as though they were sexual relationships. Perhaps only within the historical development of sexuality as an institution could lesbian eroticism have come to be so classified. I will argue that it is probably not in women's interests to support that classification. The considerations I offer have implications also for heterosexual and male same-sex eroticism, although I do not explore them.

Three possible confusions I wish to dispel at the outset. First, it is no part of my argument that lesbian relationships characteristically are or should be more spiritual than physical. However physical, sensual, or orgasmic, I will argue they probably should not be considered sexual. Second, I am not advocating that lesbians not take responsibility for reproduction. The idea is, rather, that taking responsibility for reproduction should be a project distinct from taking responsibility for erotic intimacy. Third, I am not rejecting identity politics. I am skeptical specifically of the politics of sexual identity.

What follows has three parts. Part I analyzes taking responsibility as undertaking to stand behind something. Part II examines the social construction of sexuality, which involves sexuality as an institution. Part III distinguishes the erotic from the sexual and argues that, in certain respects, the erotic offers women a better standpoint than the sexual for taking responsibility for intimate relationships. I leave for a future investigation problems presented by institutions built on the erotic.

I Taking Responsibility

Duty theorists study responsibility as a triadic relation of the form, "A is responsible to B for x," or "B can hold A responsible for x," where "A" and "B" range over persons and "x" ranges over actions or events. The interest of duty theorists has been in the assignments of such things as credit and blame, punishment and reward, generally, in holding people to certain conduct. Responsibility, in this sense, is a correlative of rights. If A is responsible to B for x, then B has a corresponding right against A regarding x. So understood, responsibility is about controlling people, more specifically, about the distribution of such control.

Responsibility can be taken for things, beings, and states of affairs, as well as for actions or events. Where the object of responsibility is not an action or event but is something that has a welfare, or requires upkeep or maintenance, the responsibility relationship may be simply dyadic, of the form, "A is responsible for x." Now the focus is on maintenance or caretaking. If you take responsibility for the house and I take responsibility for the car, each of us is concerned with the care of the thing in question, regardless whether we also are accountable to each other or to anyone else for it. The recent work of Carol Gilligan (1982) and Nell Noddings (1984) suggests that modern academic theorists have paid far less attention to responsibility as caretaking than to responsibility as the correlative of rights. The former gives the sense of responsibility that I find most appropriate to the idea of taking responsibility for oneself.

Taking responsibility for something with a welfare requires the ability to do such things as taking charge, influencing, guiding, shaping, maintaining, developing. Admittedly, these activities involve the exercise of control. Control, here, however, is a means to the further end of well-being. When responsibility is conceived as a triadic relationship, as the correlative of rights, the parties' interest in control is not simply as a means to something further. Where rights are at stake, the parties involved have an interest in maintaining a certain distribution among themselves of control over each other.

As Joyce Trebilcot (1984) pointed out, taking responsibility does not require identifying oneself as an author, originator, or cause. We may simply identify ourselves as backers, supporters, maintainers. In so doing, we become committed to the value of that for which we take responsibility—not necessarily to its success, but often to making something of it or to making good on our failure to do so.

Taking responsibility in this sense is captured by the metaphors of standing behind, backing, supporting, all of which convey the ideas of giving or being prepared to give added substance to something and being committed to its value. In supporting ourselves, we actually enter into our own development in a positive way. We may not have been behind something to begin with, but we can stand behind it now and for the future. Such undertakings reveal who we are, what we value. They not only reveal it but are also partly constitutive of it.

Because coming out as a lesbian has been conceived by feminists in terms of taking responsibility for ourselves, many of us have not been entirely happy with the popular liberal view that variety in physically intimate relationships is something that ought to be tolerated and that an individual's predilections in such matters are, after all, nobody else's business. In coming out, as in marrying, women have been prepared to stand behind their intimate relationships in a public way, although not necessarily as permanent relationships. Both women and men in relationships of same-sex physical intimacy are apt to view coming out as a major step in the development of character. The liberal view suggests that physically intimate relationships outside of marriage are nothing that one could or should stand behind. Ignoring them seems an act of toleration whereby a point is made of overlooking what might otherwise prove troublesome. Tolerating is a way of excusing, and excusing presupposes something viewed as unfortunate to be excused. From the liberal point of view, coming out, then, begins to look like a display of very bad taste, at the very least ungrateful to the liberal spirit of others if not an offense against public decency. On the other hand, if coming out is viewed as an act of taking responsibility, it is the tolerant reception that begins to look like the offense. Toleration communicates a negative value judgment of what is tolerated, together with a decision not to hold the agent accountable, an attitude that is bound to be felt as condescending under the circumstances.

While taking responsibility involves being committed to the value of something, it is sometimes possible to take responsibility for what turns out badly as well as for what turns out well. The value to which one is committed need not be a pragmatic one; failure is not necessarily incompatible with goodness. We may be committed to the value of something as an embodiment of ideals we believe in, despite its lack of success. Or, we may be prepared to make something of it or to do something about it. However, if the way in which one is taking responsibility is by identifying oneself in a certain way, then a certain success is required: I do not manage to identify myself to others in a particular way if they fail to or refuse to recognize me in that way.

Also, taking responsibility for something need not commit one to the idea that the thing is good throughout. If I take responsibility for my life, for example, I take responsibility for bad parts of it as well as for good ones. This does not mean that I deny that there are any bad parts. Nor does it mean just that I own them as mine. It means such things as that I am committed to not being defeated by the bad parts, that I am committed to such things as repairing or compensating for damage I do, seeking to understand the causes, converting misfortune into opportunities for positive development—in general, to exercising care (not to be confused with cautiousness) in the way I lead my life. Taking responsibility, in this sense, often requires faith and hope. It seems incompatible with cynicism, if not with despair.

Taking responsibility for ourselves is also a matter of degree. It would be silly and arrogant to take responsibility for everything that we are and do. Nor is it possible. One has to be in a position to stand behind something.

When is a party in a position to back something, to stand behind it?

Being in a position to stand behind something may require being able to carry out tasks that constitute backing it, making it good. Except for my ability to defend a thing's existing or realized values, I am unable to stand behind something when I cannot affect it and when I can neither repair nor compensate for the damage it does. As will become apparent, my abilities to do some of these things may require social cooperation, may require that my action receive a certain "uptake" on the part of others, for example. But also part of what it can mean to be in a position to back something is that backing it would be a good thing for me to do, that it would be worth my while. I am not in a (good) position to back something that is not already good if I cannot make something tolerably good of it without paying too high a price.

Writing on self-respect for *Vogue* magazine, Joan Didion presented being responsible for oneself as taking a certain attitude toward one's choices. (Didion, 1974, p. 123) "People with self-respect have the courage of their mistakes," she wrote. "They know the price of things. If they choose to commit adultery, they do not then go running, in an excess of bad conscience, to receive absolution from the wronged parties, nor do they complain unduly of the unfairness, the undeserved embarrassment of being named co-respondent." Being responsible for yourself, here, looks like being willing to lie in the bed you have made.

Joan Didion seems to understand taking responsibility as a kind of acceptance. More than acceptance, however, is required to distinguish taking responsibility from resignation. Taking responsibility involves the added idea of backing, and that involves the judgment that the thing in question is worth backing. Taking responsibility for oneself even as an adulterer involves, I should think, an ability and a readiness to do something about the harm, if any, that it caused.

For political activists or dissenters, matters are less simple than for agents who are simply facing failures to act in accord with their own better judgment. Joan Didion's discussion considers choices within a social framework not itself under criticism by the chooser. Joyce Trebilcot, as a social critic, was concerned not only about individual choice but also about the framework. Political activists may be unwilling to accept much that follows upon their choices. Often they feel others should take responsibility for some of that.

For a political activist, taking responsibility can be an ambitious and risky business. Taking responsibility in the context of practices one rejects requires doing it at the level of meaning and definition. This is the predicament of feminists with respect to intimate relationships.

To see what this means, we need to distinguish sexuality as an institution—i.e., a set of practices defined by social norms—from sexuality as behavior and experience falling under institutional norms, i.e., defined by them as sexual.[2] An analogy may help. Consider taking responsibility for one's crime. Shouldn't we distinguish between taking responsibility for the act performed and taking responsibility for its criminality? That distinction seems unimportant only if the agent stands behind the relevant laws and institutions. If I stand behind the law, my choice to disobey it is either backsliding or part of a strategy to improve or correct the law. Taking responsibility for my choice is at the same time a way of backing the law and the system to which it belongs. If I do not stand behind the law, taking responsibility for disobeying it is another matter. While I may not be free to act as though the law did not exist, neither am I required to try to improve it. But then I must be able to rely upon meanings of my conduct independent of the legal categories imposed on it.

Analogously, it is unimportant to distinguish between taking responsibility for intimate relationships (fantasies, feelings, behavior, etc.), and taking responsibility for their sexual meanings only if we stand behind the institution of sexuality, which is the source of those meanings. If we are not in a position to redefine sexual social norms, our so-called sexual identities are substantially beyond our control. Why take responsibility for them at all? Our best option may be to refuse responsibility for them.

In her analysis of taking responsibility for our sexualities, Joyce Trebilcot (1984, 426–27) seems to suggest that a way to go about taking such responsibility is to choose carefully whether or not to participate in various activities presently defined by social sexual norms. Choosing whether to participate in such activities, however, is not sufficient to give us control over our identities. For the meanings of our choices depend greatly upon the responses of others. Their responses determine which norms take effect. Refusing, on principle, to participate in heterosexual courtship, intercourse, or marriage is ordinarily considered, within the institution of heterosexuality, to be deviant, at the very least, to require justification. That institution defines lesbians as women who make perverted sexual choices. To the extent that the meanings of our choices are determined by the responses of others among whom we live, we inevitably "participate" in sexist and heterosexist institutions as long as we live among their supporters.

If we live in a sexist society, then, we need to take responsibility for ourselves at the level of practices. This requires changing the meanings of what we do. Taking responsibility here requires successfully imposing on rituals and relationships meanings that we can stand behind.

Even if we do this, some others may continue to employ their own definitions of us, as some Fundamentalist Christians today, for example, persist in defining adherents of other religions as sinners or heretics. The definitions of others do not negate our responsibility-taking, however, as long as they do not prevent us from standing behind our own. To do that we need to be able to make something of them, give them effect, implement them.

What is required for us to be able to stand behind our own definitions? To come out as a lesbian requires a context. Obviously, a closet is presupposed, from which to escape. But also there must be a place to go, other than into the courts or the psychiatrist's office. To come out successfully, we need a certain range of receptions. Comings out need confirmation. Otherwise we succeed in "coming out" only as exhibitionists, deviants, criminals, unrepentant sinners, etc. Confirming the self-image of those who come out is also taking responsibility for that image in that it offers support.

The need for social uptake in changing meanings suggests a certain moral problem in a society in which the existing meanings of "lesbian" are deeply negative. The objection is that we risk exposing those we love to victimization by others in a society that does not yet recognize the changes we would institute. It is absurd to think that you can change the meaning of something just by intending a different meaning when you use it yourself or with your friends. The question arises whether I am recommending something like that here with respect to the existing sexual meanings of lesbian intimacy.[3]

It is one thing merely to intend our actions to have certain meanings and another for them actually to have those meanings. Our freedom to act on meanings we can stand behind partly depends on our success in changing meanings. Since that is a social success, not an individual one, there is genuine moral risk here. There is a risk that the requisite validation will not be forthcoming or will not be sustained and that, consequently, one will not be able to take responsibility for the relationships in question. For an appropriately responsive community is not entirely within anyone's control.

It may be objected that my taking responsibility only requires me to try, not to succeed, because I can embrace the values I find in my relationships whether others recognize them or not. If I am right about taking responsibility, however, it is not just a matter of embracing something. What is at stake here is my ability to provide a kind of support. I do not offer real support as long as others can write off my attempt as just as perverted as the relationships I would support.

It is true, then, that in coming out, one risks exposing those one loves to a great deal of harm. However, to evaluate that, we need to consider the alternative. It is not as though one can responsibly just wait until social conditions appear propitious. For those conditions may be creatable only as the result of others, whose situations are relevantly similar, taking the risk in advance of any such appearance.

Taking responsibility for ourselves, then, can involve "moral luck." (B.

Williams, 1981; Nagel, 1979) "Moral luck" is luck that enters as a necessary aspect of either the development of one's character or the morality of one's choices. There is luck involved in the validation requisite to successfully creating meanings. Insofar as taking responsibility for ourselves involves imposing meanings on our lives that we can stand behind, that luck is a kind of moral luck.

The meaning of "lesbian" is currently undergoing change from a popular medico-legal conception as a sexual identity to a feminist conception which is in many respects presently unclear. The clarification I want to propose involves distinguishing the sexual from the erotic. It is, I believe, highly coherent with much contemporary lesbian feminist practice, although there is at present no common agreement upon language to describe what is occurring. Despite a widespread continued use of the language of sexuality, it seems to me that we have backed many relationships as lesbian that are not clearly sexual in any sense of "sexual" worth our support. To clarify that, I turn to the concept of sexuality.

II Sexuality

Should women stand behind lesbian relationships as sexual relationships, or behind lesbianism as a sexual identity? What is at stake in this question?

"Sexuality " is ambiguous among at least the following:

(I) femaleness or maleness (a heavily physiological concept)
(II) the institution of sexuality (a heavily political one)
(III) instances of behavior falling under the norms of (II), which may relate that behavior to (I).

The question whether to stand behind lesbian relationships as sexual is about the sexuality of what lesbians do. The concept of sexual behavior is systematically ambiguous, thanks to the physiological and political meanings of sexuality.[4] "Sexual behavior" seems to have a narrower and a wider sense. The narrower sense refers to behavior characteristically, at least in the absence of certain impediments, instrumental toward physiological reproduction or else controlling of physiological reproduction. The wider sense includes behavior falling under norms of the historical institution of sexuality, norms defining correct and incorrect behavior for females or for males in a variety of contexts. Such norms define what has come to be called sexual politics, insofar as they create and distribute forms of power. Perhaps all, or nearly all, physiologically sexual behavior is also sexual in the political sense, i.e., is covered by sexuo-political norms. However, not all sexual behavior in the political sense is also physiologically sexual. The institution of sexuality relates behavior in a great many ways to reproduction, and not only to physiological reproduction but also to social reproduction, the reproduction of culture, institutions, ways of life. In doing so, it structures adult intimacy.

Taking responsibility for sexuality, then, is at least ambiguous between taking responsibility for behavior instrumental toward or controlling of physiological reproduction and taking responsibility for behavior defined as sexual by social practices. Understood to include taking responsibility for one's sexual identity, it is taken at least partly in the second way.

I want to question the wisdom of taking responsibility for our sexual identities. Social norms defining sexual identities define too much else in the process. The concept of sexual identity has been developed in such a way that homosexuals inevitably appear perverted. We should, where we can, take responsibility for our reproductive potentialities and also for our intimate affiliations. But why take responsibility for sexual readings of our intimate affiliations? Why tie responsibility for physiological reproduction to adult intimacy? Viewing intimacy through the lens of sexuality amalgamates these projects.

Sexual identity is a hybrid concept, partly physiological, partly political. According to John De Cecco and Michael G. Shively, of the Center for Research and Education in Sexuality (CERES) in San Francisco, sexual identity has four components: (1) biological sex (assigned at birth), (2) one's conviction of being female or male (referred to as one's "gender identity"), (3) femininity or masculinity, as defined by social norms, and (4) sexual orientation. Sexual orientation, in turn, is broken down into at least three factors: (1) erotic fantasies, (2) emotional affiliation, and (3) sexual behavior. (De Cecco and Shively, 1985)

Of the four named components of sexual identity, only the first, viz., biological sex (femaleness or maleness), seems uncontroversially genetically determined. But even that claim needs qualification with respect to individuals of indeterminate sex who are nevertheless classified as either female or male. It is a question for women whether any of the other factors is worth preserving. In a philosophical feminist critique of transsexualism, Janice Raymond has argued that what Shively and De Cecco, following Robert Stoller, call "gender identity," viz., one's "conviction of being female or male," is better understood as one's femininity or masculinity, i.e., certain psychosocial characteristics stereotypically associated with being female or being male in a sexist society—which is what contemporary American feminists usually mean by one's "gender," as distinct from one's "sex." If Janice Raymond is right, the conception of the preoperative transsexual as a woman trapped in a man's body assumes that real women and men are determined by conformity to sex-role stereotypes, which feminists find oppressive. Her criticism has implications for so-called "transsexuals" with respect to taking responsibility for their sexuality. If she is right, the meaning of the "woman" that the transsexual wants to be is not something that anyone should stand behind. Consciousness-raising is a better solution than surgery.

Historians are telling us that the notion of an identity defined by way of sexual orientation is a relatively recent thing. Labeling persons "homosexuals," for example, as opposed simply to marking individual acts, apparently dates only from the late nineteenth century. According to Jeffrey Weeks's history of homosexual politics in Britain, the term "homosexuality" was coined in 1869 by a Swiss doctor, Karoly Maria Benkert, and did not enter English currency until the 1890s. (Weeks, 1978, p. 43) Formerly, particular acts, such as sodomy, were prohibited by secular and eccliastical law, and the prevalent assumption was that such acts might be committed by any man. As Foucault tells it, with the nineteenth century medicalization and psychiatrization of sex, the former sodomite criminal or sinner "became a personage, a past, a case history, and a childhood, in addition to being a type of life, a life form, and a morphology, with an indiscreet anatomy and possibly a mysterious physiology." (Foucault 1978, p. 43) By this he does not mean that people just discovered that homosexual agents had certain sorts of histories and lifestyles. The idea seems, rather, that as people constructed relationships among themselves, they thereby constructed themselves and others, even constructed who they, and others, had been.

Thomas Szasz has argued similarly that psychiatrists have simultaneously "discovered" and "created" the mentally ill. The category of mental illness, understood as a basis for commitment to a total institution, he says, has functioned in recent times the way the category of heresy functioned during the Renaissance. He regards both "witch" and "homosexual" as identities of deviance defined by way of social norms. He regards the homosexual as a paradigm modern day heretic (Szasz, 1970).

Joyce Trebilcot's account of coming out as a lesbian is in a certain respect similar to Foucault's account of the creation of the homosexual identity and to Szasz's account of the creation of the mentally ill. She says it is not simply a discovery but at once a discovery and a creation (Trebilcot 1984, p. 422). By contrast, contemporary gay liberationists have held that sexual orientation is beyond one's control and have often exhibited a lively interest in the possibility of genetic explanations.[5] They have tended to deny individual responsibility, arguing that laws attempting to regulate sexual orientation and therapies attempting to alter it are irrational and unfair. The social construction of sexuality suggests an alternative to this criticism of the law and psychiatry. If Foucault is right, the medicalization and psychiatrization of sex, understood as historical events, created forms of power by defining new relationships. To combat the distributions of power defined by those relationships, perhaps we need to reject the sexual identities by which they have been defined. If "lesbian" were understood as not a sexual concept, coming out as a lesbian might be compatible with rejecting rather than affirming one's sexual identity. Even the term "lesbian," unlike the term "homosexual," comes from the history of erotic poetry, not from the history of medicine or psychiatry.

What purposes are served by regarding so-called "sexual orientations" as sexual in any other sense than that indicating the sexes (or genders) of the parties involved? What purposes are served by regarding love making as sexual behavior?

Nietzsche and Freud saw embracing sexuality as overcoming squeamishness about the body. But why assume that embracing the body is embracing sexuality? At issue for women is both a history of being devalued and a history of being defined by what has been called our sexuality, either our utility for reproducing patriarchy (procreation) or our utility for phallic play (recreation). The twentieth-century Sexual Revolution has shifted the emphasis from procreation to recreation and attempted a revaluation of the recreation from a fraternal, rather than patriarchal, perspective but has done little to contest a phallic definition of intimate relationships.

Many have rightly questioned applying the concept of love-making to sex as fraternal recreation. What has not been questioned is the wisdom of viewing erotic behavior as sexual. The homophile movement of the 1950s came close with its emphasis on the love, rather that the sexuality, of same-sex partners. The love emphasized by the homophile movement, however, was not particularly erotic. For "homophiles," the important distinction was between love and sex, but not particularly between the erotic and the sexual, although perhaps it had the potentiality for that development.

Insofar as the erotic is a powerful bonding agent, it is worth pondering the implications of its conception as sexual. I want to challenge the association of women's intimate bonds with behavior interpreted as variations on or deviations from phallic play or insemination. From the latter points of view, lesbian relationships inevitably appear deviant, substitutes for "the real thing," or as perversity in reproductive behavior.

There is a sense in which lesbian relationships could become straightforwardly sexual without being deviant or perverse. With a different social construction of reproduction, lesbian relationships could certainly take on positive reproductive forms by involving joint decisions to have and rear children. Many lesbians are already doing this, although their careers as reproducers are presently precarious, given present norms governing social reproduction. To be in a good position to assume responsibility for reproductive potentialities we need a social reconstruction of reproduction worth standing behind. The point is generalizable. To be in a good position to assume responsibility for ourselves, we need to participate in a social reconstruction of ourselves that we can stand behind.

It is not my intention to claim that humanity, or even sexuality, is entirely socially constructed. That it is socially constructed in part, however, is what makes it possible to take the kind of responsibility that I am writing about. To some extent we construct ourselves in that who we are is partly determined by social interaction, typically in accord with social norms, themselves constructed by social interaction and revisable by different interactions.

According to a well-known labeling perspective in sociology, social construction, or definition, occurs on three levels: (1) interpersonal reactions, (2) collective rule-making, and (3) organizational processing. (Schur, 1971, p. 11) All three are involved in the social construction of sexualities. Instead of "collective rule-making," I think of norm construction. Norms are not always rules but often empower or disable by defining roles and relationships.[6] Instead of "organizational processing," I think of "rituals," understanding what one nineteenth-century critic of punishment referred to as "the custom, the act, the 'drama,' a certain . . . sequence of procedures" (Nietzsche, 1969, 79–80). Rituals may be given meanings by social norms. That critic also observed that what endures in the institution of punishment are the rituals (the "drama," he called it)—perhaps such things as arrest, inquisition, trial, beheading, incarceration, flogging. Less enduring are rituals' meanings, the purposes for which they are used, such things as prevention, deterrence, revenge, reform, expulsion, a compromise with revenge, and so on. The same may be true of sexuality. What endure may be the various rituals referred to as "having sex"—rituals of copulation, sodomy, other so-called "sexual acts." Such rituals have borne a variety of meanings, even religious ones. Part of the early contemporary feminist response to the institution of rape has involved the inclination to say that rape is not sex, meaning that the point of the act is not to gratify the desire for sexual pleasure but, rather, such things as putting women in their place, getting revenge on other men, etc. Yet it is undeniable that many of the rituals involved in rape are the same rituals involved in "having sex."

Taking a similar approach to "revenge," the above-mentioned critic described words as "pockets into which now this and now that has been put and now many things at once" (Nietzsche, 1969). He regarded both words and rituals as having lives of their own, so to speak, with meanings that come and go. This seems at least as true of "sex" and the rituals we call "sexual" as of "revenge" and the rituals we call "punishment."

What does it mean to "have sex?" In the sense of "sex" that refers to one's femaleness or one's maleness, one "has it" all the time. But "having sex," of course, refers to behaviors that are not inevitable. Suppose that "having sex" is defined by the historical institution of sexuality, rather than by our physiology. Sexuality as an institution has a genealogical history, an evolution, like punishment. What has a genealogy is better understood through its relationships to its many ancestors than through the search for an essence.[7] If "having sex" is institutionally defined, it may consist simply in engaging in certain ancient rituals now governed by social norms relating them to human reproduction. The imposition of a sexual meaning on such rituals may be simply their interpretation by way of the norms of an institution that also structures reproduction.

It might be objected, however, that the analogy with punishment breaks down. There is no such thing as plain punishment, prior to social practice. Yet, it has seemed to some that there is such a thing as plain sex, on a par, perhaps, with plain eating and drinking, not yet defined by social practice (Goldman, 1977). Lunching and dining are defined by social practices, but one can eat or drink without lunching or dining. Is there not likewise just plain having sex, prior to its social constructions?

The difficulty is to say what it is. There are, of course, sexual organs, as there are digestive organs. But so-called sexual behavior is not understood as necessarily involving organs. Nor is all behavior that involves sexual body parts sexual behavior. In law and psychiatry, it seems taken for granted that lesbian genital love-making is sexual behavior. If lesbian love-making were genital, that would seem a comprehensible—if not conclusive—reason for regarding it as sexual.

However, if "having sex" is enacting certain rituals involving external genitalia, or rituals preparatory to those or analogous to them, it can be argued that "having sex" is a phallic concept that cannot be applied without distortion to lesbian love-making. For, women have no external genitalia. Lesbian love-making, consequently, is never genital. What are inaccurately referred to as women's external genitalia are (1) the menstrual canal (which is neither generative nor an organ), (2) the clitoris, an organ generating only pleasure (and therefore not generative in the requisite sense), and (3) the labia (like the menstrual canal, neither organs nor generative). These parts are, of course, female, and so "sexual" in the same sense as a full beard, vaginitis, menstruation, menopause, and hot flashes, none of which enters into the definition of behavior as sexual behavior.

Women's physically orgasmic pleasures are processed through the clitoris, which makes no contribution to reproduction at any point in the life cycle and continues to function long after reproduction has become impossible. Clitoridectomy does not impair reproductive capacity.[8] What the clitoris is good for is pleasure. The role it plays in human relations is a bonding role, not a reproductive one.

It may be objected that the clitoris plays a role in reproduction insofar as it provides pleasure during a reproductive act and thereby facilitates reproduction. As there is no correlation, however, between clitoral pleasure and conception, it is misleading to say that such pleasure facilitates (physiological) reproduction. What it facilitates is bonding and perhaps love-making, only one of the rituals of which is ordinarily requisite to reproduction.

Classification of the clitoris as a genital organ appears to betray a phallic bias: either the clitoris is misperceived as a little phallus itself or its pleasures are viewed as a byproduct of copulation or as analogous to those of penile ejaculation—commonly, if mistakenly, identified with male orgasm.[9] If the clitoris is not a genital organ, then its involvement in love-making does not offer a reason for regarding that love-making as sexual, at least not on a genital conception of sexuality.

Not all conceptions of sexual behavior, however, have a genital focus. On Freud's account of infant sexuality as polymorphously perverse, just about any part of the body can be "sexualized" by becoming a focus of repeated vigorous muscular activity, such as sucking, with the result that a tension is regularly created there which needs to be relieved and can be relieved by muscular activity, such as sucking or pulling or rubbing (Freud, 1965).

But what does it mean to call this production and relief of tension sexual? Freud seems to have thought the energies involved were sexual energies. That pushes the question back a step: What does it mean to identify energies as sexual?

Two kinds of answers suggest themselves: either their sources are sexual or their directions are sexual. Nongenitally focused conceptions of sexual behavior, such as Freud's, attempt to define sexual behavior in terms of either motivation or teleology rather than in terms of the body parts involved. The search for a common motivation, however, has proved as futile as the search for other common denominators.[10] The likeliest teleological candidate is the purpose of furthering the life of the species.[11] By this criterion, however, research into health care, ecology, and environmental ethics may be clearer instances of sexual behavior than lesbian love-making.

For Aristotle, sexual pleasure is pleasure in certain kinds of touching (Aristotle, 1925). This view is similar to Freud's and enters into a popular notion of sexuality today. It is this kind of view to which I turn next. The view of sexuality as touching for pleasure may confuse the sexual with the erotic. Disentangling the erotic from the sexual seems an important step, even if not the last step, in taking responsibility for intimate relationships.

III The Erotic

"Erotic" is popularly employed as a euphemism for "sexual," especially in the context of art and pornography. However, the meanings of "erotic" and "sexual" are distinct. "Sexual" is either a biological concept or a sociopolitical one elaborated upon it. "Erotic" is not a biological concept. "Erotic" refers to certain emotional capacities or to social constructions elaborated upon them. The erotic refers to a capacity or set of capacities for pleasurable excitement of certain sorts. The difficulty is to say what sorts. The following seems at least one such: the susceptibility to joyful surprise in intimate discovery or disclosure by way of touching. The relevant discoveries are dis/coveries of another; the relevant disclosures, dis/closures of oneself. Desires and fantasies may be understood as erotic when they are desires for or fantasies of such experience. Autoerotic behavior can be understood as erotic by way of the fantasies it involves.

I want to focus on the idea of touching as a central element of the erotic. Only what is particular and embodied can touch and is touchable. Erotic communication is thoroughly carnal. Although carnal, it need not be skin to skin, however. It can occur by eye contact and even by the spoken and written word. Still, it is not touching in the requisite sense unless the party touched feels the touch. I am touched, in this sense, when someone moves me, succeeds in reaching me, makes me feel something.

Although carnal, the erotic need not be sexual. My hypothesis is that the connection between sexuality and the erotic is far more contingent than is ordinarily assumed. The institution of sexuality construes erotic play as a sexual invitation. Thomas Nage's paper, "Sexual Perversion," (1969) which some critics have claimed never gets around to sex, takes for granted the context of the institution of sexuality, according to which the erotic play he describes is construed as a sexual invitation. By way of institutional norms erotic play has come to be associated with sexuality. What eros and sexuality have in common, apart from such norms, is a historical association with rituals in which physical touching and its attendant pleasures are central. The touching required for physiological reproduction, however, is not the same kind of touching as enters into the definition of erotic interaction. For physiological reproduction, neither party need feel anything. (This may be literally the case with some forms of artificial insemination.)

The erotic makes no reference to gender. There is no reason why it should occur more frequently heterosexually than homosexually. There are, however, good historical reasons why same-sex eroticism is apt to be healthier than heterosexual eroticism. Under current sexual politics, parties to heterosexual eroticism are almost inevitably very unequal in power. Same-sex eroticism is more likely than heterosexual eroticism to be between equals or near-equals. The problem is not the bare existence of an inequality of power. Serious problems arise when such inequalities in a relationship actually become part of what is erotically exciting about it. When this occurs with inequalities that are due to oppressive social institutions, those damaged by such institutions may be drawn into supporting them for the sake of the pleasure derived from the relationships those institutions make possible. Where women are damaged by misogynist institutions, heterosexual eroticism contains this danger.

Similar dangers arise for same-sex intimacy when it is sexualized in a sexist context. The sexualization of same-sex intimacy consists in applying norms of the institution of sexuality to the parties involved. This involves the danger of attaching erotic excitement to damaging inequalities of power or to fantasized inequalities realizable only by way of oppressive practices.

Erotic interaction is a powerful bonding agent. A brief interchange can have one hooked for years. This is not true simply of the rituals of sex. Sexual behavior can also be a powerful bonding agent over time but not just overnight. A consequence of sexualizing erotic interaction in the context of oppressive sexual politics is that it sets us up for becoming locked into damaging long-term relationships. Sexuality, as a phallic institution in a sexist society, is laden with associations between inequality and erotic pleasure. It may be impossible to purge sexuality of those associations without a much wider nonsexist reconstruction of society. Meanwhile, the erotic offers, at least potentially, an alternative to the conception of lesbian relationships as sexual.

One may wonder whether "eros" has a better history than "sex."[12] In Plato's dialogues, *The Symposium* and *The Phaedrus*, eros leads to what Freud called sublimation, a turning away from the body (Hamilton and Cairnes, 1961). Further, the contemporary pornography scene, notorious for its misogyny, caters to an emotional high bearing at least a family resemblance to what I understand by "erotic."

My understanding of the erotic leaves open the question whether what is discovered or disclosed in erotic experience is good or bad and also whether the discovery or disclosure is itself desirable or not, for example, whether it is obtained by means employed with or without the consent of the parties involved, and so on. I do not claim that erotic relationships are necessarily good. At another time, I mean to explore differences between healthy and damaging erotic relationships. My point here is simply that the conception of lesbian relationships as erotic avoids a certain phallocentrism and, thereby, the homophobia of their conception as sexual. It offers, in those respects, a better standpoint for the feminist enterprise of taking responsibility for intimacy.

A large part of one's intent in coming out as a lesbian is to reject the charge of perversion. The idea is not to embrace some perversions as good things, after all, but to support one's identity and relationships as, at the very least, no more perverted than other intimate relationships that already have society's blessings.[13] The conception of lesbianism as an erotic, rather than sexual, identity removes the basis of the charge of perversion. For the health and success of erotic interaction understood as an emotional exchange is not contingent upon the sexual characters of the parties involved.

What the erotic captures about lesbian relationships is emotional intimacy, excitement, and a certain appreciation of our bodies. Lesbians should be able to participate in reproduction as fully as anyone. Apart from the institution of sexuality, the lesbianism of a relationship implies little about the potentialities of such participation. It has to do, rather, with what turns us on, i.e., with what excites us, what we appreciate in women. What turns us on tends to be a source of the driving energies of our lives. Coming out as a lesbian is an important part of taking responsibility for what turns us on and thereby for what drives us. This is fundamental to taking responsibility for ourselves. It is a choice to embrace intimate attachments that we can stand behind. In a homophobic and misogynist society, coming out as a lesbian potentially emancipates our intimate relationships from their historic ties to reproduction and phallic recreation. It thereby potentially emancipates us from important forms of our historic complicity in perpetuating the machinery of sex oppression. We may need to reject sexual identities in order to do it.

Notes

1. This project has many roots, including my "Love, Friendship, and Eroticism: An Essay in Carnal Knowledge," read to the Society of Women in Philosophy, E. Lansing Michigan, 1979, and "The Symbolic Significance of Sex and the Institution of Sexuality," read to the Society for the Philosophy of Sex and Love at the Eastern APA, 1984, New York City. It benefits from Sarah Hoagland's *Lesbian Ethics* (1988), which I was privileged to see in draft, from Carol Gilligan's discussions of responsibility (Gilligan, 1982), and from Alison Jaggar's work on the social construction of human nature (Jagger, 1983). I have been influenced by sociological theory with a symbolic interactionist perspective, which led me to George Herbert Mead's *Mind, Self and Society from the Standpoint of a Social Behaviorist* (1934).

   Finally, I have come to agree with an idea articulated by Carolyn Shafer, relayed to me conversationally ten years ago by Marilyn Frye, that "having sex" is a phallic concept, that only men can literally "have sex," that to see lesbian love making as "sexual" is probably to see fingers and tongues as phallic substitutes or to misperceive the clitoris as a vestigial phallus. Cf. Frye, 1983.

2. This is something like the distinction John Rawls found it necessary to emphasize in dealing with the justification of punishment (Rawls, 1955).
3. This kind of objection was raised by Sarah Hoagland in correspondence.
4. For recent philosophical discussions tending to ignore this ambiguity, see the papers by male authors in Part I of Soble, 1980.
5. Cf. turn-of-the-century homosexual rights activists. See Steakley, 1975. For recent gay liberationist perspectives see, e.g., articles by De Cecco and Shively in *The Journal of Homosexuality* over the past decade. See also Noretta Koertge, 1985, formerly published as *The Journal of Homosexuality* 6: p. 4 (Summer 1981).
6. Foucault objects to the repression hypothesis about sexuality that it focuses upon only a "no-saying" conception of power by presenting sexuality as regulated by rules forbidding various forms of behaviors. This conception of power, which he calls a "legal" conception, does not adequately capture even the way power works within the law, as was pointed out long ago in Hohfeld's 1919 account of fundamental jural relations. Laws also *create* power by defining roles and relationships.
7. Cf. Nietzsche, "Only that which has no history is definable," *On the Genealogy of Morals*, I. p. 13.
8. For more on the nature and consequences of clitoridectomy see Mary Daly 1979, ch. 5.
9. On the physiology of the clitoris see Masters and Johnson, 1966.
10. Clearly, not all sexual behavior is engaged in because any of its participants have the desire to reproduce, nor is communication or the desire for pleasure common to all such behavior.
11. This was the view of Schopenhauer, Freud's philosophical predecessor on sexuality. (Schopenhauer, 1966).
12. Sarah Hoagland, for example, argues that it does not.
13. Nagel (1969) suggests, at the end of his otherwise interesting essay, that perverted sex might actually be better as sex than unperverted sex. This seems to me either incoherent or a way of saying that it may be more fun.

6

Fallen Angels: The Representation of Violence against Women in Legal Culture

Kristin Bumiller

Introduction

One of the most frequent sources of the public's contact with legal ideas is through the reporting of trials about notorious crimes and persons. For the casual observer, these trials are worthy of attention because they capture the imagination or generate uncertainty about the law's ability to deal with human tragedy and depravity. Yet avid interest in media reports spawned by notable criminal cases is more than a spectator sport, these reports are the means by which symbolic representations of victims and criminals are produced for consumption in popular culture. The messages that are disseminated in democratic societies by the media about the causes and consequences of crime and the behavior of the principal actors in courtroom dramas are a prolific source of powerful legal symbols. This essay examines the ways in which symbolic trials concerning sexual violence, despite ostensibly promoting justice in individual cases, may actually reinforce dominant preconceptions about women, men, and crimes of sexual violence.

From the perspective of the mass audience, all criminal trials are symbolic, since defendants and victims come to represent social roles. Each trial has within it a message about the way to reconcile the social vision of a good society with justice in the individual case (Kirchheimer, 1961). Yet these public morality plays, often about disturbing and incomprehensible acts of brutality against isolated victims, evoke in the mass consciousness conflicted emotions: genuine soul-searching for a more humane society mixed with superficial evaluations of dangerous stereotypes and

---

A longer version of this paper is published in the *International Journal of the Sociology of Law*. This research was supported by a grant from the Law and Social Sciences Program of the National Science Foundation.

misconceptions about criminals and victims (see Enzensberger, 1974; Lazere, 1987). Even though the stories are controversial, they serve to portray the event as a tragedy and thus relieve anxieties about the sources of violence and the legal system's ability to control them (Edelman, 1977).

The subject of this inquiry is a major symbolic trial that focused attention in its community and the wider world on the American justice system's treatment of sexual violence and ethnic prejudice. My mode of analysis is influenced by linguistics, feminism, and poststructuralist political philosophy. The symbolic trial is viewed as a signifier within the dominant legal culture: it is a forum that projects authoritative messages through language and legal form about identity and social relationships in a struggle between the antagonistic world views of the defense and the prosecution (Bordieu, 1987). The symbolic power of the law is projected through linguistic attributions concerning the character and motives of defendants, victims, and legal professionals (see Santos, 1982). Because dominant modes of constituting the self (as a woman, criminal, or victim, for example) are maintained through the conventions of legal language, symbolic trials are moments when the rejection of those categories may come about through resistance to legal discourse (Bordieu, 1987; see also Foucault, 1977).

Drawing on political and feminist theory (see Spivak, 1987; Moi, 1985), the following passages interpret messages about sexual violence that originate from sources outside and within a controversial rape trial. Interpretations are presented from three vantage points. First, one form of communication that mediates legal issues for the mass public, the newspaper stories that report the initial incident and the legal proceedings, generates accounts that structure perceptions of the crime. Second, accounts are provided from the principal lawyers that reflect their professional identity and their assumptions about the scope and purpose of criminal law. A third dimension is presented through the interpretation of the trial proceedings, and in particular the victim's testimony. This discourse reveals how her speech in a courtroom both conforms to legal ways of understanding violence and yet embodies resistance to accepted modes of expression. The analysis will show how multiple levels of discourse in a symbolic trial, in particular the public and professional language, frame public perceptions and constitute barriers to the articulation of the victim's perspective.

This essay presents a story about women and violence that is rarely written about or discussed in the context of a legal case. Generally, the story line that captures the public interest involves the curious circumstances of the individuals brought into the drama as well as evaluations of their moral character. The public audience plays the role of a jury of one's peers; each person evaluates the credibility of the charges based upon incomplete and fallible renditions of the facts. The themes developed here, however, do not turn on the factual premises of the case. The symbolic import of the trial depends less on the witnesses' adherence to or betrayal of the truth, and more on the way the stories told resonate with images of victims and thus form the context for interpretation.

This rape trial displays the multiple meanings implied in a woman's image of innocence. Simply stated, when the claim that a woman has been sexually assaulted is made, it is often based upon her blamelessness in contributing to her own harm. Thus, the claim to innocence is not easily made, for the shadow of guilt lingers (as with the defendants). More significantly, the multifaceted meanings of innocence widen the scope of judgment about a woman's worth. The "innocence" of a female accuser is lost with her initial charge that she has been touched by sexual violence, and is further eroded as her moral purity becomes an issue in court.

The trial turns on her "innocence of experience" or "freedom from guilt"; this has powerful symbolic consequences, for it reinforces the presumption that punishing violent men is justified to the extent that women are worthy of trust and protection. This presumption is symbolically as threatening as the actual violence of rape, for it exposes a woman's intimate life in the courtroom. The accuser is forced into the role of an "angel" who must defend her heavenly qualities after her fall from grace. The symbolic message is, in some degree, an expression of the legal system's high tolerance for violence against women and its low threshold for the measure of her unworthiness. The various meanings attached to the concept of a woman's innocence in the following interpretations of a major rape trial illustrate the vulnerability of the woman as an accuser in contemporary legal culture.

The Public Trial

The 1984 rape trial of six Portuguese immigrant men in New Bedford, Massachusetts, was a celebrated moment of media attention to issues of sex and violence.[1] The political language of the media reporting of the New Bedford incident encouraged the public audience to vicariously imagine and draw judgments about the sequence of events in the bar called Big Dan's. The media constructed the story in a way that intensified and polarized issues for purposes of the alternative agendas of the feminist and Portuguese communities (e.g., Edelman 1977, 1988; see also Smart and Smart, 1978, pp. 91, 101–2). Rather than inscribing these acts of violence with meaning, the newspapers reported a lurid "spectacle" in which a "gang" of Portuguese men engaged in "senseless brutality" against a lone woman pinned down on a pool table. Although violent sexual assaults occur frequently in New Bedford and other communities across the country, this case was the subject of immense publicity because it was depicted as an inconceivably brutal gang rape cheered on by pitiless bystanders.

Six Portuguese immigrants were tried for aggravated sexual assault and sexual assault in a Falls River, Massachusetts courtroom about one year after the incident in Big Dan's. Because it received massive local and international newspaper coverage, the rape became an important symbol in popular culture and a focal point for the mobilization of feminist groups. The extensive publicity surrounding the Big Dan's incident's disputability may have arisen from the uniqueness of the circumstances, yet by subjecting the issue of gang rape to public scrutiny, the media constructed powerful images of the case through selective reporting of information and structuring of perceptions for the popular audience. While the power of the media to set agendas and to mobilize interest groups is often regarded with suspicion, the media's role in the creation of dominant images is ignored by skeptics unaware of the more subtle role of news accounts in constructing the conceptual framework within which conflictual events are interpreted and understood.[2]

In the *New Bedford Standard-Time*'s characterization of the incident, the implied motives and intentions of the victim and defendants moved in and out of focus within a larger picture which included legal authorities and community organizations. Although a considerable amount of reporting space was allotted to the defendants (their arrest, court hearings, personal information, and statements by their attorneys), the language employed by the press, at least superficially, placed the spotlight on the victim. One news story, for example, described the rape as the "victim's ordeal," in which "ordeal" broadly referred to the acts of violent sexual aggression, the trial, and the publicity surrounding the trial. For the most part, references to the victim ignored her as an individual who had her own specific responses to rape. Either the victim was named by her formal legal status and demographic qualities (e.g., the "complainant," "young woman," "21-year-old city woman"), or more elaborate discussion of the victim was carried out through references to "generic" victims of rape (e.g., anti-rape activists' statements of solidarity with the victim and special reporting features about rape crisis centers' efforts to respond to the psychological trauma of victims).

The majority of stories were unqualified in their description of the brutality of the crime and full of general sympathy for the victim and hostility toward the perpetrators. The newspapers told of a mob scene: "[according to police and witness reports] the bar was whipped into a lurid, cheering frenzy, as they watched the sexual assault." A rape reform activist is reported to have said: "The rapists knew exactly what they were doing. It went on so long, they obviously had a chance to consider what they were undertaking. The bail is ridiculously low." Her words are one example of the panoply of law-and-order demands that gain their intensity from the symbolic invocation of enemies. Thus, the Portuguese defendants metaphorically took on the instinctive qualities and look of uncivilized people, for example, one news report quoted a Portuguese man in the neighborhood referring to the accused as "barbarians."

Although the references to the victim tended to be sympathetic, there were ambivalent undercurrents in her portrayal. A New Bedford reporter attributed a heavenly innocence to the victim through the rhetorical questioning of an investigating police officer: "Where will she go from here? She'll probably have to leave New Bedford. . . . She won't be able to handle the memories. Look at her angelic face. It's *almost* full of innocence. She'll never be innocent again." She is not attributed earthly innocence, but the innocence of an angel fallen from grace.

The most conspicuous aspect of the event in terms of its symbolic representation in popular legal culture is not the portrayal of either the victim or the defendants, but the emphasis on the setting of the crime. The tone was set by the first major local newspaper story about the rape, which included a large photograph of Big Dan's Tavern. Thus, attention was drawn to the incompatibility of the setting with expected norms of human behavior. The fact that the incident occurred in a *public* place, in a barroom and on a pool table, is discordant with the social conception of consensual sex as a private and intimate act. The public nature of the crime has significance beyond its location; the image of a gang, yelling, mocking, and humiliating the woman, jars common sensibilities about personal dignity in social interactions. The early coverage employed the shock of these circumstances as a rhetorical device to establish that illegitimate sex occurred. The effect was to inhibit further speculation about the woman's responsibility for the violence. Reporting about the scene of the crime implied that "no woman" would want "that" to happen. In such cases, the woman's private intentions regarding her intimate behavior are considered irrelevant as long as the news reporting focuses on a bar portrayed as a "sore spot" where only the "riff-raff go."

The language describing the setting of the crime creates a picture of the personalities of the actors and sets the framework for popular interpretations. The structuring of public perceptions about this particular incident intensified hostilities over the description of the social setting of the rape, which in this case involved immigrant defendants from a primarily ethnic community. Because popular cultural interpretations emphasized setting, the terms of political discourse were polarized between the response of the Portuguese community that New Bedford is a decent place to live and the demand of advocates of women's rights that women must have the freedom to associate safely in public places. For the "Take Back the Night" protesters, the setting of the crime clarified the underlying moral issue, that regardless of this woman's character and circumstances, *any* woman should have the freedom of movement to enter a public bar without the fear of being gang-raped. Supporters of the Portuguese defendants objected to newspaper reporting that, in their view, employed inappropriate references to the ethnic origins of the defendants. Moreover, concerns were raised that characterizations of Big Dan's as a bad establishment in a marginal neighborhood in the city were responsible for creating the impression that New Bedford was the Portuguese "rape capital" of the country

At the level of the public trial, the news media both linguistically and visually created a story about brutal and public sexual violence and narrowed the interpretative framework for understanding the crime. In the actual trial, the setting of the rape was also re-created, but often by testimony that recast the scene in terms of precise movements indicated by pointing to a scaled down replica of Big Dan's in front of the witness stand. For the defense attorneys, once the case was brought to trial, their stated objective was to reconstruct the image of the bar so that a plausible story about human behavior would account for and justify the men's actions.

The Courtroom Trial

My ethnographic observations, obtained from interviews three years after the trial, offer an interpretation of the events that differs from the symbolically constructed accounts by the media.[3] From the perspective of the principal legal actors in the trial, the professional discourse of the law protects defendants from unbridled public hostility. The attorneys chose to analyze events by employing a language of equilibrium that employed commonsense personifications of good and evil, as well as of commendable and unworthy character.

From the defense attorneys' standpoint, the case was notable for its mundane nature rather than its notoriety; the case was nothing other than "a routine sexual assault case," "a dull, dull case," or "a classic case based on the mistrust of government witnesses." For these professional participants, the trial was similar to other rape trials and operated according to a predictable set of norms and procedures. The most perceptive of the defense attorneys recognized (similar to the social scientist) that social reality is reconstructed for the purposes of any trial. Several of the attorneys involved readily admitted that the reality of what happened in Big Dan's was unclear and were willing to entertain three possibilities: (1) that a brutal rape occurred; (2) that "something consensual" happened in the bar that night; or (3) that "something consensual" crossed the line into a criminal act. As a group, they openly discussed which image of the bar fit their reading of the facts and would best serve the interests of the defendants. As good criminal defense lawyers, their objective became to turn this incredible scenario into a story that made sense to a jury.

These lawyers confronted the ambiguity of the case but not without acknowledging the life-and-death consequences for a "lone defendant fighting for freedom" or experiencing the sheer scariness of one's heart pounding in making one's way through the mob on the courthouse steps. The defense attorneys identified with what they saw as the human side of the case. For one lawyer, the defendant was "gentle" Joseph Viera and the victim was a survivor: "she is no weeping willow or shrinking violet. She is a tough woman defending something. She has a big interest in the trial—her most important relationships are at stake. That is her public position, not what the people in L.A. think about her, but what the people around her and closest to her think of her." For the advocate, intuition about the victim is necessary to convince the jury that she was both consciously and unconsciously self-protective; that is, not to create the pretense that there was no rape, but to convince the jury that since the first experience of the victim after the attack was a confrontation with an accusatory grandmother, then she should no longer be seen as capable of expressing unadulterated truth. As the lawyer explains, "Why should I subordinate my perceptions about what the battle is about in the courtroom to [feminists'] demands that society devalues the victim because her boyfriend is a schmuck, because she is not married, or had a child out of wedlock—when the fellow next to me has his life on the line?" The bottom line for this defense attorney is that society cannot put its faith in the victim because she "has no commitment to justice."

The moral passion of the defense attorneys both recognizes and buries one truth. As actors in these roles they live with the dilemma that no language is able to express all aspects of the truth—yet all language carries the force and power of the word—and these words that may be employed to condone violence against women carry the force of the law.

The Victim's Trial

The victim's testimony in the courtroom, reviewed from the videotaped record of the proceedings,[4] provides another kind of symbolic interpretation that connects the presentation of events inside the courtroom with the social construction of sexual relationships. The victim's accounts give authority to the perspectives of women and other excluded voices that are revealed neither by controversies generated by legal analysis nor by public speculation about personalities and circumstances. Yet, these accounts confront barriers to a full understanding of the person, or self, as an actor in the social world (Cassirer, 1985; Merleau-Ponty, 1964; Taylor, 1985a). The move to ground understanding in discourse, in particular the discourse of women and other victimized groups, can be seen as a straightforward strategy to give authority to their speech. But their perceptions of social reality, and our ability to reflect upon and understand their reality, are bounded by their capacities to express themselves in language. The political implication of this epistemological problem is that the discourse of excluded groups provides us with socially constructed "ways of knowing" that are partial and as a result can be employed to undermine their interests (Belenky et al., 1986). As my reading of the trial will show, however, these interpretations give utterance to the strengths as well as the vulnerability and duplicity of victims. These expressions, therefore, must be reconciled within a political context and ultimately evaluated in the larger scheme of institutional life.

The predominant theme of the trial was the inquiry into the "innocence" of the victim, who I call Diana. Both the prosecution and the defense produced theories to account for her motivations in going to the bar and the appropriateness of her behavior. As defense attorney Lindahl questioned: "At first your only intention was to buy cigarettes . . . ; at some point you decided to stay . . . *That's the decision* you regret most about that night?" Defense attorney Edward Harrington posed the question: "If you're living with a man, what are you doing running around the streets getting raped?" (see MacKinnon, 1987, p. 80). This frame of reference inevitably flows from the definition of rape that forces the prosecution to show nonconsent in order to prove that a sexual assault has been committed. The state of mind of the victim is the window to the *mens rea* that establishes the culpability of the defendant. Since the social construction of rape in the courtroom or in society ignores the victim's perception of the attack, she becomes the object of a theory about nonconsent that uses information not only about her behavior on the day of the rape but also about the moral choices she has made throughout her lifetime.

The best defense in a rape trial, therefore, is often the indictment of the victim. That is why the defense attorneys attempted to incriminate Diana by posing a series of questions intended to raise doubts about the sincerity of her charge of rape: Was she desperate to have sex that night? So desperate that she would agree to sex in a public place? Was her behavior irresponsible or inviting? Was she too drunk to know what was happening?

The testimony of witnesses who actually heard and saw Diana that night, along with her own testimony, provides us with an account of her motives, words, and actions. Each element of evidence, however, derives its authority from the source and form of communication. For example, Diana's own accounts were different immediately after the rape from what she said at the trial and were given in the form of recollections, written police reports, and reports of witnessed confrontations in the bar or police station. Even as stories unfold in the courtroom, the value of the "facts" the court will call evidence has been predetermined by the social mechanisms that privilege certain forms of communication. In this case, it means that the simple and direct recollection of the facts she gave in court would stand against the enormous collection of documents already recording the events of the crime and her life.

As she testified in a calm monotone, she tried to present herself in society's image of an innocent victim rather than revealing weakness and anger. Adopting the pose of the innocent victim required her to show that her actions conformed to what is expected of a person of good character: consistency, sobriety, and responsibility. While the defense attorney's questions constrained her ability to explain her actions, her responses were also limited by the prosecution which was concerned that her testimony would contradict the police officers' official version and the testimony of witnesses who were in the tavern during the rape (see McBarnett, 1984). The defense attempted to question her credibility by pointing out inconsistencies in the accounts she gave to the police; even her private conferences with a rape counselor were introduced into evidence. Faced with such constraints, her strategy was not to reveal the "whole" story, but to construct a narrative that she felt would best establish her innocence. In a firm voice she recounted what she believed to be the truth about her victimization.

Given the focus on her innocence, the task was to convince the court of her capability to be cognizant of and explain all that had happened to her. This meant she had to draw a line in her description of her own emotional distress that preserved the credibility of her statements. When subjected to an extensive cross-examination that disputed the version of the facts she gave immediately after the rape, she defended her ability to perceive and report events in a state of mind that was (in her words) *near* hysterical and *slightly* confused.

The major challenge to her credibility rested on the record of her "exaggerations" in the police report written the night of the attack. In subsequent police reports she retracted the claim the there were fifteen men involved, including six who had sexual intercourse with her, and said she "lost count." She also modified the statement that "the men had knives" to "one man held a knife in front of her face" (then again, she "admits" he did not *say* anything threatening to her). She was continually questioned by the defense attorneys about these inconsistencies, to which her response was frequently that she "doesn't know" how to account for them.

Ultimately, none of her explanations captured the shock or trauma she had experienced. Instead, she offered admissions that she was tired and slightly confused. She said, "the events are clearer now than then"; and about the first police report, "I don't remember anything I said"; "I was tired, I didn't want to talk to anybody and I wanted to be left alone." Defense attorney Lindahl's effort to get her to justify her statement to the police produced this moment in the trial:

Lindahl: Did you tell [officer Sacramento] 12 or 15 men were involved?

Diana: Every man there was involved.

Lindahl: Did you say six men had sexual intercourse with you; when in fact two men had intercourse?

Diana: Yes.

Lindahl: Is this your testimony to the jury today? If you said twelve or fifteen; if you said sixteen or more; if you said—

Diana: *I believe everybody that was there was guilty!*

Lindahl: Objection!

[At this point the jury was asked to disregard the witness's statement.]

At the same time she spontaneously blurted out that everyone was guilty, she was able to characterize her "exaggerations" as a product of the horror she experienced in the bar that night. Yet Lindahl's next question was, "Maybe you were so upset you exaggerated." Diana's response was, "no." Her denial indicated both that she felt uncomfortable about the manner in which the prosecutors were using the law to try to place blame on her and that she was willing to defend her own view of moral responsibility that accounted for her rage against all of the men in the tavern.

Incriminating statements about Diana were not only used to undermine her credibility, they were also developed into theories about consent by comparing the victim's character with the moral position of other women who were principal actors in the retelling of the story. These comparisons are poignantly brought forth in the testimony of the women who were with Diana during the day she was raped. The first witness called by the defense was Rosetta, who testified about their activities during the afternoon before Diana went to Big Dan's. Rosetta was asked a series of questions about their consumption of drinks at the Knotty Pine, an Italian restaurant and bar, where they stopped to get soup for their boyfriends. Defense attorney Harrington appeared disappointed with her testimony, as if he expected her to provide a more definitive answer to whether or not Diana had any alcoholic drinks that afternoon. However, the defense was able to establish that Diana had asked Rosetta if she would like to go out with her for a drink. The defense attorney initiated the following exchange on cross-examination:

Waxler: [Diana] wanted more to drink?
Rosetta: Yes.
Waxler : What did you say?
Rosetta: I told her she should *just* go home.
Waxler: Did she respond?
Rosetta: No.
Waxle r: Did she say anything further?
Rosetta: No.

The purpose of this exchange was to attempt to establish that Diana intended to go out drinking when she left the house at dusk, but Rosetta insinuated that she disapproved of Diana's desire to get out of the house and, and in so doing, implied that Diana's own restlessness was responsible for her being raped at Big Dan's. Her testimony also enabled the defense to draw a contrast between Rosetta, who had recently married her boyfriend and made the wise decision of staying home, and Diana, who lived with the father of her two children and made the fateful decision to go out that night.

Another incriminating voice came from the other woman who had been in Big Dan's. Marie was introduced to the court as a reliable person with professional credentials: she is employed as a nurse and is much older than Diana (probably in her forties). (She was referred to as the "fat lady" in the testimony by the men in the bar who did not know her name.) She went out that night to get something to eat, but when she discovered the restaurant across the street was closed, she decided to see if she could get a sandwich at Big Dan's. Marie was a regular in the bar, and in fact, knew several of the men quite well. Previously, she had helped the defendant Victor Rapozo get a job. Marie gave the following description of Diana's actions in the tavern:

Harrington: What did you see her do?
Marie: She went to the bar to get a drink.
Harrington: Were you seated at the table?
Marie: Yes.
Harrington: Did she come to the table?
Marie: Next thing she did is, [she] came over and asked if [she] could sit down.

Harrington: Then?

Marie: I said you can sit down, but I am leaving shortly.

Harrington: What observations did you make about the young lady?

Marie: She was bubbly; she was bouncing 'round the chair; she never stood still, her pupils were very large and her eyes were glassy.

A few moments later, Marie added that during their ten minute conversation Diana had told her that "she didn't have sex for several months, I think nine months," and that her "boyfriend or ex-husband [suggested that she] should get out and meet people because she is a lonely person."

A third confrontation with the morality of other women came from her closest relative and substitute parent, her grandmother. This confrontation was also recorded for the official record because it was overheard by the police officer accompanying her to the hospital and by the nurse. Her grandmother, when she first saw Diana in the hospital, called her a drunk, accused her of shaming the family, and asked her why she was not at home with her children. Diana was reluctant to talk about her grandmother's denouncements, and at one point insisted that they were irrelevant:

Lindahl: Do your remember the conversation with your grandmother?

Diana: I don't want my grandmother brought into this.

Lindahl: The reason you didn't remember is because you didn't want to talk about your grandmother?

Diana: Yes, it is.

Lindahl: It was true you didn't remember?

Diana: It wasn't a lie. I don't think it should have been brought up.

Lindahl: Isn't it true, whenever you don't want anything brought up, you say I don't remember?

Diana obviously cared deeply about her grandmother's opinion of her, yet she explained her grandmother's reaction by asserting that she must have been so upset that she did not realize her words were harmful. Diana tried to present the story as if there had been no direct conversation, as if her grandmother had been screaming and as if most of the actual conversation had been directed at her grandfather. The re-enactment in the trial of her grandmother's assault on her character not only revealed the powerful forces of condemnation at work in her private life but brought these painful experiences into the realm of public judgment.

Using the morality of other women to incriminate Diana exemplifies how the social conception of rape finds authority in the woman's duty to protect herself. The defendants, however, relied on more overt challenges based on their ordinary treatment of women. As defendant John Cordeiro told the court, in his testimony on his own behalf, he was surprised to hear the next morning that the police were looking for him because there had been a rape in Big Dan's Tavern. He said, "A rape? Nobody raped anybody." When asked in the trial if he knew what rape was, Cordeiro responded. "It is when you tear off their clothes . . ." In Cordeiro's account of that night, he left Big Dan's for a short while, and when he came back he saw Diana on the pool table with defendant Joe Viera on top of her. He watched defendant Rapozo put his penis in her mouth and then did the same thing, while Diana was "smiling and laughing at them." Cordeiro was relatively unconcerned about talking to the police the next morning, because all he believed he had to do was to "tell the truth . . . *the truth never hurts.*" His confidence turned out to be misplaced, but his lack of concern reflects the unproblematic state of mind of the rapist. There was initially no reason for him to doubt his own opinion about what the woman wanted to have happen to her that night.

Defendant Daniel Silva's story was less frank and based upon more complicated assumptions about how Diana had communicated her desire to be raped. Silva claimed that he had met Diana a few months before and had had a short conversation with her in a cafe named Pals Four. By his account, Diana approached him and asked if he had any drugs. After a few more words, she asked, "Do you want to play, fool around?" He reportedly responded "yes" and claimed she "looked very happy." He explained to her that he could not take her home, however, because he lived with his mother. As they continued to fool around with each other, the only thing that concerned Silva was that he "thought she was holding me too tight; like a hysterical woman; like she wanted something." Daniel Silva portrayed the situation in Big Dan's as an ordinary "pick-up" in a bar, at least until the other men started making fun of him and then participated in the attack.

The challenges from the women and the defendants were based upon assumptions about how men and women communicate sexual aggression and desire. The proceedings became a search for facts that would explain a cause and effect sequence in which the defendant makes "reasonable" judgments about her desires and the victim either rebukes him or acquiesces in his actions. In this construction of the social interaction, there are "spaces" open for speculation about typical behavior that allows the defense to draw upon images in society that hold women responsible for their own victimization.

Implications for Feminist Strategies

In this essay, the New Bedford trial was analyzed as a spectacle that projected symbolic messages about sexual violence: it presented a story, reconstructed in different media, about a woman's life and her responses to a violent sexual assault. The trial was a moment at which the violation of women's sexuality was reproduced for mass public consumption in a manner to satisfy the internal logic of the legal system.

Although the ultimate conviction of four of the defendants might be seen as symbolic vindication of the victim's innocence, my reading of the trial suggests that even in a situation of multiple acts of violence (in the presence of witnesses) the victim was subject to the vulnerabilities of a woman as an accusor. From the initial media presentation of the case, it appeared that the "public" nature of the violent act served to affirm the assumption of the victim's "innocence" while vilifying the Portuguese defendants and their conduct in the community. As the "facts" became public knowledge, however, the unnamed complaining witness was portrayed as a confused young woman of unreliable character. The public persona of the victim was transformed by a reconstructed account that scrutinized her behavior in the tavern by comparing it to "reasonable" standards of women's propriety. Within the legal forum, her fearful assertion of violation was obscured by questioning that implied personal irresponsibility in protecting herself from male aggression while raising suspicion about her sexual motivations as a woman: she was forced to defend the propriety of her actions while being held suspect for female capriciousness.

Feminist reformers have tried to use the trial forum to raise public awareness about the prevalence of rape and other violent crimes affecting women. The rhetorical stance of these reformers, however, has accepted the presumption of legal realists that trials have an educative function. As a result, the publicity generated by organized courtwatchers and statements of outrage about particular cases are intended to educate an insensitive audience that violence against women had become commonplace both on the streets and in the courtroom (see Pitch, 1985; Fineman, 1983). This analysis, however, demonstrates that publicity encouraged by rape reform advocates may have failed to focus discontent, while generating ambiguous messages about the motivations of victims and the nature of feminine "innocence."

The legal realist's vision of the symbolic trial is adhered to by the professionals in the courtroom, despite realism's arguable inability to capture the social meaning of controversial events. Both the physical setting of the courtroom scene and the procedures and language of the trial create the image of law as separating out the truth from the hysteria of the victim. The prosecutors and defense attorneys act as guardians of this order and are resistent to any form of dialogue that attempts to make sense of the violence in a way that does not fit the legal models of guilt or innocence. For example, in the New Bedford rape trial a motion for mistrial arose from District Attorney Kane's reference to police officer Carol Sacramento's statement. "How did this happen?" Kane repeated it several times during his opening statement, as if this was the question he wanted to leave foremost in the jury's mind. Defense attorney Coffin argued that this inappropriate statement was inadmissible as evidence and therefore should not have been included in his opening statement. Moreover, he claimed that "How did it happen?" is an ambiguous question because it could have meant either "How could this rape have happened?" or "How could these consensual acts have happened?"

Kane's response to the motion for mistrial was that the court should recognize that Sacramento's amazement was part of the proof that the rape occurred: since the rape was an extraordinary event, it was important to point out that those who first heard the complaint that night would have responded to it in an extraordinary manner. Yet the prosecution's willingness to stimulate our bewilderment was limited. As participants in professional legal discourse, the prosecutors tried to discourage speculation about how society's approval of violence against women created the conditions for the rape at Big Dan's. From the prosecution's perspective, the case was simply about a tragedy that involved a confused young woman. In fact, the District Attorney attempted to explain the inconsistencies in his case by arguing, in his closing statement, that this was a story without "heroes." Diana was portrayed as a character in a human tragedy who must confront, like all tragic figures, her own faults and vulnerabilities.

But to call this trial a tragedy is to individualize Diana's misfortune and ignore the way that the ordinary has been given larger than life significance. It is a tragedy only if one believes that the event is otherwise inexplicable and that the cause of the attack did not grow out of the group dynamic in the tavern but arose instead from an evil that lurked within the victim. The District Attorney's analogy to a tragedy was meant to reassure the jury that the trial is the best method to bring forth the truth, and that these truths must self-evidently account for the rape.

Yet, the legal system is itself implicated in the tragedy unless one is willing to agree with defendant John Cordeiro that the "truth never hurts." As the trial is interpreted in its symbolic context, one sees how truths that are partial may become powerful instruments that can assign blame and absolve guilt. From the perspective of legal professionals, partial truths are defensible as part of a larger battle in the pursuit of justice. Defense attorney Lindahl, for example, defended the trial to the press because, "in our attempts to protect those who are truly victims, we better take care that we don't victimize not only the men accused, but all of us if we give up the confrontation inherent in a trial."[5] But the symbolism of this trial involved more than rituals of confrontation; the trial produced messages which served to disempower women both inside and outside of the courtroom. Lindahl's concerns focused on the search for justice in the individual case, and were warranted if the only threat to justice is the excessive power of the state and the unbridled vengeance that stems from victimization. Otherwise, she has ignored the way that law has unleashed metaphors that attack basic notions of human decency. The celebrated trial has an impact far greater, and a message more complicated, than the realists envisioned. Their claim that these contests affirm a legalistic society's reliance on procedure can be made only at the risk of ignoring these trials' cultural significance and meaning.

The narrative constructed in this essay suggests that those who purposely desire to use the trial forum to send a message condemning sexual violence confront a dilemma-ridden strategy. The more vehemently reformers maintain that "objective" evidence can be provided to prove the abuse of victims, the more necessary it becomes to establish the victim's innocence according to commonly held notions of verifiability (Griffin, 1986). The reliance on objective evidence, therefore, forces the defenders of victims' rights to resort to tactics that narrow or limit the telling of the woman's story. The claim of objectivity may also have the effect of making it more difficult to establish the woman's "innocence" in more ambiguous situations where rape differs from the overt violence of "real rape" (Estrich, 1987), which is marked by a relationship of strangers, the use of a weapon, and a public scene. The forms of communication that are appropriate in a courtroom and that are disseminated by the media conform to conventions of the "public" discourse of news reporting and the "professional" discourse of criminal procedure. If reformers strive toward transforming the social construction of rape, even abandoning the model of consent, then changes in the public understanding of the crime may only come about with challenges to the dominance of legal discourse.

Notes

1. Four of the six defendants were convicted, see *Commonwealth* v. *Rapozo, Cordeiro, Silva, and Viera* (Mass. Super. Ct., Mar. 17, 1984).
2. The following analysis is based upon content analysis of national and local newspaper reports on the incident and the trial, including the *New York Times*, the *Boston Globe*, and the *New Bedford Standard-Times*. All quotations in this paper are from the *New Bedford Standard-Times*, March 1983 -April 1984, unless otherwise indicated.

3. Interviews were conducted with five defense attorneys, one prosecutor, and the presiding judge.
4. The entire trial was videotaped and televised by a local New Bedford public television station. The videotapes were obtained from the archives at the Harvard Law Library. All excerpts from the trial are my own transcriptions from the videotaped record.
5. Quoted in a signed article in the *New York Times*, "The Rape Trial," written by Sidney H. Schamberg, March 27, 1984.

III

Recognizing Pleasures and Pains

Although this section contains works by three feminist legal scholars, the views of a fourth, Catharine MacKinnon, provide an important theoretical backdrop. MacKinnon's work has focused on women's subordination as a social class and an insistence that harms suffered by women as women be legally recognized. The crucial importance of grounding feminist methodology in legal theory in women's actual lived experiences continues as a common theme.

Robin West argues that women's suffering is not legally recognized because it is not even seen *by the male power structure whose perceptions and priorities have created the institutions of law. West asserts that if legal practices are to reflect the realities of women's lives, women need to attend to and accurately describe their subjective experiences. At stake is nothing less than the rejection and rehabilitation of male-centered conceptions of human nature, conceptions embedded in political theories which fail to adequately represent women's interests.*

Ruth Colker, like West, appreciates the epistemological difficulty for women who are damaged by societies that undervalue them to nonetheless determine their genuine nature and interests. Like West, too, Colker is concerned with women's experiences of sexuality as sources of both feminist insight and controversy, and criticizes MacKinnon for paying insufficient attention to experiential data when that data would contradict theory. Unlike West, Colker believes that the concept of "authenticity" is more useful than the concept of pleasure in evaluating women's well-being. Her perspective would impact the methodological, as well as substantive decisions, made by feminists in developing political-legal strategies.

Adrian Howe's focus, by contrast, is on concrete strategies for making harms suffered by women legally cognizable. She proposes utilization of the concept of social injury, a notion originally introduced in making white collar crime legally actionable. Conceptualizing harms to women as injuries to a social group not only categorizes these harms as injuries, *but also defines them as* socially *based rather than private or individual. Howe argues that her proposal builds on, and furthers, already articulated feminist theory, yielding strategic and theoretical benefits.*

7

The Difference in Women's Hedonic Lives: A Phenomenological Critique of Feminist Legal Theory

Robin L. West

Introduction

Women's subjective, hedonic lives are different from men's. The quality of our suffering is different from that of men's, as is the nature of our joy. Furthermore, and of more direct concern to feminist lawyers, the quantity of pain and pleasure enjoyed or suffered by the two genders is different: women suffer more than men. The two points are related. One reason that women suffer more than men is that women often find painful the same objective event or condition that men find pleasurable. The introduction of oxymorons in our vocabulary, wrought by feminist victories, evidences this difference in women's and men's hedonic lives. The phrases "date-rape," for example and "sexual harassment," capture these different subjective experiences of shared social realities: for the man, the office pass was sex (and pleasurable), for the women, it was harassment (and painful); for the man the evening was a date—perhaps not pleasant, but certainly not frightening—for the woman, it was a rape and very scary indeed. Similarly, a man may experience as at worst offensive, and at best stimulating, that which a woman finds debilitating, dehumanizing or even life-threatening. Pornographic depictions of women which facilitate by legitimating the violent brutalization of our bodies are obvious examples. Finally, many men are simply oblivious—they do not experience *at all*—external conditions which for women are painful, frightening, stunting, torturous and pervasive—including domestic violence in the home, sexual assault on the street, and sexual harassment in the workplace and school.

A considerably longer version of this paper, with more extensive phenomenological description and discussion, can be found in *Wisconsin Women's Law Journal* (1987) 3: 81–145.

Feminists generally agree—it should go without saying—that women suffer in ways which men do not, and that the gender-specific suffering that women endure is routinely ignored or trivialized in the larger (male) legal culture. Just as women's work is not recognized or compensated by the market culture, women's injuries are often not recognized or compensated *as injuries* by the legal culture. The dismissal of women's gender-specific suffering comes in various forms, but the outcome is always the same: women's suffering for one reason or another is outside the scope of legal redress. Thus, women's distinctive, gender-specific injuries are now or have in the recent past been variously dismissed as trivial (sexual harassment on the street); consensual (sexual harassment on the job); humorous (nonviolent marital rape); participatory, subconsciously wanted or self-induced (father/daughter incest); natural or biological, and therefore inevitable (childbirth); sporadic, and conceptually continuous with gender-neutral pain (rape, viewed as a crime of violence); deserved or private (domestic violence); nonexistent (pornography); incomprehensible (unpleasant and unwanted consensual sex) or legally predetermined (marital rape, in states with the marital exemption).

It is not so clear, though, *why* women's suffering is so pervasively dismissed or trivialized by legal culture, or more importantly what to do about it. As I will argue in a moment, feminist legal theorists do not typically frame the problem in the way I have just posed it. Nevertheless, it is not hard to construct two characteristic feminist explanations of the phenomenon, and the strategies they entail. The "liberal-legal feminist" would characterize the legal culture's discriminatory treatment of women's suffering as the reflection of a "perceptual error" committed by that culture. Women are in fact *the same as*—and therefore *equal to*—men, in the only sense which should matter to liberal legal theory. Women, like men, are autonomous individuals who, if free to do so, will choose among proffered alternatives so as to fashion their own "good life," and thereby create social value. However, the legal culture fails to see or acknowledge this central sameness—and hence equality of women and men. Because we are not *perceived* as identical to men in this way, we are not treated as such. Our choices are differentially restricted, and as a result we disproportionately suffer. The liberal feminist's strategy is directly implied by her diagnosis: what we must do is prove that we are what we are—individualists and egoists, as are men—and then fight for the equal rights and respect the sameness demands. Equal respect will in turn ensure, through the logic of formal justice and the Equal Protection Clause of the Fourteenth Amendment, that our suffering will be alleviated by law—just as is men's suffering—through a liberating expansion of our opportunities for choice.[1]

The radical legal feminist's explanation of this phenomenon is also not hard to construct. The blanket dismissal of women's suffering by the male legal culture is not a reflection of a misperception. Indeed the larger culture's perception is accurate: women are *not* as autonomous or individualistic as men. The liberal is wrong to insist that women and men are equal in this way. The reason the legal culture tends to dismiss women's gender-specific sufferings is that women don't matter. Those in power ignore women's suffering because they don't care about the suffering of the disempowered. Hierarchical power imbalances do that to people—they make the disempowered less than human, and they make the empowered ruthless. The radical feminist's strategy follows directly from her diagnosis: what we must do is dismantle the hierarchy. The Equal Protection Clause—at least if we can interpret it (and use it) as an "Equality Promotion Clause"—might help.[2]

The recent explosion of feminist writings on the multitude of problems generated by women's "difference"[3] prompts me to suggest a third explanation of this blanket dismissal by the legal culture of women's pain and thus a third strategy. The blanket dismissal of women's gender-specific suffering by the legal culture may be (partly) a reflection of the extent to which the pain women feel is *not understood*, and *that* it is not understood may be because it is *itself* different, and not just a product of our difference. Thus, it may be that women suffer more because we suffer differently. The pain we feel is itself different (as are our pleasures). (Is there anything quite like the pain of childbirth?) If this is right, then the legal culture has committed a perceptual error, but the error is not, as the liberal feminist believes, in perceiving us as different where we in fact are the same. The perceptual error is in failing to understand the *difference*—not the sameness—of our subjective, hedonic lives. If the pain women feel is in fact different than what is experienced by men, then it is not really surprising that the injuries we sustain are trivialized or dismissed by the larger male culture. It is hard to empathize with the pain of another, when the nature of that pain is not understood. If the pain women feel is not shared by men then it is not surprising that men cannot readily empathize with women who suffer much less share in the effort to resist the source of their injuries. The strategic inference I draw is this: if we want to enlist the aid of the larger legal culture, the feel of our gender-specific pain must be described before we can ever hope to communicate its magnitude.

Focus on the "difference" of our hedonic lives also suggests a different way to address the related problem of "false consciousness." As feminists know all too well, it is not just the legal culture which trivializes women's suffering, women do so also. Again, if we focus on the distinctiveness of our pain, this becomes less surprising. An injury uniquely sustained by a disempowered group will lack a name, a history, and in general a linguistic reality. Consequently, the victim as well as the perpetrator will transform the pain into *something else*, such as, for example, punishment, or flattery, or transcendence, or unconscious pleasure. A victim's response to an injury which is perceived by the victim as deservedly punitive, consensual, natural, subconsciously desired, legally inevitable, or trivial will be very different from a response to an injury which is perceived as simply *painful.* We change our behavior in response to the threat of what we perceive as punishment; we diminish ourselves in response to injuries we perceive as trivial; we reconstruct our pasts in response to injuries we perceive as subconsciously desired; we negate our inner selves in response to injuries we perceive as consensual and we constrain our potentiality in response to injuries we perceive as inevitable. We respond to pain, on the other hand, by resisting the source of the pain. The strategic inference should be clear: we must give voice to the hurting self, even when that hurting self sounds like a child rather than an adult; even when that hurting self voices "trivial" complaints; even when the hurting self is ambivalent toward the harm and even when (especially when) the hurting self is talking a language not heard in public discourse. Only by so doing will we *ourselves* become aware of the meaning of the suffering in our lives, and its contingency in our history. Only when we understand the contingency of that pain, will we be free to address it and change the conditions which cause it through legal tools.

If my argument is correct, then it would seem that feminist legal theorists should be hard at work providing rich descriptions of women's subjective, hedonic lives, particularly the pain in those lives, and more particularly the pain in our lives which is different. And yet *we aren't,* by which I mean, feminist *legal theorists* aren't. Feminists, by contrast, *are,* as are feminist lawyers. But feminist legal theorists, I believe, are dangerously neglecting the phenomenological, subjective, and hedonic distinctiveness of women's lives, and the relevance of this aspect of our difference to legal criticism. I can think of four possible reasons for this neglect. The first three are problems which plague discussion of all aspects of our differences. The fourth reason is philosophical, and is the subject of this essay.

The first reason is linguistic. It is *hard* to talk about our pain and pleasure, and it is hard to talk about our pain and pleasure because they are different. Our language is inadequate to the task. As women become more powerful, this linguistic barrier is eased: we now possess, for example, the legal and social labels that at least identify some of our experiences as injurious such as "sexual harassment" and "date-rape." But we still lack the descriptive vocabulary necessary to convey the quality of the pain we sustain by virtue of these experiences. The second reason is psychological. Before we can convince others of the seriousness of the injuries we sustain, we must first convince ourselves, and so long as others are unconvinced, to some extent, we will be as well. This is a circle that must be broken, not inhabited. The third and underlying problem is political. The inadequacy of language and the problem of "false consciousness" are but reflections of what is surely the core obstacle to the development of the feminist discourse on the nature of gender-specific pain, which is an unwilling and resisting audience. When we struggle to find the words to describe the pain (or pleasure) in our lives, and the effort is rewarded with dismissal and trivialization, the fully human response is to silence ourselves.

However, at least one reason—and perhaps the main reason—that feminist legal theorists have neglected the hedonic dimension of our difference—and the subject of this article—is not the difference problem, but the emerging logic of feminist legal theory itself. By virtue of the models of legal criticism that feminist legal theorists have embraced, we've literally defined the subjective, hedonic aspect of our differences out of existence. Unlike feminist political theorists, feminist legal theorists have followed largely derivative normative strategies. That is, feminist legal theorists have adopted *nonfeminist* normative models of legal criticism, and then applied those models to women's problems. I have no objection to the strategy of adopting already available models; I do object, though, to the *particular* models feminist legal theorists have adopted. The major normative models of legal criticism thus far embraced—liberal legalism and radical legalism—*themselves* deny the normative significance of the subjective pleasure and suffering of our lives. Because of the normative models employed by modern legal feminists, the internal, phenomenological reality of women's hedonic lives—and its difference from men's—has become virtually irrelevant to feminist legal theory.

Thus, I will argue that *liberal-legal* feminist theorists—true to their liberalism—want women to have more choices, and that radical-legal feminist theorists—true to their radicalism—want women to have more power. Both models direct our critical attention *outward*—liberalism to the number of choices we have, radicalism to the amount of power. Neither model of legal criticism, and therefore, derivatively, of feminist legal criticism, posits subjective happiness as the direct goal of legal reform, or subjective suffering as the direct evil to be eradicated. Neither model directs our critical attention *inward*. Consequently, and unsurprisingly, neither liberal nor radical feminist legal critics have committed themselves to the task of determining the measure of women's happiness or suffering.

Which is not to say that liberal and radical feminist legal theorists are unconcerned about women's subjective well-being. Rather, each group dismisses the normative significance of women's pain and suffering because of the essentially strategic choices made by the underlying (nonfeminist) politics embraced by that group, and the depictions of human nature those choices entail.

The cost *to women* of feminist legal theorists' endorsement of the antiphenomenological methodology and antihedonic norms of the models they endorse is very high. It renders liberal and radical feminist legal theorists peculiarly uncritical—*as feminists*—of the visions of the human and thus of the normative assumptions of the models for legal criticism which they have respectively embraced. The antiphenomenological methodology of radicalism and liberalism rule out the only inquiry which could conceivably determine the value *to women* of the model itself, and that is whether the description of the human which each model embraces is true of women. It is only by focusing directly on what both models definitionally exclude—our phenomenological, hedonic experience—that we will be able to ask this question.

Part One of this article provides a brief critique of the conception of the human—and thus the female—that underlies liberal legal feminism. Part Two presents a phenomenological critique of the conception of the human—and thus the female—which underlies the radical feminist legal criticism. Again, I will argue that in both cases the theory does not pay enough attention to feminism: liberal feminist legal theory owes more to liberalism than to feminism and radical feminist legal theory owes more to radicalism than it does to feminism. Both models accept a depiction of human nature which is simply untrue of women. Thus, both accept, uncritically, a claimed correlation between objective condition and subjective reality, which, I will argue, is untrue to women's subjectivity. As a result, both groups fail to address the distinctive quality of women's subjective, hedonic lives, and the theories they have generated therefore have the potential to backfire—badly—against women's true interests.

In the concluding section I will suggest an alternative normative model for feminist legal criticism which aims neither for choice nor equality, but directly for women's happiness, and a feminist legal theory which has as its critical focus the felt experience of women's subjective, hedonic lives.

I Liberal Feminism: Consent, Autonomy and the Giving Self

Perhaps the most widely held normative commitment of mainstream legal theorists is that individuals should be free to choose their own style of life, and to exercise that freedom of choice in as many spheres as possible—economic, political and personal. The conception of the human and the relation between the individual and the state which implicitly motivates this commitment is relatively straightforward. According to the liberal vision, value is produced in our social world through satisfaction of the subjective desires and preferences of the individual. That satiation is in turn manifested and facilitated through the individual's voluntary choices. The individual's choice will reflect that individual's judgment of what will best satisfy that individual's own desires. It follows that whatever is freely consented to by an individual is what is good for that individual, and, if free of adverse effects on others, is good for society. The way to maximize value in the social world is therefore to maximize the opportunities for the exercise of choice through voluntary transactions between individuals. A law which either facilitates or mimics consensual transactions between freely choosing individuals is a good law on this model, while a law which frustrates such transactions is a bad law. Individual freedom is the ideal toward which law and legal reform ought press, and coercion or restraint on freedom is the evil.

The contribution of feminist liberal legalism has been to extend the umbrella of this normative vision to women as well as men. The liberal legal feminist insists that the depiction of the human embraced by liberal legalism—which I will sometimes refer to as the "liberal self"—is also true of women, and that therefore, the relationship of the state to the individual must be the same for both women and men. What it means for women to be equal to men in the liberal feminist vision is basically that women and men are the same in the only sense that matters to the liberal legalist: women as well as men create value by satiating their subjective desires through consensual choices. Because women and men are equal in this way—because they share the same definitive human attribute—women should be equally free to choose their own life plans, and women should be equally entitled to the respect from the state that freedom requires.

Liberal feminist legal theory carries with it the same problems which now plague liberal legalism, but multiplied. Modern liberal legal feminists, like modern liberals generally, have failed to examine the essentially descriptive claims about the human being that underlie their normative model. The liberal claim that human beings consent to transactions in order to maximize their welfare may be false. If it is, then the liberal claim that social value is created through facilitating choice will be false as well. But furthermore, *women* may be "different" in precisely the way which would render the empirical assumptions regarding human motivation which underlie the liberal's commitment to the ethics of consent *more false for women than for men*. Thus, it may be that women generally *don't* consent to changes *so as to* increase our own pleasure or satisfy our own desires. It may be that women consent to changes so as to increase the pleasure or satisfy the desires of *others*. The descriptive account of the phenomenology of choice that underlies the liberal's conceptual defense of the moral primacy of consent may be wildly at odds with the way women phenomenologically experience the act of consent. If it is—if women "consent" to transactions not to increase our own welfare, but to increase the welfare of others—if women are "different" in this psychological way—then the liberal's ethic of consent, with its presumption of an essentially selfish human (male) actor and an essentially selfish consensual act, when even-handedly applied to both genders, will have disastrous implications for women.

I want to suggest that, indeed, many women, much of the time, consent to transactions, changes, or situations in the world so as to satisfy not their own desires or to maximize their own pleasure, as liberal legalism and legal feminism both presume, but to maximize the pleasure and satiate the desires of others, and that they do so by virtue of conditions which only women experience. I will sometimes call the cluster of "other-regarding," other-pleasing motivations that rule these women's actions the "giving self," so as to distinguish it from the "liberal self": the cluster of self-regarding "rational" motivations presumed by liberal legalism. Thus my descriptive claim is that many women much of the time are giving selves rather than liberal selves. If we take the liberal's description of the motivational core of the human being as accurate and central, then this motivational difference between most men and women implies that women who define themselves as "giving selves" are not human.

I believe that women become giving rather than liberal selves for a range of reasons—including our (biological) pregnability and our (social) training for our role as primary caretakers—but in this section, I will focus on only one causal hypothesis, which (I think) has great explanatory force. The causal hypothesis is this: women's lives are dangerous, and it is the acquisitive and potentially violent nature of male sexuality which is the cause of the danger. A fully justified fear of acquisitive and violent male sexuality consequently permeates many women's—perhaps all women's—sexual and emotional self-definition. Women respond to this fear by *reconstituting* themselves in a way that controls the danger, suppresses the fear. Thus: women define themselves as "giving selves" so as to obviate the threat, the danger, the pain, and the fear of being self-regarding selves from whom their sexuality is taken. We respond to the pervasive threat of violent and acquisitive male sexuality by changing ourselves, rather than responding to the conditions which cause it.

The danger, the violence, and the fear with which women live and which informs our self-definition are not a part of men's world. Men, unlike women, do not experience the fear of violent sexuality as a part of their self-definition. Furthermore, the danger and the threat that causes women's definitional fear are largely invisible to men. Left and liberal men do not see women shake with fear. They do not see women getting harassed on the street; when men accompany women, as all women know, harassment stops. For the same reason, they do not see women sexually harassed at work. They do not see women battered in the home. They do not see women being raped, by strangers, dates or husbands. They do not see women violated, abused and afraid. To these men, violence against women, the pain women feel as a result of it, and the fear of its recurrence, are invisible. It is not surprising that the claim that women's lives are ruled by fear is heard by these men as wildly implausible. They see no evidence in their own lives to support it. This simple fact, more than anything else, I believe, commits women and men to live to two separate realities. This invisibility and the ignorance it produces is almost as damaging as the fear itself.

How does a pervasive and largely invisible danger, and an equally pervasive and invisible fear, affect women's lives? Women cannot, and do not live in a state of constant fear of male sexual violence. One way (there are others) that women control the danger—and thus suppress the fear—is by redefining themselves as "giving selves." Most simply, a woman will define herself as a "giving self" so that she will not be violated. She defines herself as a being who "gives" sex, so that she will not become a being *from whom sex is taken*. In a deep sense (too deep: she tends to forget it), this transformation is consensual: she "consents" to being a "giving self"—the dependent party in a comparatively protective relationship—for self-regarding liberal reasons; she consents in order to control the danger both inside and outside of the relationship, and in order to suppress the fear that danger engenders. Once redefined, however, and once within those institutions that support the definition, she becomes a person who gives her consent *so as to ensure the other's happiness* (not her own), so as to satiate the other's desires (not her own), so as to promote the *other's* well being (not her own), and ultimately so as *to obey the other's commands*. In other words, she embraces a self-definition and a motive for acting which is the direct antithesis of the internal motivational life presupposed by liberalism.

I have no interest in arguing that all women are giving selves all of the time. I want only to suggest that enough women have lived with enough fear and danger in their lives to justify the inference that significant numbers of women have defined themselves in a way that undercuts the commitment to the ethical primacy of consent which underlies the liberal feminist legal theory. The means used by women to ward off the threat of acquisitive and violent male sexuality—primarily by learning to give ourselves to consensual, protective relationships within which we define ourselves as "giving"—are not the product of false consciousness or brain-washing. But nor are they value-creating voluntary and mutual relationships worthy of celebration. They are no less and no more than the product of our victimization: they are coherent, understandable responses to very real danger. Until we create a better world, they are also all we have. A liberal feminist theory of law which presumptively values consensual transactions on the assumption that the giving of consent is motivationally self-regarding, without addressing the fear that molds women's self-definition, runs the risk of missing altogether the real causes of women's misery.

II Radical Feminism, and the Ethical Primacy of Power and Equality

Radical feminist legal theory begins with a description of women which is diametrically opposed to that embraced by liberal feminists. Liberal feminists assume a definitional *equality*—a "sameness"—between the female and male experience of consensual choice, and then argue that the legal system should respect that fundamental, empirical equality. In sharp contrast, radical feminists assume a definitional *in*equality of women—women are *definitionally* the disempowered group—and urge the legal system to eradicate that disempowerment and thereby make women what they presently are not, and that is equal. Radical feminism thus begins with a denial of the liberal feminist's starting assumption. Women and men are *not* equally autonomous individuals. Women, unlike men, live in a world with two sovereigns—the state, and men—and this is true not just some of the time but all of the time. (See MacKinnon, 1982 reprinted in Keohane, Rosaldo, and Gelpi, 1982 and MacKinnon, 1983.) A legal regime which ignores this central reality will simply perpetuate the fundamental, underlying inequality.

The cause of women's disempowerment, as well as its effect, is the expropriation of our sexuality. Women are the group in Catharine MacKinnon's phrase, "from whom sexuality is expropriated," (Keohane, Rosaldo, and Gelpi, 1982, p. 2 and pp. 14–15) in the same sense that workers are, definitionally, the group from whom labor is expropriated. Women are the gender from whom sex is *taken*. The threat of male violence and violent sexuality both defines the class woman and causes her disempowerment and the expropriation of her sexuality, just as the threat of starvation and material deprivation both defines the worker, and causes his disempowerment and the expropriation of his labor.

This much, radical feminist legal theory shares with radical feminism, and with this much I am in full agreement. Where radical feminist legal theory has departed from radical feminism, I believe, is in the normative argument it draws from the insight that women are, definitionally, the group from whom sexuality is expropriated. The argument, I believe, owes more to radical legalism than to radical feminism. The argument has three steps.

First, radical feminist legal theory, like radical legalism, begins with a highly particularized although largely implicit description of the human being. People are, in short, assumed to be such that there exists a correlation between objectively equal distributions of power— including sexual power—and subjectively happy and good lives. Domination makes us evil and submission makes us miserable; substantive equality will make us both moral and happy; and both claims are true because of, and by reference to, this conception of our essential human nature.[4]

Second, both radical legalism and radical feminist legalism draw from this depiction of the human being the normative inference that it is the imbalance of power which facilitates expropriation (of work for the radical legalist, of sex for the radical feminist legalist), rather than the expropriation itself, which is *definitionally* bad, and then the further inference that it is definitionally bad *whether or not the expropriation it facilitates is experientially felt as painful* (Keohane, Rosaldo, and Gelpi, pp. 19–29). The strategic consequence immediately follows: radical legal reform should aim to eradicate hierarchy and thereby attain a substantively equal social world. Thus we should oppose not what makes us miserable—the violent expropriation of our work or our sexuality—but the hierarchy of power which facilitates it, for by doing so we will better target the true cause of our misery. (p. 19; also see pp. 25–26, n. 59) Thus, radical feminist legal theory shares with general radical legal thought a refusal to ground its opposition to expropriation (whether of sex or work) in the subjective suffering of the disempowered which such expropriation entails.

Finally, radical feminist legal theorists share with radical legalists a methodological insistence that the correlation between objective equality and subjective well-being is foundational and definitional; it is therefore not something that can be discredited by counter-example. Both groups of theorists accordingly refuse to credit the *phenomenological* evidence that the essentially descriptive claims that underlie the normative commitment to substantive equality may be false. (pp. 28, 5–6, 20 n. 42, 19–20, 6 n. 7) Thus, to radical legalists generally, and to radical feminist legalists in particular, the extent to which the disempowered desire anything other than their own empowerment, and anything at odds with an equalitarian idea, is the extent to which the disempowered are victims of false consciousness. Phenomenological reports by the disempowered of pleasure and desire that counter the radical correlation of equality and subjective well-being thus reinforce, rather than cast in doubt, the radical's definitional assumptions. They reflect the permeating influence of our objective condition, not the limit, imposed by subjective pleasure and desire, of the normative ideal.

The striking political contribution of *feminist* legal theory has been to extend the umbrella of the normative argument of radical legalism to include women as well as men, and thus to address hierarchies of gender as well as hierarchies dictated by class and race. The radical feminist legalist's commitment to gender equality stems from her empirical insistence that in the only respect which should be of concern to radical legalists, women and men are *the same*: women, like men, *suffer* from relative disempowerment and inequality, and will therefore benefit from empowerment and equality. Women, like men, just are such that objective inequality will cause us subjective misery, and empowerment will be our script for salvation. What we should do with law, then, if we mean to address the problem of women's suffering, is disable the objective hierarchies of gender that cause it.

The inclusion of women under the radical legalist's normative umbrella is a great triumph, but it is costly: the adoption of radical legalist methodology by feminist legal theorists has also occasioned a damaging methodological divide between radical feminism and radical feminist legalism. Radical feminist legal theorists, true to their radicalism, refuse to consider whether or not the definitional implication it assumes between objective equality and subjective well-being resonates with women's desires and pleasures, and hence whether the conception of the human on which that implication is based is true of women. The radical feminist legal theorist—to the extent that it is radical—will—must—deny that substantive equality in any sphere could ever be less than ideal or that empowerment of women could ever work to our disadvantage. Thus, to radical feminists, that women on occasion take pleasure in their own submissiveness, is simply a manifestation of their disempowered state, not a meaningful counter-example to the posited egalitarian idea. For feminists, this radical legalist methodology should raise serious warning signals. First, we should remember that the ideal and the description of "essential human nature" on which it rests as itself drawn from a male, if "left" intellectual tradition, and is therefore not an ideal we should readily assume will be true of women. But second, and perhaps more fundamentally, it is feminism's most crucial insight that *our experience* must be primary—and not be trumped by posited ideals or definitions.

Radical feminist legal theorists' failure to credit phenomenological reports of conflict between egalitarian ideals and women's subjective, hedonic, felt pleasures is generally benign, for one simple reason: the area of conflict is not great. By and large, women want the goods which substantive equality will deliver. Over vast areas of our lives, there is no conflict between our desires, our felt pleasures, and radical feminist ideals.

In one area of our lives, however,—namely our erotic lives—there has emerged a conflict between the radical feminist legal theorists' conception of an equalitarian ideal and women's subjective desire. The radical feminist's commitment to equality, and identification of the expropriation of our sexuality as the consequence of our relative disempowerment entails the normative conclusion that sexual inequality *itself* is what is politically undesirable. Thus, male dominance and female submission in sexuality *is* the evil: they express as well as *are* women's substantive inequality. But women report—with increasing frequency and as often as not in consciousness-raising sessions—that equality *in sexuality* is not what we find pleasurable or desirable (Snitow, Stansell, and Thompson, 1983; Califia, 1988; Rubin, 1978). Rather, the experience of dominance and submission that go with the controlled, but fantastic, "expropriation" of our sexuality *is* precisely what is sexually desirable, exciting and pleasurable—in fantasy for many; in reality for some. This creates a conflict between theory and method as well as between stated ideal and felt pleasure: what should we *do* when the consciousness that is raised in consciousness-raising finds pleasure in what is definitionally regarded as substantively undesirable—sexual submission, domination and erotic inequality? The conflict between felt pleasure and stated ideal has become a dilemma for radical feminism, but it has created an unprecedented debacle for our very young radical feminist legal theory, and one which threatens to be fatal.

Radical feminist legal theorists—distinctively, in feminist literature—respond to the conflict between political ideal and subjective, erotic pleasure by adamantly refusing to address it, and it is that refusal more than the dilemma itself which is threatening the survival of radical feminist legal theory. In the feminist legal literature two strategies of avoidance have emerged. The first—advocated by Catharine MacKinnon—regards the undeniable reality of the pleasure many women find in the eroticization of controlled submission as simply an example—perhaps an example *par excellence*—of the false consciousness of the oppressed (MacKinnon, 1982). The desires reflected in fantasies of erotic domination are false because the object of desire is submission, and submission is precisely what is definitionally *un*desirable. The second strategy—advocated by Sylvia Law and Nan Hunter—constitutes in essence a retreat to liberal principles. Fantasies are private and beyond political analysis; the role of law should be to expand, not shrink, the options available to women, including the option, if freely chosen, of masochistic desire, fantasy, practice and pleasure.[5]

I have examined elsewhere the pornography debate which these two feminist responses have generated. Here, I want to focus on what the two factions share: *both positions, at critical theoretical junctures, abandon feminist practice.* As a result both positions definitionally exclude the very issue which should be of greatest concern to feminists, and that is the meaning and the value, to women, of the pleasure we take in our fantasies of eroticized submission.

The first response—the dismissal of the desire for erotic submission and the pleasure obtained from it, as instances of false consciousness *as revealed by consciousness-raising itself*—is, I believe, wildly out of line with the methodology of consciousness-raising, as that method is more widely understood in feminist practice. There is a striking—and—revealing—discontinuity between the criteria by which fantasies of erotic submission are judged as "false," and the criteria by which other felt desires are discovered through consciousness-raising to be "false." Feminist consciousness-raising, and the correlative meaning of "false" in the phrase "false consciousness," is governed, I believe, by three methodological principles.

First, a woman discovers the "falsity" of her felt pleasures and desires in consciousness-raising *when she discovers that they are not her own*—when she discovers, quite literally, that she has been seeking the pleasure of others, not herself. Second, she discovers the "falsity" of her desires when she discovers, again quite literally, that she has been lying, either to herself or others. The desire (or the pleasure) is discovered to be "false" when she discovers that what she has been calling "desirable" is *not* in fact—*to her*—desirable. And third, and perhaps most centrally, she discovers the "falsity" of her desires when *she herself*—not outside observers—feels their falsity.

The feminist position that the desire for and pleasure obtained in erotic submission are "false," I believe, violates all three of these methodological principles. First, the judgment that women's desires for erotic submission are "false" is typically made by reference to the *content* of those desires, not their source. The desire for eroticized submission is false because of the content of the desire itself, not because it has been discovered to constitute, in masked form, the desires of others. Second, the desire is judged false not because it is determined to be *a lie*—not truly felt to be pleasurable but only reported as such—but solely because of its content, solely because it is a desire for sexual submission. And, finally and most revealingly, the discovery of the falsity of these desires has not typically come from the women who have them, but almost always from the women who do not. The desire is judged to be false, not because the subject herself has come to feel it as false, but because someone else has come to judge it as such. The judgment of falsehood is almost always against the will as well as the opinion of the woman who has the desire. This truly is a profound departure from feminist methodology which is also truly offensive—consciousness-raising is not about the imposition of judgments of truth or falsity on the desires of others.

Consciousness-raising, more than any other feminist methodology, has given women a means by which to break the chain of deception in which we live. By learning to identify the falsehoods we utter, we have learned to create a self who can assert a truth. Consciousness-raising is the discovery of the power of *truth*, not just *a* truth. If we abandon this method, we run a high risk of losing ourselves again in yet another morass of deception. We run the risk of once again having to *feel* subjectively what is forbidden to *be* objectively, and we will once again end up paying the piper.

If feminists abandon consciousness-raising as a method in favor of an authoritatively pronounced objective ideal, many women will pay by foregoing a source of sexual pleasure. This is not a trivial sacrifice. When we deny what gives us sexual pleasure, and when we thereby deny ourselves that sexual pleasure—we deny not just one but two important aspects of ourselves. We become, yet again, *not entitled;* this time—and, let's not forget, not for the first time—not entitled to sexual pleasure. We become, once again, sexually *errant.* [God damn: Wrong *again*!] We become, if we forego the sexual pleasure we have learned to own, once again, the conveyors of sexual pleasures for others, and once again, our role will be dictated by someone else's conception of sexual right and wrong.

So—the third response to the problem posed by women's enjoyment of erotic submission, endorsed by a small but growing number of radical feminists, is to understand rather than judge these pleasures in their historical context and in their full experiential truth. The former requires study of history; the latter requires information which can only be gained through consciousness-raising, and with no political prejudgments. Such an understanding, I believe, is essential to any dynamic future for radical feminism. First, only by such a process will we achieve any meaningful understanding of these pleasures. We will not achieve that understanding so long as we allow stated ideals to trump and silence felt pleasure. But second, I believe, only by understanding our felt pleasures will we achieve any meaningful understanding of our stated ideals. We cannot possibly give content to the substantive equality we seek until we understand the erotic appeal of submission. If we can identify what human needs are met through eroticized submission, perhaps we can better understand, and identify, the human needs which will be met or frustrated through political, legal and economic equality.

III Conclusion: Women's Difference, and an Alternative Standard for a Feminist Critique of Law

Although liberal and radical legalism are typically contrasted, as I contrasted them in the bulk of this paper, I want briefly to suggest in this conclusion that it is by virtue of an assumption that liberalism and radicalism *share* that their respective chosen proxies for well-being—choice and power—are so at odds with women's subjective, hedonic lives. Both liberal and radical legalism share a vision of the human being—and therefore of our subjective well-being—as "autonomous." The liberal insists that choice is necessary for the "true" exercise of that autonomy—and thus is an adequate proxy for subjective well-being—while the radical insists the same for power. But this strategic difference should not blind us to their commonality. Both the liberal and the radical legalist have accepted the Kantian assumption that *to be human* is to be in some sense autonomous—meaning, minimally, to be differentiated, or individuated, from the rest of social life.

Underlying and underscoring the poor fit between the proxies for subjective well-being endorsed by liberals and radicals—choice and power—and women's subjective, hedonic lives is the simple fact that women's lives—*because of our biological, reproductive role*—are drastically at odds with this fundamental vision of human life. Women's lives are *not* autonomous, they are profoundly relational. This is at least the biological reflection, if not the biological cause, of virtually all aspects, hedonic and otherwise, of our "difference." Women, and *only* women, and *most* women transcend *physically* the differentiation or individuation of biological self from the rest of human life trumpeted as the norm by the entire Kantian tradition. When a woman is pregnant her biological life embraces the embryonic life of another. When she later nurtures children, her needs will embrace their needs. The experience of being human, for women, differentially from men, includes the counter-autonomous experience of a shared physical identity between women and fetus, as well as the counter-autonomous experience of the emotional and psychological bond between mother and infant.

Our reproductive role renders us non-autonomous in a second, less obvious, but ultimately more far-reaching sense. Emotionally and morally women may benefit from the dependency of the fetus and the infant upon us. But *materially* we are more often burdened; we differentially depend more heavily upon others, both for our own survival, and for the survival of the children who are part of us. Women, more than men, depend upon relationships with others because the weakest of human beings—infants—depend upon us.

The goals the liberal and radical seek—increased freedom and increased equality, respectively—are surely intended to benefit the subjective well-being of human beings. That is, they are intended to benefit the well-being of autonomous creatures. These goals will simply not serve women, if women are not "autonomous." If women's "difference" lies in the fact that our lives are relational rather than autonomous, and if autonomy is a necessary attribute of a human being, then women's difference rather abruptly implies that women are not human beings. Politics that are designed to benefit human beings—including liberal and radical legalism—will leave women out in the cold.

This is not a novel insight: that women are not human as human is now conceived has in a sense always been the dominant problem for feminism. But the two characteristic ways in which modern feminist legal theorists have responded to this dilemma are both, I think, flawed. The liberal feminist's solution is to deny it. The fact that women become pregnant, give birth, and nurse infants is a difference that *does not count*. It does not make us any less "autonomous" than men. The radical feminist's proposal is that we seek to *become* autonomous creatures. To the extent that we become autonomous by gaining power, we will *become* beneficiaries of the legal system designed to promote the well-being of just such people.[6] This radical vision is at root deeply assimilationist—by gaining power, we become equal, as we become equal we become less "relational"—meaning less victimized—as we become less relational we become more autonomous, and as we become more autonomous we become more like "human beings"—more like men.

A very new and third response, which I think has great promise, is that feminists should insist on women's humanity—and thus on our entitlements—and on the wrongness of the dominant conception of what it means to be a "human being." We should insist, as Christine Littleton has argued, for an equal "acceptance of our difference" (Littleton, 1981). This third course is surely more promising—it has truth and candor on its side—but without hedonistic criticism it is insufficient: *which* differences are to be accepted? The root of our difference may be that our lives are relational rather than autonomous, which is reflected in our needs and has its roots in our reproductive role. But even thus defined, our "difference" has many dimensions. If "difference" includes our differential suffering, or our differential vulnerability to sexual assault, or our differential endurance of pain, or our differentially negative self-esteem, then "acceptance" of those differences will backfire. We need more than just acceptance of our differences; we need a vocabulary in which to articulate and then evaluate them, as well as the power to reject or affirm them.

My proposal is that we address the multiple problems posed by our differences from men by adopting a critical legal method which aims directly for women's subjective well-being, rather than indirectly through a gauze of definitional presuppositions about the nature of human life which almost invariably exclude women's lives. We should aim, simply, to increase women's happiness, joy and pleasure, and to lessen women's suffering, misery and pain. As feminist legal critics we could employ this standard: a law is a good law if it makes our lives happier and less painful and a bad law if it makes us miserable, or stabilizes the conditions that cause our suffering. A shift toward this direct hedonism, I believe, would do four things for our developing feminist legal theory.

First, a move toward hedonistic criticism would free us from false conceptions of our nature. Our present "equality" discourse (whether cast in terms of equal freedom or equal power) has forced us to accept dominant visions of the "human being" whose equality we seek. Second, a move toward hedonistic criticism would facilitate an unclouded articulation of the quality of women's hedonic lives. When we try to squeeze descriptions of our lives into parameters laid out for us, the results are often not just distorted, but profoundly anomalous. We are trying too hard to assimilate, in our theory as well as in our professional and personal lives.

Third, I believe, a shift toward a discourse that would focus attention on the pain in women's lives, and away from the oppression and subordination we suffer, would make us more effective. If we are ever going to make progress in alleviating women's misery—surely an important goal for feminist legalists—we must insist loudly upon the normative significance of our hedonic lives. Lastly, by forcing into the public discourse descriptions of women's subjective, hedonic lives, the conception of the "human being" assumed by that discourse—the substantive description of experienced human life which the phrase "human beings" denotes—might change so as to actually include women. For this reason alone, women need to develop descriptions of the quality of our hedonic lives.

There are two problems. Women's subjective, internal pain, because it is so silent and invisible—and because it is so different—is quite literally incomprehensible. To state the obvious—men do not understand, have not shared, have not heard, and have not felt, the pain—the numbing terror—of an unwanted pregnancy. They have not heard, shared or felt the tortuous violence of a stranger rape or the debilitating, disintegrating and destructive self-alienation of either violent or nonviolent marital rape. Men do not know that women's "frigidity"—our endurance of unpleasant, unwanted, nonmutual, and nonetheless fully "consensual" sex—is not only neither funny nor a "sexual disorder," but is painful, and thus injurious. Relatedly, men have no conception of what "nonviolent" forms of rape are even about, for the simple reason that they have no sense of what could possibly be painful about sex, when it is not accompanied by a threat of violence. This communication breakdown is not slight or incidental, it is total. Men's conception of pain—of what it is—is derived from a set of experience which *excludes* women's experience.

The second problem is this: women have a seemingly endless capacity to lie, both to ourselves and others, about what gives us pain and what gives us pleasure. This is not all that surprising. If what we need to do to survive, materially and psychically, is have heterosexual penetration three to five times a week, then we'll do it, and if the current ethic is that we must not only do it, but enjoy it, well then, we'll enjoy it. We'll report as pleasure what we feel as pain. It is terribly difficult to get to the bottom of these lies, partly because we convey them not just with our words, but with our bodies. Whatever else women have learned to do, women have learned to not speak the truth.

Both problems strike me as surmountable. Women must start speaking the truth about the quality of our internal lives. The pain women feel may be unique, but women and men (I believe) are alike in this way: both women and men resist pain when it is our own, and (most) women and (most) men will sympathetically resist pain suffered by others, when that pain is meaningfully communicated. And even if that is unduly optimistic, it is at least clear that *without* a clear articulation of the content and meaning of our pain, it will not be sympathetically resisted by men who do not share it. But more fundamentally, women will come to recognize the truth about our inner lives only when we start to speak it. Women's inner reality simply does not fit the Kantian conception of human nature that underlies so much of our liberal and radical legalist commitments. It is only by starting with our own experiences that we will be able to develop a description of human nature which is faithful to our lived reality, rather than one which ignores it. From that set of descriptions, and only from that set of descriptions, can we construct or reconstruct, our own political ideals whether they be autonomy, equality, freedom, fraternity, sisterhood, or something completely other, and as yet unnamed.

Notes

1. Because of her interest in the recent equal treatment/special treatment debate, Wendy Williams has emerged as the spokesperson for classical, liberal-legal feminism. See e.g., W. Williams, 1984–85 and W. Williams, 1982.

   The pornography debate has triggered a rebirth of liberal-legal feminism, or at least, a feminism which draws on, rather than distinguishes itself from traditional liberal-legal commitments to individualism, freedom and autonomy. See, e.g., Burstyn, 1985; Rubin, 1978; Snitow, Stansell, and Thompson, 1983 and Vance, 1984.

2. See, e.g. Taub and Schneider, 1982; MacKinnon, 1982; MacKinnon, 1983; Finley, 1986 (partial critique, partial endorsement, of radical feminist focus on gender hierarchy); Scales, 1986. For an early articulation of some of the principles now basic to radical legalistic analysis, see Fiss, 1976.
3. See, e.g., Eisenstein and Jardine, 1984. The classic works are Gilligan, 1982 and Chodorow, 1979. In the legal context see, e.g., Scales, 1981; Freedman, 1983; Law, 1984.
4. See MacKinnon, 1982. This comes through strongly, although still implicitly rather than explicitly, in MacKinnon's exchange with Carol Gilligan, in Buffalo Symposium, 1985.
5. See the Amicus Brief filed by Nan Hunter and Sylvia Law on behalf of the Feminist Anti-Censorship Taskforce, in the United States Court of Appeals for the Seventh Circuit, in American Booksellers Association v. William Hudnut, 1985.
6. Compare MacKinnon, who wants to "get the boot off women's necks," with Dinnerstein, who wants to share the burden of childrearing. Both view women's lack of autonomy as the obstacle to full participation in society, a nd accordingly as the cause of women's misery. Compare MacKinnon in Buffalo Symposium, 1985 with Dinnerstein, 1976.

8

Feminism, Sexuality and Authenticity

Ruth Colker

As a radical feminist, I seek to discover and understand my authentic female sexuality as part of my authentic self. Radical feminist theory has assisted me considerably along that journey although I have also begun to question some of the assumptions within radical feminist theory concerning the primacy of sexuality in our lives and the corresponding primacy of confronting sexual issues through the law. Because radical feminist theory teaches us that our subjective perspective influences our politics, I need to place my critique within the context of my personal life to make my political perspective more clear.

I made the choice to pursue relationships with women in 1975 as a political choice—believing that relationships with men were difficult, if not impossible, to achieve under patriarchy and recognizing that I could make the deepest possible commitment to feminism through a woman-centered and woman-identified life. My sexual choice was embedded in my broader conception of how I wanted to lead my life politically. Nevertheless, I acknowledged that I was deeply attracted to some men and occasionally found myself in intimate relationships with a man. When I was in an intimate relationship with a woman, however, I found that my personal and political life were in harmony in a way that they never were when I was in a relationship with a man.

In 1986, I ended a seven-year intimate relationship with a woman and began an intimate relationship with a man. In 1989, as I write these words, I am involved intimately with a man. I have begun to question whether my previous decision to seek intimate relationships only with women was too sex-specific and inconsistent with my authentic self. I

For a more complete version of this essay, see Colker, *Feminism, Sexuality & Self: A Preliminary Inquiry Into the Politics of Authenticity* (Boston University Law Review [1988] 68:217).

have also begun to wonder whether I have placed too much emphasis on my sexual self as part of my authentic self. At this point in my life, the satisfaction and authenticity that I find in my life seems more dependent than ever on the political/legal work that I do on behalf of women, gays and lesbians rather than on the sex of my sexual partner. Sadly, however, I find that other radical feminists often "judge" my feminist politics by my choice of sexual partner rather than by my political/legal activities in the community.

My personal stories with respect to this reaction are painful to recount. In one weekend, two lesbian couples told me that they could never again feel close to me if I pursued a relationship with a man; that they could no longer trust me to represent the gay community in political action. A gay political leader in my community said that there are no true bisexuals, only cowards. And a lesbian political leader said that I shouldn't be involved with a man because I was such an important role model for lesbian lawyers.

Thus, I find myself wanting to determine whether I can choose relationships with men and continue on my journey towards authenticity. Many radical feminists have told me that my concept of authenticity is inconsistent with feminist theory, unhelpful, and more generally, is simply wrong-headed. I believe that we have an authentic self because assuming that we do *not* have an authentic self makes no sense to me. For example, through our feminist work, we try to peel away social influences that limit our authenticity or freedom. If we are successful in our attempts to peel away those influences, what would be left? It only makes sense for me to assume that what would be left would be our authentic selves. Moreover, that authentic self must embody both a state of being as well as an ideal self. Otherwise, there is little point in trying to peel away those influences. Similarly, I consider the source of our feminist visions. They must come from some intuitive sense of each of our human possibilities. We need some measuring rod through which we can construct a critique and be confident that we can be more fully human than we are now, or, again our feminist struggles would make no sense. Therefore, I believe that our perception of and faith in our authentic self is fundamental to our continued passion to discover and experience our freedom or authentic self.

We must expend considerable energy trying to discover and experience our authentic sexuality because forces such as patriarchy have limited our sexuality. Women's struggles to discover their authentic sexuality have two major components. The first component encompasses trying to determine our sexual preference within a homophobic and heterosexist society. Catharine MacKinnon argues that women's expression of their sexuality has been limited by many forms of sexual objectification, such as sexual harassment, pornography, rape, and prostitution. She offers the striking observation that women can rarely, if ever, freely choose heterosexual sexual expression. Indeed, she says that such an apparent choice can be evidence of a woman's collaboration with her own oppression. Thus, according to MacKinnon, society structures women's perceived desires within heterosexuality so that they find pleasure in their own subordination (MacKinnon, 1987).

The second component of women's journey to discover their authentic sexuality is the struggle against a narrow and strongly normative conception of "good" sex within a particular form of sexuality. MacKinnon argues that women have not been able to define what sexual expression they desire within heterosexuality; instead, they have been limited to experiencing sexual relations on men's terms. Her inquiry has led her to ask the striking question of whether women and their sexuality even exists. She says: "If women are socially defined such that female sexuality cannot be lived or spoken or felt or even somatically sensed apart form its enforced definition, so that it *is* its own lack, then there is no such thing as a woman as such, there are only walking embodiments of men's projected needs. For feminism, asking whether there is, socially, a female sexuality is the same as asking whether women exist" (MacKinnon, 1982, p. 534).

Thus, radical feminist theory and MacKinnon's work, in particular, have been crucial in exposing the difficulty of a woman's journey toward the discovery and expression of her authentic sexuality. She has helped show how society coercively limits that expression to heterosexuality and that, within heterosexuality, women suffer much oppression and subordination. She has linked women's sexual abuse to women's overall subordinate status in society

Radical feminist theory, as exemplified by MacKinnon, raises, but does not resolve, several fundamental dilemmas within radical feminist theory: how important women's authentic sexuality *should* be to their authentic self, how women can *know* when they have discovered their authentic sexuality, and how women can construct their sexuality politically while retaining their authenticity. In this essay, I will evaluate radical feminism's consideration of these dilemmas and sketch a preliminary resolution of them.

I Search for Authentic Sexuality: Feminine or Feminist?

The fact that women are not presently experiencing their authentic sexuality does not mean that women should necessarily place a priority on trying to discover their authentic sexuality. An emphasis on sexuality within a woman's life may be feminine but not feminist. Patriarchy has made sexuality a crucial component of women's lives by making it central to women's oppression and subordination. Because women have never had the freedom to experience their authentic sexuality, it is impossible to know whether expressions of sexuality would be central to a woman's free and authentic life. In a transformed society, the importance of sexuality in a woman's life might dissipate or disappear. In existing society, the energy that women expend on developing sexual connectedness, love, compassion, etc., may be evidence of their brokenness and subordination rather than their authenticity.

This possibility was suggested to me during the 1987 Feminism and Legal Theory Conference. The topic was "Women and Intimacy" and addressed the importance and problems with intimacy in women's lives. As speaker after speaker catalogued the ways in which society helps distort women's expression of their sexuality and how women struggle against those influences, it became clear that women's subordination has helped shape their craving for intimacy. The epitome of the destructiveness of this craving is probably the battered women's syndrome under which women are not able to escape from an intimate relationship despite its physical destructiveness in their lives.

Even if sexuality should be a significant component of a woman's authentic self, it may not be realistic for a woman to try to discover and experience her sexual self in our present society. At the 1987 Feminist Legal Theory Conference, the participants disagreed about the political utility of women devoting significant energies to discovering and experiencing their authentic sexuality. For example, Sarah Salter suggested that women should take their sexual brokenness as a given and then speak about the brokenness. Several other participants added to that comment by suggesting that women are and should be demanding compensation from society for channeling women into "feminine" work through efforts such as comparable worth. Finally, several participants disputed my claim that there even is such a thing as an authentic self to unmask by arguing that society entirely constructs a woman's sexuality.

MacKinnon never endorses the concept of authenticity. But she does suggest that women can glimpse their freedom in sexual relations although she also calls it a "rare and valuable and contradictory event" (MacKinnon, 1987, p. 218). Why is it a valuable event? Because sexuality is an important component of a woman's authentic self? Because a woman's glimpse of her authentic sexuality can be politically transformative? MacKinnon does not tell us, because she does not consider these to be important questions.

Feminists who have presented probing discussions of the role of love and compassion in women's lives include Audre Lorde and Adrienne Rich. Lorde discusses the concept of the "erotic" (Lorde, 1984, p. 53).

She recognizes that patriarchy has often distorted the erotic by turning it into pornography but also insists that women's expression of their erotic selves can be a powerful source of liberation for them. She defines the erotic as an intrinsically dynamic force within women's lives (Lorde, 1984, p. 55). She tries to acclaim the importance of women discovering and experiencing the erotic within their lives.

Although Lorde recognizes that the erotic can be synonymous with women's suffering and self-negation, she also believes that women can transform the erotic into a positive source of power to struggle against oppression. Thus, in contrast to MacKinnon, Lorde argues that women should try to develop positive erotic expressions within their lives as well as struggle against the subordinating images of women within pornography. Whereas MacKinnon offers a negative critique of pornographic images, Lorde offers both a negative critique and an analysis of the positive aspects of women's discovery and expression of their erotic selves.

Adrienne Rich has explored the role of love and compassion within women's lives in a variety of contexts. Like Lorde, she recognizes both the destructive and life-building implications of women's love. For example, in her introduction to the tenth anniversary edition of *Of Woman Born*, (Rich, 1986) she describes the balance that she tried to strike between exploring the negative and positive aspects of motherhood. Despite the difficulties of creating an institution of motherhood that is free rather than oppressive, Rich claims that such a struggle is worthwhile because it can bring women closer to their "claim to personhood" (Rich, 1986, p. xviii). Thus, Rich connects authentic expressions of love and compassion through motherhood to movement to full personhood or authenticity.

Many progressive theologians offer a similar description of the role of love in our lives. For example, Etty Hillesum, a Jewish writer who was influenced by Christianity, used her love as a source of strength to persevere during the Holocaust (Hillesum, 1983, pp. 180–83). For Hillesum, who was struggling with the daily realities of life in a concentration camp, a focus on the power of her inner love was able to give her increased strength to fight her daily oppression. Hillesum used that love to fight the racism of anti-Semitism as well as to discover herself as a woman. Her work suggests that women can transform their love into a source of power for fighting many arenas of oppression—not only patriarchy.

Hillesum's conception of the role of love is political. She was able to use her love to retain control over her own feelings and inner strength. Rather than allow the Nazis to define her as less than human, to deny the value and significance of her life, she persisted in living a life that gave her meaning and satisfaction. In addition, the strength from her love enabled her to act as a source of inspiration for others who were struggling with feelings of despair and to help transform the world into a freer society. Similarly, Dorothy Day's and Simone Weil's love and compassion were the foundation of their work on behalf of working people (Day, 1963; Coles, 1987a, 1987b; Petrement, 1976).

Although Lorde, Rich and Hillesum come from different philosophical traditions, they all assert that authentic expressions of love can help create a better world. They do not emphasize the physical intimacy that can be associated with love. Instead, they emphasize the discovery of a spiritual love which is not based on dependency or weakness. They believe that this kind of love can be politically transformative and is essential to our ability to create a freer society.

This conception of the politics of love seems consistent with the radical feminist conception of sexual politics. Feminists often argue that society has overemphasized the importance of the physically intimate and procreative aspects of sexuality. They suggest that women might define sexuality quite differently if they could define it from their own perspective. By thinking of love broadly, removed from the arena of physical intimacy and procreation, women might be able to begin to consider the positive life-building potential of love within their lives removed from the subordinating sexuality that they have often experienced under patriarchy. This spiritual conception of love would seem to be able to guide women in determining how to relate to themselves as well as others. This conception of the role of love and sexuality in women's lives could make the radical feminist maxim that the "personal is political" a more meaningful statement because it would expose the full range and importance of the love and compassion that women create in their lives.

I therefore conclude that women's journey to discover and experience their authentic sexuality is an important journey but one which must be pursued carefully. Women need to be especially attentive to the possibility that they may be too willing to acclaim a particular sexual expression as authentic out of their broken need for intimacy or to overemphasize the importance of the sexual self as part of their fuller self. In addition, as I will discuss in Part III, women need to be conscious of the possibility that intimacy with men may lead to subordination or create tactical problems by interfering with the ability to develop women-only space for political work. On the other hand, the positive use of women's love and compassion may be more politically transformative than we have previously recognized. Thus, it makes sense to embark on legal challenges to protect and expand our "right to love."

II Discovering Authenticity Through Feminist Methodology

Feminists generally endorse consciousness-raising and experiential discourse as fundamental to feminist methodology. Nevertheless, their writing often does not reflect feminist methodology.

The absence of an experiential discourse, for example, weakens MacKinnon's general statements about sexuality. At one point, MacKinnon says "[E]ither heterosexuality is the structure of the oppression of women or it is not" (MacKinnon, 1987, p. 60). Such a general statement does not purport to reflect on the variety of meanings that heterosexuality has in women's lives. For some women, intimate relationships with certain men may be an authentic and affirming expression of their sexuality. For other women, possibly the vast majority, such relationships may be one aspect (but not the "structure") of their oppression. A more contextual discussion of sexual relationships may illuminate those different experiences and give us a better understanding of how certain relationships can oppress women as well as how women can overcome that oppression. This may be more useful than making global statements about what forms of sexual expression are liberating or oppressive for all women.

When MacKinnon does use an experiential discourse, she selectively validates women's voices. She affirms women's descriptions of their lack of freedom but does not affirm women's alleged glimpses of freedom (MacKinnon, 1987, p. 218). She also does not provide us with tools to determine which voices to describe as authentic. In short, MacKinnon's assertion that "feminism has not changed the status of women" (MacKinnon, 1987, p. 2) reflects her general denial of the possibility of movement towards authenticity or freedom within any particular woman's life.

MacKinnon's skepticism about movement towards freedom or authenticity emerged in a public conversation with Mary Dunlap (MacKinnon, 1987, p. 305). Dunlap asserted that she, and many other women, have experienced nonsubordination in their lives. She asked that all the women in the audience stand who had experienced non-subordination. Apparently, a substantial, although not overwhelming, number of women in the audience then stood.

MacKinnon rejected the authenticity of these women's claims of nonsubordination and accused Dunlap of misunderstanding her. MacKinnon claimed that Dunlap's assertion of nonsubordination: "turns a critique of a structural condition into a statement of individual inevitability, an indictment of oppression into a reason for passivity and despair" (MacKinnon, 1987, pp. 305–6).

It is possible that Dunlap misunderstood MacKinnon but it is also obvious that MacKinnon misunderstood Dunlap. Dunlap was not asserting that women have achieved equality and should give up the feminist struggle. She was not asking the women who stood up to stop fighting for non-subordination throughout their lives. Dunlap was simply insisting that many women have had a glimpse of non-subordination in their lives which they should not be afraid to acknowledge. She apparently finds MacKinnon's unwillingness to acknowledge progress or movement towards authenticity as inconsistent with her and other women's life experiences.

I have no trouble with the idea that it is *difficult* for women to describe the world accurately given the socialized lenses through which they see the world. But why should we affirm women's descriptions of subordination but not women's descriptions of progress? MacKinnon says that "feminism is built on believing women's account of sexual use and abuse by men" (MacKinnon, 1987, p. 5). She validates women's cries of pain and humiliation within traditional sexuality but not women's cries of freedom or authenticity.

One possible reason MacKinnon discounts descriptions of freedom, but not subordination, is that descriptions of subordination are inconsistent with patriarchy, because patriarchy induces women to believe that they are not subordinated. In other words, a woman who describes subordination must have struggled to overcome the limiting ways in which patriarchy distorts her vision. Although that explanation may clarify why it is *easier* for women to describe subordination authentically than to describe freedom authentically, it does not provide us a justification for completely discounting claims of freedom. If women can overcome patriarchy sufficiently to see their subordination then women should be able to overcome patriarchy sufficiently to see their freedom.

Robin West ties MacKinnon's selective validation of women's voices to methodological issues. She criticizes radical feminists, such as MacKinnon, who completely discount women's descriptions of pleasure under sexually submissive arrangements, although those statements of pleasure have emerged from consciousness raising (West, 1987, pp. 115–16).

West asserts that the reason that MacKinnon discounts women's descriptions of pleasure, even though attained through consciousness raising, is that MacKinnon has an underlying, but unjustified assumption about women's happiness: that women cannot be truly happy under conditions of submission (West, 1987, p. 118). Instead of assuming that subordination produces submission which in turn produces women's unhappiness, West challenges radical feminists to explore more fully women's direct assertions of pain and pleasure.

West claims that women should try to avoid pain and move toward pleasure (West, 1987, p. 142). She questions MacKinnon's assertion that the eroticization of controlled submission is closely tied to women's overall subordination, because she asserts that MacKinnon has not connected those observations to pleasure and pain, and more specifically, has not used consciousness-raising to make that connection (West, 1987, p. 118).

I do not understand why West asserts that pleasure and pain are the appropriate standards to use in thinking about women's well-being. From a feminist perspective, we must ask: "how can we, as women, achieve our full womanhood and full personhood?"; "what do women want?" Pleasure may be one component of achieving a full life of womanhood and personhood but I do not believe that attaining that single component is sufficient to bring about such a life. Feminist theorists need to explore more fully what constitutes women's well-being.

MacKinnon has considered women's well-being by asking how women would define their injuries through rape, pornography, and sexual harassment. She has examined that part of women's pain. I assume that West applauds that part of MacKinnon's scholarship and would agree that MacKinnon has been asking the correct questions. The crux of West's criticism is a consistency argument—MacKinnon has been less comfortable asking what sexual expressiveness contributes to women's well-being. Instead, she has simply asserted that women cannot flourish through sexual submissiveness. Thus, MacKinnon has used her anti-subordination perspective to consider women's pain but not to glimpse women's freedom or authenticity.

In order to evaluate both MacKinnon's and West's assertions about women's well-being, we need a framework within which we may learn about women's experiences. West turns to consciousness-raising for that data but I am not entirely satisfied with that discussion, because she has not been sufficiently critical of consciousness-raising. She seems to assume that so long as an expression of pleasure or pain is acknowledged through consciousness-raising then it is authentic; it has not been tainted by patriarchy or other forms of coercion. I am not as comfortable as West in the ability of consciousness-raising to help us see our authentic feelings of pleasure and pain. If we accept the radical feminist critique that sexuality is the root of women's oppression, then we should be hesitant about the ability of consciousness-raising to unearth this aspect of women's oppression. In addition, consciousness-raising takes many forms. Its outcome often depends upon the particular group of people involved or the techniques they choose. Moreover, few of us are actively engaged in formal consciousness-raising at this stage of our feminism. Perhaps we have a study group; most likely we have a small group of friends with whom we engage in intimate conversations. We may not be fully subjecting our assertions of authenticity to feminist methodology. And, as I have discussed earlier, even if they are fully subjected to feminist methodology, they may not reflect out authenticity because of the imperfections of feminist methodology.

For example, West provides us with examples of women who perceive that they have received pleasure from submission through participation in pornography but she does not tell us exactly what form of consciousness-raising was used to uncover those feelings. It is therefore hard for the reader to evaluate the authenticity of the observations. We need to place our use of the phrase "consciousness-raising" in context to show how it helps uncover authenticity. I am searching for a middle ground between West and MacKinnon which is skeptical, although not dismissive, of women's assertions of both pleasure and pain or subordination and nonsubordination even when those claims are made through consciousness-raising so that we can begin to understand difficult issues like women's experience with pornography.

III Tension Between Authentic Expression and Political Construction of Sexuality

Even if women could discover their authentic sexuality, they would still have to try to *experience* that sexuality in order to move toward their authentic self. Several participants at the 1987 Feminism and Legal Theory Conference suggested that women should choose not to seek intimate sexual experiences with men, because those relationships cannot be experienced freely under patriarchy.

If radical feminists are correct that women are unlikely to experience intimate relationships with men authentically under patriarchy, they raise a troubling problem about expressions of authenticity. Is a woman who glimpses that her authentic sexuality can include relationships with men destined not to be able to experience that aspect of herself? And, if women are going to interact intimately with men, anyway, how can those interactions best move them toward discovering and experiencing their authentic sexuality? Formulated in this way, I do not question the authenticity of some women not experiencing intimate relationships with men when they perceive that such relationships would not be consistent with their authentic sexuality.

I am not as skeptical as many radical feminists of the possibility of movement toward freedom or authenticity within a woman's intimate relationship with a man. Although society tries to define sexual expressiveness narrowly, women may be able to work to overcome those forces in their internal lives. In order to consider how women can experience authentic sexual relationships with men, I would first like to consider how the sex of a woman's partner is important to society on an external level. I will then turn to how significant that factor is, or should be, within women's internal lives.

By the external level, I refer to the power of compulsory heterosexuality. Because of the external pull of compulsory heterosexuality, an exclusive expression of lesbianism may help a woman escape the oppressive aspects of heterosexual marriage within our society. In addition, an exclusive expression of lesbianism can be an act of political resistance, as a statement to society that women do not need men for personal or sexual fulfillment.

For a woman who glimpses that her authentic sexuality would not include intimate relationships with a man, the obvious choice of sexual expression would be lesbianism. For a woman who perceives that sexual relationships with a man would be consistent with her authentic sexuality, a difficult struggle may lie ahead. As a precondition to such a relationship being satisfying, the feminist must maintain her woman-centered political perspective and life work. It would be difficult for her to share some aspects of that life work with a man because much of it necessarily occurs in woman-only space. It is probably harder to stay intimately connected with someone if one cannot share a major part of one's life experiences with him. It would seem to take an extraordinary man who could maintain the necessary connectedness with a feminist's community while not being able to participate in her woman-only space.

This brings me to the basic question of what are the preconditions of intimacy. If non-subordination is a precondition for intimacy and true non-subordination must exist on both an internal and external level, the task for women is to create an environment of non-subordination. Is there any way that external subordination can *not* impinge on a male-female relationship?

For example, I feel the pull of compulsory heterosexuality and know that even if I choose to pursue intimacy with a man *despite* rather than *because* of compulsory heterosexuality, that choice will nevertheless reinforce that institution in the minds of others. As I write this essay, I feel these pressures everywhere—from conversations with my mother to the knowledge that my immigration difficulties would disappear automatically if my Canadian boyfriend and I married. When my friends get married, I usually donate money in their name to the Louisiana Sexual Privacy Project and send them a note saying that I am sure that they will be happy to know that their gift is being used to make it possible someday for gay people to experience the privilege that they are now enjoying. I am often surprised that my straight friends are not really aware that gay people cannot get married although when they think about it they realize that they have never known a married, gay couple. Hence, I have to realize that the choice of a heterosexual relationship might undo my prior work in insisting on a woman's right to be accepted and affirmed in her choice of an intimate female partner.

A tension therefore exists between the external forces of patriarchy and expressions of our authentic selves. To consider how women might resolve this tension, I find a racial analogy useful. My life as a woman who "glimpses" that her authentic sexuality could include intimate relationships with men is like my life as a white person. As a white person,

I have a responsibility to confront directly the racism that I see in my daily life. Because I cannot experience life as anyone other than a white person, I must live up to the responsibilities of my privilege rather than try to escape that privilege by denying the significance of my whiteness. Similarly, as a woman involved intimately with a man, I have a responsibility to confront directly the homophobia and heterosexism that I see in my daily life. Rather than try to experience an inauthentic sexual expression, limit expression of my authentic self, or deny the political significance of my sexual expression, I need to live up to the responsibilities of my position of privilege. We always have the same responsibility to overcome sexual oppression. Rather than run from relationships with men to avoid collaboration with their oppression, women need to work to overcome the conditions that make that oppression possible. The way in which the external component of subordination affects a relationship may depend on how conscious women are of those forces.

These issues raise the question of choice—a question that MacKinnon raises in her discussion of collaboration. (MacKinnon, 1987, pp. 7–8) Although a feminist may be able to discover her authentic desire to pursue a relationship with a particular man, she must be able to sustain the expression of her desire within an externally constraining environment. A relationship with a man could become an inauthentic expression of a woman's sexuality because of her inability to fit that expression freely into her external environment. For a politically conscious feminist, the external forces of compulsory heterosexuality may make certain expressions of her authentic sexuality difficult, if not impossible, because those external forces would make a choice of heterosexuality feel subordinating. Thus, it is crucial that we develop legal-political strategies to limit, and eventually eliminate, the effects of compulsory heterosexuality.

Nevertheless, we need to consider the question of whether feminists are operating entirely within a regime of compulsory heterosexuality. Since many feminists have created strong support networks with other feminists, they have been able partially to overcome the pull of compulsory heterosexuality. Although I agree with feminists that compulsory heterosexuality does exist, I do not assume that it is the only or the necessarily determinative force in women's lives as feminists.

Feminists may be placing too much significance on sex or gender within their lives because society places such emphasis on sex or gender. Feminists may be overlooking that their authentic selves can and should be nurtured in an intimate relationship. Ideally, we should aspire to seek intimate relationships with people on the basis of their authentic self rather than their biological sex. A woman's exclusive choice of women as intimate or sexual partners is a sex-specific choice that seems to contradict a movement toward the discovery and expression of her authentic self.

It could place too much emphasis on one factor—the biological sex of one's partner—rather than the broader question of what should be most important in a relationship. An exclusive expression of lesbianism (or heterosexuality) would seem to suggest that the sex of one's partner is so significant that it must circumscribe the possibilities within a relationship. Feminism needs to assist us move away from sex-specific choices toward authentic choices.

My consideration of the journey toward authenticity prevents me from arriving at the conclusion that the only authentic expression of female sexuality under patriarchy is celibacy or exclusive relationships with women. The lesson for me is that intimacy is not easy; women need to be on guard for internal and external conditions which inhibit the development of fully satisfying intimacy. Women need to question whether their search for intimacy is itself an aspect of their brokenness. Women need to place each individual relationship in context to see how to react to and prevent external influences which might limit their journey toward authentic sexual expression. These external forces may affect any intimate relationship that women seek—be they with a man or a woman. Women's openness to a range of sexual experiences may necessitate a political diligence that is tiring and sometimes frustrating but it may, also, help move them toward the expression of their authentic selves—a goal worth struggling to attain.

IV Conclusion

This essay is the beginning of a larger project for me because it has helped me to formulate some basic questions raised by radical feminism. What is the relationship between authentic expressions of sexuality and authentic self? What is authentic sexuality? Can we even begin to understand authentic sexuality until we better understand love and compassion generally? How can we best conduct the journey toward authenticity? These are all fundamental questions which theologians have been asking for thousands of years. It seems appropriate, therefore, for feminists to begin to explore that literature more fully so that we can sift out some of the answers to these questions.

9

The Problem of Privatized Injuries: Feminist Strategies for Litigation

Adrian Howe

There is, I believe, a great deal that feminist legal theorists can contribute—must contribute—to the clarification of the muddle that is presently women's internal lives. Specifically, . . . we should be clarifying the nature of the injuries we sustain so as to minimally insure that the legal system we are increasingly empowered to use will respect and understand them. (Robin West, 1986)

An amazing notion: if there is an injury, there should be a remedy. (Catharine MacKinnon, 1985a)

I

My starting point is women's pain—not our physical pain (although that cannot be separated out)—but rather that pain we feel, as gendered women, at an intimate, hitherto private level. The question of the centrality of women's pain to feminist legal theory was raised by Robin West when, in the process of clarifying the nature of women's legally unrecognized "gender-specified injuries," she called on feminist legal scholars to set about describing, phenomenologically, our gender-specific pain in order to "communicate its magnitude" and thus insure its legal recognition (West, 1986; 1987). As phenomenology is neither my field nor my forte, this paper takes a different but complementary journey. Its theoretical starting point is the unlikely field of criminology. I have argued elsewhere (Howe, 1987b) that criminology is incapable and unworthy of reclamation. But within criminology there is one significant though neglected concept—that of "social injury"—which scholars have begun to theorize in ways that have extended analysis of the legal regulation of harmful corporate decision-making. "Social injury," I believe, has a potential to be theorized in ways which may lead to the progressive development of feminist legal theory that Robin West and others have called for.

My intention then, is to seize upon the concept of "social injury" in order to prise it out from criminology and develop it around *our* pain. I

This paper is an elaboration of my article " 'Social Injury' Revisited: Towards a Feminist Theory of Social Justice," (*International Journal of the Sociology of Law* [1987]15). A version of it also appears in *Studies in Law, Politics, and Society* Volume 10 edited by Susan S. Silbey (JAI Press).

mean the pain caused by the "hidden injuries" of all gender-orientated societies—that lived, internalized experience of lower gender status as personal failure; that felt sense of a lack of a "badge of ability" which is central to the effectiveness of the ideology of equality (Sennett and Cobb, 1973; Freeman, 1982).[1] I will argue that this resulting self-identity is an injured one—not a privatized, personal injury, but a *social* one. Importantly, we have begun to name the injuries associated with lower gender status. Over the last two decades our once privatized injuries such as domestic violence (now criminal assault in the home), have become public issues. But while some of our injuries are thereby becoming legally cognizable, others are still dismissed in the legal culture (West, 1987). Moreover, we ourselves are divided over whether some of our injuries should be made actionable at all.

My argument is pitched at several different levels. First, it is offered as a contribution to the development of feminist legal strategies. The specific legal strategy advocated here is that we publicize and thus politicize those injuries—those intimate intrusions into our lives—which we want to make legally cognizable. More broadly, the paper is submitted as a contribution to the process of developing "collectively, and within an international framework" (Smart, 1986, p. 111) a more adequate—because more experientially grounded—feminist theory of law. More broadly still, it is offered as a contribution to two current feminist projects—the "deconstructive project" which identifies and deconstructs male perspectives on "human" experience and the feminist "reconstructive project" which, according to Sandra Harding and Merrill Hintikka, identifies "distinctive aspects of women's experience which can provide resources for the construction of more representatively human understanding" (1983, p. x). The distinctive aspect of women's experience which I am suggesting we focus on within legal discourse is that of our injuries: we should value them, politicize them and, when necessary, demand that they become actionable.

II

The concept of social injury became part of the criminological repertoire when Edwin Sutherland took up the challenge of white collar crime over forty years ago. By broadening the definition of crime to "legally defined social injury" for which the State provides a penalty (even if it was only a penalty in civil law), Sutherland achieved the distinction of bringing white collar crime within the scope of criminology. White collar crime, he said emphatically, was "real crime." Sutherland's explicit purpose in studying white collar crime was to correct the socioeconomic bias which excluded business practices from consideration as crime in order to "reform" criminology by bringing the crimes of the powerful within its scope (1940). My concern, however, is not to participate in the sterile debate of the 'tis/tisn't kind about whether corporate harm and, by extension, sexist harm, should be criminalized. Nor am I interested in engaging in any of the disputes about the best way to refine Sutherland's definition of crime. It is relevant, however, to revisit briefly the conceptual terrain on which "social injury" resurfaced over the forty years since Sutherland reflected on white collar crime, in order to assess its potential for development by feminist legal theorists.

Overall, social injury did not have a very stimulating journey within post-Sutherland criminology. On the one hand (the right hand), Paul Tappan complained that Sutherland's definition of crime as legally defined social injury went too far. "The concept of socially injurious conduct," he said in his now classic response to Sutherland, "Who is the Criminal?," does not "define what is injurious. It sets no standard. It does not discriminate cases, but merely invites the subjective value judgments of the investigator" (1947). On the other hand (the left hand) critics complained that Sutherland's definition of social injury did not go far enough. While commending him for pointing out that business practices previously regarded as merely violations of the civil law were "crimes because they were social injuries rather than private wrongs," they criticized him for taking a "legalistic position," one which accepted that the State defined which social injuries were crimes. From this perspective, there were two problems with this "legalistic" stance: it did not account for socially injurious acts which were not defined as crime (the examples given were genocide, racism, sexism and poverty) and it did not consider that there were socially "non-injurious acts" which were defined as crime (for example, the so-called "victimless" crimes). One response to this dilemma was to explicate social injury with reference to "historically determined rights of individuals" and, tellingly, to "make man, not institutions, the measure of all things," when reconstructing standards of criminality (Schwendinger and Schwendinger, 1970).

Another leftist response to the perceived inadequacy of Sutherland's notion of crime as social injury was to claim that the "relevant" social injury—"the type of social injury common to what are depicted as white collar crimes" was more appropriately called "exploitation" or "appropriation" (Pepinsky, 1974; 1976). Still another response by those feeling the need to advance beyond Sutherland was to criticize his white collar "perspective" for focusing on social injuries which had a "diffuse economic impact" (such as company fraud) and glossing over offences which had serious—that is, harmful physical effects, such as killing employees and consumers. In this view, white collar crimes should be redefined as "organisational crimes," described as "illegal actions taken in accordance with operative organizational goals" which did serious physical or economic harm to employees, consumers or the general public (Shrager and Short, 1977).

These, then, were some of the developments which social injury underwent in post-Sutherland theorizing about white collar crime. Insofar as the concept of social injury itself was involved in the mapping out of this new discursive field of white collar crime, the theorizing boiled down to a debate over the definition of "serious" crime. On one side were those who said that serious crime was that which caused the most harm or the greatest harm to the greatest number. On the other side were those who reasserted the so-called "common sense view," based on "crime severity" surveys, that serious crime was murder and burglary, not misappropriation of funds—a view which was allowed to conclude that business "malpractice" could result in a lot of physical harm, but that this harm was "less basic" in that it was less disruptive than direct attacks on person and property (Brown, 1978, pp. 90–94).

Social injury also made appearances in mainstream criminology and in related discourses. For example, in the late 1970s A.K. Bottomley made a case for a "victim-orientated criminology" which would take its interpretation of crime from the victim's perspective of "individual and social harm" (1979, p. 31). At the same time, he recognized that:

> . . . for the foreseeable future criminologists will have to accept that the public still holds to a very personalised view of crime and victimisation, and are very slow to associate many of the more recent social harms with these traditional categories (1979, p. 38).

Interestingly, Bottomley cited "social harm" along with "deviance" as the "contemporary issues" in criminology (1979, p. 161). But as we all known it was deviance, not social harm or injury, which pushed its way, past saturation point, into criminological and sociological theorizing in the '60s and '70s—a development which prompted two Australian criminologists to insist that we talk less about "deviance" (in their view, a "methodologically unsound category") and more about harm to others. They advocated—somewhat simplistically—a "sociology of dominance" which would tell how "powerless people" doing "little harm to anyone were repressed by being labelled deviant" and a "sociology of exploitation" which would tell how the illegal practices of powerful people, which did considerable harm to powerless people, is covered up (Wilson and Braithwaite, 1979, pp. 5–10). At the other end of the political spectrum, the concept of harm or injury has reverted back from its emergent social or collective form to its old individualistic mode in "law and order" jeremiads about predicting "dangerousness." Here "dangerousness" is defined as a "propensity to cause serious physical injury" or "serious bodily harm to another person" while the dangerousness of unsafe factories, for example, is ignored—proof, if any were needed—that the concept of injury is not inherently progressive (Bottoms, 1977).

The concept of harm or injury has also made an appearance in the justice debate where the spotlight shifts from the motivation of the offender to the degree and kind of harm occurring. The right or "just deserts" theorists maintain that the length of a sentence should be determined by the harm—"moral harm"—of the act and demand that serious crime—typically, street crime—be punished more severely, the seriousness being determined by the harm produced. Center and left justice theorists, on the other hand, emphasize the idea of *social* harm and want to criminalize the injurious acts of the powerful. However, marxist critics of the justice model such as Dean Clarke (1978, p. 53) have been quick to point out that the crucial question—that of the "criterion for the comparison of socially harmful acts" has not been "properly confronted" by the justice theorists—thereby highlighting the critical issue: the problem is to determine the "relevant" social injury, not its mere existence.

Again, the question of the meaning of social injury has been raised within the American Critical Legal Studies movement by Mark Kelman and Richard Abel, amongst others. While Kelman is scathingly critical about the way in which what he calls "traditional radical criminology "has overstated the contingency of crime to the point where standard index crimes—common variety crimes like burglaries—are viewed almost as "class-biased nonharms," but where "corporate harm-causing" is prioritized beyond commonsensical understanding, he nevertheless insists that we have to question our "near-universal acceptance of the harms routinely tolerated" and our "condemnations of those that seem incidental or disruptive" (Kelman, 1982, pp. 218–221). He provides an interesting and very relevant example—one which provides a clue to a way in which we can develop the meaning of social injury within feminist discourse:

> A woman may ultimately be just as abused and exploited [I would say "injured"] by the sexual harasser as the rapist; the fact that the sexual harasser so closely resembles the boss in his ordinary mode . . . should ultimately be used by radicals to undermine the legitimacy of power, not to defend harassers as obviously noncriminal (Kelman, 1982, p. 222).

Finally, Richard Abel has made some relevant comments about injury in the process of unpacking capitalist tort law. Class, race and gender, he said, "will affect the extent to which and the way in which the experience of injury is transformed into a claim for legal redress." For example, class, race and gender will affect "the sense of entitlement to physical, mental, and emotional well-being"; they will affect "the feeling of competence to assert a claim and to withstand retaliation," and they will affect "the capacity to mobilize the legal process." Interestingly, Abel cites what he sees as women's relatively recent resistance to "abuse by their husband's" as an example of such a growing sense of entitlement to well-being and—by implication—a growing sense of injury. Presumably Abel would include women in the group of people now at risk of injury but who would be assured of regaining "control over the threat of injury" by advocates, like himself, of a socialist approach to injury and illness (Abel, 1982, pp. 189–196). Presumably too, Abel and Kelman would agree that any new "sophisticated typology of preventable social harm" (Edgeworth, 1984, p. 149)—one which might be designed by those committed to effecting a paradigm shift in commonsense understanding of social injury—would include harm to women.

III

In all these different discourses the concept of "social injury" has been developed in ways which Sutherland could not have foreseen. Nor could he have possibly foreseen that I would suggest that feminist legal scholars analytically privilege the concept of "social injury" within feminist legal theory and, ultimately, within legal discourse. This concept, developed in relation to women's social injuries, could, I suggest, become a valuable tool for feminist theorists and lawyers wanting to devise litigation strategies in which women's substantive differences—for example, the way we feel the pain of sex stereotypes substantively differently from men—will be taken into account by law reform. The notion of social injury, perhaps self-evidently, could be especially useful to those of us interested in extending analysis of the group-based—that is, social—nature of women's "private" injuries within an anti-discrimination context.

The case for prioritizing the concept of social injury within feminist legal theory is a strong one. Most importantly, the concept of injury has a long and therefore legitimated history within legal discourse. Indeed, injury's strength is that it is legally cognizable: it has actionable status. Many forms of injury have been actionable, as the history of torts and contract law and the evolution of worker's compensation demonstrates. That injury has always been an actionable claim is, I suggest, of vital significance for feminist legal theorists. Consider, for example, that it has been the "hurtfulness" of the oppression of women, the "damage done to women" by sex stereotypes and our socialization as inferior which, according to Juliet Mitchell, has concerned feminists since the French Revolution (Mitchell, 1984, p. 68). Consider too a recent feminist philo-

sophical definition of oppression—oppression in its "everyday, common-or-garden, O.E.D. sense":

> it refers to the condition of being oppressed, where, to oppress, means . . . to press *injuriously* upon or against; to subject to pressure with *hurtful* or overpowering effect (my emphasis) (Finn, 1982, pp. 147–148).

If we were to rename our oppressions as injuries and insist that injury has always been a legally actionable claim, we would be in a strong position to join the discussion taking place within criminology and Critical Legal Theory about "relevant" social injuries and to insist that any new "sophisticated" typology of preventable harms developed there includes harm to women. More broadly, we would be in a strong position to intervene progressively in the development of a new commonsense understanding of socially injurious behaviors which should become legally actionable.

I am not trying to reinvent the wheel: naming and renaming our oppressions as injuries has been an important feminist strategy—one, moreover, which has already been deployed within feminist legal theory. Canadian, American, British, European and Australian feminist legal theorists have commenced the important task of developing a feminist jurisprudence which takes as its starting point women's different perspective on the wrongs we experience and which is suggesting new solutions to such injuries as pregnancy discrimination, rape laws, sexist stereotypes, employment discrimination, sexual harassment, and pornography (see, for example, Cole, 1984; MacKinnon, 1979). This is not the place to review these feminist interventions in legal theory, but it is vital to note that it is the very prevalence of the notion of injury or harm in feminist legal theory—especially in feminist critiques of anti-discrimination law—which provides another reason for focusing on and extending our analysis of women's injuries, albeit in the broader context of *social* injury.

While it would be tedious to provide to a definitive listing of the appearance of the concept of injury or harm in feminist legal analyses, it is useful to consider some examples to see how injury, although not always a focal concern, is a dominant if previously untheorized theme. In Australia, feminist legal theorist Margaret Thornton has questioned the capacity of affirmative action measures in this country to prevent the occurrence of "future harms." She has been concerned to assess the capacity of these measures to go beyond the traditional civil law model which deals with specific, individualized conduct, and to "foreclose the possibility of harmful conduct of a general kind"—for example, by correcting a "generalised harm" such as the under-utilization of women in the workplace (Thornton, 1985a, p. 123). Similarly, Meg Wallace has questioned the capacity of Australian anti-discrimination law to eliminate what she calls "harm by discrimination" (Wallace, 1985b, p. 23). The concept of injury has also loomed large in arguments for affirmative action programs in the United States. For example, in the "compensatory justice" argument, affirmative action is presented as awarding reparations to injured parties for their past and ongoing discriminatory injuries. While the injuries caused by sex discrimination are often "more subtle than their racial counterparts," they are similarly "all-inclusive" in the sense that compensatory justice is now due to women and racial minorities "as groups"—because the injury against the groups was "all-encompassing." On the other hand, the "distributive justice" model argument for affirmative action, the aim is not to "repay past injury but to neutralize its present effects" (Duncan, 1982, pp. 510–521).

However, affirmative action is very difficult, some would say impossible, to implement in practice, partly because of the resistance of its opponents—privileged white, anglo-saxon men and their agents—who claim that affirmative action injures them. Yet for as long as affirmative action measures are caught up with the ideology of liberalism and the "merit principle" (Thornton, 1985b), that claim will be unfounded. On the contrary, such anti-discrimination and affirmative action measures should be seen for what they are: socially injurious to the vast majority of women. For as Frances Olsen amongst others, has shown, these measures, while pretending to end discrimination, instead create yet another reason for women to blame themselves when they fail in the job market (Olsen, 1983, p. 1555).

In all these analyses, the centrality of the concept of social injury has been a continuing but dormant theme. It came alive in the women's litigation strategy orchestrated by Ruth Ginsburg in leading sex discrimination cases brought by male plaintiffs before the United States Supreme Court in 1970s. While these cases have been seen as unsatisfactory in that they did not "always develop the harm perceived by women for the Court" (Taub and Schneider, 1982, p. 135), Ginsburg saw the male plaintiffs as useful for women in that their cases could highlight for the Court the way in which so-called "benign" discrimination hurts women by perpetrating injurious, stigmatic stereotypes. For while a male-dominated judiciary is able to see the slight but tangible burden placed on men by, for example, laws providing tax exemptions for widows but not widowers, it is not usually able to see the hidden, internalized injuries suffered by women because of harmful gender stereotypes. In order to educate the court about the injurious effects of false stereotypes labelling women and men as inherently different, Ginsburg chose to litigate issues which she could "frame as hurting both men and women," rather than issues like pregnancy discrimination where the harm falls predominantly on women. Her ultimate aim was to show that while the male plaintiffs suffered direct economic harm, women suffer indirectly from "benign" discrimination and, consequently, "the ultimate harm of all statutory sex distinctions" falls on them (Cole, 1984, pp. 52–85).

This strategy was predicated on a concept of harm by stereotype—a concept which is cognizant of the hidden, internalized nature of the injury caused by sex stereotyping. A related but alternative approach to social injury in relation to women has been taken by Robin West. Building on the idea that women suffer differently from men, West explored the way "women's injuries are often not recognized or compensated *as injuries* by the legal culture" (her emphasis). Far from being actionable at law, women's "gender-specific injuries" are dismissed as trivial (sexual harassment on the street), consensual (for example, marital rape), or "participatory, subconsciously wanted, or self-induced" (for example, father/daughter incest) (West, 1987).

While this is a novel way of framing the problem, the idea that some social injuries are gender-specific has been implicit in the newly emergent feminist jurisprudence which emphasized women's "difference" and insists that women's real differences must be taken into account by the law. Additionally, law itself causes harm. Canadian and American feminist legal theorists have recently been at pains to make clear that law which "attempts to ensure equality of treatment by banning or avoiding differential treatment regardless of substantive differences"—for example, law which relentlessly applies gender neutral norms—can "further disadvantage," that is, injure women (Miles, 1985, p. 65). Such law provides them with what Kathleen Lahey has called "equality with a vengeance" (Lahey, 1987). Divorce law reform provides a good example, as Martha Fineman's analysis of Wisconsin's "reformed" divorce law illustrates. After exploring the tension which exists between "symbolic" law reform—which takes the form of rule equality and which provides equal treatment—and "instrumental" law reform, which provides "result equality," Fineman concludes that divorce law reform "can cause damage to women." In her view "equality of treatment is an abstraction which harms women in divorce" (Fineman, 1983).[2]

Conversely, law's abstentionism from sites of women's gender-specific injuries can also have harmful effects on women. As one study has pointed out, there are many forms of injury which are legally cognizable in the public sphere, but not in the private sphere, despite the "fundamental similarity" of the conflicts. Tort law has traditionally been held to be inapplicable to injuries inflicted within on going family relationships—injuries which fall disproportionally on women and children. And criminal law has had little impact on injuries short of death, inflicted in the still sacred private sphere—injuries such as rape which are inflicted almost exclusively on women and girls. Insofar as the law is absent from the private sphere, it devalues and thus harms women who are, by implication, unworthy of legal regulation (Taub and Schneider, 1982, pp. 121–22).

The concept of injury, then, saturates feminist legal theory, especially American feminist legal theory. Sometimes the concept of injury is undeveloped; sometimes, as in the analysis of the harm of discrimination, it becomes more salient. Increasingly, however, feminist scholars are resorting to the notion of women's injuries in their confrontations with law—for example, in their conceptualization of sexual harassment and pornography as harms to women. Yet, with few exceptions, they have not theorized injury. In my view, such a theorization is essential for the development of feminist legal scholarship. We need to demonstrate that a partial definition of social injury is inherent on gender-ordered legal systems. Just as Critical Legal Theorists have shown that capitalist tort law is gripped by a class bias (Abel, 1982), so feminist legal scholars need to demonstrate how law, especially law pertaining to injury, is gripped by a gender bias. Again, this work has begun. Feminist analysis of rape law is the obvious example. Catharine MacKinnon says it best and in a way which anticipates the kind of privileging of the concept of social injury—women's social injury—which I am suggesting in this paper. In her view, the problem with rape law is that:

> the injury of rape lies in the meaning of the act to its victims, but the standard for its criminality lies in the meaning of the same act to the assailants. Rape is only an injury from women's point of view. It is only a crime from the male point of view (1983, p. 652).

And again:

> When a rape prosecution is lost on a consent defence, the woman has not only failed to prove lack of consent, she is not considered to have been injured at all (1983, p. 653).

MacKinnon concludes that rape law "reflects the sex inequality" of society in "conceiving a cognizable injury from the viewpoint of the reasonable rapist" (1983, p. 654).

As is well known, MacKinnon extended her gynocentric injury analysis to pornography and sexual harassment within an anti-discrimination framework and, in the process, transformed feminist legal theorizing in the United States. To rehearse her arguments for interpreting pornography and sexual harassment as harms to women and as violations of civil rights would be tell you what you already know. It would also risk becoming involved in the debate over the controversial MacKinnon-

Dworkin pornography ordinance. While that controversy is fascinating to feminists who have no First Amendment to feel committed to,[3] my concern here is not to enter the fray, but rather to consider MacKinnon's conceptualization of injury in her discussions of these harms to women.

Let us first consider her interpretation of the harm of pornography. While that interpretation is controversial, and while Robin West, for one, has condemned it for abandoning "feminist practice" and for failing to take account of the "felt subjective desire" of many women for "eroticised submission" (West, 1987), it is, nevertheless, a theoretically significant one. First, it takes as its starting point women's experience of pornography and their testimony about the pain it has caused them. Second, it does analytically privilege the notion of injury to women in ways which anticipate the development of the conceptualization of women's injuries as *social* injuries which I believe is crucial for the advancement of feminist legal theory,and consequently, of women. Her contribution is seen clearly in the way in which she distinguishes her view of the pain of pornography from traditional versions. Thus, pornography is not a "moral harm": indeed, to define the pornographic as obscenity is to misconstrue its harm. Rather, "its harm is the harm of male supremacy made difficult to see because of its pervasiveness . . ." Indeed, the issue for MacKinnon is not what the harm of pornography is, but how to make it visible. This she sees as a huge problem insofar as pornography's invisibility—and this is critical—is a measure of its "success in constructing *social* reality" (my emphasis: MacKinnon, 1984, p. 335). Furthermore, it is a harm difficult to grasp by those following legal reasoning such as "First Amendment logic" because it is not "linearly caused in the 'John hit Mary' sense." MacKinnon rejects such a positivistic (that is—"individuated, atomistic, linear, isolated 'tort-like' ") conception of injury because the harm of pornography "does not work like this." Further, it privitizes the injury and fails to take account of its group-basis. Most significantly, pornography hurts women "as members of the group 'women' " (MacKinnon, 1984, pp. 337–8).

Critically too, MacKinnon argues that the liberal critique of pornography as "dehumanizing" is also inadequate. While the condemnation of pornography as "dehumanizing" is "an attempt to articulate its harm," this misses the specificity of the harm to women. From her feminist perspective, pornography dehumanizes women "in a culturally specific and empirically descriptive—not liberal moral—sense . . ." (1984, p. 341). Her ordinance, then, was designed to get at this specificity by naming the harm done to women—"our damage, our pain, our enforced inferiority." Accordingly, it defined pornography as "a systematic practice of exploitation and subordination based on sex which differentially harms women." This differential impact is crucial to MacKinnon's meaning: for "as a *social* group, men are not hurt by pornography the way women as a *social* group are" (my emphasis, MacKinnon, 1985b, p. 27). In this way, MacKinnon moved away from a moral concept of harm to a concept of a group-based-social harm. This, and not the controversy she aroused, is what is relevant to my argument. MacKinnon's naming of pornography as an injury to women as a social group was an extension of the naming strategy which she first applied to the injury of sexual harassment—"the first legal wrong to be defined by women." Again it is her emphasis on the social dimension of this injury—"the social reality women experience"—which is critical here. The creation of a legal cause of action for the injury of sexual harassment has brought a new awareness of this "social reality" which "urges the priority of defining women's injuries as women perceive them" (MacKinnon, 1981). Such an awareness has obvious ramifications for the theorization of social injury.

MacKinnon's elaboration of her controversial "inequality" approach to sex discrimination need not detain us. We need note only two crucial and interrelated themes: her prioritizing women's "lived-through experience" and of the "*social* reality of women as a sex" (my emphasis). This social dimension of women's lives is not only one of the most persistent themes of *The Sexual Harassment of Working Women*, it is central to an understanding of the "inequality" approach in which the "social position" of women has a special place (p. 103). Indeed, one of her focal concerns is "the *social* context" of women's lives—the "level of communality that makes sexual harassment a women's experience"; its "social impact"; the "*social* dynamics" of women's suffering which are not reflected in the law, especially tort law which fails to redress injuries to "public and shared *social* existence" such as sex in employment. Similarly, she is concerned with tort theory's failure to "capture the broadly *social* sexuality/employment nexus that comprises the injury of sexual harassment"; its failure to treat these incidents as integral to women's "*social* status" and its failure to analyze the *relevant* dimensions of the problem—namely, the "*socially* determinate character" of gender (1979, pp. 6, 47, 57, 87–88). Furthermore, sex discrimination for MacKinnon consists of "the systematic disadvantage of *social* groups" (or the "systematic depravation of one sex because of sex"), and the main point of reference for anti-discrimination law should be "the *social* situation and experience of women"—the "*social* experience" of battering, rape and other assaults (p. 116, p. 129: My emphasis).

As MacKinnon's analysis develops, it becomes apparent that this social dimension of women's experience is as intrinsic to her understanding of the "systematic damage done women" through their regulation to "secondary *social* status" (p. 143) as it is to her critique of tort law. Tort's inadequacy as a remedy for sexual harassment is that it personalizes what is, in effect, a social injury—one which has a psychological impact on women's "socialized sense of self-worth" (p. 160). More bluntly:

> . . . tort is conceptually inadequate to the problem of sexual harassment to the extent it rips injuries to women's sexuality out of the context of women's social circumstances as a whole (p. 171).

In short, tort law "omits the social dynamics" of women's subordinate position: it considers individual and compensable something which is fundamentally social. Crucially, MacKinnon's point here is not that sexual harassment is not a personal injury, but rather that it is "a social wrong and a *social injury* that occurs on a personal level" (pp. 172–73: My emphasis).

In the final analysis then, MacKinnon actually names sexual harassment as a "social injury." Indeed, all her analysis has lead, logically, to this outcome. Furthermore, in the process of elaborating her conceptualization of women's injuries as socially-based, she has done well phenomenologically: she has helped immensely to clarify the nature of our injuries to insure that they become legally recognized. She has described "the pain, isolation, and thingification of women" and their pacification into "nonpersonhood" (1982, p. 520); she has defined the damage to our sexuality as "the absence of life, of the ability to live in security or wholeness" (1985a, p. 27). And, equally important, she has empowered women to speak out publicly about how what she calls "our real injuries," such as pornography, have hurt them. In effect, by politicizing their injuries she has given them standing to speak.

IV

My conclusion from all this is that MacKinnon's naming strategy—her naming of our pains as socially-based injury— has been vitally important in winning them public and legal recognition. But it needs to be extended. Just as she developed our understanding of discrimination theory by showing how "the best attempt at grasping women's situation in order to change it by law"—the analyzing of sex and race—"gets a lot" but also "misses a lot," so her "inequality" approach to discrimination gets a lot (including the all-important social dimension of women's pain), but falls short of elaborating a theory of that pain as social injury (1985b, p. 9). My suggestion is simply that we keep MacKinnon's focus on women's experience but that we shift our focus from inequality to social injury by superimposing a social injury framework on her inequality framework.

This strategy has the following advantages. First, it enables us to step outside and transcend the futile, restricting formal-versus-substantive-equality debate which appears to have fragmented the American feminist legal community. At the same time, it not only alleviates the fears of MacKinnon's critics that her inequality analysis will deteriorate into yet another form of "detrimental protectionism" (Taub 1980, p. 1691); it also provides a means of reconciliation on ground where they agree—namely, that the "social meaning of female sexuality" (MacKinnon, 1979, p. 174) is "a deeply embedded meaning, deriving over time from women's historic necessity of exchanging sexual services for material survival" (Taub, 1980, p. 1688). Furthermore, the social injury strategy has a subsidiary benefit in respect of the "equality" debate: by shifting the focus from inequality to injury it makes redundant interpretation and misinterpretation of MacKinnon's position.[4]

Second, this strategy crosses discursive boundaries in order to find women's injuries a place in the broader theoretical movement which is developing the concept of injury in ways which are intended to transform commonsense understanding of relative social harms and to impact progressively on law. For example, in Australia alternative criminologists have started to develop a concept of "aggregate social harm" which they define as "those injuries, diseases and material losses that are suffered by individuals and are a consequence of deliberate policy or international behaviour." It is conduct which is "collective" and foreseeable "in an objective sense" even if there is no direct connection between the perpetrator and the ultimate damage. In a most relevant way, these criminologists have suggested that the allocation of individual responsibility for proximate harm "fragments any real analysis of aggregate social harm" and deflects attention away from non-criminalized but foreseeable social harms as industrial accidents, pollution and the manufacture of unsafe cars (Prisoners Action Group, 1980, pp. 45–46). Feminist legal strategists could usefully add women to this list. We could also profitably intervene in the process of redefining foreseeable injury.

Similarly, it would be strategically useful to add women's injuries to the list of substantive areas which Critical Legal Scholars have suggested need to be examined with a view to ascertain the process by which "unperceived injurious experience (unPIE)" is transformed into "perceived injurious experience (PIE)" (Feltsiner, Abel and Sarat, 1980–81, p. 634). While naming is already a feminist strategy, construing women's social injuries as yet another area needing attention may help to legitimate women's sense of entitlement to a remedy. Moreover, a feminist version of a more-broadly conceived PIE may help male-dominated courts to see women's injuries as "harm of a kind in which the state has legitimate interest" (MacKinnon 1985, p. 61). On the one hand, then, the social injury strategy avoids the pejorative overtones of "special treatment" and "sex specific" law; on the other hand, it finds legitimation for women's social injuries outside feminist legal discourse. Such legitimation can be found, for example, even in the unlikely field of Anglo-American criminal jurisprudence where, thirty years ago, Jerome Hall expanded the "principle of harm" to such "intangibles" as "public safety" and, crucially, "the autonomy of women" (Eser, 1965–66, p. 371).

Third, the social injury framework provides a strategic response to the problem of the privatized nature of women's pain—a problem which has been widely canvassed in a range of feminist discourses, including feminist legal discourse. Within these discourses there has been a consensus that the public/private dichotomy has been inimical to women in that it implies a false distinction between "public issues" and the pain women feel at the private level. Importantly, the solution to this problem has been seen to lie in the creation of a language in which women's experience will be "communicated and understood in a societal perspective" and in which women's oppressive privatized social reality, currently mystified by judicial ideology, will become public knowledge (Dahl and Snare, 1978, pp. 8–13). To the extent that the women's rights litigation strategy has fulfilled this task by emphasizing the "systematic pattern of social discrimination" underlying our privatized injuries, feminist legal scholars have commended it. Yet today many are beginning to question the potential of the rights strategy to achieve "social reconstruction" for women (Schneider, 1986). Feminists may have "exploded the private"—they may have demonstrated that "the measure of the intimacy has been the measure of the oppression"—but, ultimately, insisting that "our private degradation" become public issue has not been enough (MacKinnon, 1983, p. 656). The vocabulary of law still has difficulty framing our claims, arguably because we have missed out a crucial step. To ensure that the "special sort of fragmentation and loss of women"—our distinctive "mode of alienation" which is our privatized reality (Bartky, 1982)—is not lost in its translation into a legal claim, we need to demonstrate that the injuries we feel at the private, intimate level are socially-created (indeed, social) injuries before we demand that they become public issues. At the same time, analytically privileging social injury in a feminist legal framework will provide a necessary step in the deconstruction of the public/private dichotomy.

Finally, the social injury framework provides a strategic way out of the dilemmas posed by disenchantment with the "equality" focus of feminist legal analysis. In the face of pervasive disillusionment with law reform in general and the women's rights litigation in particular, we are urged to develop a "more compelling sex discrimination jurisprudence" and to encourage an explicit debate in judicial decisions about "the harms caused by sex discrimination" (Freedman, 1983, pp. 960–68). We are urged to adopt a 'gender discrimination approach' which focuses on 'the harm done to women as a group' in order to politicize the deeper forms of discrimination which "remain immune to conventional legal analysis" (Note, 1986, pp. 1272–3). We are invited to adopt strategies which will bring attention to the "concrete way in which various attributions of difference" have harmed women and which will deal with "the systematic and more subtle subordination that we must confront now that the easy cases have been won" (Finley, 1986, p. 1170, p. 1181). And we are reminded that at the heart of several "feminist legal clusters" is "the idea that harm and pain and hurt that are gender-correlated must end, must be prevented, must be remedied" (Dunlap, 1985, pp. 13–15).

In all these emergent priorities a social injury focus is promising. But it is equally applicable to agendas which are less explicit about the idea of harm. To those feminist legal analysts who are concerned about the defects of a gender-neutral analysis of prostitution or pornography and who advocate an approach which addresses "that materiality of gender" (Boyle, 1985, p. 107), or who prefer "materialist strategies" which "entitle or empower women" to the "legal equality" approach (McCloud, 1986, p. 319), I suggest that social injury is a materially-grounded concept because it is based in the materiality of women's gender-specific injuries. To those who assert that equal rights are "too restricted in legal content" to provide an adequate feminist agenda and who suggest that the challenge is to "move beyond liberal legalism" by developing a more constructive approach focusing less on gender difference and more on the disadvantages that have followed from it (Rhode, 1986, pp. 151–55), I reply that these disadvantages are properly and strategically construed as social injuries. And, finally, to those who say that analyses such as MacKinnon's which focus on the harm of pornography are "a step in the right direction . . . but don't go far enough in critiquing the nature of social control" (Olsen, 1984, p. 521), I suggest that a social injury analysis would go further.

IV

Finally, I have tried to anticipate feminist objections, points of resistance to my proposed strategy. First, the vexed question of "subjectivity." In an updated version of Paul Tappan's concern that the concept of socially injurious conduct did not define what is injurious or discriminate cases, but "merely invites the subjective judgments of the investigator"(1947), David Trubek has expressed reservations about "the complex subjective dimension" of the notion of an "unperceived injurious experience." This raises an important question about injury. Asbestosis, for example, is unproblematic because it is "serious, harmful and apparently preventable, so that everyone . . . would agree that a bad thing has happened." There is a "consensus of valuation" here, but not necessarily with other PIES (Trubek, 1980–81). Indeed, even the advocates of this approach agree: "unPIE is inchoate, PIE in the sky so to speak." That is:

> It can only be bounded by choosing someone's definition of what is injurious. Frequently this will not be a problem. An injurious experience is any experience which is disvalued by the person to whom it occurs. For the most part people agree on what is disvalued. But such feelings are never universal.

Moreover, it is people's "social position" which determines whether they perceive an experience as injurious, claim redress or get their claims accepted (Feltsner, Abel, and Sarat, pp. 634–36). This has obvious implications for women whose PIE *is* their social position.

Feminists have echoed these concerns, warning us that claiming our injuries as social will not be enough: we need to determine which are the harms "we want to eradicate," which pornography hurts us, which is the *real* injury (West, 1987). But feminists are divided over the "real" injuries. Consider, for example, the reaction of these two Dutch feminist legal analysts to the criminalization of pornography in the Netherlands:

> Unlike, for example rape, the seriousness and social injuriousness of which is undisputed, there is no such consensus on the harmful effect of pornography. Indeed, the harm it does is most likely to be on an ideological and immaterial level.

From their perspective, "too much time was spent proving and disproving the social injuriousness" of pornography and, most problematically, "the definitions of injuriousness were not always the same" (Brants and Kok, 1986, pp. 271–75). However, these issues do not constitute an argument to dispense with the social injury approach: rather, they should be taken as a directive to subject it to close scrutiny and to encourage a continuing dialogue about our social injuries.

A second possible objection to my proposed injury strategy is that it ignores questions of race and class. I might be accused of idealism and of treating women as a single class, thereby obscuring the class-differentiated and race-differentiated effects of their socially-injurious experiences (McCloud, 1986). To this I reply that women can share injury and recognize difference: taking women's social injuries seriously does not preclude taking their different needs into account. Yet another objection may be raised that in as much as the social injury strategy is dependent on an evaluing of our injuries, it encourages a victim mentality. Certainly, we do not need a feminist legal strategy in which women are constituted as victims: such a categorization has been seen—in sexual offences legislation (Smart, 1982, pp. 55–6) and in women's self-defence litigation—to reinforce an undesirable victim status. Certainly too, we must realize that the reluctance of victims of discrimination to move beyond the perception of discrimination to claim the protection of anti-discrimination law is "due to a resistance to the negative image of the victim." And we must understand not only that victims are reluctant to "cross the boundary between normalcy and victimhood," but that legal ideologies—including anti-discrimination or equal opportunity ideology—"can constrain the social vision of the victim" (Bumiller, 1987, pp. 435–8). However, the social injury perspective would insist that we perceive women as survivors, not victims, and that, in a broad sense, we are all victims to the extent that the "systematic exclusion of segments of society from society's benefits injures the social whole" (Ellis, 1984–85, p. 604). But my strategy will still need to come to grips with the constraining nature of legal ideology and, more particularly, with negative evaluations of anti-discrimination laws as actually legitimating race and gender equality (Freeman, 1982).

In the final analysis then, I must face the danger that social injury will go the way of all feminist legal initiatives: that however we theorize our claims, they will become transmogrified into legal categories which mask the nature of women's socially-based oppression. Undoubtedly, this constitutes our biggest challenge: to be or not to be involved in and committed to restructuring law for women. For some, "harm by discrimination"—is not actionable at law and as far as women are concerned, law has not proved to be the useful "form of social criticism" nor the deliverer of "at least some of the goods" which David Trubek claimed it to be (Wallace, 1985a; Trubek, 1977). Others are less pessimistic. While they recognize that anti-discrimination laws fit the model of "conformative institutions" which "contain, incorporate and moderate" conflict within capitalist societies, they insist that these institutions also have "an ambiguous character"—one which "creates new opportunities for pressing demands" (Gregory, 1979). They also warn against the dangers of abstentionism from law reform, such as perpetrating women's exclusion and disempowerment (Cole, 1985, p. 93).

On one side then, are those who maintain that concern with law reform diverts "the energy of the women's liberation movement into a narrow focus on legally articulate claims" (Polan, 1982, p. 300) or who insist that "the use of law in women's struggle for emancipation is a problematic tactic for feminists" insofar as male legal and judicial hegemony means that for the foreseeable future "the conception and execution" of legal change is going to be "masculine" (Kirkby, 1985, p. 153). On the other side are those such as Elizabeth Kingdom who reminds us that while in the past law has been "dismissed by sections of the left and feminists as being irredeemably reactionary and hence politically impenetrable," legal practices have been "a site of feminist intervention" (Kingdom, 1980, p. 75). Similarly, Carol Smart has argued that our legal "disappointments" notwithstanding, we need to continue engaging with law. In particular, she has suggested that "the willingness of courts to be influenced by non-legal criteria is a sign that yet other considerations can be brought into the legal forum" (Smart, 1984, pp. 239–40). Social injury, I suggest, is a strong candidate. Further, she has offered her concept of "the uneven development of law"—which recognizes that law both facilitates and obstructs change—in the hope that it will open the possibility of seeing law as "a means of 'liberation' " (Smart, 1986, pp. 116–8).

In the wake of feminist disenchantment with law and with the concept of rights in particular as a means of pressing feminist claims in law (Kingdom, 1985), Smart and Julia Brophy have suggested a new starting point—women's experience, not "abstract notions of law, justice or equity" (1985, p. 3). In this way, they give expression to a growing recognition that our theorizing must "escape imprisonment within the dominant discourse" (Thornton, 1986) and become experientially-grounded in women's lives. Similarly, Scandinavian feminists have insisted that we must privilege women's lives, not legal definitions. For Dahl, for example, the project of building women's law involves prompting "dignity, integrity and self-realization as basic needs of women today." From the social injury perspective, it is significant that her notion of integrity is "especially connected to the right to be left in peace, both physically and psychologically" (Dahl, 1986, pp. 244–45), for it is the physical and psychological damage caused by women's social injuries which we need to highlight in our fight to maintain our integrity. On the one hand, then, feminist legal scholars are condemning legal liberalism for having no language to adequately conceptualize our oppression; on the other hand, they are calling for innovative discursive practices grounded in women's lives. At yet another level altogether, they are deciding that there may be no single response to women's legal issues: the approach we take is simply a question of strategy. In the still inchoate state of feminist legal theorizing, I offer my social injury strategy as an affirmation of my faith in the progressive possibilities of feminist interventions in law.

Notes

1. I have here appropriated the idea of a "lived, internalized experience of lower class status as personal failure" from Freeman's analysis of the "hidden injuries" of class-structured societies (Freeman, 1982). Freeman, in turn, was appropriating Sennett and Cobb's notion of "the hidden injuries" of class (Sennett and Cobb, 1973).
2. To take another example, Aiken argues that statutes governing juvenile sexual activity "harm a young woman's freedom to act" (Aiken, 1984, pp. 374–5). Similarly, Olsen has

argued that while boys and girls "may both be harmed by early sexual activity" they are "harmed differently and we gain nothing by pretending the harm is the same" (Olsen, 1984, pp. 516–17).

3. I am not suggesting that non-American feminists would not be divided over the pornography ordinance—merely that the debate would be less virulent. Beth Gaze has suggested that if a federal legislative right to freedom of speech is enacted through the proposed Bill of Rights in Australia, "the problem of what are acceptable restrictions on free speech will be raised" (Gaze, 1986, p. 127).
4. Olsen, for example, has placed MacKinnon in the "substantive equality" camp, but claims that "MacKinnon's argument could also be interpreted as more than just an argument for substantive equality . . . as a complete departure from rights analysis" (Olsen, 1984, p. 397). More recently, she has named MacKinnon, along with Rifkin and Polan, as a "law as patriarchy" feminist legal theorist for whom the law is male in its essence (Olsen, 1986). This categorization is at odds with MacKinnon's own description of her *Signs* position (1983). She claims she was analyzing the state as male "not in its eternal essence (in the liberal mode), but in the interests it embodies and expresses" (Buffalo Symposium, 1985, footnote p. 87). See also McCloud (1986, footnote p. 295) for the view that MacKinnon transcends the theoretical dichotomy of formal versus substantive equality which mars sexual equality jurisprudence.

IV

Recasting Women's History

Our view of the past informs our understanding of the present and our vision for the future. It is just as true that our present perceptions shape and illuminate our understanding of the past. Who we are, what we value, that to which we have become sensitive determine our historical focus. In historical accounts constructed by white males, women and non-European men have generally played at best supporting roles. Recent work undertaken by feminists have populated history with a new cast of significant actors and motives. Previously treated episodes in women's history are seen in new light when they become the focus of feminist vision.

Barbara Omolade's study shows how families headed by single mothers have been integral to Black communities throughout American history. The origin of Black single motherhood lay in the social death of Afro-Americans. In spite of their treatment as nonpersons, both legally and culturally, however, Black single mothers maintained families which were sources of strength, continuity, love and commitment. Omolade argues that improvements in legal status have not brought about an end to the social death of Afro-Americans. Black single motherhood continues today, as in the past, to be both a forced condition and a chosen response to oppression.

Elizabeth Clark sheds new light on the nineteenth century women's movement. Male dominated legal history has tended to portray the women's rights movement as embodying the republican sentiments and values of America's founding fathers and as naturally culminating in women's victory of the formal right to vote. The values of antebellum women's rights advocates, however, were to a large degree antithetical to those of the dominant male political culture. Clark contends that the impetus for women's rights was not any desire to be "equal" to men, but rather recognition by women that their relative powerlessness prevented them from adequately protecting themselves and their families. Clark also argues that an appreciation of the religious underpinnings of women's quest for rights is necessary for an adequate understanding of women's rights history.

Focusing on a fascinating but little known episode in women's legal history, Sybil Lipschultz discovers a significant, but previously overlooked division between progressive era men and women who advocated protective labor legislation. Seen in this light, gender becomes central, not just to her analysis of women's labor laws, but also to her treatment of the community that sponsored this reform. The early 1920s saw a drive by social feminists to achieve "industrial equality." Recognizing and accepting the fact that most women's domestic responsibilities prevented them from undertaking the same wage-work schedules as men, social feminists advocated policies designed to neutralize women's resulting economic disadvantage. Aiming for equality of economic results rather than sameness of "opportunity," social feminists fought for the passage of a minimum wage for women. As Lipschultz shows, however, this movement hit an impasse when required to translate its ideals into legal argumentation. Legal ideology interpreted equality as sameness, but social feminists were trying to achieve equality through difference. Both the liberal male lawyers who advocated a minimum wage for women and the conservative male court that rejected it equated different treatment with inequality. Law's apparent inability to encompass notions of equality which recognize and respect material differences in person's lives is, alas, not simply a problem of the past.

10

The Unbroken Circle: A Historical Study of Black Single Mothers and Their Families

Barbara Omolade

Introduction

Families and households managed soley by Black women have been an integral part of American society since the days of the British colonization of North America and, as such, have been at the nexus of race, gender and class within the United States. Because racism permeates and transcends all social relationships, economic and political arrangements such as slavery, segregation, and desegregation have not operated in the public arena alone, but have seeped into the private arenas of sexuality, marriage and family,and the personal lives of Blacks and whites, men and women.

The history of Black single mothers and their families is part of the history of American family life. Three principles have shaped the development of American families:

> First, there was the puritanical tradition, which condemned fornication with the threat of fire and brimstone. Second, there was a highly developed sense of racial purity frequently codified in laws against miscegination. And third, there was a strong moral commitment to a patriarchal family life. (Patterson, 1982, p. 261)

Black families have been shaped by sexual conservatism, a patriarchal family life and a strong sense of racial pride. However, Black single-mother families have existed outside the patriarchal family, and often reflect the reality of sexual intercourse outside marriage. In their earliest

---

A more extensive version of this paper, including analysis of contemporary conditions as well as additional historical material, has been published in *Wisconsin Women's Law Journal*, (1987) 3.

states, such families reflected interracial sex (that is, white male sexual exploitation of Black women slaves.) In fact, both Black and white family life was undermined by the actions and guilt of ruling elite white men who violated their own social codes by having sex with Black slave women. In addition, this elite group ignored the desires of Black women and men to have marriages and families of their own.

Black single-motherhood first evolved as the manifestation of the slave woman's legal and cultural social death. Her capacity for both social and biological reproduction of slavery assured maximum profits and social control for the racial patriarch or ruling elite. However, Black single-motherhood was also a viable family type which Black men and women adopted in response to a system which did not recognize their right to a legal marriage and family. Within the slave community, single-mother families coexisted with outlawed two-parent families. After emancipation, during Reconstruction and during the segregation era, Black single-mother hood continued to provide a survival strategy for Black families still relegated to second class citizenship and social marginality by racism, apartheid, pogrom and poverty. During the desegregation era of the last thirty years, Black people have achieved legal recognition as citizens and have forced the dismantling of segregation and apartheid. But new forms of racism have emerged, characterized by racially-based economic injustice, contentious gender and class relationships within the Black community and use of the media to amplify the social sciences which camouflage, promote and shape public policies that continue racism and strengthen white nationalism. Today, Black single-motherhood is both chosen by and imposed on Black women attempting to address social and economic changes.

In each era, Black single-motherhood has been interwoven both with Black estranged and nonresidential fatherhood and the emasculated patriarchal status and power which has accompanied the social death of Black men. The sexism of the ruling elite is not only directed at women; it is also aimed at stunting the development of Black manhood, whether it takes a patriarchal or non-sexist form.

This essay examines Black single-mother families and their historical development during three eras: slavery, segregation and desegregation. It focuses on the beginnings and contemporary condition and experiences of these families. The concept "social death," which is the theoretical framework for this study, comes from Orlando Patterson's cross-cultural study, *Slavery and Social-Death.* The study includes a Black feminist perspective and expands Patterson's concept "social death" beyond the institution of slavery into the second class and marginal position of Black people within a racist society. In addition, the study examined another theoretical framework, the dialectics of oppression, and found that the debased condition and position of the oppressed always led to their conscious resistance and desire for freedom. Black resistance to social death took the form of creating viable families, whether patriarchal or female-headed, and of developing extended kinship networks along with political and protest strategies.

To consider Black women as historical human beings, all we have been taught about the assumptions and givens of historical development, societal progress and personal and political power must be unlearned. These notions have been given to us through the prism and eyes of white men, whose wealth, privilege and power have been based upon the subjugation and domination of men and women whose skin is darker. To understand the story of those darker-skinned men and women we must become both expansive and thorough, visionary and scientific, Africanized and feminist. The traditional framework upon which we have based our person and our politic, our commitment to law and society, our experiences and learning about the family and home must change if we include the history and experience of Black single-mothers.

Slavery and Women

> All fixed, fast-frozen relations, with their train of ancient and venerable prejudices, and opinions, are swept away, all new-formed ones become antiquated before they can ossify. All that is solid melts into air, all that is holy is profaned, and men at last are forced to faced . . . the real conditions of their lives and their relations with their fellow men [sic]. (Berman, 1982, p. 21; quoting Marx 1848)

In describing the vision of the modern environment and the impact of the profound transformational capacities of capitalism, Marx unwittingly also described the transition of Africans from free men and women into captured and chattelized slaves. In a larger sense he also described the essence of their relationship to a society which designated them mules of the new world economy and used racism to banish them to the realm of the socially dead.

Social death shadowed every African captive chattelized into lifelong servitude in the Americas. The now familiar story of holocaust and uprooting was underscored by color, cultural and language differences between African and European people. To be socially dead was more than being separated from the music and tastes of one's motherland. It was to exist perpetually outside the circle where people decided things, allocated resources, made laws, communicated with God, wrote histories of the past and made plans for the future. The socially dead could neither choose, nor dream; they could only watch others choose and dream.

Yet as everything traditional and familiar was fleeting and transitory for the African captives, they clung to that which remained both solid and intangible: love, spirit, freedom, and of course, family. The bare relationship of exploitation and hatred between Black and white men, and the social distance between their worlds and histories were contrasted by the connection and commitment between and among Black men, women and children.

As Patterson's study of slavery demonstrates, "the definition of slave, however recruited, is a socially dead person" (Patterson, 1982, p. 5). Slave women were subject to a particular kind of social death. "In all slaveholding societies slave couples could be and were forcibly separated and the consensual "wives" of slaves were obliged to submit sexually to their masters; slaves had no custodial claims or powers over their children and children inherited no claims or obligations to their parents" (Patterson, p. 6).

Without marriage or human right, the female slave is a sexual vessel as well as chattel. There is no patriarchy to protect her unless the master assumes the role of protector, that is, if she is his concubine and has his children. Her men have no power or status; they are socially dead and thus are unable to come to her aid, unable to father the children they sire. There are no laws to protect her because she has no place in the law.

Furthermore, as subordinate members of patriarchal societies, especially those with slaves and class hierarchy, women become socially relevant solely because of their connections to men. The patriarchy is a worldwide system in which men are the heads of their households and families and women become socialized and organized into subordinate positions. Patriarchy is a system which requires control of women's fertility and sexuality in monogamous or polygamous marriages and is based upon a sexual division of labor regulated by male chauvinism.

In terms of worldwide historical considerations, the patriarchy at one time was perhaps a humane attempt at an arrangement in which women and children had protection and stability. The patriarchy has persisted, in part, because women gain from their relationships with men: as daughters, wives, mothers or sisters. In African societies, women had social recognition as members of the society. They had social and political rights and responsibilities. They had the right to join women's societies, which often shared birth control and sexual information. Women's bonding was a recognized part of the society. The men were also in a social relationship to women in which male domination had limits and responsibilities.

The advent of slavery changed these basic relationships because the traditional patriarch, the Black man, lost his status and economic and political power, which included wardship and protection of his women. Both Black man and woman fell under the domination of the racial patriarch, the white man. This fall was disastrous because all women, even those under bondage and racism, benefit from being connected to the patriarchy of their own men, no matter how weak or emasculated the status.

Under racism and bondage, Black women lose recognition and status as "women." The only "women" are those whose men have ultimate control and domination over people of color. Thus, it becomes understood and axiomatic—to be white and female is to be "woman". and to be white and male is to be "man." Black men and women are neither man nor woman; they are nonbeings, e.g. chattel, nigger, underclass.

In the years immediately following the Jamestown settlement, white and Black men and women comingled as slaves and servants. Many Blacks, whites and Native Americans were pressed together as unfree laborers with varying statuses. Not all whites were free and not all Blacks were slaves.

> Moreover, those Blacks who were imported before about 1660 were held in various degrees of servitude, most for limited periods and a few for life. (Nash, 1974, p. 149)

The first legislative enactment making reference to Blacks was a statute in 1639 which stated that:

> All persons except Negroes are to be provided with arms and ammunition or be fined at the pleasure of governor and council. (Higgenbotham, 1978, p. 32)

In 1665, the first English slave code in New York provided that slavery was for life. By the 1680s when the first major slave codes were issued in Virginia, and Blacks were denied the right to assemble, move freely, or defend themselves, Black skin began to mean perpetual servitude and stigma. The freedom of "free" Blacks was also limited and proscribed.

During this period, the status of unmarried women servants and slaves, and their children, was also the focus of special legislation. Black and white women were usually outnumbered by their male counterparts. Interracial sexual relationships, common-law and legal marriages existed along with monogamous marriages among Black servants, slaves and free people. However, the status of the children of bound women, especially of interracial parentage, most concerned the ruling elite.

In 1662 the Virginia legislature penalized the unmarried mother indentured servant by requiring an additional two years of service, regardless of her race. However, by the 1690s the treatment of Black and white "unwed" mothers differed. Eventually, Black women slaves or servants were not punished for bearing children fathered by white men, while white women servants were punished for bearing children fathered by Black men. "A woman servant who had an illegitimate [sic] child by a black or mulatto was fined 15 pounds and if unable to pay was sold for 5 years after her time of service expired" (Higginbotham, 1978, p. 45). If the unmarried mother was a free white woman she was also "subject to a 15 pound fine or 5 years of service." In 1664, all marriages between the races were prohibited and interracial couples were banished in 1691 statutes. By 1792, whites were penalized by imprisonment if they married a Black person. But interracial relationships between white men and Black women servants and slaves were commonplace and existed outside the laws.

In fact, English traditional precedent was broken in the 1662 statute which required that "children got by an Englishman upon a Negro woman shall be bound or free according to the condition of the mother." English common law and worldwide patriarchal customs always required that the status of the child follow his father. In order to prevent a free or quasi-free mulatto class from developing, which could undermine slavery, and to assure the maximum profits of a slave labor force, which could so easily reproduce itself, the racial patriarch treated Black women and children as distinct entities. He legally isolated them from Black men and regarded them differently from white women servants.

Because the right of slaves to marry each other or to marry whites was outlawed, Black women were also denied any form of patriarchal protection. Furthermore, sexual activity between white men and slave women could not be considered rape, because these women had no legal voice or choice not to submit. By forcing Black children to follow their mother's status and condition, slave masters could deny any responsibility for paternity, thereby enslaving their own children. In addition, Black men were prevented from assuming any responsibility for the children they sired. By requiring slavery to become the lifelong condition of Black men and women, the position of Black women would almost always be unmarried, raped, enslaved, and/or childbearing.

Slave Family Life: It Was Never Our Wish to be Separated

From the beginning, slaves, the socially dead, captive African, men and fathers, women and mothers, took in all that the slave master and his hypocritical system put on them: whippings, torture and unrelenting toil. Yet they turned it around to work for themselves and their progeny: language, religion, law, and family became Afro-American tools and weapons which slaves used to hone their humanity. In spite of restrictions on marriage and family, from the beginning slaves constructed both. When they could, they wrote and received love letters from distant "husbands" and "wives.." When they could, they traveled long distances to see their families. Children knew their fathers or heard about them from their mothers.

In rejecting and ignoring the negative notions associated with Black single-motherhood, especially the separation of marriage from family, Black women assumed the role of family head. In the absence of spouses and mates, the Black single mother assumed that she and her children were a family. She protected, nurtured and fought for a new kind of family, one which emerged outside the patriarchy of her man yet remained within the oppressive sphere of the racial patriarch. Her family developed within a slave community which provided sustenance, love and resistance from the horrors of slavery. The slave community also socialized, protected and reproduced human beings who were born into families and who expected to have families of their own.

Large slave families met the financial interests of slave masters, some of whom could boast that "a plantation of 50 or 60 persons had been established from the descendents of a single female in the course of the lifetime of the original purchasers" (Gutman, 1976, p. 132). But large families also met the personal needs of slave men and women. Even when large families were begun by a single female, her children formed both two-parent and single-parent families. The birth register from the Good Hope Plantation in South Carolina, studied by historian Herbert Gutman, revealed important information about the slave family. The register was "an unusual historical document because it listed fathers' as well as mothers' names and because it covered a lengthy period of time, from 1760 until 1857. From the first to the last recorded slave birth, 175 men, women and children made up the Good Hope slave community. Of these 28 families, all but 5 of them contained a mother, father and their children" (Gutman, pp. 46–47). Two-parent households usually occurred on large plantations and coexisted with single-parent families.

The birth records also revealed another quite common practice among slaves: prenuptial intercourse and pregnancy. Many young women had children before settling into long-term marriages, a practice common to many pre-industrial societies but one which would cause considerable alarm and confusion much later, in the 1980s. In some cases a woman had children by one man in her teens, but settled into a long-term marriage with another man and had the rest of her children by him.

Prenuptial intercourse, bridal pregnancy and teenage motherhood were frequent aspects of slave family life. Most young, unmarried slave mothers lived with their families of origin when they could.

However, in spite of Good Hope and other plantations which supported long term and stable two- and one-parent households, family separations were an all too common occurrence which increased the number of single-mother families. Fear of separation was constantly hanging over families. Stable marriages and committed relationships were used by slave masters to keep their slaves obedient. Lewis Clarke, an ex-slave, explained, "if a woman slave had a husband and children, and somebody asked her if she would like her freedom? Would she tell 'em, yes? If she did, she'd be down the river to Louisiana in no time, and her husband and children never know what become of her" (Blassingame, 1977, p. 153).

Some slave men left their women and children behind, thus creating Black female heads of families. Henry Bibb, in a letter to his former owner, attributed his flight from home and family to his treatment.

> "To be compelled to stand by and see you whip and slash my wife without mercy when I could afford her no protection, not even by offering myself to suffer the lash in her place, was more than I felt it to be the duty of a slave husband to endure, while the way was open to Canada." (Blassingame, p. 49)

His wife and children undoubtedly continued to endure the whip and hard work without him.

George Pleasant, a hard-working father and husband wrote, "If I live to see Nexct [sic] year I shall have my own time from master by giving him 100 and twenty dollars a year . . . I hope with gods [sic] helpe [sic] that I may be abble [sic] to rejoys [sic] with you on the earth" (Blassingame, p. 19). Fathers and husbands worked to purchase themselves from their masters and then to redeem their wives and children from the same servitude. Because they were legally prevented from remaining in slave-holding areas, such free husbands and fathers were separated from their wives and children for long periods of time. They often tried to raise the money with the help of nothern abolitionists, though sometimes women and children were separated and sold before the money could be raised.

Black women sadly remained separated from the men they loved. One such wife writes, "I have no news to write you, only the children are all well. I want to see you very much, but am looking forward to the promest [sic] time of your coming. Oh, Dear Dangerfield, com [sic] this fall without fail, mony [sic] or no mony [sic]. I want to see you so much" (Blassingame, p. 117). Many single mothers never saw their husbands and mates again, though they frequently sought to find them after slavery ended. Other Black single mothers were widows such as Phoebe on the Good Hope plantation who "was still living with five of her nine children. Jack had been the father of the first four; Tom the father of the rest" (Gutman, p. 47).

By the eve of the emancipation, the slave community had become a powerful and distinct social construction which had persevered and protected the slave. The slave community, perhaps begun with the sexual exploitation of a single young slave woman, was often a network of blood and fictive kin which supported resistance to the slave system.

Ironically, Black single mothers, as unprotected "non-women" who lived alone, became human beings in their own right and were thus "annulled as woman, that is, as woman in her historical stance of wardship under the entire male hierarchy" (Davis, 1981, p. 7). Black slave women could "freely" participate with other members of the community in resisting slavery. They could attempt to protect their own children, a role usually reserved soley for the patriarch. For instance, Moses Grandy, an ex-slave, remembered his mother hiding his brothers and sisters in the woods to save them from being sold and fighting back when her young child was about to be sold (Frazier, 1939, p. 42). When slavery ended, Black mothers who were unmarried, widowed or separated from their mates had become a distinct family which complimented and often fostered two-parent households. These families and extended families in turn made it possible for Black single-mother families to survive. Help with childcare and childbearing, emotional support for lonely women, sharing of food and shelter, as well as protection from torture and hard work characterized the mutual support which had developed in slave communities.

These communities persisted in spite of the legal and economic contours of slavery and national politics. The expansion and shift of the slave economy from the upper to the lower South during the early nineteenth century forcibly separated slave families over long and unsurmountable distances.

> About one in ten (slave) men and women born between 1835 and 1845 had experienced a forcible separation by 1864, a percentage sufficiently high to indicate that in the pre-Civil War decades the peculiar institution retained its grimmest quality, the breakup of marriages and the damage thereby inflicted on husbands and wives, parents and children. (Gutman, p. 146)

Black single-mother families made it possible for slaves to spread family and kinship cultural values in the same way as two-parent families. New fictive kinship relationships among slaves on plantations far from their families of origin helped slaves survive the trauma of separation. Afro-American culture was also spread by slaves who moved into the lower South, thus fostering creation of Blacks as a homogeneous people, not merely diffused slave groupings.

During slavery, the slave and the slave master were in constant struggle: the slave master attempted to restrict the slave, while slaves pressed to expand their rights and opportunities for a free life, which especially included the right to a family within their own communities. They struggled for marriage and families in spite of the pronouncements of a North Carolina Supreme Court Justice, who, writing in 1853, expressed a common opinion:

> Our law requires no solemnity or form in regard to the marriage of slaves, and whether they 'take up' with each other by express permission of their owner, or from a mere impulse of nature, in obedience to the command 'multiply and replenish the earth' cannot, in the contemplation of the law, make any sort of difference. (Gutman, p. 146)

Justice Taney's decision in the Dred Scott case was more to the point and reiterated the social death of slaves, regardless of their efforts to resist:

> We think they are not, and that they are not included, and were not intended to be included, under the word "citizens" in the Constitution, and can, therefore, claim none of the rights and privileges which that instrument provides for and secures to citizens of the United States . . . [T]hat neither the class of persons who had been imported as slaves, nor their descendants, whether they had become free or not, were then acknowledged as part of the people. (Commager, 1958, pp. 340–41)

Black Families after Slavery: The Land and Love Unrealized

Slaves fought against the law and the economics of slavery, and included themselves as "people" and "citizens." They worked with abolitionists and free brethren and sisters to topple the slave system. Neither war, amendments nor proclamations alone ended slavery. The political mobilizations of abolitionists, the campaigns of Harriet Tubman, John Brown, and other conductors on the underground railroad, the changing national economy, and Black labor's withdrawal from the southern plantations during the war combined to end slavery. The slave family and community which sustained and nurtured the slaves and their progeny helped to prepare the slave for freedom.

After slavery ended, large numbers of the newly-freed people legalized long-term slave unions by marrying. They desired to legalize their families and begin a new self- and community-defined legitimacy. The dislocation and devastation of the war and continued attacks by former masters caused the ex-slaves hardship, but they persevered in creating self-sustaining farm communities based on the labor of family and kin. The slaves hoped Black women would at last be able to care for their husbands and children without having to work outside their own homes and farms.

Many women did settle into marriages in which men headed their families and households, upholding both African and American patriarchal values about monogamy, sexual modesty, and divisions of labor based on gender. However, there were significant numbers of Black female-headed households and Black single mothers. Young Black single mothers remained within the households of their parents, and female-headed households tended to belong to widows or older women who had been separated from their husbands and spouses for long periods.

Values about the negative aspects of childbearing outside marriage were in part fostered by the churches and schools established in the Black community. Many ex-slaves wanted to put the horror of sexual abuse against slave women behind them and establish families headed by married couples. Harry McMillan, a former slave said, "They are thought low of by their companions unless they get a husband before the child is born and if they cannot the shame grows until they do get a husband" (Gutman, pp. 444–45). Conversely, the journalist Nordhoff said, "It was held no shame for a girl to bear a child under any circumstances" (Gutman, p. 66). Special words described the status of children born prior to or outside of settled unions, namely "stolen" or "outside" children.

Outright promiscuity was condemned in all Black communities, even though prenuptial intercourse, teenage marriage and pregnancy continued in most. When children were conceived outside of common-law or legal marriages, the mothers and children were stigmatized but rarely ostracized or banished. Women could overcome sitgmatization by becoming faithful Christians and church-goers, and faithful and hard working wives. Thus, social stigma against "illegitimacy" coexisted with the social reality of Black single mothers and their families.

Internal community concerns over values and morals as they pertained to single mothers were overshadowed, however, by the political and economic realities of late nineteenth-century Black southern life. The promise of Black enfranchisement, economic self-sufficiency and social equality were eroded by pogrom, lynching and racial violence. These horrors affected many of the very Black men who strove to build their family life on the economic base of private farm ownership. Prosperous, even modest, Black farmers became dangerous Black men in the eyes of the white power structure, especially, though not exclusively, in the Black-belt South.

The migrants to Kansas who left the South to improve and protect themselves from pogrom often left in family groups. When ex-slaves did not, Black single-mother families were created: "I have no family along with me; I have a wife and two children down south; I brought my parents with me" (Gutman, 1976, p. 434). James Brown, on the other hand, brought his wife, three orphans, his mother-in-law and five of her six children with him. She had no husband (Gutman, 1976, p. 435). Women whose husbands were lynched or run out by night riders had to rely upon themselves and kin to help support their families in the rural southern Black communities. A letter from Joseph Starks asking the Kansas governor for advice about migration provides a glimpse of those troubled times for Black men and women alike.

> We want to come out, and have no money hardly. We have to be in secret or be shot, and [are] not allowed to meet. . . . We have about fifty widows in our band that are workmen and farmers also. The white men here take our wives and daughters and do [with] them as they please, and we are shot if we say anything about it. . . . We are sure to have to leave or be killed. (Gutman, 1976, p. 437)

By the 1880s, "[w]omen at least forty years old headed a large percentage of father-absent households and subfamilies; many of these had been conventional two-parent households in which the husband had died." (Gutman, 1976, pp. 444, 489) (or perhaps had been killed or run out of town). Gutman studied four urban and four rural areas and found that 28% of the households and subfamilies in urban areas were headed by women, and, in rural areas, 16% were headed by women. Single women and mothers often moved to urban areas in search of wage-earning work to sustain themselves and their families.

Furthermore, as Black families continued to slip more and more into the mire of peonage and poverty all family members were needed to work for wages or shares. Economic pressures prevailed over marital custom. In order for families to survive most Black women went back to work in the fields and kitchens of white men under slave-like economically and sexually exploitative conditions. But the ideology and hope of the Black patriarchy remained, assisted by Calvinistic religious principles spread by Black churches, Black schools and the emerging Black ruling elite. Many extolled the virtues of marital rather than common-law unions, monogamous rather than serial monogamistic relationships, and childbearing after marriage rather than birth outside of marriage. Those who abided by the virtues of monogamous marriage were accorded status and respect. Men who worked to take care of their families and women who were loyal to their men were regarded as the ideal and preferred family. As long as the options for Black women were only patriarchal marriage or severe economic struggle alone, women as well as men strove for the ideal of monogamous marriage, in spite of the forces which hampered them from obtaining it.

The cheap dependable labor of Black women as domestics and busy-season farm hands also motivated local white politicians, police and merchants to prevent, in some cases by statute, Black women from staying home to work on their family farms. Thus, soon after the end of the Civil War, whether married or single, Black women had become wage-earning workers to support the depressed wages of Black men. Black girls were socialized to become mothers, wives, and workers, often workers first. By the early twentieth century it became evident that rigid sex role divisions would never be realized for large numbers of Black families. Black family members were constantly called upon to adjust and shift to forces stronger than their will, desire, culture, and ideology. Family breakups were not merely the mark of chattel slavery, they were the mark of wage slavery and peonage as well.

Black people had become quite adept at making their families and households into havens from oppression. However, they were often havens where male dominance and power relationships also prevailed. Black women were the "slave of a slave" within their marriages. Poor Black men, though oppressed and dominated themselves and dependent upon their women's wages, could also be abusive and brutal toward their wives and children. Black women often looked the other way while their men fathered children by other women. Undoubtedly some Black women also suppressed their own lesbian desires and ignored their husband's homosexual relationships. Abortions, viewed as un-Christian and sinful, were nevertheless performed "underground." Women were often vague about the fathers, birthdates and relationships of some children in the family. Young Black women working in the cities sent many of their "outside children" back home to the rural South or Caribbean to be raised by their kin.

The period of legal segregation lasted nearly a century, from the 1896 "separate but equal" decision of Plessy v. Ferguson until the 1954 decision in Brown v. The Board of Education, which overturned the 1896 doctrine. During that time, Black people suffered the quasi-free status of all manumitted slaves. Though not designed to include people of color and white women, the American commitment to legal democracy became a powerful weapon in the stuggle to end racial segregation in the United

States. But this commitment was offset by American color prejudice and racism. Both the commitment and the aversion amplified the movement and the struggles of Black people.

The racism, peonage and pogrom in the South caused Black people to move into urban areas, so that by mid-century the majority of Black people had become urban dwellers. The exodus had become even more poignant because of the low status and wages of Black workers. Black women merely exchanged southern for northern domestic servitude, with some increase in wages and some personal mobility. Black men moved from rural farm work and menial labor to northern menial labor and the lowest level of industrialized work, lower than white women or immigrants, both in terms of wages and job security.

The movement of Blacks into urban areas was accompanied by more than poverty and lower caste status, however; a Black cultural renaissance, the strengthening of Black education and religious institutions and the expression of profound political and ideological concerns also emerged. The century began with white social scientists questioning Blacks' humanity; twenty years later whites were dancing to Black music, reading books by Black authors and slowly developing a personal and cultural fascination with Black individuals and expressions, while still maintaining a racist society and protecting white interests.

By the 1920s questions about class solidarity were raised by Black workers in every sector of workers' organizations, from the work place to the unions to the Communist Party. Marcus Garvey assembled the largest group of Blacks ever in one organization to preach Black pride, self-development and racial separation. Meanwhile, other Black leaders, such as A. Philip Randolph and W.E.B. Du Bois, continued to press for civil rights, in spite of lynching and coon shows or class and nationalist movements. But the protests and the writings, and the emergence of a distinct Black culture and sense of peoplehood, often masked the underlying similarities in values, especially family values, shared by most Blacks and whites. Puritanical values about sexuality were backed by references to the Bible. Regular church attendance was an integral part of the Black as well as white experience. Certainly both Blacks and whites at least professed the same basic Protestant religious and spiritual value system, and though Black theologians assert a more liberatory tradition, this difference does not negate the common religious heritage and roots shared by the two groups.

Similarly, Black people lived in family groupings, fell in love, married, and raised children. In fact, Black people extended their family concerns for the future of their own children into an intensive and extensive social movement for welfare, education and other health benefits for children. Both the white and Black communities adhered to rather strict notions of proper sexual conduct. Prostitution in the Black community was confined to areas, or "houses." Young people were warned against associating with "those" women and listening to their music (jazz, blues), though daring men and women frequently did. Also, customers of prostitutes were frequently white men as well as black men. Homosexuality was taboo and not viewed as a valued social practice in the Black community, though gay men and lesbians were treated individually and often viewed with pity and sympathy, rather than hatred.

But single-motherhood occupied a different place in the Black community than in the white community. It seems that unless they were widowed, white single mothers were viewed as prostitutes and brutally ostracized. But Black single mothers, if they worked hard to provide for their families, were generally accepted into working class communities everywhere, though less accepted in Black middle-class communities.

Analyses of the Black family, generally reflecting both Black patriarchal and white racial standards, have been common in the twentieth century. Nearly all studies and discussions have focused on the Black family's economic destitution and either its lack of or its possession of strong survival and cultural mechanisms. Most have failed to discuss the sexist position and oppression of women within the family and community as powerful rationales for marital breakup. Nor have they included the strengths and choices of Black women as factors in creating and sustaining Black single-mother families.

Social Movements and New Racism

During the segregation period, most Black families did adapt to the norm of two-parent married families with strong male heads but were still neither equal to whites nor free from oppression. In fact all Black family members regardless of family type were attempting to survive the continued terror and subjegation of apartheid in the South and the vicious "ghettoization of Black life" in the North. During the years immediately after WWII, the dismantling of segregation was uppermost in the minds of Black family and community members, especially those who wanted a better life for Black children. Few stopped to demand that those children come only from two-parent homes.

The movement for civil rights was an all-embracing Black community effort to change the practices of a society that had long denied them equal access and opportunity. Its original goals were to end legal segregation, provide movement and access to public facilities regardless of race, promote integrated schools and equal employment. The goals were moderate and fell within the existing parameters of the legal system.

The influences of the civil rights movement quickly spread to many other aspects of the society. White women who had participated in the movement unearthed their own history of protest and current personal grievances. This reaction created second wave feminism and a women's movement which attacked women's oppression within the patriarchal family as well as second class citizenry within the larger society. The women's movement pushed for flexible gender roles, shared power relationships and respect for diverse families (Evans, 1979). Feminists further pointed out that the traditional white nuclear family, the standard against which Black families were being measured, was not an ideal to be emulated because a woman's place within that idealized family was one of abused and dominated appendage to her husband and his property.

Both the civil rights and women's movements demanded jobs to accompany social equality as the economy was simultaneously being transformed from an industrial to a service employment base. The service-based economy increased the employment of women within the economy. By 1970, for the first time in 250 years of wage work, Black women were no longer employed predominately as domestic workers or farm laborers. Thirty-two percent were employed as white collar workers and 21% were working in sales and clerical jobs. These social and economic changes accelerated Black women's "de-mammification." "De-mammification" was also accompanied by changes in Black men's and women's consciousness, perceptions and feelings, as Black women moved from the mammy role in private households into clerical and secretarial roles in public corporations and bureaucracies. For many women the consistent meager wage gave them the wherewithal they needed to dissolve unwanted marriages and relationships. Black single-motherhood during the post segregation era made a radical shift: Black women no longer considered themselves primarily tied to their legal or common law husbands.

The social movements of the 1960s and the "de-mammification" of Black women changed the personal, familial and societal norms, but it did not transform the economy or the political power in the nation. By the 1970s, another social movement gained momentum. Predominately white male, middle class and middle American, it embraced and promoted the traditional values of Puritanism, patriarchy and racial purity of the founding fathers and pushed American nationalism to new heights of militarism and chauvinism. The conservative movement equated the American way of life with two-parent, hard-working Christian families. By the election of President Ronald Reagan in 1980, it had gained national authority.

The conservative social movement exacerbated the new racism of the desegregation era. The Black community, which had become a visible stimulus for interpreting social problems and promoting public policies to meet them, became less and less powerful. The civil rights movement had effectively responded to and ended the racism of segregation, lynch mobs and overt hatred. But the new racism was more systematic, subtle and rational. In fact charges of racism were viewed as inaccurate and obsolete. The proponents of the new racism saw economics and motivation, and not color or culture, as the principal reasons for Black inequity. "They don't want to work" was the response to charges of racial discrimination and lack of jobs. "No more handouts" was the answer to demands for increased government spending to help the oppressed. "They have themselves to blame" was the reply to demands for government actions on homelessness and destitution. (For one of the best recent examples of these policy ideas see Murray, 1984.)

Under the new racism, ideology replaced sociology and rhetoric replaced attention to economic reality in examining Black people's condition and position. Black single mothers, especially poor teenagers, had become the symbol of all that was wrong with Black people and women and their movements.

Poverty is the contemporary form of continuing the social death of Black people that has always been the design of a racist society. To be Black and poor is the current version of being Black and a slave. But being poor, stripped of all its ideological and moralistic veneer, only means that one does not have the resources to meet one's needs. Just as slavery was not a system that could make human beings chattel, poverty is not a condition which makes the poor inhuman.

Current social policy perpetuates the deliberate creation of a strata of people—Black men, women and children—who live outside the society of men and women who decide things, allocate resources, make laws, communicate with God, write histories of the past and make plans for the future. The new racism promotes the fabrication of an underclass (or is it a permanent caste) system that masks the displacement of the Black working class or those denied economic enfranchisement within the society.

In the long history of Black people in this land, we have tried everything: marches, petitions, speeches, nonviolent and violent campaigns. Still social death separates us from the power and wealth we deserve. We might have to try all those things and more, for we remain at the mercy of those who want us to have neither power nor wealth. We've gone around to come around, back to the beginning, where all we have to fall back on are the men and women who love us and nurture and protect us: our families.

11

Religion and Rights Consciousness in the Antebellum Woman's Rights Movement

Elizabeth B. Clark

The meeting of feminists at Seneca Falls in July of 1848 marked the nominal beginning of the movement which in the nineteenth century was labeled "woman's rights." For us that term has become commonly interchangeable with "suffrage," and we often assume that "woman's rights" describes a seventy-odd year campaign to gain civil and political power and protection from a government which—although it had perpetrated outrages against women and slaves—had an unquestioned legitimacy as the guarantor and enforcer of rights.

Historical interpretations of the woman's movement have reaffirmed this picture, stressing the republican origins of women's claims and their easy fit within the tradition of American constitutionalism. The movement's biographers have placed feminists' arguments well within the secular political tradition of the nineteenth century. They have treated "natural rights" as a form of "super-right"—more emphatic, an appeal to historical tradition, but not qualitatively different from constitutional claims—and natural law language as formulaic fist shaking (Kraditor, 1965; DuBois, 1978).

Historians have overstated both the secular identity of antebellum feminism and the centrality of suffrage to that movement. The rather abstract language of rights used by the Founding Fathers was common currency in America, and women drew on it for help in fashioning their arguments and in making public appeals. But feminists did not don the Founders' philosophy of rights as a perfectly fitting suit of mail. Many were initiated into organized feminism through the philosophies of liberal Protestantism so prevalent in antebellum reform thought. The con-

---

This essay appeared in fuller form as "Religion, Rights, and Difference: The Origins of Rights Consciousness in the Antebellum Suffrage Movement" in *Wisconsin Women's Law Journal.* (1987)3.

tent of their rights thinking was informed by a deeply religious sensibility which stressed the interconnections between rights and responsibilities, between civil and domestic relations, and between the workings of the state and of the home. Suffrage did not automatically take pride of place in the panoply of rights women sought in the period before the Civil War, but stood as one goal among many, and not the most important.

Further, rights consciousness was originally rooted in domestic concerns for many women, who saw them as a means of achieving protection for themselves and their families while pursuing the ends of social justice. Such an understanding of rights was in full accord with the liberal Protestant imperative for the full development of the individual and his or her full participation in society. The demand for rights did not emerge theoretically full-blown from any woman's head, but was born the usual way, amid a welter of personal and familial concerns.

Finally, although "equality" was the watchword of the movement, in the antebellum period it referred largely to a negative proposition; the removal of the false and artificial restraints of woman's sphere, restraints which prevented her full entry into public life. "Equal" was not "like," and although feminists ideally hoped that the destruction of spheres could bring about the growth of common sympathies between men and women, their attitudes toward male culture were rooted in the genuine, material differences in men's and women's lives which existed in education, opportunity, political entitlement, and social expectation in nineteenth-century America. Although women demanded equality, they also predicated their entry into the political world on a moral sensibility which most saw as uniquely feminine, and which served as the basis for their political agenda and their theory of rights.

Women's Legal Culture

To understand what significance "law" and "rights" had for mid-nineteenth-century female activists, we must interpret their concepts of power and governance according to the Protestant ethos which informed their world vision. Within this Christian framework, the possession of power was construed in a peculiar way. Both evangelical revivalists and Garrisonian abolitionists—two groups which influenced budding feminist thought profoundly—were suspicious of power and of its potential for corruption in human hands, where it could so easily work against God's designs. The power of the husband, the father, the slaveowner, the legislator, the judge—all were potentially abusive, or abusive by the fact of their existence, as intrusions between God and the individual (Perry, 1973). For many Christians, morality remained sharply antithetical to concepts of power or human governance, an attitude which in many respects early woman's rights advocates shared. Certainly in the 1850s the Christian ethos still shaped women's apprehension of power relationships, and of what kind of action they could most effectively undertake in the world.

Given the early woman's movement's understanding of power—apprehension over its direct exercise, fear and distrust of the institutions of government, seeing morality and official power as antithetical, belief in change worked from within rather than from without—it is difficult to interpret the demand for woman's rights strictly within the framework of secular liberal political theory. Most feminists were more pragmatic than the Garrisonians; they lacked the wild, intense piety which prepared that group to renounce all human organizations on the spot, including their own, in favor of some form of mutual self-government which their faith had not yet revealed. Still, a strain of anti-institutionalism was strong within feminism in the antebellum years. Women repeatedly resolved to

> rely no longer on organizations of any kind—upon neither national or state, secret or public societies of any description . . . but to depend upon . . . [our] own energetic, determined, and individual effort for . . . the final triumph of our glorious principles.[1]

This was hardly the stuff of legal positivism.

The majority of feminists believed that legal and political change—changes in statutes, court rulings, the common law, interpretations of women's political rights—were symptomatic, and could only reflect deeper change on the level of public opinion worked by individuals coming to a real understanding of natural laws. Even Elizabeth Cady Stanton, certainly one of the best versed of the feminists in legal matters and a fiery advocate of political measures, opined that "[P]ublic sentiment is higher than laws—laws in advance of the people are mere chaff."[2] Most reformers believed that reeducation of the moral sentiments was the way to bring public opinion around, and that old laws could not withstand new leanings: "The ballot box is not worth a straw, until woman is ready to use it . . . The moment that woman is ready to go to the ballot box, there is not a constitution that will stand in the country."[3] Far from looking to government for remedies and favors, there was a strong emphasis on self-help and a belief that, by readying themselves and their neighbors, activists could bring about the desired transformation without seeking direct political change or soliciting governmental intervention.[4] Women strove, not for new laws to reshape public life, but to promote moral sentiments and their adoption by the whole community. Women judged progress, not by citizens' begrudging acceptance of a law eked out through determined assaults on the legislature, but by a reorientation of each individual conscience toward God, and a consequent righting of public opinion.

This vision is at odds with the positivist view of law and government which plays an important part in our conceptualization of rights. Rights consciousness today implies recognition of a mediating state power to protect against encroachment, and usually looks to human government or a constitution as the source and guarantor of rights. Between 1848 and 1860, however, positive or positivist attitudes were not a major feature of women's legal repertoire, which held only a nascent recognition of the law's transformative potential. For the many who believed that divine and natural laws ruled the world in intimate detail, human legislation loomed small. The determined belief in law as a constitutive or transformative force grew as women became politicized and moved outward from the revival-style convention to engagement with state and national legislatures. But in the early years, the shared wisdom was that law was a creature of public sentiment, and any legal revision which did not derive from an underlying shift in the common mindset had a futile career ahead of it.

For most, a budding hope that law would provide them redress or protection was seriously compromised by the belief that the vision of law as external authority instead of as self-government constituted the problem, and that genuine reform would entail the erosion of government which sought to coerce human behavior. Feminists identified human law with the dictum "might makes right." Women viewed the evolution of society as entailing the ascendance of moral and mental over physical might, and the consequent withering away of the state as an instrument of control. Divorced from law and legal processes as they were, and with their understanding of the corrupt nature of humanly held power, antebellum feminists were not simply seeking inclusion in the revolutionary settlement, or in the system as it stood. When it came to law and governance, their attitude is best expressed by the text they so frequently quoted—"Behold, I make all things new."

Feminists consistently pitted themselves against what they perceived as a distinctly male culture of law and politics in developing their critique of male institutions. Nevertheless, the idea of a distinctive woman's politics or legal culture has not received much play in the scholarship. Despite a commitment to "equality," nineteenth-century feminists did not define it as sameness: they entertained strong beliefs in equality, likeness and dissimilarity, and a womanly mission, simultaneously.

Certainly the claim of equality between men and women, a staple of woman's rights rhetoric, radically contradicted deeply entrenched social thought on gender roles. Rarely has a society postulated such elemental differences between men and women as mid-nineteenth-century American society did. Feminists' assertion that women had the same souls, same moral duties, same intellects and hopes as men opened the way to a more fully integrated public sphere than was ever possible before: we are still dining out on the capital of that ideal. The assertion of equality was a protest lodged against discrimination in both law and custom, against whatever rules or attitudes restrained women's natural energies or kept them in a dwarfed or crippled state. In the early years they envisioned legal equality entailing the abolition of all laws which weighed disproportionately on women. After that, women's unobstructed energy would surely bring them into full parity.

But while the ideal of equality held great meaning for women, it did not eradicate their understanding of their social and familial roles and their larger interests as being distinct from men's. In twentieth-century society, where civil equality is held up as the highest stage of the citizen's development, justice is blind to individual characteristics, and the fungibility of the bearers is the measure of rights. This kind of equality—ignorant of gender, race, role, duty, station—was initially incomprehensible to most feminists. Instead, they argued in the name of equality for rights that would allow each to fulfill her role and attain her highest individual destiny decreed by God, whatever it might be. An important degree of difference was built into this idea of equality, which did not

> mean either identity or likeness . . . of the two sexes, but equivalence of dignity, necessity, and use; admitting all differences and modifications which shall not affect a just claim to equal liberty in development and action.[5]

The apprehension of their own special interests and duties which imbued women's politics in the 1850s did create some friction. The popular cultural idealization of woman's superhuman goodness, her angelic nature, raised the hackles of those who suspected men of packing women off to heaven prematurely to limit their influence on earth. But although they were prickly and resistant to what they considered demeaning characterizations on the part of men, women reformers had their own ideas of their goodness and what role it would play in a reformed society. In envisioning a political future women saw themselves endowing men with their own traits far more often than they saw themselves taking on the traits of men. In the years before the Civil War, woman's rights activists were inspired by a sense of equality; but they were also motivated by a discontent with the existing order which fell out along gender lines, and emphasized the differences, both natural and cultural, between the sexes. When arguments for woman's rights came largely from abolitionism, equality was a natural focus.

But as women developed their own well-articulated positions, they began to enumerate their grievances with male management. The belief in woman's moral mission to clean up politics and society was one to which many women openly or tacitly adhered from the movement's beginnings. Difference was both the agent of change in this scheme, and the problem to be overcome. Women had little doubt that they would perform the duties of officer better than men, firmly opposing poverty, intemperance, and their social roots, and promoting "all just and beneficent purposes."[6]

Nor does the movement's moral consciousness necessarily suggest that it was politically immature, insular, or domestic in its focus. If anything, it suggests broader concerns, a fuller life within the reform community, than was true of suffragism after the war, when narrower legal and political concerns took precedence. Many of the pacific dictates of liberal Christianity—"feminine submissiveness"—were known in another guise as politically oppositional stands taken by reformers convinced that problems like slavery and territorial aggression would diminish under their rule.[7] Calls to non-violence and reason in place of force were grounded in a Christian tradition, but served in the antebellum years as a potent charge against the government which perpetrated such crimes. By adding the feminine to the masculine element, women were rejecting the political sphere men were carving out for themselves, one seemingly cut loose from the constraints of traditional moral principles of governance. Women felt strongly that the absence of either element would bring results fatal both to justice and morality. Above all, women manifested a wish to substitute the principles of non-coercion, non-violence, and consensual government for the Hobbesian arrangements of the day.[8]

Women activists vigorously disputed their critics' charges that they were being unsexed through their political activities, and affirmed their own femininity and security in their roles as wives and mothers. No one rebutted those charges more effectively than Frances Gage when she complained,

> They (men) cannot get up a picture of a woman's rights meeting . . . but they must put cigars and pipes in our mouths, make us sit cross-legged, or hoist our feet above their legitimate positions—making us behave as nearly as possible as disgustingly and unbecomingly as themselves . . . They have . . . so long associated their vulgar thoughts and feelings with constitutional rights and privileges that they seem to think them inseparable . . . [9]

Gage in her pithy way put her finger on a thread which runs consistently through women's concerns in this period—resentment and dislike of male political culture, from which women were so excluded. Male opponents of the woman's franchise often argued that polling places were too rough for women; feminists deplored this self-confessed pollution of civic functions, finding man in his role as political animal repugnant, whether as lawyer, judge, voter, or clubman.

This attitude translated into often made claims that male legislators could not represent women adequately, not because they would not, but because the difference in their natures and interests meant that men were not capable of such representation. Ernestine Rose argued cleverly that, if man's nature was different, he could not understand woman's needs sufficiently to make laws for her; and if the same, there was no reason to exclude women from full political participation.[10] Cool argumentation aside, even Stanton clearly felt the outrage and slight when she asked,

> "Shall the most sacred relations of life be called up and rudely scanned by men who, by their own admission, are so coarse that women cannot meet them even at the polls without contamination? . . . How can man enter into the feelings of . . . [a] mother? Shall laws which come from the logical brains of man take cognizance of the violence done to the moral and affectional natures which predominate, as it is said, in woman?"[11]

Antoinette Brown Blackwell tended toward essentialist rather than cultural explanations of men's and women's differences, but her conclusion was the same: "The law is wholly masculine: it is created by our type or class of man nature. The framers of all legal compacts are thus restricted to the . . . thoughts, feelings, biases of men . . . we can be represented only by our peers."[12]

It was this dangerous isolation of the masculine from the feminine which feminists hoped to remedy, feeling that "so long as woman is required to take care of the morals of the community and men to take charge of the politics, having . . . separate interests in these two great matters, we shall have a strange and incongruous state of things."[13] Traditional networks of women's influence—local, personal, religious networks which operated through churches, voluntary organizations, and familial contacts—had been strong in pre-industrial America. Through these networks women had wielded social influence disproportionate to their formal standing. But the growing cult of electoral politics—male politics—and the shifting of power away from the local to more centralized levels, undermined women's leverage in the community (Wellman, 1980; Hewitt, 1984; Baker, 1984). The early feminist agenda is remarkable, not because it tried to vault women from the private into the public arena leaving the wall intact, as scholars have suggested, but because it sought to eradicate spheres entirely, and with them the growing and dangerous split between public governance and private morality. Such a distinction made little sense to women reformers. Rather, through the interdependence of the sexes they hoped to integrate public with private, legal with moral, in a common standard of universal governance. Women's denigration of male political life for its insularity and its brutishness betrays both resentment and understanding of the dangers which the isolation of politics posed for women, a politics conducted outside their scope of influence.

Law, Nature, and Rights

Feminism also evolved an articulate critique of the exclusive legal world, criticism informed by moral and religious concerns. The legal system came in for a constant barrage of criticism from feminists who occasionally took gratuitous swipes at other professions, but reserved their most biting criticisms for clerics and lawyers. Most often, women depicted lawyers and judges as morally and spiritually corrupt, "winebibbers" with "bullet heads and red faces," who commonly resorted to "fisticuffs and duelling" rather than restraint and reason.[14] Like religion, law represented human corruption of a divine institution, but a particularly egregious instance of male corruption. The drinking, swearing legislator who would rather resort to brute force than logic and reason was pictured as a throwback to a less advanced stage of civilization, and as the opposite of the "Christian Gentleman" who was many reformers' and evangelicals' manly ideal (Rosenberg, 1973).

Women revealed the level of frustration and outrage they felt with male legislators in many ways, claiming that law had placed women in an intolerable position by refusing the legal right of divorce, while refusing at the same time legal protection of maternal rights, property, and earnings for wives of drunkards and insolvents; "woman cannot obey nature's first law of self-preservation without violating man's (laws)," a fact which inspired "indignation and hatred of our laws and law-makers." Elizabeth Cady Stanton was fond of saying that law gave women such protection as "the wolf the lamb, or the eagle the dove."[15]

At least on paper, the *Lily* encouraged women in acts of self-help like the burning or trashing of their husbands' haunts, and congratulated one unusual woman on horsewhipping the barkeeper, citing it as a justifiable act of self-defense.[16] Abolitionists' manifestoes on human rights and natural law had laid a strong groundwork for a critique of human laws like those enabling slavery and rumselling as counter to the laws of

God and Nature (Hosmer, 1852; Hurlbut, 1845). The *Lily's* correspondents boldly and repeatedly urged women to ignore the law's shabby cloak of legitimacy, and act according to higher right: "Resistance to tyranny is obedience to God . . . if the vampyres of the law will continue to suck the life blood of their fellow men and spread destruction and death all around them, then let women step boldly forward and take matters into their own hands."[17] The question of damage to taverns was dismissed with the argument that a tavern "ceases to be property when it is employed to destroy the people."[18]

Again, in the antebellum years women were brought to this pitch not as much by high-minded notions of equality as by a vivid apprehension of their wrongs. Here the problem of alcohol took on great significance. In licensing the liquor trade legislators were acting, not just to withhold rights, but to commit clear wrongs, with grave consequences for women. Woman's righters were uniformly temperance advocates as well, and felt that it was in permitting the sale of alcohol that government truly showed itself to be morally deformed. They castigated the rumseller; but far guiltier than the rumseller was the law, which "threw its arms around him who was causing the ruin . . . [with] legalized poison." Women reformers in this period judged what they perceived as male law by a higher standard, and found it wanting. They could see little difference between "the guilt of killing a man by arsenic or alcohol, or between stealing his property by first stealing his reason, or breaking into his house at midnight, and carrying it off when the owner is in peaceful slumber." As one woman declared, "God did not say, 'Thou shalt not kill with a pistol.' "[19] In the one case, the law would punish the slayer; in the other it protected him, at the expense of the wives and children of drunkards. A great deal of time and energy went into redefining crimes, and comparing various statutory crimes to those of the rumseller. Was the highwayman who pulled the trigger guiltier than the one who held the horses? Were either more guilty than the man who sold drink to an alcoholic?[20]

A deeply Christian conception of moral consequences underlay this assessment of man's law. Women saw that with liquor, legislators were concerned, not with preventing or punishing wrong, but with limiting liability. They felt strongly that legal doctrines of causation and the treatment of the liquor trade as an issue of economic regulation only obscured the nature of the transaction. Moral consequences could not be rightly limited by legal doctrine. "We touch not a wire but vibrates in eternity . . . we see not in this life the end of human actions. The influence reverberates."[21] This was as true for evil as for good, and for the *Lily*'s writers it was impossible not to see the misfortunes of many homeless, abused, hungry women and children pouring straight from the rumseller's bottle in a chain of accountability which no legal sanction could interrupt. For "sin perpetuates itself forever. Like the ocean ripple, its influence is beyond all calculation . . ." No amount of legal hair-splitting could excuse men from their Christian duty, nor protect them on the day when "God will call upon them to answer, 'WHERE IS THY BROTHER?' "[22]

This sense of woman's wrongs at the hands of the intemperate was extremely fertile ground for rights consciousness, as women felt an increasing duty to protect themselves, each other, and their children from man's depredations on their persons and property. Those who invoke "rights" usually endow them with transcendental qualities, but "rights" itself is not an ahistorical concept with constant meaning over time. Rather, it denotes a set of values or demands used in a particular political context which gives them meaning. Antebellum feminists seized the language of rights and transformed it with their own ideas and concerns. This does not mean that women rejected the republican ideals of the founding generation. Revolutionary rhetoric, the enlightenment vision of inalienable human rights, was a critical tool in helping women to envision a new status, and express their demands to a male public. But the language women spoke among themselves appealed to a larger sensibility.

A telling instance of this discrepancy occurred at a woman's rights meeting in Ohio which was held in 1850 for the purpose of influencing the work of that state's upcoming constitutional convention. The official "Memorial" written to be presented to the men's convention began, "(W)e believe the whole theory of the common law in relation to woman is unjust and degrading, tending to reduce her to a level with the slave, depriving her of political existence, and forming a positive exception to the great doctrine of equality as set forth in the Declaration of Independence." Citing the need for freedom and equality, for protection of maternal interests and property rights by the government, it is a business-like appeal to republican sentiments, in which each mention of rights is specifically qualified as "political and legal"—protection of property, custodial privileges, and the vote. The "Memorial" contains no broad enumeration of personal or economic entitlements, and is devoid of any hint of rights as divinely derived, or any religious language.

By contrast, the corresponding "Address to the Women of Ohio" passed by the woman's rights meeting on the same issue opens with the sweeping assertion that "How the people be made wiser, better, and happier is one of the grand inquiries of the present age."[23] The "Address" exalts the role of God above that of the legislature in the creation and definition of rights. Dismissing the "cold sympathy and tardy efforts" of the "dough-faced serviles" in the legislature, the address is a paean to the "Rights of Humanity . . . What is their design? How do we know them? They are of God . . . their design is happiness." In the "Memorial" woman's entitlement is predicated on "the great doctrine of Equality as set forth in the Declaration of Independence," without elaboration. In the "Address" by contrast a broad range of rights are cast as directly contingent on the discharge of responsibilities, enabling individuals to "attain the end for which God the Father gave them existence." Ohio feminists urged women to seek not just political rights but education and occupation as well—"The full exercise of the heavenly graces . . ." The fact that the business of women's rights was carried out in two distinct languages signifies that women themselves identified their values and politics as in some way separate from men's.

This adjustment of language to audience crops up repeatedly, and illustrates women's complex relationship to the American rights tradition. Early documents addressed to legislators predictably pleaded in a secular language of rights based on equality and the revolutionary settlement, commonly citing principles like "no taxation without representation." Female lobbyists occasionally invoked their duties as mothers in favor of their cause, but by and large their arguments were couched in the familiar phrases of the revolutionary settlement. Women's writing to women proved a far richer admixture, not limited to claims for political and legal rights, but seeking a range of economic, domestic and personal entitlements and opportunities. Religious language and imagery permeates their discourse, while arguments from liberal theology undergird their vision of total reform.

Feminists stood both within and without the republican tradition. While genuine in their appeal to the revolutionary heritage, there was also a strong strategic element in their choice of words. As opponents of despotism, arbitrary power, orthodoxy and hierarchy in church and state, they honored the Founders and valued dearly the philosophy which had so effectively countered those evils. But the revolutionary settlement was incomplete and had unjustly excluded women and slaves. Further, mid-century reformers constituted a political opposition, and remained highly skeptical that the current crop of statesmen and legislators possessed the requisite virtue to pursue the goal of liberty in their own policies. Using the unadorned language of legal and political rights, feminists were appealing to a critical common tradition, in the language—meaningful both to themselves and within larger political circles—they thought would best make their case. At the same time, their appeal was not to the actual creations of the Founding Fathers, but to a normative ideal of natural rights to which feminists gave unique definition. Most women themselves seemed more at home with the spiritualized discourse which is the argot of private letters and diaries as well as women's newspapers and public proceedings.

For the ideology of woman's rights, unlike revolutionary rhetoric, was shaped in the fervor of millennial perfectionism. On closer scrutiny both the form and content of rights theories employed by feminists differed markedly from the traditional strain of republican rhetoric. Rights for women were definitely not conceived in the cool, secular dispassion of American constitutionalism. The end of the eighteenth century represented a low point in religious fervor and activity of all kinds: church attendance dropped precipitously; except in the West there was little by way of organized religious movement; and in the love feast of toleration which attended the church-state settlement, religious concerns receded formally and informally as a predominant force in the establishment of a public order. This tepid public piety did not fuel a fervent, God-centered view of natural law or natural rights. By the early federal period, natural rights was a concept which statesmen sought to contain, because of its volatile and potentially explosive reach. The exuberant rights language of early political documents was toned down, and the enumeration of precise and specific entitlements replaced the sweeping claims of the earlier period (Rodgers, 1987, chap. 2; Wright, 1931, pp. 179ff).

Feminists did not tread in this cautious path (Hurlbut, chap. 8; Kraditor, 1965 chaps. 3 and 4; Wright, pp. 176–9; Smith, 1927, chap. 3). In common with laborers, abolitionists, and other dissident groups, women sought to reopen the great constitutional questions of inclusion and entitlement, wielding a theory of natural rights which went well beyond the meager portion allotted in the state constitutions. The onset of the first woman's movement came after the Second Great Awakening had stirred the country to new heights of millennial passion and transformed the public's understanding of social change. Nineteenth-century reformers did not share their forebears' utilitarian vision of power as something to be balanced and shared. The emphasis on free will, the belief in the possibility of perfection and the newly benevolent designs of a well-disposed God—all worked to dispel the fear of unchecked liberty which dominated political debate in the constitution-making era. Women showed unbounded faith in the workings of an inner law: "emancipate from external bondage and the internal law written upon every heart makes itself audible" (E. Smith, 1851, p. 34). Such protean concepts as natural law and natural rights were plastic in the hands of feminists, who followed traditional rhetorical forms with conviction while giving them new meaning.

One innovation lay in feminists' perception of the relation of rights to natural laws. A concept of ancient lineage repeatedly refashioned by thinkers both within and without the church, natural laws in the revolutionary era diminished in importance while natural rights theory grew explosively (Wright, pp. 173ff). In America, natural rights became a largely secularized concept. Its proponents did not derive such rights from a divine source, but looked increasingly to human government and constitutional guarantees for their provenance, rendering a system of natural laws quaint and redundant.

Natural law regained its rule in the philosophy of the early woman's rights movement, where all rights were immediately derived from a divinely sanctioned order governed by the system of natural laws which was a pillar of reformers' faith. To claim human government as the source of rights was to confuse the cart and the horse—"It is God that gives our rights. *Government is the offspring of rights, not the parent.*"[24] Feminists, abolitionists, and other disaffected antebellum reformers frequently dismissed the Constitution as but another human law to be judged by God's standards (Hosmer, pp. 46–47 and chap. 14; Hurlbut, p. 33). Women saw rights as springing directly from the divinely ordained natural order, proclaiming that "the true rights of humanity are founded in the laws of nature, and consequently are natural rights."[25] Rights claims for antebellum feminists were not in the nature of strict bids for inclusion in a grant of powers and protections from human government. Rather, they expressed the terms on which individuals could best live out God's designs for human happiness. In the years before the Civil War the vote itself was repeatedly described by the valise theory of suffrage—as a way of obtaining the rights to domestic protection, property, education, remunerative work, personal autonomy, and all the other entitlements which women so desired. The specific rights women sought heralded not an alteration but a transformation of society. "Nature" in early feminist thought became a powerful normative force, a measuring stick rather than a descriptive tool (Wright, pp. 3, 176–79; T. Smith, pp. 106ff). What was "natural"—and this was almost always defined by what contributed to the full realization of human potential—became the ideal state toward which to strive. At the same time, nature—spruced up into a civil order by the Founding Fathers—regained an earthiness in feminist thought rooted in the physical functions of life itself.

For feminists and abolitionists both faced the problem of elaborating compelling grounds on which full rights should be extended to women and slaves—a difficult task since the constitutional guarantees of inalienability, freedom, and equality had produced such partial entitlement. Women's passionate arguments from moral equality only partly filled the bill. Both groups, typically suffering from a lack of education, were commonly stigmatized as mentally deficient and without the proper intellect or character to cultivate civic habits. In response to their opponents, reformers also fashioned arguments from the lowest common denominator of physical life—needs common to all. Abolitionist tracts elevated "the right to see, or to eat, or to walk" to stand beside life and liberty as "conditions of being. We have them from God when we have existence, and so long as existence remains those rights must remain, unless taken away by Him who gave them" (Hosmer, pp. 46–47). The pursuit of "happiness," always a somewhat vague component of revolutionary philosophy, took on a new specificity in claims to food, clothing, jobs, education—claims measured by needs and wants. "The Creator . . . has endowed man with certain innate desires, emotions, and faculties, the gratification and exercise of which are the means of his happiness. Here is the consummation of man's rights—the right to gratify his natural desires; to supply his natural wants; to exercise his natural functions, as the means of attaining happiness" (Hurlbut, p. 16).

Such abolitionist writing—particularly Elisha Hurlbut's treatise on human rights—proved very influential for feminists, who agreed that natural rights "emanated from the nature and wants and emotions of mankind."[26] Women and slaves did not know Latin, but they could know hunger, and from the capacity for hunger sprang the entitlement to food—"that is to say, physical existence acknowledges a higher law, whether we intellectually and morally acknowledge it or not" (Hosmer, p. 20). It was this assertion of the essential, physical fact of humanity as granting status that was behind Sojourner Truth's cry, "Ain't I a woman?" And the right to provide for these wants was guaranteed by the God who created them, for it was a critical aspect of the new, benevolent deity that he would impart no hunger, no yearning, without granting a means of its satisfaction (E. Smith, 1851, pp. 116–18; Hurlbut, pp. 13, 16). This concept of rights as following physical function ordained by natural laws is at odds with the idea of inalienable rights as settled during the struggle for independence. But it provided far greater scope for claims to economic and social justice than the revolutionary model, which effectively limited feminists to claims to political rights.

Feminists' conception of rights can perhaps best be contrasted with revolutionary republican tradition by comparing the terms "underlying" and "overarching." For the Founding Fathers, natural rights were pulled down from the sky, a set of external restraints to limit the actions of human government. In the early reform movement, by contrast, much of the focus of natural rights shifted to the internal. In a return to an older tradition, natural rights were seen as emanating from natural laws discovered, not in anterior principles like "no taxation without representation" and "one man one vote," but in the ordinary patterns of everyday life. Women did not look to outside sources or rules to control human behavior, but sought to bring human behavior into harmony with an inner working which comprehended material and spiritual forces alike.

The belief that God gave no need and no capacity which he did not mean to be fulfilled was expanded on by woman's rights advocates, and became what was probably the most common argument of that group before the war. Frequently the rationale for the dismantling of "woman's sphere" and taking up rights and duties in the wide world was put in functionalist terms, rather than in the language of inalienable human rights. Lucy Stone in one convention offered her own definition of "natural":

> when God made the human soul and gave it certain capacities, he meant that those capacities should be exercised. The wing of the bird indicates its right to fly; and the fin of the fish the right to swim. So in human beings, the existence of a power presupposes the right to its use, subject to the law of benevolence.[27]

It was this functionalism that lay behind the recounting of the stories of renowned and competent women popular in speeches and tracts. What *had* been done indicated an ability, and where there was an ability lay a God-given right to use it. More than in an ideological commitment to political rights, women first perceived of rights as originating in the capacities and talents handed out by God, which it was their duty as well as their pleasure to use fully. Initially, power and rights were conceived in this context of self-development: "for what is power in the sense in which it is so often applied to women, but the liberty to employ one's facilities in one's own way unobstructed . . . ?"[28]

Rights arguments were strongly addressed to the development of individual capacities in the context of the fulfillment of duties in the 1850s. No clear distinction was made in this period between rights stemming from concerns for family and social justice, and those which contributed to civic competence and personal development. Most often the two were pictured as mutually reinforcing, with woman's increased freedom enhancing her capacity to serve herself and others, including her family.[29] Stanton in a speech to the American Anti-Slavery Society in 1860 gave voice to a cherished reform belief that "rights never clash or interfere, and where no individual in a community is denied his rights, the mass are more perfectly protected in theirs" (DuBois, 1981, p. 78). Most feminists subscribed to the thesis that individuals had rights in order that they might do right. The frequent pairing of "rights" and "duties" was not accidental. Women were sincere when they repeatedly argued that it was because of their equal moral accountability to God, and the resulting duties to themselves, their families, and society, that they deserved and needed rights.[30]

Since women's duties were so much concerned with family, it should not be surprising that there was a significant domestic component in the developing ideal of woman's rights, and that natural rights were often pictured as concrete ways for women to protect or further the interests of their families. The *Lily* and the *Una* were published, not just for the several hundred pioneers of the movement, but also for many thousands who were still puzzling out their positions. Its letters and articles chronicle the conversion of many women to politics on the ground that it was woman's right and duty to assert her claims for protection.[31] The archetypal tale—"learning woman's rights by woman's wrongs"[32]—is of the woman in poverty or abused at the hands of drunken husbands; a key question becomes, "Has this woman had her rights?"[33]

Nor was this elaboration of woman's rights confined to some conservative wing of the movement; in the antebellum years there was considerable harmony of position. Although Stanton and Anthony moved from organized temperance to woman's rights in the mid-1850s, they and other woman's righters remained advocates of the temperance cause, finding it a "hard matter to speak of the cruel wrongs inflicted on women by the liquor traffic, without at the same time saying that her rights have been trampled upon."[34] Many women initially resistant to the assertion of rights became enthusiastic converts: their new ideals were rooted, not in higher political theory, but in concrete concern for the "sacred ties of family relations." Mothers turned to rights for the sake of their children, seeking assurance that they would be able to feed and clothe them, and keep them nearby.[35] Many women sought "equal rights for (women) in the family, in order that its highest uses and harmonies may be insured."[36]

Nevertheless, this theoretical harmony between rights for the self and duties to others was not to survive the Civil War. Even before then the two strains had begun to be discernible. The broadest category of rights included

> the general question of woman's Rights and Relations (which) comprehends such as: HER EDUCATION, *literary, scientific,* and *artistic*—HER AVOCATIONS, *Industrial, Commercial,* and *Professional*—HER INTERESTS, *Pecuniary, Civil,* and *Political in a word, her RIGHTS as an Individual,* and her FUNCTIONS as a *Citizen.*[37]

Many middle class feminists stressed forcefully the incidents which contributed to personal freedom and development—the right of sexual autonomy within marriage, of education, work outside the home, independence—and were content to see economic parity rather vaguely as the inevitable consequence of women's personal and civil gains.[38] Antebellum activists understood their rights and duties as a seamless web. Only in Stanton's work do we see fully foreshadowed the conflict between individual women's rights and the interests of family and community which was to split the suffrage movement so bitterly in the last years of the century.

To the extent that it is possible to isolate two different strands of rights thought here, the question arises of whether one is superior to the other, or more truly feminist in outlook. Even leaving aside contemporary debates between "equality feminists" and "cultural feminists" it is unclear that this standard can be usefully applied to nineteenth-century feminism. For one thing, what could "formal equality" mean to women in the absence of any federal or state regulatory mechanism to ensure it? In the 1850s, the possibility of constitutional amendments like the fourteenth, fifteenth, or nineteenth, was remote. In many ways the woman's movement's political aspirations developed reciprocally with the growth of the government's capacity to administer equal protection standards. As we have seen, most antebellum feminists were initially highly skeptical of the power of government to work change by law; Hannah Tracy Cutler once declared that she never saw the words "law reform" or "revised statutes" without thinking happily of a bonfire.[39]

More important is the question of whether "domestic rights" really represented an inferior brand, and what consequences the repackaging of women's early broad vision into the demand for political rights had for the movement as a whole. One critic has charged that

> The concept of 'rights' in general [is] a concept that is inherently static and abstracted from social conditions. Rights are by definition claims staked within a given order of things. They are demands for access for oneself, or for 'no admittance' for others; but they do not challenge the social structure, the social relations of production and reproduction. (Petchesky, 1984, p. 7)

While this accurately diagnoses a contemporary malaise, antebellum woman's rights claims spilled over legal categories: not limited to what governments could provide, they were the markers of a state of harmony with natural laws which mandated the satisfaction of all human wants. Their revolutionary character lay in representing, not claims to an established order, but new ways of reenvisioning social relations and the relations of power.

Nor did feminists see rights as any kind of absolute or unlimited entitlement. The linking of rights to responsibilities, and their firm placement within a system of natural laws, meant that rights were not seen as discrete, but as functioning within a larger context as a set of reciprocal obligations. Far from granting a power to be exercised against others, restraint was built in.

> The great laws of our own beings demand justice to ourselves and justice to our neighbors. We cannot infringe either law without disorder and pain, and . . . the Infinite Creator looks benignly upon his creature who

> thus obeys the laws of his own nature, and reverences those appertaining to every other. (E. Smith, p. 118)

Yet such restraints were not galling. Perfect freedom still lay not in total autonomy but in acting out God's will, so that "the most free are the most bound."[40] Rights were a precious new license for women to employ their talents for themselves and others, and women saw them, not only as individual entitlements, but as the context for a happier and more fulfilled life for all human beings. Rights were not static entitlements, but the conditions of a dynamic new freedom: "rights . . . will galvanize women into civil liberty: [and] you will find her capable of being in it, and sustaining it."[41]

Conclusion

When the antebellum woman's movement took up the concept and language of rights, it was not a case of incorporating the meanings and usages of the Founding Fathers whole into women's vocabulary. Rights rhetoric evoked a political tradition meaningful to women as well as men, a set of promises for women as gender blind as the assurances of the new God of liberal theology. But the genesis of rights, their meaning for women, lay initially in Christian-based concepts of social justice, the fulfillment of needs, and each person's development according to their divinely ordained talents. In the early years the problem of power was itself a critical hurdle for women's activism. Understanding its corrupting nature, seeing the evidence all around them in the political arrangements of men, how could women justify their own accession to power? A good deal of argument within the broader movement was directed toward the idea, not of seizing or sharing power, but of its *dissolution,* on the theory that when men ceased their corrupt administration, the problem of power would resolve itself into a natural harmonious balance between the sexes. Much of the rest of the discussion was taken up by mutual assurances that, should women gain their political due, their natures would protect them from the misuse of power through corruption and greed.

Despite their hesitance about the assumption of power, the antebellum feminist campaign was a time of political maturation, overcoming scruples and fears about acting in the political world. Women reformers began to prepare themselves, not just to speak in the role of outcast-prophet, but to take up the tools of government for their own ends. In the spring of 1852 the *Lily* published separate short blurbs side by side on two cases at law successfully argued by women. In one, the woman is armed with nothing but her knowledge of right and faith in good justice;

her appeal reaches past the minds and straight into the hearts of her listeners, who acknowledge that she has shown up their law as irrelevant and grant her the decision. In the second, the female advocate is beautifully prepared with a wealth of incisive arguments which dumbfound her opponents and lead to her uncontested victory on highly technical points of legal doctrine.[42]

These two cases represent a progression: the woman's movement in the 1850s is a microcosm of political change, a moment of transition in individuals' basic attitudes toward government. Despite their initial disaffection with government, workers in combined woman's and temperance movements came to recognize that politics and law were increasingly becoming creatures of the central state, and were passing out of local control. Politics was a man's game, one played away from home. Women resented their own exclusion, and distrusted the ability of male legislators sitting at a distance to represent their interests, and to meet the diverse needs of the banker, the housewife, and the drunkard. The imperative for women's entry into politics became clearer and clearer to feminist reformers in the decade before the War.

Theirs was a romantic vision; its romanticism was partly redeemed and partly betrayed by the political maturation of its proponents, a process that started even before the war. In fact, the *Lily* illustrates that it was through the temperance activities of the 1850s that many women were brought around to the use of political means, including the ballot. The Maine liquor law of 1851 gave reformers a heady taste of the sweeping change which legislation could accomplish so much more effectively than the painful, uncertain process of personal conversion to abstinence which had been the temperance workers' model. The Main law was the "philosopher's stone in the pocket," capable of effecting spiritual and behavioral regeneration instantly, and the *Lily* followed the progress of similar laws with intense interest.[43] Under Amelia Bloomer's management, editorials, articles, and letters in almost every issue starting in 1850 exhorted women to take up political tools to accomplish their social ends.[44] Over the years of the *Lily*'s publication (1849–1856) readers of all persuasions wrote in to attest to their conversion to political methods, at least to the combination of legal and moral suasion. A growing number found that moral suasion alone "will not do," was "worse than useless," and made little impression on the legislators who, corrupt or not, were calling the shots.[45] Citing the inability of mothers to protect sons from the liquor "monster," one former anti-feminist found that "there came a complete change over my feelings on the subject." A sense that they were "warring with harmless weapons" brought many reform women to a more assertive political challenge to the supremacy of the male liquor cartel.[46]

The new philosophy of women's political power did not require women to jettison moral ideals, but it did require a transformation of the imagery of mortality and power. Most importantly, it required the acknowledgement that the institutions of government were not inherently opposed to morality, but with the right composition could act to improve social conditions.

After the Civil War the rights movement became a suffrage movement in earnest, with the ballot's earlier focus as a carrier of other rights downplayed. Because of the movement's fuller engagement with the political process, and the growing involvement of government in mediating and enunciating the rights of its citizens, women increasingly conceived of rights in legal terms. The emphasis on legal rights, narrowly conceived, diminished discussions of economic and social entitlement. Feminists like Antoinette Brown Blackwell found the movement's agenda narrowed after the war, too neglectful of issues like education and work. Although the untested antebellum vision was probably naive, and certainly immature, in its conviction that the well-being of the community lay simply in the perfection of individual rights, the shift in focus toward legal remedies represented both a gain and a loss. Women gained a basic political agenda which could be pursued to ultimate success; and limited their claims for transformative social change inherent in their early vision.

Notes

1. *Lily,* vol. 3 no. 3, p. 21 (March 1851).
2. *Lily,* vol. 1 no. 11, p. 86 (Nov. 1849).
3. "Proceedings of the Woman's Rights Convention Held at Cleveland, Ohio . . . 1853" (1854) (hereafter cited as "Cleveland"), p. 168.
4. Speech of Abby Kelly Foster in *Woman's Rights Commensurate with Her Capacities and Obligations: A Series of Tracts* (1853).
5. Paulina Wright Davis, "On the Education of Females," tract no. 3 in *Woman's Rights Commensurate with Her Capacities.*
6. "Cleveland," p. 30, p. 91.
7. *Una,* vol. 1 no. 3, pp. 37, 41 (April 1853); "Cleveland," p. 92.
8. *Una,* vol. 1 no. 3, p. 41 (April 1853).
9. *Lily,* vol. 4 no. 2, p. 14 (Feb. 1852).
10. "Cleveland," p. 36.
11. Elizabeth Cady Stanton, "Address to the Legislature of New York, Adopted by the State Woman's Rights Convention, Held at Albany . . . Feb. 14 and 15, 1854" (Albany, 1854), p. 7.
12. "Proceedings of the Woman's Rights Convention Held at Syracuse . . . 1852" (1852) (hereafter cited as "Syracuse"), pp. 20–21.

13. *Una,* vol. 1 no. 1, p. 14 (Feb. 1853).
14. *Lily,* vol. 1 no. 7, p. 55 (July 1849).
15. *Lily,* vol. 4 no. 7, p. 58 (June 1852).
16. *Lily,* vol. 4 no. 9, p. 77 (Sept. 1852).
17. *Lily,* vol. 4 no. 9, pp. 77–78 (Sept. 1852).
18. *Lily,* vol. 4 no. 7, p. 59 (July 1852).
19. *Lily,* vol. 2 no. 6, p. 45 (June 1850).
20. *Lily,* vol. 2 no. 2, p. 15 (Feb. 1850).
21. *Lily,* vol. 1 no. 2, p. 15 (Feb. 1849).
22. *Lily,* vol. 2 no. 7, p. 51 (July 1850); vol. 1 no. 11, p. 86 (Nov. 1849).
23. Both of these documents are to be found in the *History of Woman Suffrage,* ed. Elizabeth Cady Stanton, Susan B. Anthony, and Matilda Joslyn Gage, vol. 1 (1881), pp. 105–110.
24. "Proceedings of the Woman's Rights Convention Held at Akron, Ohio, May 28 and 29, 1851" (1851; reprint, 1973), p. 41.
25. *Lily,* vol. 4 no. 2, p. 11 (Feb. 1852).
26. *Lily,* vol. 2 no. 10, p. 73 (Oct. 1850).
27. "Proceedings of the Seventh National Woman's Rights Convention Held in New York City . . . 1856" (1856) (hereafter cited as "New York"), p. 42.
28. *Una,* vol. 1 no. 1, p. 7 (Feb. 1853).
29. "Syracuse", pp. 62–63; "Boston", p. 8; "Cleveland", p. 8.
30. *Lily,* vol. 2 no. 10, p. 73 (Oct. 1850).
31. *Lily,* vol. 1 no. 10, p. 77 (Oct. 1849).
32. "New York", pp. 4, 76.
33. *Lily,* vol. 3 no. 5, p. 34 (May 1851); see also vol. 3 no. 11, p. 86 (Nov. 1851); and "Boston", p. 24.
34. *Lily,* vol. 4 no. 3, p. 22 (March 1852).
35. *Lily,* vol. 4 no. 5, p. 35 (May 1852).
36. "Report of the Woman's Rights Meeting at Mercantile Hall, Boston, May 27, 1859" (1859), p. 8.
37. "Syracuse", p. iv.
38. "Cleveland," pp. 10, 17, 41, 55–56.
39. *Una,* vol. 1 no. 3, p. 41 (April 1853).
40. "Syracuse," p. 81.
41. "Proceedings of the Woman's Rights Convention Held at . . . Rochester, New York, Aug. 2, 1848" (1870; reprint, 1969), p. 7.
42. *Lily,* vol. 3 no. 6, p. 42 (June 1851).
43. *Lily,* vol. 5, nos. 1 or 2 (Jan. or Feb. 1850) (page and date undecipherable), speech of Antoinette Brown.
44. See for example *Lily,* vol. 2 no. 10, p. 73–74 (Oct. 1850).
45. *Lily,* vol. 4 no. 5, p. 39 (May 1852); vol. 1 no. 8, p. 61 (July 1849).
46. *Lily,* vol. 3 no. 10, p. 77 (Oct. 1851).

12

Social Feminism and Legal Discourse, 1908–1923

Sybil Lipschultz

Introduction

There is a "male standard" in law, Florence Kelley proclaimed through the early 1920s. Kelley, the executive secretary of the National Consumers' League, believed existing legal rules and rhetoric represented only men's interests. If women were subject to these male rules, she reasoned, equal treatment would yield unequal results. Kelley wanted equality for women, but she was firmly committed to an equality based on women's differences from men, rather than an equality grounded on gender neutrality. She tried to introduce to American law a female standard, one that created new legal rhetoric, concentrating on women's distinct experiences. This equality-through-difference approach was summed up by the phrase "industrial equality," which women who agreed with Kelley used to explain their approach to law and social change (Kelley, 1924; NCL, 1922; LWV, 1924).

Historians have dubbed these women "social feminists" (O'Neill, 1969; Lemons, 1973). They were the women who staffed the many reform organizations that grew between the late nineteenth century and the New Deal. Many had political roots in the settlement houses, where they began to create child- and woman-centered reforms which built the foundation for the welfare state. Among their important reforms was protective labor legislation for women. These laws limited the hours women could work, provided a variety of on-the-job health and safety measures for women, and attempted to put a legal floor on the wages a woman could earn (Hill, 1979).

Historians tend to cast the social feminists as rather static in their approach to reform, depicting them as women who valued general social

Reprinted with permission of the *Yale Journal of Law and Feminism* (1989).

reform over feminism and who unquestioningly accepted women's dependency on men (O'Neill, 1969; Lemons, 1973). Although it is true that until 1920, social feminists did not challenge women's dependency, a longer view of social feminism reveals that it underwent important changes in the 1920s. In the 1920s, social feminist claims to industrial equality demonstrated a growing egalitarian spirit and a more feminist approach to law and women's lives. This version of industrial equality feminism, however, was an alternative to the equal rights model, or equality-through-sameness, commonly associated with the National Woman's Party and the standard history of American feminism. The alternative of equality-through-difference is best exemplified by the social feminist campaign for a woman's minimum wage, based simultaneously on women's value as workers and as domestic caretakers.

The new vision of industrial equality presented some significant problems for social feminists, however. They were committed to a strategy of legal remedies for women's social and economic problems. To carry out this strategy they needed lawyers, and they joined with some of the leading liberal attorneys of their day. Louis Brandeis, for example, agreed to argue *Muller v. Oregon,* the famous women's hour limitation case, for the Consumers' League in 1908, and he continued to argue women's labor law cases for the League until his Supreme Court appointment in 1916. Felix Frankfurter took Brandeis' place as legal counsel for the League, and became responsible for litigation in *Adkins v. Children's Hospital,* the women's minimum wage test case. He and other lawyers close to social feminist groups such as the Consumers' League, did not share the industrial equality vision. Rather, the lawyers whom social feminists needed to take their case for equality-through-difference to court expressed views about women and equality that were in sharp contrast with social feminism.

Social feminists were saddled with lawyers who basically believed in women's inferiority, and who read proposals for highlighting women's differences as formulae for inequality. These lawyers were generally liberal in their politics, but they were also the emissaries of the received tradition in law, and they transmitted values and ideologies deeply embedded in dominant interpretations of the Constitution. By separating female social feminists from the male lawyerly company they kept, I have found important differences along gender lines in a group historians have formerly treated as harmonious (Weinstein, 1968; Lubove, 1968; Kolko, 1963; Gordon, 1988; Pivin and Cloward, 1971).

Important changes in social feminism can be viewed through the window of two major Supreme Court cases. *Muller v. Oregon,* decided in 1908, is the quintessential example of the social feminists' early acceptance of dependency. *Muller* won hour limitation for women on the basis of women's relative physical weakness and other claimed *biological differences,* as well as their lack of suffrage rights. Social feminism was transformed, however, by 1923 and reliance on biological dependency was no longer acceptable. These changes were evident in the less successful *Adkins v. Children's Hospital.* This post-suffrage case denied women the right to a minimum wage because they had purportedly won "equality" with men when the Nineteenth Amendment was ratified. Taking their cue from the suffrage victory, social feminists argued that women were entitled to a state-imposed floor on their wages because of *economic differences*—they earned less than men. Furthermore, they argued that women's differences from men demanded legal attention, especially the *social differences* of childrearing and domestic caretaking. During the 1920s, the social feminist stress on social and economic differences, and an accompanying refusal to discuss biological differences, marked an important change in the movement. Encouraged by legal victories, social feminists were pushing beyond their own prior limitations.

It was litigation strategy, however, that eventually limited social feminism. Forced to put their ideal of industrial equality into legal discourse, social feminists faced a legal ideology strictly at odds with their perspective. The cruel irony of working with lawyers who did not share their views on women cut deeply into social feminist attempts to enact industrial equality. Failure to prevail in *Adkins,* moreover, curtailed the social feminists' sense of legal possibilities, much to the detriment of their movement. Equality-through-difference, or industrial equality, was not an idea whose time had arrived. Instead legal discourse shaped and re shaped this idea until it was no longer recognizable. At the same time the litigation process re-shaped the social feminist movement until adherents finally gave up on industrial equality.

This article brings to light "industrial equality," the social feminist political vision of equality-through-difference, which was prominent in the 1920s. It argues that industrial equality shaped advocacy of protective labor legislation during the twenties, separating litigation in that decade from the earlier period. This article further shows how those changes put social feminists at variance with the liberal male lawyers who took their labor law cases to court. This was a particularly important issue with Felix Frankfurter, who argued the women's minimum wage test case before the Supreme Court. In that case, *Adkins v. Children's Hospital,* social feminist Molly Dewson wrote a brief which attempted to articulate industrial equality within the confines of existing legal rules and concepts. Understanding the *Adkins* brief in the context of industrial equality promotes a new explanation of social feminism and the law in the 1920s. Thus, this article concludes that social feminists were hampered by a friendly lawyer who did not understand the feminist dimensions of the case, and a hostile Court which insisted on a vision of equality based on sameness. As a result, the social feminist case for industrial equality was severely limited by legal institutions and legal discourse of the 1920s.

Industrial Equality: Social Feminism in the 1920s

Social feminists who supported women's minimum wage laws did so because they wanted to correct women's inferior status and lower wages. It was this kind of attention to difference, one that sought separate laws for women to bring them up to "industrial equality," that was attentive to women's double burden, women's devalued labor, and hindrances to women's political participation. These women were eager to extend equal rights beyond suffrage, but they stressed that positive action was needed to get closer to actual equality, since women were held back by their distinct social role. They believed that the necessary action was best addressed through legal channels. After all, it was through law that they had won the right to vote and had gained previous protective labor laws.

The issue of minimum wages for women in the 1920s is part of a larger history of "protective" labor laws. Today these laws are often associated with restrictions on women's employment which now constitute sex-discrimination. It is, therefore, sometimes difficult to understand early twentieth-century perspectives on them. Social feminists who supported these laws in the twenties called them "women's labor laws," consciously rejecting the idiom, "protective labor laws," which they had used in the previous decade. There is significance to this shift in rhetoric. Social feminists no longer thought of themselves as "paternalistically" (maternalistically?) taking care of other women; instead, they saw this as positive action for women. However, social feminists' intent notwithstanding, separate women's labor laws, as constructed in the early twentieth century, did result in restriction and contributed to women's secondary and inferior position in the labor force (Boris, 1987; Baer, 1978; Erickson, 1982; Kessler-Harris, 1982).

The National Consumers' League, the National Women's Trade Union League, the League of Women Voters and the Women's Bureau were the primary social feminist organizations in the 1920s, and the women who staffed them believed strongly in equality for women. Even though they campaigned against the Equal Rights Amendment, they had a profound belief in the ability of law to provide equal rights for women in society. Advocating the women's minimum wage as part of this political campaign, they attempted to correct social and economic inequity through legislation and litigation that focused on bringing women's labor standards up to a new level.

This practice of invoking different treatment to achieve similar results was the keystone of industrial equality. The League of Women Voters announced its belief that "equality of opportunity does not and cannot mean identity of opportunity" (LWV, n.d.). If women, as unequals, were treated the same as men, then women would not fare as well. Women's lower wages, their relative lack of skill and the fewer opportunities open to them required some kind of positive action. Women's labor laws were one such action; they might "raise the position of women in industry to one more nearly approaching equality with that possessed by their male fellow workers." Far from "discrimination," women's minimum wage laws would inch women toward "equal industrial footing" with men (Hicks, 1927).

Removing women's "economic disabilities" was not easily accomplished, and social feminists did not always believe legislation alone could do the job. Women's labor laws were once part of a proposed constellation of solutions, including education, technical training and union organization (Johnson, 1924). But male unionists shunned the prospect of women in their unions—or even separate unions for women; the law, conversely, seemed potentially open to upholding legislation for women on the grounds that they were different from men. Women's labor laws appeared attainable, and despite the fact that social feminists had to spend years securing them, gaining the laws provided social feminists with political legitimacy (Dye, 1980; Payne, 1988). Women from the League of Women Voters acknowledged that legislation was "remedial," addressing "results of economic disabilities," not attacking the cause, but "as long as these causes remain, so will special legislation be necessary." One of the most important causes, social feminists were aware, was "persistence of the traditional attitude toward women's work and education" (Johnson, 1924, p. 17).

A legally mandated increase in wages might begin to correct traditional attitudes that suggested women's labor was worth less than men's, but wage laws had their limitations. Despite the fact that social feminists insisted on female self-sufficiency and the role of women as supporters of families, the standard women's "living wage" was based on the needs of a single woman living away from home, with no one to support but herself. Although social feminists made it known that women often supported others, the wages set by minumum wage laws did not begin to address the economic troubles besetting women with dependents. Social feminists of the twenties took an important step in recognizing the social and economic roles of women, but their wage scheme suggested they believed women with dependents should have acquired a partner to share in breadwinning. This position assumed the benefit of reinforcing traditional family values. Yet, simultaneously, it advanced the value of women, and encouraged independence for at least some (single) women.

On the other hand, social feminists sometimes pushed beyond their own limits. One of their proposals suggested that part-time work should pay twice the hourly wage of full-time work. Because women who worked part time did so to spend the rest of their time with domestic responsibility, social feminists wanted to compel employers to compensate for this dual role (District of Columbia Minimum Wage Board, 1920). Once again, social feminists accepted the double burden, but suggested rearrangement of work-time and compensation which would allow women to fill the two roles without suffering economic loss, and without being required to construct a male biography of their working life (MacKinnon, 1987).

This proposal goes a long way toward explaining what social feminists meant by industrial equality, and why they saw this attention to women's difference from men as a means to achieve equality. They accepted the double burden as reality. What they were looking for was a way to make a doubly burdened life more livable. Reduced hours of labor created time for children, and higher wages produced money to support those children. Social feminists believed it was possible to convince the state—through legislation and litigation—to cooperate in this scheme, in the name of feminism and the family. To them, this was "industrial equality" and justice. They also saw it as realistic.

What they viewed as unrealistic, however, was changing family relations so that men would shoulder half the burden of domestic responsibility. They called that proposal a "utopian dream." Although it was an appealing dream, they were thoroughly convinced that men were not going to change. It seemed easier to alter the terms of an industrial economy than to transform conditions of personal relationships (Frankfurter and Dewson, 1922; Gilson, 1923; Hoagland, 1923). Constant awareness of the need for change on the domestic level, coupled with refusal to try to alter these conditions presented something of a strain within social feminists' "realism" (Grimes, 1924).

Awareness of working women's many roles, however, helped social feminists maintain sensitivity to those who were called to the "double draft" of industrial labor and household work. Wage-earning men, by comparison, were a "privileged class;" they had far fewer responsibilities at home than did their working wives. Women faced the choice either of neglecting their families for the sake of their own independence, or of catering to family needs, while sapping their own "vitality" (NCL, n.d.).

To achieve citizenship on par with men, women needed legal measures to alleviate their double burden. Rather than protect women in motherhood, social feminists worried that women were "stunted" by their lack of civic involvement, and they urged facilitation of that participation, lest the public be deprived of their viewpoint. As voters, women were "for the first time . . . sharing in the government," and so the National Consumers'

League declared its new task for women: "we must see to it that industrial life is compatible with citizenship in democracy" (Ibid.)

Women were also different from men in their lower wages, a problem compounded by being classed into the least skilled and most draining jobs. They earned "just enough to keep body and soul together," and this didn't leave much left for "social questions." Political citizenship was contingent on "industrial citizenship," and thousands of women did not exercise their rights "largely because of economic conditions," (U.S. Department of Labor, Women's Bureau, 1926). Women's labor laws were an attempt to create a healthy workplace, with high enough wages, so that working women could enjoy rights more often exercised by men. In the wake of suffrage, this was separate treatment to create equality and political integration (Kelley, 1924; Hicks, 1927; Gordon, 1986; Kraditor, 1965, Cott 1987).

Social feminists still claimed a right to state protection of women's labor for reasons that set women apart from men—for gendered reasons—but they also proudly drew on women's full citizenship and began to include enjoyment of full participatory rights as a reason to protect women. Combined with notions of women's independence, self-sufficiency and the benefit of work was recognition that many working women were hindered in these "rights" by the double burden, exploited labor and consequent low wages. All these issues encouraged social feminists to think in terms of industrial equality, and with suffrage behind them, they believed they had all the more reason to think prospects for a women's minimum wage were better than ever.

But these politically active women were stuck with old legal methods for their new ideas, and it was a struggle to maintain a style of reasoning for minimum wages that had been successful with hours restriction. One problem was that social feminists simply no longer believed in the older characterization of women. Although they still advocated distinct legal measures for women, they did so to bring women into the former male sphere of power, and to give women advantages formerly reserved for men. Social feminists aimed to bring their new concepts to the Supreme Court for validation, as they had done before, and they expected their lawyerly sympathizers to comprehend this goal. But lawyers adhered to the prior vision of women which had guided past protective labor laws: a vision that set women apart from men because they were different and, therefore, unequal.

Lawyers and Women's Equality

The 1920s discourse on women's equality contained three alternatives. Competing for dominance were the social feminist vision of industrial equality, the National Woman's Party campaign for the Equal Rights

Amendment, and the view from the male legal community. The liberal male lawyers who supported separate women's labor laws, were allied with, but sharply distinct from social feminists. Dividing the movement along gender lines, these men had no commitment to the broader goals of industrial equality. To them, separate treatment meant inequality for women—something they favored.

Whereas social feminists were developing a critique of equality through identical legal treatment male lawyers tended to oppose women's equality of any kind. Social feminists favored women's labor laws as means to equality, and they were troubled by posed contradictions between formal legal equality (ERA) and separate treatment (women's labor laws). Contradiction between these two methods was partly imposed by lawyers. To them women's equality was a liability, denying what was in their view an exalted status for women in society.

Most lawyers in 1923 viewed the ERA as a threat to privileges women enjoyed based on inequality. Equality would eliminate better treatment of women, and therefore hurt them. One lawyer thought the "chief difficulty with the amendment seems to be the word 'equality' " (Szold, 1922). Lawyers stressed differences between men and women as a "well recognized fact" which mandated "special and restrictive laws" for women (Garfield, 1922). Social feminists were not uncomfortable with the word "equality," which they themselves used; they were only concerned with how equality was to be defined. Rather than speaking of women's labor laws as restrictive, they had begun to advocate them as a means to empower women, especially through wages. But their legal advisors disagreed. For them the purpose of these laws had nothing to do with "civil and legal rights of women," even though social feminists had defended the wage law as a matter of full enjoyment of "rights." Women's labor laws, to lawyers, served only to protect women from "hardships, wrongs and evils" (Garfield). Male lawyers stressed physiological differences between the sexes, which social feminists were then downplaying. And to lawyers, accounting for differences meant precluding equality (Lewis, 1922).

Women in the League of Women Voters and Consumers' League consulted with several lawyers in their reform circles on the question of equality. They wanted to know the extent to which women's labor laws and formal equal rights were contradictory. Although social feminists had begun to see women's labor laws as promoting industrial equality, their lawyers were forthright in asserting that previous protective laws had been based on inequality. *Muller v. Oregon,* declared one lawyer, would never have been successful if it hadn't been premised on women's inequality. By upholding women's employment statutes, the court "did create legal inequalities in respect of sex" (Kane, 1922; Pound n.d.; Pound, 1922; Borchard, 1922).

Felix Frankfurter, the Consumers' League lawyer, who would argue *Adkins* before the Supreme Court, was one of the staunchest opponents to women's equality, in part because he was such an advocate of women's labor laws. To his legal mind, that meant stressing women's inequality. Declaring that the law must account for diversity in women's "nature," Frankfurter insisted laws should treat females sometimes as "persons" and other times as "women." Although social feminists often discussed women's diversity, they never saw it as a matter of nature; they instead viewed social roles and labor conditions as impediments to women's equality. Frankfurter's distinction between women and persons was a far cry from social feminists' claims of "women first" as an approach to women's predicament, but it also mirrored feminist ambivalence about sameness and difference (Hicks, 1927; Frankfurter, 1922).

Protective laws relied on separate treatment of men and women, and this both reflected earlier social ideals of womanhood and encouraged behavior that reinforced this ideal in the economic sphere. Lawyers who wrote on equality, even those who supported women's labor laws, expressed the dominant legal view in these matters. Separate treatment, legally, meant inequality. In part, hours restriction had been successful because American social feminism had been in accord with these legal principles and broader social outlooks. Although social feminists did not advocate women's inequality, they did stress women's separateness and difference. In so doing, they were able to gain women's labor laws. After suffrage, social feminism and the ideology of industrial equality were at odds with legal ideology.

In the twenties, while social feminism was in transition, women continued to speak about the women's minimum wage as a matter of equality. Social feminists—unlike their lawyers—did not see protection as "a sign of weakness or inferiority," rather its achievement indicated "the power and importance of women in industry" (King, 1922). They were in favor of "positive gains" (NWTUL, 1922) for women, which could be obtained, they theorized, not by adopting sameness in law, and subjecting women to a "male standard," (LWV, 1924) which would encourage inequality, but by stressing different treatment for similar results (Wing, 1924, NCL, 1922).

There was a division between lawyers and social feminists. Although in advocating women's minimum wage laws, social feminists can be seen as attempting to feminize the law, lawyers remained resistant to the possibility. Frankfurter probably captured this best in his discussion of Crystal Eastman, a supporter of ERA. "I am aware that Crystal Eastman once upon a time knew something about law, but that was long ago and far away. Now she disregards her former learning and writes as a 'feminist' " (Frankfurter, 1924). To Frankfurter, legal ideology and feminist politics were mutually exclusive, and his view was echoed by most male lawyers and judges: thinking like a lawyer excluded thinking like a feminist. Those who favored industrial equality assumed law and social feminism could be merged, and, in fact, made the merger the fundamental point of women's minimum wage laws. Frankfurter enthusiastically supported women's minimum wage laws, but the social feminist notion of bringing gender distinction to the law to promote equality escaped him (White, 1990).

Frankfurter was significant to the social feminists because he was to argue their case on behalf of women workers' wages in the Supreme Court. But he was more than that. He was the emissary of legal ideology, well-trained and versed in dominant legal thinking. His knowledge comprised an unknown deficit for the social feminists' cause; it embodied the very limitation of the law for social feminism.

Lawyers represented, if nothing else, the received legal wisdom, and they hinted at what was to come in *Adkins,* where the social feminist claim to industrial equality was incomprehensible to the justices. Significantly, this was true even though the Court was dominated by conservative judges who were politically distinct from the liberal lawyers who were in alliance with Consumers' League leaders.

Contemporary liberal observers feared a conservative mood at the Court in 1923, especially in light of recent anti-labor decisions and several conservative Harding appointments. "The economic complexion of the Court will have to change materially before we can hope for greater liberality," one lawyer told the League of Women Voters. He suspected that anti-labor sentiments, combined with the proposed ERA, which cast women's labor laws as inegalitarian, were certain to bring an adverse decision in *Adkins* (F.F. Kane, 1922; *American Steel Foundaries v. Tri-City Central Trades Council,* 1921; *Truax v. Corrigan,* 1921). Yet, he failed as did all other observers, to see that suffrage was equally threatening, in the eyes of the law, to women's labor laws. Although social feminists feared the effect of the ERA on the women's minimum wage, it was suffrage that had actually changed the legal status of women and had encouraged social feminists to significantly alter their reasons for defending the women's minimum wage. And it was suffrage, itself, that could be turned against these laws.

Social feminists were attempting to influence law, as they believed their past advocacy of women's hours laws and suffrage had done. However, legal ideology had also influenced social feminists. Their success in previous litigation had partly relied upon women being in a separate legal class, as the *Muller* decision had noted (*Muller v. Oregon,* 1908). Other factors, too, had put previous women's labor laws in a favorable light. Putting motherhood first among women's roles and stressing women's physical inferiority was not a challenge or a threat to the judicial outlook on gender roles. Women's differences from men suggested to the Supreme Court and to dominant legal thinking that women were unequal. Now social feminists wanted to rely on difference to gain special treatment that might, in their view, encourage legal equality. This was a different matter. Influenced by suffrage and the equal citizenship it implied, they were drawing on a strain in American law that probably bore little relationship to the protective "police power" of the state, which had justified previous protective labor legislation.

The police power was an important exception to "free contract" ideology which enabled the state to intervene in the bargain between employer and employee to mandate certain conditions of labor, concerning the health, safety or morals of the community. Women's differences, both physiological and social, became the basis of police power exceptions in women's labor laws, and the community interests protected were often the real or potential offspring of the working women, rather than the women themselves. In part, the courts were sympathetic to this argument because disenfranchised women were seen as wards of the state, which made it easier for the courts to justify legal interference in the "bargain" between employer and female employee (Baer, 1978).

As the social feminist acceptance of female dependency gave way in the 1910s to a new vision of industrial equality in the 1920s, social feminists found themselves arguing for women's minimum wages in a style no longer compatible with the police power rule they had previously used to their advantage. They now faced a new legal problem. How were they to establish a link between the police power and yet remain true to their ideology of industrial equality? The brief created by Molly Dewson was an attempt to mediate this political problem.

Social Feminism and the Adkins Brief

By 1923 when the women's minimum wage test-case, *Adkins v. Children's Hospital* reached the Supreme Court, the character of the wage issue was clearly separated from other women's labor laws. Social feminists, in their new vision of economic rights and industrial equality, were challenging the established boundaries of state intervention in the economy. Their feminism had led them to a direct departure from the economic status quo.

Hours legislation and health and safety measures involved intervention in the economy, but the cost to employers could always have been made up in reduced wages. A state-imposed floor on wages signaled to conservative employers, and to a majority of the Supreme Court, a "redistributive" culmination to the era of "progressive" reform. This redistributive capacity was, of course, very moderate, but on the heels of the Red Scare it raised the specter of socialism. Enemies of minimum wage laws for women argued these laws involved "changing the rules" of economic principle, and that they were illegitimate because they were concerned only with money. If low wages were dangerous, they offered, then so was capitalism itself. The Constitution, they feared, was being used to tamper with capitalism (Ellis and Folk, 1920; *Children's Hospital v. Adkins,* 1922; Ross, 1977–78).

Both sides brought their competing views of economic policy to the Supreme Court. Although economic policy issues dominated the case, and the social class issues raised by it are very significant, judicial comment on women's legal status is equally important to understanding *Adkins.*

The brief presented by the National Consumers' League in *Adkins* represented the culmination of a generation's work and evolving ideas on women in society. Meticulously prepared by Molly Dewson, it drew on many social feminist claims to industrial equality, selecting pertinent data from amassed investigations of women's organizations. In preparing the brief for the Consumers' League, Dewson did most of the sociological and economic work for attorney Frankfurter, who worked on the legal arguments and appeared in court (Ware, 1987).

Dewson told the Court that work was not degrading to women. Where previously social feminists had argued to preserve women's health from the horrors of industrial labor, now they argued that work itself was far less damaging to a woman than low wages. No longer interested in accepting female dependency or curtailing opportunities, social feminists now favored expanded rights for women in the form of a right to decent wages. But the brief, and this argument, was limited by the need to prove a police power exception to free contract.

To convince the Court a police power exception was compatible with women's minimum wage laws, Dewson had to demonstrate women were separate from men in order to distinguish them as a "class" needing protection. After suffrage, this was more difficult to do, because women had the same political rights as men. Although potential starvation represented an important threat to a woman's health, social feminists saw the need for minimum wages as more than a safeguard to health. Viewing the state less as a caretaker and more as an agent of freedom for women, social feminists wanted to transform dependency into an alternative form of equality. Social feminists wanted women's minimum wage laws not primarily to protect women's health, but as an answer to working women's economic disadvantages (Hartog, 1987).

In their brief, social feminists celebrated the value of women's work. As economic and social justice, "underpayment of large groups of women" was "contrary to all standards, economic as well as social." The minimum wage offered the "first step toward the elevation of women in industry to a plane where due recognition is given the full value of their work" (Frankfurter and Dewson, 1922). Dewson selected material that stressed women as breadwinners, with family members dependent on their support. In an effort to overcome the long standing myth that women worked only for "pin money," she relied on reports that stressed women's labor as crucial to family support. ("Protective Legislation vs. 'Equal Rights,' " 1923; Wandersee, 1981; Anderson, 1951)

Dewson argued, women worked to support children if husbands were absent or unemployed. If a man was disabled or had deserted his wife, she was solely responsible for her family. Young single women often worked to support parents, a responsibility young men often escaped. Divorced or widowed women supported themselves and their children, as well; they had no other source of income, and their own wages had to suffice. In sum, women made an important economic contribution to family life, whether they were single or married, and social feminists vigorously pointed to this in their brief. A community larger than women themselves needed a woman's wages. Older assumptions that only men shouldered such economic responsibility did not apply (Frankfurter and Dewson, 1922).

The double burden separated women from men, the social feminists' brief declared, and part of the difficulty was child care. To afford such care for their children, many women needed increased wages. Working women were shouldering the "double social significance," but the solution was not depending on someone else. They simply needed more money to afford their many dependents, and they needed fewer hours of labor to allow more time for caregiving. Social feminists were attempting to alter the dominant culture's view of the American family. They did not challenge the family arrangement; instead they emphasized women's contribution to that family as something socially worthy and deserving of decent wages (Frankfurter and Dewson, 1922).

To argue that women's wages were based on actual responsibility to others, however, did not demonstrate a direct relationship between women's wages and their health and welfare, a connection which was necessary to prove the need for a police power exception to free contract. To provide such a link, Dewson couched wages in terms of a cycle of " 'poor wages,' 'poor health,' 'poor wages' " which was a "descending spiral into the regions of destitution . . . Individual suffering," and the larger general "social loss" from low wages, which would bring "community decline," and was "degrading to workers themselves." Degradation was widespread, but it oppressed men as well as women (Frankfurter and Dewson; Seligman, 1921; Ely, 1920). Dewson and Frankfurter needed to distinguish women from men to make an effective case for the women's minimum wage. Portraying women as strong, responsible workers and admitting that work itself was less harmful to them than low wages, suggested the similarity between men and women. The right to a decent wage did not appear particularly gender bound (Frankfurter and Dewson, 1922).

As industrial equality, the women's minimum wage was, to social feminists, a question of increased economic equality. Social feminists wanted wage laws for women so they would earn more money. There was a link between starvation and public health, but it was not gender specific. What was gender specific was women's devalued economic status. The brief for the minimum wage stressed poverty, which implicated the police power more than did other principles of industrial equality. But it was also closer to an argument for universal wage laws for men as well as women, and it interfered with the free contract ideology dominant in the twenties and the tandem philosophy of laissez-faire.

Thus, the major principle that women needed a legal floor on their wages because they earned less than men, and that economic disadvantage needed correction so that women could enjoy rights to equality and citizenship, was lost in the *Adkins* brief. Although the most important contribution of industrial equality was the merging of equality and difference, it had no real place within the police power. Furthermore, given Consumers' League legal counsel Felix Frankfurter's views on women's equality, it is not surprising that this aspect of industrial equality disappeared from the case. Largely defending a reversal of inequality, social feminists faced a police power rule that was not intended to promote equality, but to preserve public welfare. If women were entitled to such welfare because they supported others and were valuable to their communities, then men would also be entitled. From the Court's perspective, this extension made the women's minimum wage all the more threatening. Most significant for social feminism, however, was the process by which legal rules—in this case the police power—forced out more radical ideas so they would have no voice in the courtroom (White, 1990).

The Adkins Decision

Justice Sutherland, one of Harding's recent conservative appointees, spoke for the Supreme Court's majority. He was quick to point out the difference between wage and other labor laws. To him regulated wages meant a different kind of state involvement with the economy. But the *Adkins* case also represented a new view of women, and this was not lost on Sutherland. Politically distant from the liberal lawyers consulted by the Consumers' League, the very conservative Sutherland offered a new twist on the legal dilemma of equality and difference. Comparing this case to the hours test-case, *Muller,* Sutherland noted that hours legislation had been upheld based on differences between men and women. And he was right. Looking at the world around him, he observed, however, the "ancient inequality of the sexes has continued with diminishing intensity." Why, since suffrage, inequality had almost reached the "vanishing point!" The result of this newly won equality for women, he reasoned, was that women had to be free to negotiate their own wages (*Adkins v. Children's Hospital,* at 525, Majority Opinion at 552–53).

Sutherland's denial of inequality, however, did not extend to overruling *Muller.* The result was curtailed hours without the benefit of increased wages. Sutherland saw no irony in declaring women free to work for any wage offered, but too inferior and dependent to choose hours of labor. The combination of low wages and restricted hours was worse for the woman who worked than no laws at all (Lustig, 1982).

Enlisting the theoretical equality of women to defeat the women's minimum wage, Sutherland found an effective means of turning social feminism against women. Sutherland's view of equality was that it meant sameness and identical treatment. Inequality had brought social feminists to recognize difference, but to Sutherland, equality and difference could never be reconciled. And by upholding hours regulation while striking down a floor on wages, he denied the possibility of self-sufficient womanhood, increasing chances of female poverty and dependency.

Oliver Wendell Holmes dissented. He saw no difference between wages and hours; if one could be regulated, he reasoned, why not regulate the other? He regarded his own opinion as "plain common sense," and intended it to "dethrone Liberty of Contract from the ascendancy in the Liberty business" (Holmes, 1953). Nevertheless, Holmes could not resist commenting on women's equality. He, unlike Sutherland, was certain suffrage did not create women's equality. "It will take more than the Nineteenth Amendment to convince me there are no differences between men and women, or that legislation cannot take those differences into account." Despite the fact that the politically liberal Holmes was more of a friend to women's labor laws than Sutherland, he too, assumed it was inequality that mandated attention to difference. Equality, to his mind, too, was sameness. Much like Frankfurter, he used women's inequality to defend minimum wages for women. (*Adkins v. Children's Hospital,* 570)

Judicial opinions drew on economic policy, free contract ideology, and the role of the state in minimum wage laws. All the justices seemed to be aware that the wage law would probably extend to men (*Adkins v. Children's Hospital,* 548–52, 566). The embodiment of twenties' conservatism in Harding's Court was hostile to this path of policy development. The established economic-legal order of the twenties was clear on the issue of wages: tampering with them was inappropriate. Wage legislation appeared to jeopardize capitalism itself; conservatives were not about to compromise free contract ideology for a policy that they misconstrued as "bolshevism." Employers accepted hours legislation, because they were able to rationalize hours limitation as part of industrial efficiency and, therefore, in their long-term profit interests. Wage legislation was perceived differently, however, because wages were directly linked to profits in the employer's mind. A state-imposed floor on women's wages looked like a profit cut, or at least interference with employer control. Profits were more sacred than motherhood.

Economic policy, however dominant, was not the only significant aspect of *Adkins*. All the justices and lawyers involved somehow grappled with women's equality and difference. Certainly, Sutherland used women's equality to rationalize his opposition to labor laws, but Holmes used women's inequality to defend the minimum wage. A contradiction had developed between equality and labor reform for women. Were women entitled to these reforms because they were entitled to equality, as social feminists suggested? Or did they need protection because of their inherent inequality, as Holmes argued? Did Constitutional equality mean "identity of treatment," as social feminists had feared, and as Sutherland articulated? Social feminists had been trying to suggest that women's equality could be defined legally in women's difference, without loss and without contradiction. The contradiction imposed by legal ideology distorted feminist theory.

Social feminists believed that suffrage was a good reason to expect the Supreme Court to uphold women's minimum wage laws. But the Court turned this gain against women. Denying the validity of women's minimum wage laws, the Court used equality rhetoric—and especially suffrage—against feminism. Hiding behind a mask of equality for women, the Court defeated what most of the justices saw as a bid for the "redistributive" state.

Suffrage, and the equal citizenship it implied, had empowered social feminists and had provided the groundwork for the idea of "industrial equality." But as Florence Kelley observed, Sutherland essentially argued that since suffrage, women had won the equal right to starve (Kelley, 1925). Ironically, social feminists had thought introduction of the ERA might create this problem; nobody dreamed suffrage alone had this legal capacity.

While victories in the suffrage movement and in women's labor law cases had encouraged women to act and had instilled in them a deep faith in legal process as an agent of social change, law also revealed the capacity to hold back the social feminist agenda by turning equality rhetoric against women. This was especially true when social feminist demands moved into the sphere of direct economic consideration. Even though social feminists advocated the women's minimum wage in defense of industrial equality, their lawyers and the judges they encountered in *Adkins* never quite comprehended this concept. To them, separate laws for women were a matter of inequality. The only legal friends these social feminists found were those who defended women's labor laws because they favored women's inequality.

Conclusion: Social Feminism and Legal Discourse

The political vision of equality-through-difference marked an important change in social feminism, distinguishing twenties social feminism from that of the 1910s. Between 1890 and 1920, social feminists accepted female dependency and used it to accomplish reforms, such as protective labor legislation. During the 1920s, however, they rejected the old dependency line, and argued in a new voice for what they now called women's labor legislation. That new voice spoke of a special equality for women, one social feminists called "industrial equality."

The new vision of industrial equality put social feminists at variance with the male lawyers in their political coalition, including those who would argue women's labor law cases in court. This became a problem; although these lawyers were needed for their prestige and national prominence in legal matters (and legal technicalities), they were not sympathetic to the new social feminist vision. They represented received law, not just the attitudes of lawyers, but also the ideology of law embedded in its language and its structure. The brief, written by social feminist Molly Dewson and lawyer Felix Frankfurter, was an attempt to articulate a new strategy for approaching law and a changing ideology of women's rights within the confines of legal language and structure.

Once they faced putting industrial equality into legal discourse, social feminist found themselves less able to articulate their vision, and even less able to achieve their goal of equality-through-difference in law. The Court's response to the brief highlights some of the difficulties in 1923 of getting a legal recognition of women's differences without sacrificing women's equality. In law, differences were linked to inequality and equality was connected to what Florence Kelley called the male standard for personhood. What was to become of people who did not conform to the male standard but wanted equality at law? In 1923 they had two choices: either conform and be equal or be different and be denied equal rights.

V

Perspectives on Marriage and Family

Although the institutions of marriage and traditional motherhood are frequent targets of feminist criticism, most women marry and have children. There often appears to be a conflict between the material conditions of many women's lives and the idealized expression of feminist goals. The papers in section V each focus on an area in which theory has failed to account for circumstances. These papers illuminate the tension between feminist goals of both restructuring oppressive social institutions while aiding individual women in their struggles to improve the lives they fashioned under the old rules.

Eileen Boris's discussion of the Vermont knitters highlights the complexity of controversies over women's "right" to work for wages in their own home. Contracted piecerate homework is most attractive to women who are primary caretakers of their children. Working in the home, however, can be viewed as both facilitating women's economic exploitation and reinforcing their traditional private family role. To this extent homework may be construed as inimical to the goals of feminism. On the other hand, homework gives women committed to traditional family standards some financial power. In addition, alternative outside work opportunities for women often involve low pay or rigidly structured working conditions. Thus homework may be the most satisfying option for particular women, a reflection of the differences in the positions among women that varies with factors such as race and social class.

The articles by Mary Coombs and Martha Fineman also highlight areas in which reforms of legal policy undertaken to confirm or advance feminist ideals may actually operate to the detriment of many women. Coombs describes how feminists earlier in this century sought to abolish suits for breach of promise to marry, their rationale failing to conform to feminist ideals of marriage as a mutually chosen companionship of equals. The real world of many such plaintiffs clearly failed to mirror the ideal, however; women who brought these actions often suffered real economic and other life-opportunity losses as well as the hands of reluctant suitors.

Fineman's discussion of the symbolic choices influencing criteria for the distribution of property in divorce reveals that the tension between the ideal of marriage as a partnership of equals and the reality of marriage as an institution that helps to alleviate the dependency that arises when children or other unequalizing factors are present still exists. Policy embodying the presumption that spouses have contributed equally to the marriage and thus are entitled to assets equally divided symbolically recognizes and advances the feminist ideal of equality; at the same time, however, such equality is insensitive to the differential needs that motherhood and traditional marriage choices create in many women, a difference which does not vanish when children are grown or when the marriage ends. Once again it is apparent that the conflict between the rhetorical or symbolic and the practical desire to meet the needs of women is further exacerbated by the fact that legal policy disproportionately reflects middle and upper class experience and norms.

13

Homework and Women's Rights: The Case of the Vermont Knitters, 1980–1985

Eileen Boris

Introduction

Picture Mrs. Audrey Pudvah as the *New York Times* described her in March 1981, "working at her knitting machine in a quiet room looking out on snow covered fields, tall trees, and craggy hills." While earning nearly four dollars an hour, more than the minimum wage, she also "can keep an eye on her two young children and keep the woodburning stove stoked and the house spotless." Mrs. Pudvah's knitting, however, was then illegal. It violated a 1942 administrative ruling under the Fair Labor Standards Act (FLSA) that banned industrial homework in knitted outerwear. Yet she claimed not to "feel the least bit exploited . . . she thinks that her job knitting ski hats in her own pleasant log home at her own pace is a pretty good deal."

In the early 1980s, the plight of Audrey Pudvah and other New England knitters became a cause célèbre among free market conservatives who argued for lifting the homework ban because it deprived workers of their constitutional "right to work." For the Reagan administration, ending the ban fitted nicely into its plans to deregulate the economy. But Audrey Pudvah herself offered another set of reasons for homework: "All the time the Government says to be more family-oriented and spend time with your children and to save energy," she explained. "That's what I am doing. I don't have money for an extra vehicle, extra clothes, or for baby sitters that I would need to go out to work" (Shabecoff, 1981). Given

---

For fuller documentation, see the original version of this article in *Signs: A Journal of Women in Culture and Society,* 13 (Autumn 1976) : 98–120. This article also appears in Eileen Boris and Cynthia R. Daniels, eds. *Homework: Historical and Contemporary Perspectives on Paid Labor at Home* (Urbana: University of Illinois Press, 1989), pp. 233–57.

her responsibilities for children and household, and given the low wages available to women in the workplace, homework made sense.

While the media portrayed the homeworkers as mothers challenging the Goliath of big government, the knitters presented themselves as craftswomen, "worksteaders," and pioneers of "the American cottage industry" who also cared for children and tended wood furnaces. Though they saw themselves as controlling their own labor, these women were not independent contractors in the legal sense but employees, industrial homeworkers paid by the piece and thus subject to FLSA. Their fight to knit ski caps and sweaters at home began in the partisan preelection atmosphere of 1980 as a routine Labor Department suit against homework wage and hour violations. It ended in late 1985 when the Department of Labor, after a four-year battle with the International Ladies' Garment Workers' Union (ILGWU), rescinded the rule prohibiting industrial homework in knitted outerwear but instituted an employer certification program that would comply with FLSA.[1] The public debate that occurred in the course of changing the knitwear regulations questioned the exploitative nature of home labor and the "fairness" of labor standards legislation toward women—both assumptions underlying the homework ban. From the perspective of the knitters, the regulatory state seemed to ignore women's dual role as family nurturers and wage earners in its attempt to protect workers by disallowing homework.

This recent controversy marks a profound shift in the decades old debate surrounding homework. Since the New Deal, defenders of homework have pointed out its advantages for women who must work and care for their children at the same time. Advocates of the Vermont knitters, most of whom identify themselves as political conservatives, added to this defense a critique of protective legislation that echoed feminist demands for equal rights: they claimed laws that ostensively "protect" women from poor wages and long hours actually intensify employer discrimination against women by making women as expensive to hire as men and thus limiting women's opportunities in the labor market (Baer, 1978).

The homework advocates' arguments rely on the major tenets of classical liberalism: equal rights, equal opportunity, the separation of the private from the public, and the right to work (Eisenstein, 1984). Using the rhetoric of sex equality, defenders of homework have labeled a homework ban discriminatory because it bars women from sewing or knitting at home while permitting men to work at carpentry or other home-based labor. Such gender classification in the homework restrictions, Ruth Yudenfriend of the National Center on Labor Policy argued, fails to meet the Supreme Court's test of serving "important government objectives" and thus "discriminate[s] against women by eliminating their rights to raise their children and earn a living at the same time." "Prohibitions against industrial homework disenfranchise women from the workplace," reiterated Mark A. de Bernardo of the U.S. Chamber of Commerce. "It is therefore a women's issue" (U.S. Dept. of Labor, 1981a, pp. 26–33; U.S. Senate, 1984, p. 127). Feminist rhetoric has found a particularly strange home in the voice of new right conservatives like Senator Orrin Hatch (R-Utah), who equates "right to work" with "rights of women .... the right to be able to support your family ... in the privacy of your home."[2] Thus, homework regulation, historically supported by labor unions, restricts the "right to work," long associated with business's defense of the open shop. For some conservatives, a pro-homework stance complements their assault on government regulation of industry, union power, and the welfare state because it characterizes labor as an individualized, rather than a collective, experience. Such conservatives have extended "right to work" as a woman's right to maintaining women's place within a male-dominated society: at home, earning wages, while caring for children. Capitalism and patriarchy have joined forces for their mutual benefit.

Opponents of homework also have shifted their arguments from the historical stance of women reformers, labor unions, and New Dealers, who advocated mother care of children and prophesied the downfall of domestic life if work for pay was introduced into the home. Today, opponents assert the adverse impact of homework on wage standards for women in the workplace, and most advocate day-care for women who work outside the home. However, they continue to present the homeworker as a victim of unscrupulous employers, who is without the economic, political, and legal resources needed to defend herself. Jay Mazur, the current president of the ILGWU, has argued, "To license industrial homework is to license exploitation" (Mazur, 1986). Yet he and other opponents of homework fail to address the social and cultural conditions affecting all women that make homework a solution to some women's double day. By maintaining a separation between home and work, anti-homework liberals keep the home free from homework but not from the unwaged labor that is the cornerstone of power inequities between men and women. The gender economy, however, intertwines with the political economy. Homework not only belies any separation between family and economy, it also forces us to rethink their connection.

The debate over industrial homework appears to have only two sides: rescind the 1940s prohibitions against homework in the garment-related industries or maintain them. Yet despite the "prohibitions," homework in most industries is legal as long as employers comply with the wage, hour, child labor, and record-keeping provisions of FLSA. Opponents of homework question the effectiveness of this or any regulation, because the wage and hour administration lacks the funds needed to enforce certification and record-keeping systems of employers and because historically, at least, it has been impossible to monitor whether homeworkers are receiving fair piece rates. In fact, reformers in the 1930s suggested regulation as a form of prohibition because they understood that if employers paid minimum wages to homeworkers, the cost-cutting advantage of this system would be lost, leading to a decline in homework in most trades (Boris, 1988). Indeed, this strategy (along with unionization) seemed until the 1970s to have worked.

This paper attempts to take the debate over homework regulation beyond these simple dichotomies. A feminist analysis recognizes the complexity of the fact that while some individual women consider homework their best option, homework may not be beneficial for women as a group. Such an analysis recognizes that unwaged labor in the home (women's responsibility for nurturing and housekeeping) supports the traditional division of labor in the marketplace. Thus, although homework has been a strategy for individual women to cope with limited opportunities in the workplace, it has done so at the cost of reinforcing the subordinate position of women as a group in the economy and perhaps also in the family. To fully understand homework, then, we need to explore the interaction of social, economic, and cultural forces that make homework both appealing and exploitive, and we need to listen to the voices of homeworkers themselves, both in the past and in the present. Only then can we get beyond current policy options to imagine those social conditions (such as accessible, affordable dependent care or community located workshops) that would enable women truly to choose between working within or outside of the home.

The History of Homework Legislation

In their defense of homework, the Vermont knitters challenged arguments against homework that originated nearly a century ago. In the chaos of rapid industrialization, reformers fought to regulate homework as part of a larger quest for labor standards for all workers, protective legislation for women, and maintenance of the family wage. These reformers, especially the women of the National Consumers' League and the Women's Trade Union League, sought maximum hours, minimum wages, child labor regulations, and workplace safety measures to protect the health of young female industrial workers, whom they saw as potential mothers. Such measures, however, also would increase the cost to businesses of employing women. Some employers, consequently, forced women out of the workplace. Along with improved wages for men, gained through unionization, reformers believed that the laws would allow wives and children to remain at home or at school, with husbands in the work force supporting them. The prohibition of homework, with its long hours and low wages that undercut male workers' demands for better working conditions and higher wages, was essential to their plans. Homework regulation was thus a form of protective legislation that assumed the separation of home and work. Mothers did not belong in the waged work force, a point that reformers dramatized through a portrait, mockingly entitled "Sacred Motherhood," of a haggard woman suckling an infant at her foot-powered sewing machine (Boris, 1986a; Kessler-Harris, 1985).

Since the mid-nineteenth century, women who stayed at home because of their cultural traditions and/or family responsibilities had taken in homework. These women, most of whom were married, worked because their men held seasonal, casual jobs and earned too little to sustain their families. (To a lesser extent the old and disabled also became homeworkers.) They included rural women who lacked other means to earn wages and immigrant women in the Italian, Jewish, and Spanish-speaking districts of Northeastern, Midwestern, and Southwestern cities (U.S. Women's Bureau, 1935). These women shared with reformers the belief that mothers should stay at home with children. Unable to live on the income of husbands or other family members, or on charity, such women took in homework, despite its exploitative conditions, because it was necessary for family survival.

Like the Vermont knitters, most homeworkers who answered government queries in the 1920s and 1930s cited care of children and household responsibilities as the major reasons for doing homework. Respondents also listed physical disability and old age. A few preferred homework because they could set their own pace, determine their own hours, and still earn the same wages as they would in a factory. A few felt that it was beneath them to work in a factory, and others believed that it was impossible to find factory or office work due to their lack of English skills or to general economic conditions. Still others combined homework with caring for sick relatives or taking in boarders. For the most part, then, unwaged family labor, custom, and limited economic opportunities kept them at homework. Yet when faced with a homework ban in 1933–35, 60 percent of such women took factory jobs. Of those who accepted factory positions, 83 percent were able to make alternative child-care arrangements. Only 15 percent wished they could return to homework (Skinner, 1938).

Regulation of homework began in the late nineteenth century as a crusade against tenement-made goods that middle-class consumers feared were contaminated by tuberculosis, vermin, and filth. Beginning with the 1892 New York State Tenement House Law, regulations were proposed to protect the consumer through licensing that prohibited certain items. Reformers also emphasized the demoralizing environment of the home as a workplace in ways that sustained the public/private dichotomy central to the gender stratification of labor. As Annie S. Daniel of the New York Infirmary for Women and Children put it, "Absolutely no home life is possible in a tenement workroom." Or, as one factory inspector explained, "privacy of the home" succumbed to a "stronger duty," the public interest, which would "rescue . . . all homes and make the necessary division between home and workplace" (Daniel, 1905, p. 628; O'Reilly, 1895, p. 68). Middle-class reformers desired to make working-class homes conform to their own image of domesticity. At the same time, union agreements in the garment trades attempted to stamp out homework (Boris, 1988; Shallcross, 1939).

With the New Deal, under which women reformers played a key role in shaping social welfare and labor policy, homework became federally regulated. The 1933 National Recovery Administration (NRA) established codes of fair competition that prohibited homework in over one hundred industries. When the Supreme Court declared the NRA unconstitutional in 1935, women reformers combined their efforts to win passage of the FLSA in 1938. Viewing an administrative ban on homework as crucial for carrying out the provisions of this act, the Department of Labor instituted special record-keeping requirements for employers of homeworkers to establish that FLSA could never be enforced for homework. By 1939 seventeen states also had laws regulating homework, though none was able to enforce them fully (Boris, 1985; Boris, 1988).

Participants in the debate over homework during the thirties shared a common conception of womanhood that equated women with mothers and mothers with the home. The small-business community's reason for permitting homework—that mothers could earn wages and still watch children—suggested the very circumstances under which their opponents rejected homework: a mother could not properly care for children while engaged in the low-wage piecework of sewing dresses, knitting sweaters, or soldering jewelry. As Clara Beyer of the Division of Labor Standards asked, "Is it socially desirable for a mother with a four months old baby and three other children under 6 to work 33 hours a week for $1.75; or for a mother with 4 children under 5 to work an average of 4 hours a day and receive 63 cents for her week's work?" (Boris, 1985). Women reformers and organized labor opposed homework for its effect on labor standards and interference with union organizing, but protection of the working-class family and the male wage lay at the center of these concerns. Women's Bureau head Mary Anderson reflected the prevailing sentiment when she argued, "The only thing to do about homework is to abolish it and to arrange for high wages for the breadwinner in a family so that his wife and children do not have to supplement the family income by doing homework, or, if there is no regular bread-winner, to provide pensions or relief" (Anderson, 1951, p. 244).

In the late thirties, FLSA discouraged urban employers from sending work across state lines into rural districts to avoid paying the minimum wage required by their own states. At the same time, federal courts disallowed buy-back schemes of employer-controlled rural cooperatives, according to which employers would sell materials to homeworkers and then "buy" the finished product. Homework, however, persisted in rural areas, especially in the business of hand-knitted outerwear, in which throughout the depression women had contracted for knitting from different firms under four or five names. As one woman had complained, "None of the people that do this work do it for pleasure . . . it is for the money. They must have to live and try to keep or help keep up taxes on their little homes. . . . Why should our women . . . be obliged to work at such wages? Is there any way of making things different and women as well as men get living wages?"[3] Though the number of homeworkers in this industry decreased from 20,300 in 1935 to an estimated 6,000–8,000 in 1941, the latter figure still constituted 28 percent of the industry. In the early 1940s, wage and hour administrators found widespread violations in the payment of homeworkers of knitted outerwear and, thus, prohibited homework.[4] The Supreme Court upheld this ruling, applied also to six other industries, in *Gemsco v. Walling* (1945). In 1949 Congress incorporated the prohibitions into the FLSA (*Gemsco v. Walling*, 1945; Boris, 1988).

Following World War II, in response to the apparent consensus on the need for prohibition, industrial homework became less common. Some industries' use of cheap labor abroad and/or profit from economies of scale also made the use of homeworkers less attractive. The number of homeworkers in knitted outerwear had dwindled to about one thousand by 1981, constituting about 5.3 percent of the industry's work force. This figure, though representing a drastic decline from earlier years, also represents the beginning of a resurgence in homework (both in old industries, such as knitted outwear, and in new ones, such as microcomputer assembly and word processing), which issues from the unstable economy of the 1970s. As the garment unions weakened and economic and political refugees from the Americas and Asia entered the work force in increasing numbers, garment manufacturers and their contractors began to pay less for homework, much of which had been taken on by the new immigrants. Meanwhile, industries faced with increasing competition promoted the deregulation of industry and joined ideological supporters of "free enterprise" and "the right to work" to dismantle homework regulations. Indeed, the desire to make American industry more competitive by cutting labor costs and ending government protection of organized labor informed Hatch's prohomework Freedom of the Workplace Act as much as the desire to appeal to women who wanted to work at home (Boris and Daniels, 1989).

Homework and Motherhood in the 1980s

Opponents of homework today address the issue without the "sacred motherhood" rhetoric of the past. These labor liberals contend that homework undermines labor standards (health and safety, minimum wage, maximum hours, etc.), encourages employers and employees not to accurately report wages or hours to the Internal Revenue Service, tramples the rights of undocumented workers, and condones competition that is unfair to law-abiding businesses and unions. They call for childcare in the workplace so that mothers can go to work "in decent places" instead of being forced to take work into their homes because they lack such care (Committee on Education and Labor, 1982). Proponents of homework, in contrast, argue as they have in the past that women should have the right to work at home while also caring for their children.

Homework defenders still associate homeworkers with motherhood. Before hearings in 1981 to rescind the outerwear prohibition, Vermont entrepreneur C. B. Vaughan urged that "we work together to enable the mothers of small children to stay at home to care for their children and at the same time have the opportunity to earn income (U.S. Dept. of Labor, 1981b, p. 440) In a resolution supporting homework in 1984, the Iowa Senate argued that "no rational legislative objective is served by effectively forcing mothers out of the home and into the factory."[5] Vermonters, the state's Secretary of Labor, Joel Cherington, asserted, prefer mother care to day-care because they value "the family as a building block in our society, and because of the costs associated with child care." (U.S. Dept. of Labor, 1981b, pp. 66–67) As the Center on National Labor Policy (counsel for many of the Vermont knitters) argued in one brief filed with the Department of Labor, "The children know their mother is home with them and she can teach them the skills and values which would otherwise go untaught." The knitters themselves constantly attacked day-care out of the belief that "it is important that preschool children be with their mothers," although a few complained about lack of available services in their rural regions. Others recognized that the cost of child care would consume so much of their wages that it would not be worth working outside the home.[6]

Yet in the debate about the Vermont knitters, even the most diehard supporters of motherhood as woman's noblest profession, like Senator Jeremiah Denton (R-Ala.), recognized the economic necessity for two-earner families and thus viewed homework as a necessary compromise between economic reality and cultural preferences. Acknowledging the entrance of married women with small children into the official labor force, the Heritage Foundation supported letting Americans work out of their homes. Moreover, the Center on National Labor Policy claimed that such homework offers a huge "non-monetary advantage" to society. Because of its flexible hours, homework gives women more time than a factory or office job to do nonpaid work, such as volunteer work, nurturing activities, and other traditional women's tasks (U.S. Senate, 1984, pp. 76–77; Germanis; 1984).

In the rhetoric of deregulators, welfare and dependence stand in opposition to homework and independence. The Heritage Foundation argued that prohibiting homework "would be a serious blow to thousands of women seeking financial independence" (Germanis, 1984). Similarly, Senator Orrin Hatch introduced the Freedom of the Workplace Act as part of "a comprehensive initiative aimed at removing the barriers [that] prevent families and women in transition [female heads of households] from reaching their potential and achieving economic self-sufficiency." Appropriating the phrase "feminization of poverty," Hatch perceived homework to be one tool—along with various workfare schemes and private sector training programs—that would take women off welfare and make poor women "independent." Moreover, it would allow them to work at home and care for small children (Hatch, 1983, S–16981–2).

Homeworkers themselves also associated their work with autonomy, self-sufficiency, and independence, which were otherwise difficult for them to achieve in the economy of rural New England. No precise statistical profile of the knitters and other homeworkers in Vermont and the New England states is possible; but their letters and comments reflect a range of economic and social situations, including divorced heads of households on welfare, retired couples on social security, and college-educated, homeowning, dual-earner families. Like rural homeworkers in the past, the Vermont knitters were primarily female, white native born, either mothers of young children or older women. Whether working class or middle class, all faced a labor market in which jobs for women consisted of part-time work or of low-paying service, retail, or manufacturing jobs. Economic pressure in the stagnated economy of the late 1970s encouraged them to earn wages; in an economy where women were paid three-fifths what men were paid, homework appeared to be a viable alternative to pink-collar jobs that included the hidden costs of child care, transportation, and wardrobe (U.S. Dept. of Labor, 1981a, p.189).

As Violet Jones of Hardwick, Vermont, a divorced mother of two preteen boys, wrote to the wage and hour administrator, home knitting "gives me the opportunity to become self supportive and off of state aid." A Maine woman commented on the proposed deregulation of homework, "It just doesn't make sense to ban homeknitting when it is helping people to help themselves and helping the economy at the same time." A Massachusetts woman poignantly combined her feelings about traditional mothering, her distaste for dependence on the state, and her need for "productive" labor:

> Children need a home life, and . . . I am now able to stay home and nurture my own children not rely on others for their child care. My husband is under medical care for a pre-ulcer condition and because I can knit at home I can relieve him of some of the burden of our financial support. There are many women like me. We want to be productive not just reproductive. Many of us don't want full time careers and "latch-key" children. We just want to help out, but not at the expense of our children. We need our "at home" jobs. Please help us!

Although perceiving her labor as supplementary, as the majority of homeworkers do, this Massachusetts woman found satisfaction in being able to maintain her web of familial interdependence through homework.

Many women have internalized the criterion of worth that undervalues bearing children and the tasks related to nurturing them. Yet, at the same time, many of these women criticize the organization of factory labor that interferes with their ability to care for dependents. A Norridgewock, Maine, woman protested that working in a factory was not worth the sacrifice:

> I have worked for minimum wage in mills and factories in Maine and Massachusetts in the woolen, paper, plastic and shoe industries. I know what the conditions in factories like those are and what the workers have to tolerate in the way of noise pollution, air pollution and other poor working conditions. I know what working seven to three is like; getting to work when the sun is just rising in the morning, getting home just as it is doing down, not seeing the sunshine for five days a week. I know mothers and fathers who only see their babies when they are asleep in their cribs. Believe me, "minimum wage" doesn't begin to cover it.[7]

Since the New Deal, labor legislation has regulated but hardly transformed the deadening experience of most factory work. The Vermont knitters, claiming that "working in a factory is demeaning, and working at home has dignity," have taken factory conditions to task. Although during hearings in Burlington, Vermont and Washington, D.C., the ILGWU constantly linked homework with sweatshops, the knitters imagined the home as a place of rest and took offense that anyone could call their well-maintained houses sweatshops (U.S. Dept. of Labor, 1981a, pp. 232, 268; U.S. Dept. of Labor, 1981b, pp. 460–70).

Homework, the knitters believed, fosters independence not only because it allows them to earn money but also because they perceive themselves in control of their labor. Virginia Gray of Greensboro, Vermont, testified, "Factory work with straight time, two fifteen minute breaks and at lunch is boring, I know. I believe that I can get done more at home with the freedom to do anything as I want to and to knit during the day and in the evenings if I wish to. I like a chance to do different things and that being home lets me do" (U.S. Dept. of Labor, 1981a, p. 249). Another woman wrote, "I enjoy being at home, and not having someone looking over my shoulder while I work." Lacking direct supervision, having no card to punch or bell to obey, these homeworkers report a relative autonomy over their work. They think of themselves not as laborers but as artisans, as skilled workers, making arts and crafts rather than mass-produced products.[8]

However, the control the knitters actually have over their labor varies considerably, depending on whether they design the hats or sweaters they knit, whether they choose colors and yarn, and whether they are truly independent contractors. While most own their knitting machines (which are hand-operated shuttle types that have a row of little teeth resembling knitting needle tips along the top), many have purchased them and taken lessons from the "manufacturer" who is their major source of orders. If a knitter buys supplies, especially yarn, from this manufacturer and the finished product goes back to that same person for marketing, then FLSA considers the knitter an employee, even if the "employer" did not instruct on colors and design (U.S. Dept. of Labor, 1981b, pp. 121–29; U.S. Dept. of Labor, 1981a, pp. 265–66).

Moreover, most of the knitters followed patterns determined by manufacturers. For example, the Stowe Woolens receipt order sheet for Gene Gray reveals handwritten notes: "The little border just before and after the reindeer itself is white. Thank you. Please do these sweaters last."[9] Certainly the descriptions provided by knitters suggest a predetermined quality to the work, albeit of a skilled kind. While the knitter sets up the machine by pushing out the amount of needles, the work process itself consists simply of moving the shuttle back and forth except when finishing or beginning an item. Moreover, the knitters rely on punch cards, eliminating the need to manually change needle lengths per row. For some machines, the design comes on computer-programmed cards that further eliminate the need for skill or creativity (U.S. Dept. of Labor, 1981a, pp. 268–71).

Even though the knitters are not considered independent contractors and lack the autonomy or artistry of the true craftswoman, they do sometimes finish their work by hand, and they certainly control their work pace to a greater degree than factory workers or many other kinds of garment homeworkers. The Vermont women knit between ten and thirty hours each week and choose how much work to accept over a two-week period or whether to knit at all that week. Many knitters expressed the sentiments of Jan Kuhn of Johnson, Vermont, who wrote, "Although my working conditions, i.e., small children constantly present, make it difficult to compute my hourly wage exactly, I estimate my earnings to be $5.00 per hour. Even days when my knitting develops problems or the children are difficult I still earn the minimum wage."[10] Working at home means interrupted labor, phones to answer, and clothes to wash, a style of work familiar to many women with small children. If such patterns curtail production and ultimately decrease the number of hours devoted to knitting, the knitters seem less concerned with such factory-imposed criteria than with controlling the quality and distribution of their time.

The Vermont knitters' concern for control over their own labor acknowledges a connection between women's rights and the right to work that is hardly surprising, given the origins of each in classical liberalism. These terms were not often drawn together in the past because of the residue of patriarchal thinking within liberalism itself that regarded women as dependents. Because liberalism divided social life into private and public, family and state, women and men, because its generic individual was the man who was associated with the market and the polity, its concepts of choice, opportunity, and rights applied to only one sex. Connected to nature rather than culture, women were controlled by biology and thus belonged to the private realm of the family (Eisenstein, 1984; Olson, 1983).

Women were thought of as children, "wards of the state," requiring state protection. Freedom of contract, judges reasoned, which men possessed hardly could apply to women in their condition of dependency. Thus, social reformers argued for the prohibition of homework and other labor legislation on the basis of the state's right to exercise its police powers to protect potential as well as actual mothers; the courts concurred. (A notable exception was the Supreme Court decision *Adkins v. Children's Hospital* of 1923, which struck down the Washington, D.C., minimum wage law for women. There the justices argued that women's newly enfranchised status made them equal to men and that they too had the right to compete in the marketplace free from "protective" legislation [Hill, 1979; Baer, 1978; Adkins v. Children's Hospital, 1923].)

Today some of the most outspoken homeworkers have taken up this notion of women's rights, declaring with Mary Clement of Ripon, Wisconsin, "I am tired of the antiquated idea that women must be taken care of." Many knitters reject the concept of government "protection" with the bitter comment that such protection is depriving them of their work (U.S. Senate, 1984, p. 73). Nevertheless, few homeworkers identify themselves as feminists, even when drawing on an ideology of rights. Mary Louise Norman from Denver wrote to the Department of Labor, "Not every woman is inclined to march for equal rights. Many of us prefer to stay at home with husband and children and WORK for equal rights. We believe in FREEDOM OF CHOICE. I can knit, be at home when my two teenagers need me, bake a chocolate cake, collect my neighbors' UPS packages and deliveries, keep an eye on the neighborhood for vandals . . . *and* provide city and state with taxes all at the same time. This makes me something of a Wonder Woman compared to my 'sister' marchers." While evidence suggests that knitters draw on existing kinship and women's friendship networks (e.g., Audrey Pudvah and her sister knitted for the same firm), they belong to a woman-centered, but rarely feminist, culture. Yet, one woman who sold knitting machines and had hired homeworkers in the past declared that the practice allowed women who cared for their families to feel "some independence from their husbands."[11] Although the meagerness of homework wages limited women's financial autonomy and certainly never led to complete economic independence from their spouses, homework income did supplement men's earnings and provided a check on men's absolute power over family finances.

Kathy Hobart was one of the most combative of the Vermont women. Identifying herself as a feminist, she declared, "I don't believe that a woman should be home, that she needs to be home with her children. The only reason that I choose to be home is because it keeps me from getting an ulcer." Yet even she admitted, "My children benefit most by my staying at home, I think I have a right and my children have a right to have me home with them." Hobart's stance in favor of both women's responsibility as mothers and women's right to work and be economically independent reflects the complexity of the homework dilemma: "I look at this as a women's issue because I just think women have been forced to choose . . . [between] being full-time mothers or workers finding work in the workplace, and I think for those of us who have found an alternative measure to both and can get them to work together, we should be encouraged rather discouraged. I think this is a real struggle, and in these two identities of being a worker or mother it has caused a lot of stress and anxiety for women (U.S. Dept. of Labor, 1981a, pp. 490–91; U.S. Dept. of Labor, 1981b, pp. 30–31, 53). Rather than accepting the dichotomy of work or motherhood assumed by traditional liberals, Hobart proposed a third option for women: work and motherhood.

Whether homework is a viable way to combine work and motherhood, however, depends on the conditions in the home under which both work and mothering occur. What appears a reasonable alternative for Kathy Hobart and others living in single family dwellings with employed husbands in fact opens the way for the continued exploitation of poorer, more desperate women. For many women, the self-sufficiency and alternative organization of work and home promised by homework is often illusionary. Clerical homeworkers in California, Wisconsin, and South Carolina have found that insurance companies periodically speed up their claims quotas, define homeworkers as "independent contractors" to avoid paying benefits, and force homeworkers to rent or purchase machines. For some, the opportunity to have more time for their families has also proven to be a myth. One California woman described how "her daughter would stand outside her workroom and ask, 'Mommy, are you going to be done tonight before I go to bed?' " (Boris and Daniels, 1989, pp. 183–214; Pollack, 1986).

Deregulation of homework also allows factory employers to overburden underpaid garment seamstresses with additional piecework to be done, at home. As Sarah, an undocumented worker for more than a decade, testified at New York State hearings in April 1981, "The homeworkers never get a rest. They don't go home to their families. They go home to continue to work so they can feed their families and when they go to get paid, the boss has an excuse not to pay them and they have to wait until he feels like paying and sometimes not the amount that they thought they were going to get paid." For these immigrant women, who live mostly in New York, New Jersey, Miami, and Los Angeles, the family economy exists close to the edge of survival; internalized clocks, set by low piece rates, push them on. As one woman explained, she purchased her sewing machine because "I had no choice being that "I'm a mother with children without a husband, in order to alleviate the cost of living"—though it took her two to three hours to sew a dress for which she received $1.30. Moreover, since the homeworker cannot predict exactly how long her bundle of piecework will take, she must sometimes turn to her children for help: "You have sort of a deadline and the child is brought in" (New York State, 1981, pp. 65–79, 81–92; Boris and Daniels, 1989, pp. 165–179).

Such women live lives reminiscent of an earlier generation of immigrant pants finishers, artificial flower makers, and embroiderers whose exploitation symbolized homework for reformers and unionists. Opponents of homework have these women in mind when they speak of the homeworker as a victim, "the most desperate, especially mothers with small children," "the most vulnerable," scared, poor workers "who don't know their rights" and need protection.[12] At 1982 House hearings, Senator Daniel Patrick Moynihan (D-N.Y.) expressed the classical argument for protective legislation when he portrayed homework as a system for exploiting defenseless women, "locked up in a house with a month's supply of gloves . . . to sew at 20 cents an hour," who if they complain of underpayment face deportation. Moreover, like proponents of homework, he called on the language of rights, evoking the success of the New Deal's Frances Perkins who "got those women out of those sweatshops. She got them their rights." However, whereas proponents referred to women's right to work, Moynihan referred to a very different notion of rights: women's right to be protected under the law from unfair labor practices.

Moynihan and other opponents of homework, like ILGWU's former president, Sol Chaikin, argue the portrayal of homeworkers as middle-class women handcrafting while their toddlers play by the fire distorts "the real world" (Committee on Education and Labor, 1984, pp. 38–45, pp. 66–73). Class and race stratify homeworkers not only in terms of their material conditions but also in terms of their ability to see themselves as part of a single economic system. One Vermont woman expressed her resentment of "a regulation that the manufacturers and the union people feel that we need to protect the illegal alien," as if FLSA was intended to protect only immigrants (U.S. Dept. of Labor, 1981b, p. 481).

Opponents of homework, like their predecessors generations ago, also argue for justice and moral right, drawing on turn-of-the-century concerns for health and family welfare. One state AFL-CIO official noted: "How industrial homework, as it has forced women workers to labor for long hours for low pay, as it forced mothers to 'subcontract' to their children to raise the household income, fosters a nurturing, loving home environment is beyond our belief." Another opponent relied on contemporary feminist ideas that state that "the laws have to apply to everyone, no matter where I live or what kind of a family I have." Hence, she concluded that because homework is particularly advantageous for women with children to care for, permitting it "would discriminate against those with older or no children" (Committee on Education and Labor, 1982, p. 200; U.S. Dept. of Labor, 1981b, pp. 999–100).

Advocates of women, in contrast, have rejected the portrait of the homeworker as victim even when they oppose homework generally. Grace Lyu-Volckhausen of the New York City Commission on the Status of Women, a consultant to Local 23–25, ILGWU, emphasized that homeworkers are skilled seamstresses whose self-image suffers from the lack of recognition given to their work. Representing the National Consumers' League and the Coalition of Labor Union Women, Ruth Jordan couched her testimony at the Washington hearings in the rhetoric of sisterhood. She spoke of a public policy based on women's values, the same "female difference" that her predecessors at the League had drawn on and that the Vermont knitters themselves associate with women: "I stress the caring part, because I think as women workers, we should be concerned with all aspects of nurturing. And part of the aspect is what is happening to our other sisters, whether they work in rural settings or in urban slums." She rejected any proposal that threatened to undermine national standards as pitting one group of "sisters" against another or that inhibited the ability of workers to organize, as homework historically has. For her, homework became a women's right issue but not as defined by Senator Hatch: "It is more of a woman's issue than anything else. Women already earn less than 59 percent of what men earn, and as in the knitwear case it is the women who are workers. They are denied the ability to upgrade their skills and economic well-being." Jordan argued that homework rarely brings a living wage for women and their children, that the problem with homework was that employers, not women, benefited (New York State, 1981, pp. 106–114; U.S. Dept. of Labor, 1981b, pp. 230–44; Committee on Education and Labor, 1982, p. 148).

The Future of Homework

The debate over industrial homework in the 1980s emphasizes women's precarious position in the restructuring of the U.S. economy. Unable to find jobs that pay enough for them to afford child care, unable to find adequate child care even when they can afford it, women are resorting to homework. How can feminist arguments accommodate women's need for both wage labor and child care without reinforcing the gender stratifications of labor or the ways in which class and race divide women?

The Vermont knitters' merger of home and workplace calls into question labor legislation that focuses only on the workplace, but it does not adequately challenge the home's place in the economy or of women within the home. Homeworkers are underpaid by their employers and continue to perform unpaid household labor for their families; for them, both parts of the double day take place in the home, which often leads to a continuous working "day." Their willingness to perpetuate these conditions encourages the view that all women are only secondary earners who need not have jobs that pay better and undercuts women's struggle in the workplace for flexible hours, better pay and benefits, and more control over the work process. Furthermore, combining home and work may conflict with other rights women should have in the home: the right to rest and leisure, the right to nurture and mother with dignity, the right to keep homes free from exploitative labor, whether waged or unwaged. Finally, homework discourages setting up alternative facilities for child care. Because the performance of piecework under deadlines or financial pressures leads women to tend but not necessarily care for their children, the presumed advantage of homework is an illusion for many women. By being both mothers and wage earners, they relieve men of responsibility for family labor and reinforce the notion that children should be cared for in the home by their own mothers.

If allowing homework is a poor option for women as a group, prohibiting it also fails to address the problem of women's need to perform both family labor and wage labor. We need to devise social alternatives that value the care of children but do not limit women to this activity. Some alternatives already exist. Black Americans, for example, have relied on extended kinship networks to care for children. European social democracies have devised family policies that allow mothers to stay home with small children and keep their seniority and other job rights. In the United States, proposed parental leave legislation is a first step toward dissolving the gendered identity of caretaking, although until women earn as much as men, it will be mostly women who, because they have less pay to lose by leaving their jobs, look after dependents. Single women still will have limited choices. Income transfer payments for caring for dependents could relieve women of the burden of wage earning but would do so at the cost of reinforcing the sexual division of labor unless they matched male wages so that some men might also choose to stay home. Unless implemented with other reforms—among them, accessible child care, elderly care, and comparable worth legislation—such payments will not be adequate for many women to become independent. Moreover, only when nurturing is a primary value for men as it is for women will the gender stratification be broken that now crowds women into a few occupations, encourages part-time work, and leads to lower wages for women as a group. By transforming the power relations under which women work in the workplace and in the home, we can reorganize both the political and the gender economies (Stack, 1974; Adams and Teich, 1980; Taub, 1986; Hayden, 1984).

The solution of the knitters—workplace autonomy without financial independence—cannot benefit working women as a group. Control over time allocation does not compensate for lack of control over one's product or piece rates without benefits. Historically, homework has meant exploited labor, meager wages, and excessive hours. Theoretically, these conditions could be regulated, but no evidence suggests that the state could do so adequately in the future when it so consistently has failed in the past.[13]

The ILGWU has been monitoring Labor Department regulation of homework over the last few years in order to document its inadequacy and argue for the imposition of a new ban. The Labor Department, in turn, has lifted the restrictions on six of the remaining prohibited industries and probably will also lift the ban on women's apparel, an action that unions and many women's organizations oppose. The DOL actions have been contested and will be decided in the courts sometime in the late eighties. Meanwhile, the number of knitted outerwear employers resorting to homeworkers continues to increase, not only in rural regions and the Northeast but in New York City, Los Angeles, Miami, Chicago, and Philadelphia as well—a reminder that not all homeworkers will fit the profile of the Vermont women who sparked the protest. While many of the most prominent actors in the Vermont case are again knitting, Audrey Pudvah has moved on to form her own design firm. She creates patterns for her employees, who also work at home, to program with computers (Boris, 1986b; Boris, 1989).

Audrey Pudvah does not need a certificate because computer homework is legal, though the AFL-CIO has called for its prohibition. Though knitted outerwear is a small industry, telecommunications promises to use homeworkers even more extensively. Insurance, banking, and other industries in need of a cheap, flexible, clerical work force already are resorting to homeworkers (Boris and Daniels, 1989, pp. 258–72; Appelbaum, 1987). The debate surrounding the old industrial homework prohibitions must therefore be seen as a prelude to a larger struggle over the shape and control of the American workplace, a struggle in which women's contribution to the reformulation of the gender system will play a crucial part.

Notes

1. The analysis in this article is based on extensive reading of the public record, including written comments and unpublished testimony, housed in the Division of Labor Standards, Office of Special Minimum Wage, 4th floor, Department of Labor, Washington, D.C. For these events, see *Daily Labor Report,* February 18, 1981, sec. A, pp. 11–13, and July 14, 1981, sec. F, p. 21; *Daily Report,* November 30, 1983, sec. A, pp. 1, 9–10, and sec. D, pp. 1 ff. For new regulations, see U.S. Department of Labor, Employment Standards Administration, Wage and Hour Division, 29 CFR Part 530, "Employment of Homeworkers in Certain Industries; Final Rule," *Federal Register,* v. 49, n. 215, pt. 2, Monday, November 5, 1984, pp. 44262–44272.
2. Senator Orrin Hatch, remarks on "It's Your Business: Industrial Homework: Why Not?" transcript of program no. 231, tape date: January 31, 1984; air dates: February 4–5, 1984, p. 11. Available from U.S. Chamber of Commerce, Washington, D.C. 20262.
3. O.H. Brinkerhoff, Central Square, Oswego Co., N.Y., February 16, 1935 to Franklin Delano Roosevelt, box 8385, folder "Industries (I-N)," NRA Homework Committee Papers, National Archives.
4. For conditions in knitted outerwear, see U.S. Department of Labor, Wage and Hour Division, Research and Statistics Branch, "Current Status of Home Work in the Knitted Outerwear Industry," November 1941, pp. 4–33, and Findings and Opinion

of the Administrator, "In the Matter of: The Recommendation of Industry Committee No. 32 for a Minimum Wage Rate in the Knitted Outerwear Industry and Industrial Home Work in the Knitted Outerwear Industry," March 30, 1942, pp. 13–20ff., both in the Department of Labor Library, Washington, D.C.

5. Senate Concurrent Resolution no. 105 (Iowa 1984 Bills) (see also 1984 sess., House Joint Resolution no. 49, Virginia Bills) in DOL files.
6. Michael Avakian and Edward F. Hughes, "Statement of the Center on National Labor Policy, Inc., in support of Proposed Rulemaking to Rescind Restriction on Homework in the Knitted Outerwear Industry," May 11, 1984, pp. 5, 9–10; for an example from the knitters, Debra Waugh to William M. Otter, May 11, 1984, in DOL files.
7. Violet Jones, Box 322, Harswick, Vt., to Otter, n.d., and attached untitled paper; Mary Berard, R.F.D. L1, Box 3890, Oakland, Maine, to Otter, April 11, 1984; Mrs. Ellen Z. Lampner, 48 Orchard St., Randolph, Mass., to William M. Otter, May 3, 1984, pp. 4–5; Linda Clutterbuck, R.F.D., L1, Box 1540, Norridgewock, Maine, to Otter, April 18, 1984; all in DOL files.
8. For example of the numerous references of homeworkers as crafts-workers, Robin Frost, P.O. Box 61, Anson, Maine, to "Dear Sir," n.d. in DOL files.
9. Stowe Woolens Receipt and Order Sheet for Gene Gray, exhibit no. 21 for Burlington Hearings, DOL files.
10. Mrs. Jan Kuhn, Box 74, Johnson, Vermont, to Mr. Henry T. White, Jr., January 2, 1981, in "Exhibits, Public Hearing to Commence Labor Dept. Review of 'Homeworker Rules,' " DOL files.
11. Mary Louise Norman, Nicely Knit—Denver, 1310 Clermont Street, Denver, Colo., to Otter, April 21, 1984; Wendie Ballinger, Special Stitches, 624 Westmore, Oreana, Ill., to Otter, April 21, 1984, in DOL files.
12. For example, Jill Pollack, "Stamping Out New Sweatshops," *News, North Jersey,* September 8, 1981; Frederick Siems, "Sweatshop Close-up: Filth, Crowding and Child Labor Are the Norm," *Herald Journal* (Indiana), September 21, 1979, ILGWU clippings files, New York City.
13. The possibility of regulating electronic homework is more promising, since programs already exist to monitor the number of keystrokes made by typists.

14

Abandoned Women

Mary Coombs

Miss Hanson was a servant at a boarding house when she met Mr. Johnson in 1895.[1] After a few month's acquaintance, they became engaged and began to sleep together. She vainly waited thirteen years for him to marry her, meanwhile bearing his child. Finally, she sued and recovered $8000.

Miss Hanson was not the first to respond to seduction and abandonment with a lawsuit. Miss Giese, another plaintiff, apparently persuaded the jury in the Ripon municipal court that the defendant, Mr. Schultz, with the aid of a promise to marry her, "and his persuasions thereunder, seduced, debauched and carnally knew the plaintiff, and got her with child." The pregnancy miscarried, the defendant refused to keep his promise, and Miss Giese sued. The Wisconsin Supreme Court twice reversed verdicts in her favor, holding that the jury could compensate her for the loss of virtue and reputation and the mental suffering caused by the seduction, but not for the miscarriage and its physical effects.

Seduction and abandonment did not end with the close of the nineteenth century. Miss Klitzke was in her mid-twenties in 1915 when Mr. Davis, a young man from the same small Wisconsin town, began courting her. He was away at college, but wrote her and called on her when he came home. According to Miss Klitzke's testimony, they became engaged in 1916 and she then agreed to have intercourse, though she had refused earlier. The engagement continued for several years and, when Davis

---

This paper was originally presented at the Feminism and Legal Theory Conference in Madison, Wisconsin in June 1988. A somewhat longer version is available as "Agency and Partnership: A Study of Breach of Promise Plaintiffs" (*Yale Journal of Law and Feminism* [1990]). I want to thank the participants in the conference, as well as my indefatigable colleagues, Marc Fajer, Michael Fischl, and Jeremy Paul, for their wise counsel. I particularly want to thank Susan Sponnoble, University of Miami School of Law, 1989, for her research skills, her insights and her support.

went into the Army during World War I, he wrote and begged her to remain true. On his return, however, he sought to break off the engagement, explaining that "he had a lot of money coming from home" that he would lose if he married her. A week later, he married someone else. She sued and recovered $6500 in compensatory and punitive damages.

The cause of action under which each of these women sought compensation was breach of promise to marry. The plaintiffs in breach of promise actions presented themselves as frustrated seekers after the American dream, women's division.[2] The injuries they suffered included the loss of economic advantage of a promised marriage, the humiliation and pain of being jilted and (in some cases) the additional psychic and economic costs of allowing themselves to be seduced in reliance on the promised marriage.

To accept such claims as valid would be to assume that the plaintiffs' stories were credible and that the harms they exposed were real. Two elements stand out in these stories. First, women wanted very much to be married and to have the security of being someone's wife. The loss of that opportunity was a genuine economic harm. Second, women who would otherwise remain chaste until marriage might be seduced by their fiancés' assurances that they were "as good as married." In giving up their virtue without assuring their future, these women were harmed. They suffered shame and humiliation; their chances for future happiness were dashed, for they were no longer eligible to be "blushing brides."

This picture of the role of women in American life contrasted radically with the picture that many contemporary feminists endorsed. Feminists' views of the proper role of marriage were inconsistent with a recognition of its monetary aspects. While traditional romanticism was rejected, the commodification of marriage was also ideologically uncomfortable. Women were to achieve economic independence through careers providing respect and fair wages. Marriage was to be an emotional partnership, rooted in continuing mutual affection. Furthermore, women were to discover their sexual nature. The rules of sexual behavior were to be the same for men and women.

Both the presumption that women were seduced into sexual activity and the claim that the loss of virginity was a devastating harm to women contradicted the emerging feminist view of women's sexuality. Thus, there were understandable reasons for feminists not to endorse the cause of breach of promise to marry plaintiffs.

At least some of the women who brought such suits, nonetheless, appear to have suffered real harms, for reality had not—indeed, has not entirely—caught up to the feminist ideal. Furthermore, bringing such a suit is itself an untraditional action for women. The plaintiffs did not simply accept the harm that had been done to them, but took action to improve their situations. They were not, then, simply victims, but agents in their own lives (Gordon, 1988a). Agency in this sense has been succinctly defined as "the way in which people make history, although not under conditions of their own choosing" (Interrante & Lasser, 1979, p. 26; cf. Marx, 1983, p. 287).

The breach of promise to marry action is rarely invoked anymore and the injury that it is purportedly aimed at treating—broken engagements—no longer seems a harm appropriate for legal redress.[3] A marriage can be immediately followed by a divorce at will in many states and such a brief marriage usually has few or no financial consequences. Similarly, premarital sex is now sufficiently common that the loss of one's virginity is unlikely to have significant consequences. I would like here, however, to project us back into a past when the cause of action, though perhaps in its twilight years, had some significance and examine the goals and needs of the plaintiffs and the kinds of criticisms to which these women and their cause of action were subjected, both by the mainstream press and by other women. In this essay I want to explore the ways in which feminists of an earlier era did and could have responded to the actions of women who sought control over their world within the boundaries of traditional roles and ideologies.[4]

Finally, I want to consider how contemporary feminists might respond to such agency. We can find similarly problematic parallels in the actions of organized right-wing women or the resistance of many divorcing mothers to joint custody. These intersections of agency and traditional roles present both opportunity and danger to feminists. I speculate briefly about how feminists, by encouraging self-empowerment of more traditional women and their concerns, can bring them within the concerns of the feminist movement in a process of mutual transformation.

The Cause of Action: A Brief Summary

Breach of promise plaintiffs had to fit their claims for recognition and compensation within a doctrinal structure that corresponded only roughly with their real complaints. The essential claim was contractual: the defendant had agreed to marry the plaintiff and then breached that contract.[5] The plaintiff could thus recover, under standard contract theory, the monetary value of a marriage to the defendant. Damages or harms not usually compensable in contract actions were also potentially available: for humiliation and mental suffering; for seduction, when the plaintiff had yielded in reliance on his promise to marry her; and punitive damages, if the defendant had been particularly outrageous in his treatment of the plaintiff.

The range of admissible evidence was unusually broad. Furthermore, the determination of liability and damages was peculiarly in the hands of the jury. The variety of potential bases for damages and the lack of any precise criteria for measuring their value meant that the judges had little basis for controlling the verdict, a source of concern to defendants and critics.

The cause of action was severely criticized and, ultimately, in some jurisdictions, legislatively abolished. Some of the criticism reflected traditional lawyerly concerns, such as a formalist dislike for the admixture of tort elements in a contract cause of action (see Gilmore, 1974) or pragmatic concerns over certain remedial and evidentiary peculiarities. The critics, in both the academic and popular press, however, were extraordinarily virulent. Their criticism frequently embodied views of women and of marriage that changed over time, but were consistently contrary to those underlying breach of promise claims.

Critics asserted that the cause of action was "misused."[6] Women who brought such claims were adventuresses, golddiggers,[7] and schemers. Even when there had been a broken engagement, the woman who brought a suit was seeking only cash, not comfort (Brown, 1929; Lawyer, 1894). The classic example is the fictional protagonist, Lorelei Lee (Loos, 1963). Furthermore, critics contended, jurors were too easily swayed by the tearful melodrama created for their benefit, especially by an attractive woman.[8]

The most scathing attacks were on the use of such suits for settlement. High verdicts encouraged defendants to settle, a tendency allegedly exacerbated by the reluctance of decent men to have their private affairs exposed for the benefit of the sensationalistic press. Critics and legislative opponents referred to the process of complaint followed by settlement as extortion or legalized blackmail (Brown, 1929, p. 495; Feinsinger, 1935, p. 979; N.Y. Civ.Rights L. 61-a, 1987).

Especially in the time period before World War I, critics recognized that women might be hurt by men's unjustified breaking of an engagement. They saw little, if any, overlap, however, between the women who were harmed and the women who sued. These critics acknowledged marriage as central to a woman's life plans. A lengthy but ultimately unconsummated engagement, or a seduction that left the woman unchaste and thus probably unmarriageable caused her real harm. She would never have the chance to be the angel of the house that every Victorian woman, in their eyes, properly aspired to be (Degler, 1980, p. 153; Griswold, 1982, pp. 44–45). If the law could, it should provide some relief for such victims. The breach of promise cause of action, however, could never be the source of that relief. The deserving woman was a lady, a creature of delicacy. Her pain and humiliation would only be increased by bringing a lawsuit where she must recount a story of private pain and humiliation, of unfulfilled promises of eternal love, of sexual importuning and its consequences. No lady would willingly expose these details to a jury and, through the press, to the public at large (Brown, 1929, p. 493; Coombe, 1988, pp. 100–01). Furthermore, a court could only offer money; a lady would never consider money an appropriate recompense for the hurt feelings she had suffered. In essence, the fact that a woman brought a cause of action exposed her as the sort of woman who deserved no sympathy.[9]

Later critics, who fanned the agitation to abolish the cause of action, rejected its fundamental premise. They were hostile to the economic vision embedded in the breach of promise suit. Marriage was to be a partnership rooted in love and affection; a "companionate marriage" (Lindsey & Evans, 1927). The proper choice of partner was essential. If, during engagement, either of the parties decided he or she would not be happy married to the other, the reluctant lover should be free to break off the engagement (Popenoe, 1934, p 442). The law should accommodate such second thoughts, not punish them. Furthermore, the "damages" from such a breach were merely emotional. Women, in this modern view, were or could be economically self-supporting; they had no legitimate claim for lifetime financial support from a man. "Seduction" was reconceptualized as a mutual activity for which damages were inappropriate (Turano, 1934, pp. 43–44).[10]

The Plaintiffs' Perspective

Many women were dependent on marriage for economic survival and a sense of self-worth (May, 1980, p. 67; Rothman, 1987, p. 252).[11] Opportunities for middle-class women to achieve economic self-sufficiency were severely limited in the nineteenth century (Degler, 1980, p. 152; Taylor, 1983, p. 192–93). Jobs available to women were (and are) poorly paying. The unmarried woman was more likely to become a spinster maiden aunt living with one of her siblings than a career woman. Even during the 1930s, when the cause of action was increasingly viewed as obsolete, most middle-class women left the workforce upon marriage to become full-time homemakers, wives and mothers (May, 1980, pp. 63, 117). Indeed, even today women with husbands present are economically better off than single women (See Gelpi, Hartsock, et al., 1986).

Any woman with a valid breach of promise claim had lost at least one opportunity to marry. Furthermore, particularly where the courtship was lengthy or where her "marriage value" had otherwise been reduced (e.g., by seduction), she was now less likely ever to marry. Seduction imposed emotional as well as economic costs on women. Some women, even in Victorian times, and certainly more as the twentieth century wore on, perceived themselves as active participants in their own sexual lives.[12] Other women, however, engaged in intercourse reluctantly and only at the urging of men (Cott, 1978). Furthermore, in the 1920s and 1930s—indeed, even as late as the 1950s—losing one's virginity could be a serious matter. A woman who was no longer chaste had lost something both of psychic value and of value on the marriage market: she was "damaged goods" (Thomas, 1959, p. 214; Sinclair, 1987, p. 78). Breach of promise law could provide partial compensation for these genuine hardships.

What did the plaintiffs seek to achieve by filing suit? Despite the fears of some that men would be coerced into marriage, by the time the woman had determined to bring a suit, she was not concerned primarily with the lost opportunity to marry the defendant. Rather, what she sought compensation for was the pain she had experienced and the constriction of her future life plans. If these were caused by his actions and her reliance on his promises, a legal response would be appropriate.

The harm suffered was particularly acute when the liaison led to the birth of a child.[13] The mother's life, if not "ruined," was at least extraordinarily difficult. The illegitimate child, under the common law, had no claim for support from the father (Vernier, 1936, vol. 1, p. 9). State statutes frequently allowed some sort of bastardy action by which the child and mother could obtain support from the father, but these actions were hedged about by daunting procedural limitations and frequently included extraordinarily low limits on awardable support.[14] Furthermore, the award would be for a periodic payment. Modern studies indicate that even men who have lived with and presumably come to love the children they are being required to support frequently fail to make these payments (Chambers, 1979). Surely the payment rate by fathers of illegitimate children was even lower and the amounts too small to make enforcement practical.

A breach of promise action could serve as a means to obtain a lump sum for the support of an illegitimate child (Grossberg, 1985, pp. 45–47). Breach of promise suits provided a back door to obtaining a cash settlement from the father when the front door was closed or barely cracked open.

The cause of action was not, of course, designed to serve this subterranean purpose: according to the vast majority of courts, the cost of raising the child was not part of the damages suffered when the defendant refused to marry the mother. The ideal solution for these women would have been to reform the cause of action or substitute a more responsive one. Simple abolition of the breach of promise cause of action, without the concurrent development of such legal alternatives, however, could have caused serious economic harm for these women and their children.

A spokesperson for these plaintiffs would thus be cautious about joining the cry to discard the cause of action.

Feminist Responses

One might expect an advocate for women and women's interests to be skeptical of the claim of critics that deserving plaintiffs did not exist, or were the claimants in only an insignificant portion of the cases, and empathetic to the plaintiffs' plight. Instead, to the extent that women publicly discussed or took positions on the cause of action, they generally supported the move to abolish it.[15] For example, the small number of female state legislators in the 1930s included the sponsors of the bills abolishing breach of promise in Indiana,[16] Massachusetts,[17] and Colorado.[18] In Ohio, heart-balm legislation stalled briefly as two women competed for credit for the bill.[19] The arguments used by these women in support of the legislation were similar to those of the male critics. The law, they claimed, could not heal real broken hearts; it ought not try to heal when pocketbooks, not hearts, were empty.[20] The lawsuits were seen as vehicles for extortion and blackmail,[21] while cases that went to trial were a fount of offensively sensationalistic testimony.[22]

Women legislators' statements were echoed by the two popular women writers on the subject. Anita Loos' best seller, *Gentlemen Prefer Blondes*, (1963) may have invented the word "gold-digger." The heroine, Lorelei Lee, is a flapper with a taste for gold. In one incident, she tricks one of her suitors into proposing to her in writing. The letter seems especially useful when she decides she doesn't want to marry Henry. "So the best thing for me to do is to think up some scheme to make Henry decide not to marry me and take what I can get out of it and be satisfied" (Loos, 1963, p. 197).

Dorothy Dunbar Bromley, a writer and journalist specializing in civil liberties and women's issues, mounted a more direct attack on breach of promise plaintiffs. Her 1927 article condemned them as even worse than those childless able-bodied women who "live[d] the life of parasites" on alimony.[23] Bromley also, however, criticized such suits from a feminist vantage. Their greatest defect, she argued, was that they embodied an erroneous view of woman as "still a helpless creature totally dependent upon matrimony for her welfare and subsistence" (p.8). Such a view must be combatted, "[f]or just as long as women seek to profit materially from their relationship with men—both in and out of marriage—there will be no new era for the sex as a whole" (p. 40). Meanwhile, organized women's groups apparently took little or no interest in the debates over the breach of promise action.

In the remainder of this section, I want to speculate about why this woman's cause of action produced such a reaction. Breach of promise suits can be conceptualized on at least two levels: individual and structural. For the particular women who brought them, the fact of bringing the suit and the results of the suit had certain benefits. At the same time, the existence of the cause of action and the public responses it evoked reinforced certain images of women, of marriage, and of sexuality. For feminist women, I suggest, the cause of action was perceived as an ideological impediment to woman's progress, while the particular plaintiffs were largely invisible.[24]

Feminists in the nineteenth and early twentieth century focused much of their attention on the public world: most especially suffrage and political rights and secondarily workplace rights to hold certain jobs, to protections against employer exploitations, and to decent (if not equal) pay.[25] To the extent these issues were the focus of feminists' attention, issues of marriage and sexuality were downplayed.

There were also strains within feminism that did focus on issues of the "private world" of marriage and sexuality.[26] For example, there was substantial agitation over issues of divorce reform (O'Neill, 1967). By the 1920s and 1930s, the dominant feminist approach to these issues was consonant with a modernist vision. They rejected traditional marriage, in which women played a defined and subservient role (Gilman, 1898; Degler, 1980, p. 289). They condemned the double standard; the "New Woman," like the new man, could have sexual interests (Sinclair, 1988, pp. 88–89; Cott, 1987; see generally Thomas, 1959). Marriage was to be "companionate," a freely chosen coming together of two adults for mutual affection and support (O'Neill, 1967), while each also had a place in the outside world of work (Leach, 1980, pp. 195–202). In essence, men and women were to become equal, depending on each other emotionally, but not financially. Women, like men, could aspire to an idealized prototype of the traditional husband.[27]

The vision of marriage and sexuality on which the breach of promise cause of action rested was radically different. It presumed that men and women had different roles to play. It also presumed that women were dependent on men, though simultaneously at risk of being misused or manipulated by them (compare Gordon, 1988a; Dworkin, 1983). A woman's loss of a marriage prospect entailed material harm, for marriage was a primary means of economic security. Furthermore, when a man used the intimacy of engagement to persuade a chaste woman to anticipate her wedding vows this was seduction, not consensual sex.[28] When he did so, and then refused to marry her, the woman had been harmed. She had lost her self-respect and the respect of others. Her value on the marriage market had eroded (Taylor, 1983, p. 34). All these images of women—as economically dependent, as sexually passive, and as subject to a severe double standard—were contrary to the modern images that many feminist felt women should strive to make realities.

Feminists might nonetheless have been sympathetic to the problems of women entangled in the traditional patterns of passivity and dependency if they had recognized their own vision of independent, sexually equal woman as simply an ideal. Modern womanhood, however, was frequently seen as something already achieved. If one believed that woman could be independent, that marriage was essentially a legitimation for bonds of affection, and that sexuality was a matter of choice for both parties, then the stories told by breach of promise plaintiffs made no sense.[29]

It was relatively easy to deny legitimacy to the world views of breach of promise plaintiffs, for the stories of genuine need and harm suggested earlier were not readily heard. Feminists, like other non-lawyers, were dependent on the media for their knowledge. The media chose to publicize two sorts of stories: the sensationalistic and those with human interest appeal. Most fell in the former category, and were generally chosen for the prominence of the defendant. Typically, he was a man of great wealth and fame, and the plaintiff someone not of his social class, such as a stage dancer,[30] an opera fan who was "a brunette of a striking type"[31] or a shopgirl.[32] Many readers would no doubt believe that a man of wealth and breeding never intended nor agreed to marry a woman from the other side of the tracks. Either she had invented her story of an engagement or she was a foolish dupe; in any event, she did not deserve a wife's share of his fortune.[33]

The stories hinted at in the case reports are surely more complex than those texts disclose. One can sometimes discern within them the voices of women who loved, not wisely, but too well. Furthermore, despite the impression the popular press might give of these disputes, appellate cases suggest that juries almost uniformly found for the plaintiff,[34] since few of them are appellants.[35]

If the jurors' understanding reflects the realities of the cases before them, one must ask why the press and critics misread reality. The stories that became known, I suggest, are atypical of the real world and yet stereotypical; they fit comfortably within pre-existing images of rapacious women and beleaguered men.

The apparent willingness of the women's movement to accept the popular press' picture of these women may also be the result of ideological blinders. The picture painted in newspapers and articles did not arouse feminists' suspicion because it was coherent with their images of traditional women against which they defined themselves. Breach of promise plaintiffs, like alimony-seeking wives, represented the worst of what women would be if they did not become independent (Gilman, 1898).

Furthermore, by distancing themselves from such unpopular women, feminists might appear less threatening to the male power structure. This rejection of female dependency served the women's movement in much the same way as the self-deluded claims by some second wave feminists that men would welcome changes that allowed their wives to have their own income and become economically independent (Dworkin, 1983; Ehrenreich, 1984).

To accept or advocate the breach of promise action would have imposed ideological costs on feminism (Sinclair, 1987, pp. 96–97). It may thus have been understandable for feminists to adopt the position they did. The failure to recognize the costs in such a move, i.e., the positive value to a significant group of women of the availability of a "non-feminist" claim is nonetheless disturbing. As indicated above, the breach of promise action served, though imperfectly, to redress real harms suffered by certain women. The fact of taking action on their own behalf also may have served the plaintiffs as a means of overcoming passivity and victimhood. Paradoxically, the breach of promise suit, the most effective action available to these women, required them to present themselves as passive victims, a picture contradicted by the very action of bringing suit.[36] Their agency on their own behalf is thus obscured. Neither of these aspects of the cause of action, both potentially of value to a non-sectarian feminism, appears to have entered into the calculus of the contemporaneous feminist movements.

Empowerment and Ideology

Bringing a law suit is an act of courage and self-empowerment (cf. MacKinnon, 1979; Schneider, 1986). Breach of promise plaintiffs appear to have been women who, at the moment before they filed suit, had failed to achieve their dream. One response to such failure would be to accept the harm as deserved—to see themselves as victims of life's vicissitudes. Instead, they chose to take action, to claim some agency over their lives (cf. Gordon, 1988a). To file suit is to say, first, that I will not accept the harm that happened as my lot in life, and, second, that I will take action to reallocate responsibility for that harm to those who caused it.

Bringing a lawsuit is risky as a form of self-empowerment, however. Filing suit itself does not bring material change, though it may have a psychic impact. One has, in a sense, put oneself in the hands of others.[37] Furthermore, the process of telling one's story in such a public arena is frightening and risky.[38]

Those risks are compounded for breach of promise plaintiffs, for whom the legal tools available are a poor fit. The conception these women had of how they had been harmed and what relief they wanted may have had little to do with the cause of action brought on their behalf by (male) lawyers, subject to the review and control of (male) judges and juries. The stories they needed to tell to win may have been quite different from their own stories. Given that the voice provided by the cause of action was only a distorted version of their own, it is unclear how much they were empowered by speaking.[39]

The question whether using such legal tools as breach of promise suits is ultimately empowering is an open and complex one. The value of the cause of action for women ought not, however, be dismissed out-of-hand because the theory under which the plaintiffs acted appears antithetical to feminists' vision of the long-run interests of women.

Women in a variety of situations have sought to take action to improve their lives, within the limits of traditional roles, by demanding that the bargains implicit in traditional patterns at least be kept. As feminists, we often think these efforts are ultimately self-defeating. Traditional gender relations are not, on the whole, good for women, and the benefits for women are both rarely enforced and worth less than we were taught. Rejecting traditional roles and life-patterns does not necessarily mean, however, rejecting those women who take action to improve their lives within those patterns. They challenge, by their actions, the picture of traditional women as passive, as victims.[40] Yet, just as the feminists of an earlier period apparently found it difficult to feel kinship with breach of promise plaintiffs, many feminist women today seem unable to see the positive elements in the actions of more traditional women.

Three brief examples may clarify my point: women seeking sole custody on divorce, sex workers seeking economic gain, and right-wing activist women. The first two examples involve women making non-feminist arguments in support of their own material needs. I deal separately with the last group—women driven primarily by a traditionalist ideology—for they raise rather different issues for feminists.

Many feminists seem uncomfortable in responding to women who demand recognition of and support for their bonding with their children. In the new feminist utopia, childrearing will be a non-gendered activity (Firestone, 1970; Piercy, 1976). I would find it difficult to quarrel with an ideal of a world where men, too, define themselves in large part as the nurturers of children.

The ideological goal, however, has led many women to support the trend to joint custody (Ahrons, 1980; Holly, 1976) imposed over mothers' objections. Those mothers may distrust their former husbands' capacities to serve as good single parents to the children these women have raised. Further, they often suspect that their husbands' desire for joint custody does not reflect a serious desire to parent. Rather, at best, it reflects a desire to maintain control over the lives of their ex-wives. At worst, joint custody statutes make it easier or men with no real desire for custody to coerce wives into accepting less child support than they need (Fineman, 1988; Singer & Reynolds, 1988, Chambers, 1979).

These women want legal recognition and economic support for their continued role as primary parents for their children. They want to maintain some control over their lives as they rebuild their newly constituted families. But the arguments they make are ideologically uncomfortable for certain feminists, who distance themselves from these fights.[41]

A second group of women who cause discomfort in the feminist ranks are prostitutes and other sex workers. For some feminists, heterosexuality itself is problematic; even for the less radical, prostitution seems both a degradation of sexuality and a locus of oppression of women. Yet some women who work as prostitutes claim that the problems they face are largely a result of the illegality of their work and the concomitant exclusion from legal protection (Delacoste & Alexander, 1987). Feminists once sought to assist such women and to change laws that oppressed them (Walkowitz, 1980; Rosen, 1982). The efforts were grounded in a lack of understanding of the prostitutes' lives, however, and evaporated when the prostitutes failed to show proper appreciation (DuBois & Gordon, 1984, pp. 36–39). Contemporary feminism mainly ignores sex workers.[42]

These issues can be conceptualized as conflicts between ideological and material goals. If what these women seek is the immediate improvement of their lives, then sympathetic feminists might best work with them to discover and implement alternative means of material support so that it will no longer be necessary to assert claims that reinforce traditional roles. Women who wish to have children should be able to obtain support from fathers, while abortion must be freely available. Realistic spousal support payments must be provided for older women who had carried on traditional roles, but retraining for independent lives should be encouraged for women with the potential to use it (Weitzman, 1985). Economic opportunities for women should offer better choices than prostitution or minimum wage work.

The benefit of taking control over one's life, however, is not simply result but process. Women who make claims of entitlement within traditional values, by direct action or by legal action, inherently refuse to accept passively the hand life has dealt them. The glimmerings of energy and self-motivation are important phenomena upon which the women's movement should seek to build. If women exercise some degree of control over their lives, they have taken a step toward a non-traditional role. While their stories and claims need not be taken at face value, they should be taken seriously and reread for their liberatory kernel. The rechanneling of such energies, rather than their denigration or the dispiriting process of women fighting women ought to be our goal.

A more complex problem for feminists is determining the appropriate stance toward activist right-wing women. Unlike sex workers or custody-seeking mothers, such women act, in the first instance, out of an alternative ideology, rather than concrete material needs. Even here, however, I think dismissing them as wrongheaded and dangerous misses both real ideas about women's lives embedded in the interstices of their arguments and possible openings for alliance and connection.

Two keys facts define activist right-wing women. First, they often take leadership roles and exercise significant power within their own communities and in certain legislative battles (Luker, 1984; Freeman, 1983; MacKinnon, 1987, p. 28). Second, they do so on behalf of an agenda—anti-abortion, anti-ERA, "pro-family"—that most feminists find abhorrent.

Few feminists have made serious efforts to understand why such women seek the goals they do, what role political activism plays in their lives, or how their gender relates to their political agenda.[43] Those efforts are worth making. First, we can learn about many women's lives and self-understanding by listening to some of the right-wing agenda. The traditional familial role has its comforts and its safety. In a world where men wield most economic and political power, rules that bind men to particular women can at times protect those women from economic disaster and the Hobbesian jungle (Dworkin, 1983). Furthermore, the appeals to family values strike deeper roots than we perhaps once recognized. Feminism needs to understand these appeals and recapture "family"—broadened and transformed from its nuclear, patriarchal paradigm—within its own agenda.[44] On a more concrete level, right-wing women can become—always with some trepidation—provisional allies in certain concrete causes such as enforcement of child support and protection of abused children.

Finally, we should hold open the possibility that not only the agenda but the actions of right-wing women can provide openings for feminism. This optimistic vision assumes that these patterns of action sometimes contain a core of empowerment that can be built upon. Not every action taken on behalf of women is necessarily taken "by" women, of course. Much political action of right-wing women, for example, may reflect manipulation by others, rather than any woman's view of the world. When women are acting, however, there is an opening for transformation: in the process of acting and interacting, their understanding of their own goals and processes can change.

I am not suggesting that the various channels by which traditional women stake claims, including breach of promise actions, are (or were) necessarily worthy of support. What I do suggest is that the potential value of such activities to women, individually or collectively, has been too readily ignored. We have thus been unable to consider sensibly whether the benefit is worth the cost; the benefits have been unseen by feminists both because the ultimate visions are antithetical to ours and because we have too readily accepted the picture of who these women are and what they seek to do as presented by the mass/male media. Implicit in feminism is a promise that we reach out to women and seek to help them. When, instead, we too abandon them, they have suffered twice over. Particularly when the women are acting out of their own sense of harm, we need to respond, for their sake and ours. Action is a step forward for traditional women, and women empowered are women capable of further empowerment, for all women.

Notes

1. Citations to this and other cases can be found in Coombs, 1990.
2. While for boys the Horatio Alger dream is one of entrepreneurial success, through much of American history girls dreamed of success through marrying into fame and fortune.
3. The cause of action for breach of promise did not simply die a natural death, however. It has been eliminated by statutes (commonly referred to as "heartbalm" or "anti-heartbalm" bills) in eighteen jurisdictions. Most of the abolition fervor occurred during the 1930s.
4. I make no claim that the plaintiffs serve as any sort of representative group of oppressed women. First, there is inevitably a class bias in the group. While the plaintiffs were sometimes poor, all were romantically linked to men with sufficient income to make such a suit worthwhile. At least one commentator criticized the cause of action on this basis as "available only to a few aggressive women whose connivance or good fortune has procured them pledges from men who can pay," (Turano, 1934, p. 40).
5. See generally on the development of the cause of action, M. Grossberg, 1985; J. Schouler, 1921; Brown, 1929; Feinsinger, 1935.
6. "Misuse" is, of course, a loaded term; critics state as fact, without documentation, that many suits were brought out of vengeance or greed and should not have succeeded. It is impossible to know how frequently claims were filed by women who suffered no felt harm. See Coombe, 1988, p. 98.
7. Calling the plaintiffs "gold-diggers" or "adventuresses," engaged in a "racket" in which they sought "heartbalm," was, of course, a powerful way of turning the discourse in a direction that made alternative stories difficult to believe or even hear. See Kane, 1936, pp. 65–66. On the power of discourse, see generally Fineman, 1988; Foucault, 1980, p. 77.
8. See, e.g., Vernier, 1936, at 6: "If the girl be pretty, the jury generally give her heavy damages . . . She who has her fortune before her is handsomely recompensed, while her plainer sister, who could ill afford to lose the best years of her life, is often sent empty away." It is impossible to know if attractiveness really increased the plaintiff's likelihood of success. If so, the explanation might be disbelief that the defendant was

sufficiently attracted to a plainer plaintiff to credit her claim that he had proposed marriage. This is not necessarily inconsistent with jurors equating sexual attractiveness with sexuality and thus disbelieving the claims of glamorous (as well as plain) women that they were raped or sexually harassed.

9. The bringing of a lawsuit showed that the plaintiff was one of the undeserving sort who "does not mind the laughter which alone would keep possibly deserving litigants forever out of court." Daggett, 1935, p. 47; Cf. Heller, 1961.

10. See Sinclair, 1987 on the complex and contradictory images of women's responsibility for sexual activity.

11. This dependence was recognized and repeatedly criticized by Charlotte Perkins Gilman. See, e.g., Gilman, 1911, p. 167.

12. Evidence of the active sexuality of some Victorian women can be found in the studies of Dr. Clara Mosher, discussed in Gay, 1984, pp. 135–44 and Degler, 1980, pp. 257–58. On the positive attitudes towards sexuality of women in the 1920s, see, e.g., Banner, 1983, pp. 182–83; Smith-Rosenberg, 1985, p. 283.

13. The proportion of such situations among breach of promise cases is likely higher than a reading of the case reports would suggest. We can assume there was usually a high cost in publicly exposing one's fall from chastity. If the seduction had led to pregnancy, however, that cost had already been paid and thus the willingness to file would be greater. See Coombe, 1988, p. 84 n. 59. Cf. Gillis, 1983, p. 114 (discussing economic suffering of unmarried mothers in Victorian Britain).

14. See 4 Vernier, 1936, 250. In Florida, for example, the maximum support payment for an illegitimate child was $50 per year, and that for no more than ten years. Women Lawyer's J., 1934, at 25. Nonetheless, in introducing her heartbalm bill, Indiana Rep. Nicholson proclaimed that no one with a legitimate complaint would be harmed, given the existence of "statutes governing support of wives and children [and] bastardy." Indianapolis News, February 1, 1935, at. 1, col. 5.

15. In fact, "[n]ewspapers of the time reported the [heartbalm] measure as largely a woman's cause. For example, a United Press story stated, 'The loudest champions of the legislation are women while the most bitter opponents are men.' " Sinclair, supra n. 17 at 82–83 (footnotes omitted). The lawyer for the plaintiff in Fearon v. Trainor, 272 N.Y. 268, 5 N.E. 2d 815 (1936) (testing the constitutionality of New York's heartbalm bill), criticized Mrs. Nicholson and other women supporters of such legislation for "an idea which is so shortsighted as to everlastingly damage person of her own sex." [sic] *New York Times*, Nov. 16, 1936, at 24, col. 1.

16. The first anti-heartbalm bill was introduced by Indiana's only female legislator, Roberta West Nicholson. See, e.g., *Indianapolis News*, Feb. 1, 1935, at 1, col. 5.

17. A bill was introduced by Katherine Foley, only Democratic woman in the State Legislature to "defeat gold-diggers and shyster lawyers." *New York Times*, April 3, 1935, at 25, col. 8.

18. Rep. Eudochia Bell Smith said her bill would lead to "the end of the gold-digger in Colorado courts." *New York Times*, April 28, 1937, at 16, col. 5.

19. See *Cleveland Plain Dealer*, March 21, 1935, at 1, col. 2 (describing dispute between Representatives Alma Smith (D.-Cleveland) and Blanche Hower (R.-Akron)).

20. E.g., Nicholson said that "Surely a suit to recover money as damages for the broken romance cannot soothe a woman if love was genuine," 16 Time 1 (Feb. 18, 1935); and referred to her bill as "a piece of progressive legislation, in keeping with the times." *Indianapolis News*, Feb. 1, 1935, at 1, col. 4. Similarly, Ohio sponsor Blanche Hower

said her bill "was for the benefit of society and the uplifting of womanhood." *Cleveland Plain Dealer*, May 9, 1935, at 1, col. 4.

21. Nicholson called breach of promise actions "blackmail suits . . . in which principals attempt to capitalize on some one's indiscretion." *Indianapolis News*, Feb. 1, 1935, at 1, col. 4.

22. Nicholson stated that "suits of this sort, with their attendant publicity, are a detriment to public morals." *Indianapolis News*, Feb. 1, 1935, at 1, col. 4.

23. Bromley, 1927, p. 8. She argued that the "breach of promise law . . . benefits the gold-digger, rather than the woman who cloaks herself in her self-respect and goes about making a new life." Id. at 9. Such adventuresses, moreover, were likely to succeed by preying on the best instincts of male jurors who "each have a soft spot which a clever woman can locate" and "are prone to suspect their own kind of base dealings with woman." Id. at 40.

24. Cf. Fineman, 1988, p. 730 (the voices of custodial mothers "are not heard because their concerns cannot be expressed through existing and accepted discourse or rhetorical concepts").

25. For feminist analyses of the division of the world into a public and a private sphere, see, e.g., Olsen, 1980; Polan, 1982.

26. These non-suffrage oriented movements are sometimes referred to as "domestic feminism." They are discussed in, e.g., Cott, 1987; Jeffreys, 1985; Pivar, 1973; Smith, 1973, p. 40.

27. The goal of this liberal feminist vision was for women to take an active place in the outside world, and a liberated approach to sexuality. The problematic for women of accepting such a "male" vision has been explored within "second wave" feminism. See generally, e.g., Dworkin, 1983; Ehrenreich, 1984; MacKinnon, 1987.

28. This vision was consistent with that of Victorian social puritans who saw illegitimate sexuality as the result of male manipulation of "the female's trusting and affectionate nature." Smith-Rosenberg, 1985, p. 116.

29. "This protection to women that at one time may have been a necessary and just thing now seems at times almost a travesty." Daggett, 1935, p. 41, quoted in Grossberg, 1985, p. 55.

30. Fontaine v. Whitney, *New York Times*, Jan. 4, 1933, at 1, col. 2.

31. Meffert v. Caruso, *New York Times*, April 22, 1914 at 7, col. 5.

32. Mendal v. Gimbel, *Newsweek* (April 18, 1936) at 22.

33. Fictional treatments of breach of promise plaintiffs were equally unflattering. See, e.g., Loos, 1963, Dickens, 1837; Gilbert and Sullivan, 1875.

34. Some critics suggested that male jurors were bamboozled or that plaintiffs were the beneficiaries of chivalry rather than justice. See, e.g., Bromley, 1927, p. 40. Studies of rape trials, however, suggest that men are generally disinclined to believe women's claims that they have been subject to sexual coercion by other men. See Estrich, 1986. It seems unlikely, then, that claims of seduction and abandonment were believed too easily.

35. It is possible, of course, that plaintiffs frequently lost at trial. The infrequency of such cases in the appellate reports might reflect litigation economics. Most plaintiff's attorneys were likely working on contingency fees and thus reluctant to appeal such fact-bound disputes. Defendants, by contrast, could afford an appeal and might at

least hope for a remittitur of damages or the benefit of delaying the payment of damages.

36. Compare the way in which experts' defenses of battered women who kill explain their past passivity, but not the activity for which they are being tried. See Schneider (1986a) pp 198–99.

37. There is an ongoing dispute over the value of law as means of social change. Compare, e.g., Freeman, 1978 with Delgado, 1987.

38. Many critics of the cause of action believed such stories should be kept private. See, e.g., Wright, 1924, p. 361. These arguments embody a traditional view of a natural public-private distinction and thus seem to me to be contrary to a feminist epistemology. Speaking pain is a way of making it real to the speaker, in part through the process of working through the full dimension of one's beliefs and feelings in order to represent them in linguistic form and in part through the validation of being listened to. Such public articulation of pain may also help to reconstitute it in structural rather than individualist forms. See Howe, 1987a; West, 1987.

39. There is enormous dispute within the feminist community on the extent to which women's voices are their own and how we can enhance the chances of their being heard. Compare, e.g., Menkel-Meadow, 1987 and Dubois, 1985 with MacKinnon, 1987.

    For the oppressed, there is always a tension between speaking in ones' own voice and adopting enough of the dominant language to be heard. Compare Jaggar, 1983, pp. 355–57 (need to adapt) with Lorde, 1983, p. 98 (need to acknowledge and speak out of difference).

40. Sometimes, of course, the activities of traditional women, such as the attempts of anti-abortion protestors to block access to clinics, are directly harmful to other women. In such cases, we must struggle against those activities, even as we strive to understand our opponents' motivations. See, e.g., Luker, 1984 (anti-abortion activists see pro-choice movement as threatening the value of traditional mothering).

41. At least until recently, second wave feminists have paid relatively little attention to children. See, e.g., Gordon, 1986; Stacey, 1983.

42. The focus on pornography, see, e.g., Dworkin, 1981; Lederer, 1980, creates a deep divide with the asserted interests of at least some sex workers. But see MacKinnon, 1987, pp. 10–14 (defending Linda Marchiano, whose book, (*Lovelace and McGrady*, 1980), documents her horrifying exploitation as Linda Lovelace).

43. One area in which strategic, though cautious, alliances might be made with right-wing women is around the issue of new reproductive technologies. While ultimate visions of women's place in the world differ greatly, traditional and radical women often concur in a well-grounded fear of the technocraticization and professionalization of mothering. See, e.g., Stanworth, 1987; Corea, 1986.

44. Some feminists are engaged in this work. See, e.g., Folbre, 1988, p. 57 and sources cited therein.

15

Societal Factors Affecting The Creation of Legal Rules For Distribution of Property at Divorce

Martha Albertson Fineman

I Introduction

The way that we as a society perceive marriage and the relationship between husband and wife profoundly effects the way that we select, develop and apply rules governing property distribution at divorce. I would assert that it is this societal perception that is most significant. It will shape the way that all actors involved in actual divorce proceedings—judges, lawyers, and the spouses—as well as legislators consider the fairness and advisability of various distribution factors. The general social consensus about the nature of marriage and what it entails is the background which frames arguments over the appropriateness of specific rules regulating dissolution. There have been many changes provoked by a great deal of controversy in this area.

One source of the controversy about property distribution rules, I believe, is the existence of two competing and, perhaps incompatible and unrealistic, political visions of contemporary marriage. The first is the more modern view that marriage as an institution has been transformed so as to be consistent with formalistic notions of equality between the sexes. The second is the more traditional policy stance that the family is the appropriate, perhaps solitary, institution to resolve problems of dependency or need that inevitably arise in the context of families.

Sometimes these contrasting visions of marriage are presented as representing steps in a progressive recasting of the legal nature of the marriage relationship. For example, scholars describing the form of state regulation of marriage and divorce often describe a movement from status to contract (Glendon, 1981, pp. 101–18). Generally, this movement

An earlier version of this article appeared in *The Family Law Quarterly*, 23 (Summer 1989) 2: 279–99.

is characterized as involving the gradual substitution of individual choices concerning the nature, duration, and terms of the marriage relationships, for standardized formulas imposed by the state. This development, it is argued, reflects major shifts in the assumptions underlying marriage.

Earlier views held that marriage was a basic social institution, and its external characteristics—its formation, organization, and dissolution—were appropriately regulated by the state. The more recent view of marriage as an institution existing primarily for the benefit of the individuals involved has led to a shift in the focus of state regulation. The state has abandoned, to some extent, its concern with the formalities attending entry into marriage and the designation of acceptable reasons for divorce. Instead, there is increasing focus on the internal aspects of family life with need for protection of individuals within the family structure and the desirability of the imposition of egalitarian standards as the contemporary justification for state regulation. There is less concern with the formal establishment of "family" relationships, but a correspondingly greater concern with the conduct and quality of those relationships once they are established.

This shift of state regulatory focus is consistent with the view that marriage is a voluntary (and therefore, perhaps, temporary) union of equals which either may terminate "at-will" if it does not satisfy their desires and needs. This shift in the societal understanding of marriage is reflected in the adoption of no-fault divorce and of new rules governing the allocation of economic benefits and burdens. Access to divorce is made easy under these reforms, and the state's concern centers on ensuring "equity" and "justice" between the spouses in dividing up their accumulated debts and assets.

A consensus about what constitutes "equity" and "justice," however, is not easily attained in these matters. The problem of property division upon divorce is still a controversial area of family law, and one to which no satisfactory solution has yet been found (Fineman, 1983). Confidence that the law can be revised so as to do justice, however, assumes that there is widespread agreement as to what policy or policies the law should support or propound.

Any discussion of law and legal reform must reflect the fact that there are real and unresolvable differences that emerge when discussing family law in the latter part of this century. Even if one were to believe that a unitary system of law can be developed and applied to clearly identified problems, which law should be selected? Which problems should it address? Which values should be given prominence? Whose image of the world (or at least that part of it we set aside and designate as "family") should prevail? There is no consensus about the many issues involved in this area we label "family law." Even an issue as fundamental as whether divorce should be freely allowed continues to generate some, though muted, discussion.

Journals are filled with debates about what is the best set of rules to govern property division or custody and visitation. This society is divided on issues such as the proper roles for women and men in and out of marriage; the content and extent of a parent's post-divorce obligations—financial and otherwise—to their (particularly his) children; the amount of sacrifice a man should be expected to give to maintain an "old" family when a "new" and younger one (wife) awaits.

Aside from pointing out the general differences in perceptions about problems and proposed solutions, it should also be noted that family law has tended to be concerned with the relationships in middle- and upper-class families and has tended to focus on the problems of members of those groups. They are economically privileged images that float through the literature of legislative reform and appellate cases, [mis]informing lawmakers and lawgivers as to what are the "typical" problems and the "proper" solutions.

The choice and application of various distribution rules by legislators, attorneys and judges whether in the context of the legislative process, in formal adjudication or in negotiation are influenced by these societal factors. These legal actors must develop and apply rules in a legal system where the longstanding recognition of dependency and need on the part of mothers and children within families is increasingly offset by the desire for symbolically compelling presentations of gender equality and independence. Marriage is no longer realistically presented as a lifelong commitment with well defined gender based roles establishing an interdependency that is easily comprehended and reflected in supportive legal rules. Things are more complex today—roles are less defined and marriage as an institution is in a state of flux. Unfortunately, the law of property distribution at divorce has often become the crude instrument with which we attempt to both implement equality *and* address dependency and need. When the law is expected to do incompatible or contradictory things simultaneously it is no wonder that confusion results.

II The Distribution Process

It is important to note that although the distribution of property is only one of the economic aspects of divorce, it has a unique procedural posture. It is a final decision, not subject to future modification should circumstances change. This means there are no potential future opportunities to correct errors. Because it is final, it may appear more significant.

It is also important to be aware that distribution decision may present a different type of emotional experience for spouses than decisions about other economic aspects of divorce. Families are more than legalized sexual relations or the repositories for products of those relations. They represent the convergence of a complex set of emotional and material needs which are inevitably frustrated in the divorce process. The distribution may psychologically represent to the spouses the final accounting of their contributions to the marriage—a concrete measure of their relative worths.

There is an additional fact that may cause spouses to react differently to the distribution process. With child support the emotional as well as legal justification is based on the appropriateness of continued obligations of support in the context of an ongoing, even if altered, post-divorce relationship. With children, future support obligations are based on need and premised on the assertion that divorce does not sever the responsibilities or the rights associated with parenthood.

Property distribution may in fact reflect concern about a spouse's future needs. As the image of marriage becomes more that of partnership than dependency, however, such concern increasingly is considered inappropriate. Need may be implicit in some of the factors utilized for division, but typically the stated rules explicitly reflect notions of *entitlement* based on earnings or, more recently, on marital contributions whether economic or homemaking.

A Factors Relevant to Property Distribution at Divorce

Currently a variety of specific distribution factors are typically noted in common law state statutes, or in court opinions in states with general statutory directives. These factors include: (1) The length of the marriage, (2) The property brought to the marriage by each party, (3) The "contribution" of each party to the marriage, often with the explicit admonition that appropriate economic value is to be given to contributions of homemaking and child care services, (4) The contribution by one party to the education, training or increased earning power of the other, (5) Whether one of the parties has substantial assets not subject to division by the court, (6) The age and physical and emotional health of the parties, (7) The earning capacity of each party, including educational background, training, employment skills, work experience, length of absence from the job market, (8) custodial responsibilities for children and the time and expense necessary to acquire sufficient education or training to enable the party to become self-supporting at a standard of living reasonably comparable to that enjoyed during the marriage. Increasingly, some consideration is given to (9) the desirability of awarding the family home or the right to live therein for a reasonable period to the party having custody of any children.

In addition, other economic circumstances, including pension benefits, vested or unvested, and future interests, the tax consequences to each party and the amount and duration of an order granting maintenance payments may be considered. If a written agreement was made by the parties before or during the marriage concerning any arrangement for property distribution, such agreements are often presumed binding upon the court unless inequitable. Some statutory systems that enumerate various factors explicitly end with a general catch-all for judicial discretion that allows consideration of such other factors as the court may in each individual case determine to be relevant.[1]

B Classification of Distribution Factors

There are at least four potential conceptual categories into which one could place the variety of specific factors for property distributions: (1) title, (2) fault, (3) need, and (4) contribution. These conceptual categories represent rationales or justifications for allocation decisions and may be ordered according to when they first begin to be utilized. This sequencing has been used to suggest that there has been progression from the simple common law emphasis on title to the more complex understanding of the function and purpose of the distribution system as reflecting and valuing both monetary and non-monetary contributions to the marriage. Ordering the categories does reflect a movement from the strict common law system based on title to the modern notion of an partnership based on equally valued, though different in kind, contributions to the marriage. I believe that there is a serious problem with this characterization of the movement from title to partnership and contribution as progression, however. Progress implies that we have either outgrown the bases for the old concepts, or that our initial perceptions were in error and now must be revised. A progression thesis might, therefore, characterize fault and need as "transitional" concepts—inelegant patches that allowed judges to do justice under a strict title system prior to the enlightened presentation of marriage as partnership.

I am not convinced that the circumstances that generated arguments for a distribution system focused on needs, however, are no longer in existence. I am worried that the material circumstances of divorcing women and children are being detrimentally ignored by supplanting a focus on needs with a focus on contribution as the primary distributive concept. The ascendancy of contribution may present a nice neat instance of conceptual progress to legal academics and law reformers, but for many divorcing spouses, as well as the practicing professionals to whom they turn for advice, adverse material circumstances and the needs they generate have not been left behind.

Title considerations do not seem to be the determinative ones in modern distribution schemes. Need and, to a lesser extent, fault, however, are still viable alternatives to contribution as conceptual frameworks for the creation and implementation of various specific distribution factors.[2] When fault or need were first introduced into consideration they were welcomed as helping to ameliorate the hardships of the title system, but in contemporary divorce practice both have increasingly come under attack because they carry negative symbolic connotations. In the context of "no-fault" divorce reform, for example, continued reference to fault as an explicit allocation category would obviously be problematic.

The concept of "need" presents even more complex conceptual difficulties. As a relevant consideration, however, need is not as easily moved beyond as fault. Historically, the courts could respond to the existence of dependency since marriage was viewed as a status relationship. The husband and father was obligated to provide support for the needs of wife and child, and this obligation did not necessarily cease with divorce. This duty could be extended beyond divorce through awards of alimony, through property division provisions, or through both.

Modern attacks on the legitimacy of the patriarchal family have eroded this traditional notion that the husband is predominantly responsible for the financial well-being of all members of the family and transformed our approach to the rules governing the economic aspects of divorce. The earlier status-based model of marriage has been replaced by an egalitarian or equality model under which obligations to spouses ideally end with the marriage and any ongoing economic obligation such as child support or payment of existing marital debts are considered shared and equal responsibilities.

Dependency has not disappeared, however. The care of children produces dependency, not only for the children, but for the primary caretaker. The needs that this dependency generates must be met, either by society as a whole or by individuals with legally significant connections to children. It could be argued that the existence of this dependency should not have to be wholly remedied by individual men in the context of post-divorce economic arrangements. This is compelling only to the extent we believe these men have not benefited from their wives choices and, generally by market discrimination against women.

Furthermore, it must be recognized that this dependency does not end when the child reaches 18 or any other magic age. Children's needs may change with the passage of time, but the caretaker has assumed ongoing responsibilities, with present as well as future economic consequences, such as a reduced amount of money in a social security or pension fund or increased susceptibility to requests for "loans" once the children are fully grown and supposedly "independent." Some family relationships tend to last. This is particularly true of the primary caretaking parent who is attached to her children. The obligations that such a parent may feel are not legal, but moral or emotional ones. A parent who desires to assist a newly "adult" child may not be dictated to do so by law, but that does not mean that the law should be insensitive to (or unsupportive of) her sensibilities when assessing the most socially useful allocation of property at divorce.[3]

C Need and Contribution Factors

Assessment of the various specific distribution factors listed in Section II A, reveals that four may be categorized under the concept of "contribution".[4] Five fit more neatly within the concept of "need."[5] The fact that within any system the factors are often combined and exist simultaneously reflects the tension between two incompatible contemporary images of marriage—the egalitarian partnership and the dependency models. In fact, the partnership image gives rise to the idea of contribution; each person contributes a different but valuable set of benefits to the good of the whole and the whole should be divided to reflect these contributions if it is dissolved. Need has no role to play in a true partnership of equals. The dependency image, in contrast, anticipates that a woman has been "victimized" to some extent in marriage. She is viewed as having sacrificed career goals and ambitions for the marriage. At divorce she is dependent and that dependency will continue. She, therefore, has needs that should be compensated. These models may be said to represent polar ends on the spectrum of the major transformations that have occurred in the way society views marriage and the position of women within it. In that it is not clear how either view of marriage reflects the reality of many women. If marriage incorporates the notion of women performing dual roles, as wage earner and as mother, it is not egalitarian, but potentially oppressive for many women who cannot do both, or cannot do both well.

The fact that factors based on both the dependency and partnership models of marriage exist simultaneously within any distribution system does not suggest that the selection of factors will necessarily reflect an explicit principled balancing process. Rather, it sometimes seems that within the context of any distribution task there may be unavoidable concessions to dependency within a preferred framework that focuses on contribution and equality. In our contemporary society the concept of need must create some ambivalence for those who accept equality as the social as well as the legal ideal. The predominance of the equality model evident in much of the commentary and law reform efforts illustrates that there is a strong preference for the legal presentation of women as equal partners within marriage, and as independent equal economic actors outside of it.

Feminist reformers have adhered for the most part to the ideal of equalitarian marriage in addressing the economic questions in divorce. There may be several reasons why feminists haven't argued for the employment of concepts of affirmative (or protective) action, in the area of divorce reform. First, such arguments would cast doubts on the ideal of family equality. Second, although the family is distinguishable from the market, result-oriented arguments that women should be treated differently in the family area because of their gender-related social characteristics might be transferred with very different symbolic connotations into the market. Third, generalized result equality rules may actually reinforce the idea that biology is destiny. And finally, to the extent that feminists' overriding objective is the affirmation of the ideal of equality, result equality rules which concede that equality does not in fact exist may create an impression that it cannot exist (Fineman, 1983, pp. 823–26).

In some states the equality norm is formally embodied in provisions which establish an initial presumption that all property of the spouses is to be equally divided upon divorce.[6] This rule equality presumption is consistent with the organizing concept of marriage as a equal partnership. Need is not forgotten, but equality has significant symbolic importance and the partnership model is argued as not only reflecting the preferred or correct vision of women, but also as, secondarily, addressing "need." The dependent woman through ideological fiat is considered to be benefited in being brought "up" to partnership status and made an "equal."

If, however, one rejects the comprehensiveness of either or both of the conflicting images of marriage that the stereotypes of woman as equal and woman as dependent represent, one must confront the reality that a lot of women whose mixed circumstances may require remedial rules are neglected. The stereotypes of dependency and partnership are polar opposites. Thus no single typical result can be fairly reconciled with the goal of doing justice to both. A woman who operates in both the marriage and market as an "equal" might be better off under the old common law system where she keeps her separate property and her ex-husband is liable only for child support. The true dependent, by contrast, might by her very circumstances have been able to claim all of the property and still be found in need of continued support for herself. In either case, it would seem that what is desirable in the way of reform is the creation of a range of acceptable economic outcomes which could accommodate a variety of differences among women in various circumstances. The focus on the stereotypes of dependency and equality, and the futile attempt to reconcile them, tended to narrow rather than expand the definition of what are acceptable results.

Equality as an organizing concept is also evident in other divorce law provisions. Just as the decisions concerning divisions of assets are to be made with a presumption of equality between the spouses, so are those concerning marital "liabilities." Economic responsibility for children is to be shared, with both parents responsible for the children's future support. Future support for the spouses is to be primarily their individual responsibilities, unless certain well-defined circumstances indicating need justify one receiving some temporary, limited support from the other to reeducate or rehabilitate herself for the job market.

The equality conceptualization of marriage places tremendous significance and primary focus on the symbolic nature of the "partnership" relationship between men and women. The concept of contribution in this model supplies the distribution standard. The dominance of equality means it will also provide the preferred method of valuing contributions and, thus further avoid the need for anything resembling detailed fact-finding or consideration of individualized circumstances on the actual amount of contribution. Divorce is an economic adjustment between partners, with the ideal solution being an equal division of the assets and liabilities amassed as a result of their equally valued contribution. The use of contribution eliminates the need for individualized inquiry. It is based on a fictitious past, on some socially derived, idealized notion of all spouses' actions and conduct during marriage. Contribution operates at the expense of inquiry into possible future needs.

As already noted, the partnership model is not an absolute one and there are often specific factors that are available and could be employed to allow deviation from the equality ideal. Various individual circumstances can exist that could indicate the necessity of making an unequal allocation of assets and/or liabilities at divorce to handle future needs. Even in the face of an initial equal division presumption, just the existence of need based factors provides the potential for deviations from the distribution norm of equality.

Unfortunately, in the statutory schemes and case law the need factors are neither sufficiently developed nor sufficiently clear to offset the partnership model with its easily grasped contribution factors. Even without a specific mandate that the court presume that property is to be divided equally, judges and lawyers will tend to start at 50/50 because of the social and professional conditioning that presents modern marriage as an equal partnership. Alteration of the partnership model will probably be possible only if the spouse arguing for such a deviation can meet the burden of establishing that her circumstances (needs) clearly are exceptional. The wholesale acceptance of the partnership model means, however, that the burdens of production, proof, and persuasion will be placed upon the one who would argue that the rule equality concept is inadequate given her specific circumstances.

Furthermore, even if a wife could initially meet the burdens of demonstrating that her needs should outweigh the equal contribution assumptions, her husband could argue that the application of other accepted distribution factors indicate there is no basis for deviation. The same factors that can be employed by one spouse to argue that deviation is warranted, may also be used by the other in an attempt to counter the assertion that deviation is appropriate. Because the factors are not weighted or ranked, one factor or set of factors may be balanced against others in the decision-making process. As a result, unless one spouse can assert that she occupies all, or most, of the categories (an unlikely scenario since they are inherently incompatible), her spouse may use the remaining factors to push the allocation toward the rule equality norm.

The difficulty of attempting to deviate from the equality presumption is further complicated by the fact that in using and developing the factors, decision makers have themselves failed to distinguish those grouped under the concept of contribution from those supported by need. Although they are really referencing different models and different sets of concerns, contribution arguments may be used to offset an appeal for unequal division based on need.

For example, a woman may argue that since her education or employment skills and the presence of small children make it unlikely that she can become self-supporting at a standard of living reasonably comparable to that enjoyed during the marriage, she needs more than fifty percent of the property.[7] Her husband need not dispute these assertions, but only argue that the marriage has lasted only a few years (implying she has not assisted in the accumulation of assets), or that he has aided her by assuming financial and domestic responsibilities while she went to school or work, and these equally unweighted contribution factors may be applied in his favor to negate her need-based arguments. Since he is able to argue that some of the provisions apply to him, they are likely to cancel out her arguments and it is likely that the norm of equal division will prevail. There should be recognition that the arguments are presented on different conceptual bases. She is arguing *need*, he is responding with *contribution* which does not meet nor defeat the thrust of her assertions. To the extent that contribution is an equalizing concept, only the greatly disadvantaged—the polar model dependency—will have a chance at deviation.

In addition, since the factors are not weighted or ranked, even when employed successfully they will be only partially effective in negating the preference for the rule equality model. Since equality is established as the norm, justification becomes more difficult for more than nominal deviations from a 50/50 division. Therefore, even in cases where deviation is considered appropriate, the combination of the failure to weight the factors and the expressed preference for equal division is likely to lessen the distance from the equality ideal (and consequently, the incentive for attempting deviation at all).

Even if not unduly affected by the presumption of equal distribution, the factors alone are inadequate to guide the trial court or attorneys toward more discriminating decisions based on the specific characteristics of the divorcing parties. They focus on an abstract view of the nature of the relationship between men and women, and do not direct attention to the more difficult components of an assessment of need. A woman who has not been victimized by her husband or society may still need more assets than her husband to cope with her post-divorce life as custodial parent. It appears, however, that only the wife/victim, can hope to successfully assert need as a basis for inequality. Other women, despite their needs, will be left with the equality model as their sole recourse.

D *Equality and the Contribution Concept*

The ideal of equality between spouses is at the center of our current views of marriage and therefore exerts a powerful and symbolic influence on our process of fashioning rules to govern distribution of marital assets. Marriage is considered a union, a partnership of equals. This view mandates that if the partnership ends the accumulated assets should be divided in a manner consistent with the model under which they were acquired. The norm or standard against which rules regulating the economic aspects of dissolution are measured will be that of equality.

This approach of using equality as the organizational concept in assessing appropriate rules for property division will create dilemmas. In its simplest form equality demands sameness of treatment, and differentiation in any sphere may be considered a concession of inferiority or "unequalness." Using this concept of equality has confused the questions in family law as it will in any analysis because, "it masquerades as an independent norm. In addition, framing the discussion of entitlements in terms of one individual's equivalence to others, misleadingly suggests that one person's rights vis-à-vis another's are identical." Because discussions based on equality tend not to make explicit reference to the specific substantive rights incorporated from elsewhere "equality 'blind[s]' us not only to the existence of such rights but to their specific substantive content also." It leads as well to the "erroneous assumption that, if two parties are morally or legally equivalent for one purpose, they must be morally or legally equivalent for all purposes" (Westen, 1982, pp. 575–82).

The difficulty with equality as a distribution standard for marriage dissolution should be clear. It is a concept that is often reduced to its most simple (and ultimately inequitable) form. In dividing a finite bundle of goods between two contenders, equality too often means that each receives one-half. This is the most easily understood and implemented manifestation of equality. In addition, it is the most politically acceptable. On a symbolic level, this result expresses more than just a method of division. It explicitly assumes that each individual's rights or entitlements are equal as well. There is a great deal of symbolic significance to the notion of equality and equal property division in marriage as the preferred standard.

There are also pragmatic arguments that can be made for adoption of an equality model. Equality, in addition to supporting the idea of marriage as a partnership, can be viewed as giving real "teeth" to platitudes about the value of women's childcare and work in the home. It is often asserted that the standard of equally divided property at divorce will put women in a better position economically than they would be under another conceptual system. It is argued more generally, that the ideal of marriage as an equal partnership will reduce sex role stereotypes in marriage and allow each partner to decide on the type and timing of the contributions he or she would make. Thus equality standards in the distribution of property on a conceptual level may be linked to broader ideals of placing equal value and promoting freedom of choice in marriage roles. Making equality the ongoing concept underlying divorce may be considered part of a series of conscious symbolic choices about how to best ensure a more just society.

When equality rhetoric is translated into specific rules governing distribution the results must be measured and assessed in more than symbolic terms, however. Symbolic expression may be important, but care should be taken so that as translated into legislation having direct impact on the lives of many people, the results also meet standards of fairness and justice. Unfortunately, as a symbolic characterization equality has taken on a life of its own and is emphasized to the exclusion of fine distinctions in decision making that are necessary to achieve a more individualized or just notion of equality.

III The Results of the Uneasy Contemporary Coexistence of Dependency and Equality: Need and Contribution

There are a variety of situations experienced by women at divorce that will not conform to a simplistic application of the contribution conceptualization of the equal partnership model. Adherence to this model continues, however. This failure to adequately accommodate these differences in women's material circumstances has led to a system of rules of property distribution applied to all women, but based on the experiences of only some.

One way of restating this is to say that the cost to women of deviating from the traditional housewife model is extremely high. As long as the concept of contribution is simplified and employed solely in an effort to make the housewife the equal, other circumstances are ignored. In fact, the concept can work to the disadvantage of the nonhousewife women. Such a woman not only pays with her time and effort while she is doing two jobs, for example, but also at divorce she may be viewed as not in need of assistance because she is not traditional. There is a danger that the contribution concept might in fact be used against women who are not in traditional roles, and at the same time not benefit the traditional housewife as much as it should.

The current lack of theorizing about distribution factors means we treat need and equality as unweighed alternatives when they are fundamentally incompatible on a theoretical level. It means they are placed in competition with each other, both as applied in individual cases and as a matter of policy. As they are competing concepts, we should rationally decide which one should prevail under which circumstances. As it now stands, in practice need will not have the same status as equality in fashioning allocation decisions because the law is unclear.

The present state of distribution rules lead to undesirable results. Because many cases do not fit neatly into one or the other of the competing concepts in some situations women may be overbenefited and while in others they will be undercompensated. Women who are not mothers but choose to be unemployed during the marriage may be considered overcompensated by the imposition of the partnership model. They will be overcompensated to the extent that they do not contribute wages to the accumulation of assets nor did they contribute by providing a nonmonetary service, such as childcare, for the family unit. Mothers who *are* employed (and, therefore, are not considered poor), however, may be undercompensated because the need factors will be interpreted too narrowly to remedy the needs generated by their post-divorce situation. Furthermore, because contributions are conceived of as equal in the partnership model, the fact that such women make *dual* contributions (money and household) likely will not be recognized. It will be unlikely that they will be able to successfully argue that they deserve a more-than-equal share of the assets to care for their children. The rules are not flexible enough to accommodate different classes, different ages, different educational levels or different family circumstances.

Commitment to the equality ideal, typified by use of the partnership metaphor as the appropriate analytical construct to guide divorce policy, does not permit us to face the fact that women's and children's needs in this society have continued to be undervalued and ignored. The equality rhetoric now associated with the marriage relationship must be challenged as inappropriate for resolving difficult questions in situations, such as divorce, where they stand in inherently unequal positions.

An equality view of marriage denies reality for many women who assume, during and after the marriage, more than a partner's share in the conduct and burdens associated with household and child care. The partnership metaphor slips easily into equal sharing for property, children, debts, and so on at divorce. The metaphor has symbolic content that is preserved only at significant cost to many women who must suffer equality in this one area while the rest of the society and culture continues to treat them unequally.

Notes

1. A number of states including Colorado, Connecticut, Delaware, Illinois, New York, Pennsylvania, Rhode Island, Indiana, Virginia, and Wisconsin have enacted property distribution statutes that enumerate factors that must be considered by the court. Most states have statutes which simply authorize the court to divide property available for distribution "equitably," without listing mandatory factors for the courts consideration. However the factors considered by judges in simple equitable distribution states are substantially the same as the factors which appear in the enumerated lists.

   For example, the Supreme Court of New Jersey while upholding the constitutionality of its unspecific equitable distribution requirement against a vagueness challenge, suggested guideline criteria to be followed by its courts which included the following:

   > (1) respective age, background and earning ability of the parties; (2) duration of the marriage; (3) the standard of living of the parties during the marriage; (4) what money or property each brought into the marriage; (5) the present income of the parties; (6) the property acquired during the marriage by either or both parties; (7) the source of acquisition; (8) the current value and income producing capacity of the property; (9) the debts and liabilities of the parties to the marriage; (10) the present mental and physical health of the parties; (11) the probability of continuing present employment at present earnings or better in the future; (12) effect of distribution of assets on the ability to pay alimony and support; and (13) gifts from one spouse to the other during the marriage.

   The court also offered the following list of criteria from Section 307 of the Uniform Marriage and Divorce Act:

   > (1) contribution of each spouse to acquisition of the marital property, including contribution of a spouse as homemaker; (2) value of the property set apart to each spouse; (3) duration of the marriage; and (4) economic circumstances of each spouse when the division of property is to become effective, including the desirability of awarding the family home or the right to live therein for reasonable periods to the spouse having custody of any children.

   (*Painter v. Painter*, 320 A.2d 484 (N.J. 1984).

2. Some sorts of extreme misconduct related to marital breakdown have been found relevant to the distribution issue, even in states which explicitly prohibit consideration of marital misconduct. See *Blickstein v. Blickstein*, 472 N.Y.S. 2d 110 (N.Y. App. Div. 1984), where a New York court found fault relevant to equitable distribution in "very rare" situations involving misconduct that "shocks the conscience."

   In *D'Arc v. D'Arc*, 395 A.2d 1270 (N.J. Super. Ct. Ch. Div. 1978) aff'd, 421 A.2d 602 (N.J. Super. Ct. App. Div. 1980), an appellate court found misconduct relevant where the husband had attempted to arrange his wife's murder. Similarly in *Stover v. Stover*, 696 S.W.2d 750 (Ark. 1985), The Arkansas Supreme Court held that the trial court could go beyond the statutory list of factors bearing on equitable distribution to consider fault where the wife had been convicted of conspiracy to murder her husband.

3. Noncustodial fathers may not feel the same sort of connection to "adult" children and be as responsive to their needs. See for example Wallerstein's findings:

   > A father's attitudes and feelings about his children can become blunted by divorce—a finding that took me by surprise and one that is hard to understand. Psychologists, lawyers, and judges used to think that a father's relationship with his children during marriage would, within reasonable limits, predict his attitude toward them after divorce. If he was an attentive, loving, and sensitive father before divorce, those attributes of fathering would continue long after the breakup. ... But we are finding otherwise. ... We have seen that a father's commitment to his children does not necessarily carry-over into the post-divorce years. ... Many fathers who pay all their child support over the years and maintain close contact with their children draw the line with college. While they can afford it, value education, and have cordial relations with their children, they do not offer even partial support through college. ... The majority [of these men] have college educations. But when I asked about college for their children, they don't want to discuss it.

   Wallerstein and Blakeslee, *Second Chances: Men, Women, and Children, a Decade after Divorce*, 1989.

4. The length of the marriage, the property brought to the marriage, the "contribution" of each party to the marriage, and the contribution by one party to the education, training or increased earning power of the other.

5. Possession of substantial assets not subject to division, age and physical and emotional health, earning capacity, custodial responsibilities, the desirability of (temporarily) awarding the family home to the party having custody of any children.

6. For example, see Wis. Stat. § 767.255 (1981). The statute states: "The court shall presume that all other [marital] property is to be divided equally between the parties, but may alter this distribution without regard to marital misconduct after considering [a list of factors]."

   Other states which have adopted an explicit rule that an equal division of marital assets is presumptively fair include Alaska, Arkansas, California, Idaho, Indiana, New York, Ohio and North Carolina.

7. To be successful in most jurisdictions, she would have to combine this argument with one or more of the following factors: that she has been married over eight or ten years, has devoted this time to homemaking and child care services, is of an age or physical or emotional condition where she may not be able to work, or that her services contributed to her husband's education, training or increased earning power—in other words, monopolize the factors.

VI

Feminist Strategies Within Legal Institutions

When the goals and insights of feminism contend with powerfully entrenched legal institutions feminist ideals seem inevitably to become distorted and coopted, while the law remains essentially unchanged. Although particular or partial legal changes may occur, these "victories" often lay the ground for doctrines that harm rather than help women. Equality doctrines, for example, initially seen as a tool for women's empowerment, have often been used to the detriment of women in prohibiting legal treatment tailored to remedy material and social inequalities particularly born by women in our culture.

As Mary Jane Mossman notes, feminism challenges the very structure of legal inquiry. Mossman uses case studies to illustrate how the basic processes of definition of legal issues and the determination of "relevant" facts and precedents are highly sensitive to the general cultural milieu, as reflected in the perceptions of those who administer the legal system. Her article contradicts the "official" picture of law as a self-contained politically neutral institution. Mossman argues that the structure of law makes it relatively impervious to feminist influence and that, as a matter of strategy, there is little prospect for achieving significant gains for women via court action. The dilemma she confronts at the end of her article echoes those expressed by others throughout this collection. It is the dilemma of feminist legal practitioners, scholars, teachers and students who must become proficient at "law," while questioning and challenging its legitimacy.

Elizabeth Schneider expresses a slightly more favorable assessment of attempts to achieve feminist goals via litigation.

Schneider is sensitive to the power of legal institutions to distort feminist ideology and coopt feminist gains. She contends, however, that the struggle for women's rights, including struggles in the courts, are part of, rather than an alternative to, women's political strategies. The assertion of rights and the mobilization of popular support for legal action contribute to the development of political consciousness and theory. As an example, Schneider recounts how challenging the sex-bias in a court decision rejecting a woman's plea of self-defense stimulated insight into ways the legal process itself contributes to the propensity of women who kill to base their defense on pleas of insanity rather than self-defense. The degree to which a struggle to win legal rights is politically efficacious depends on particular circumstances. She suggests that such struggles may have greater effect early in a movement's history.

In "Strategizing In Equality" pessimism gives birth to strategy. Diana Majury recounts her unsuccessful attempt to construct an adequate feminist model of equality. Brought to the realization that, on the one hand, no single model could be adequate to address the wide variety of disadvantages faced by women and that, on the other, any formalized equality model could be and eventually would be used against women, Majury abandoned her search for an abstract definition of "equality." In this article she proposes instead focusing on specific inequalities *suffered by women and devising strategies to alleviate these disadvantages within the framework of equality discourse.*

16

Feminism and Legal Method: The Difference it Makes

Mary Jane Mossman

> The fact that our understanding of Homo Sapiens has incorporated the perspective of only half of the human race makes it clear that women's studies is not an additional knowledge merely to be tacked on to the curriculum. It is, instead, a body of knowledge that is *perspective transforming* and should therefore transform the existing curriculum from within and revise received notions of what constitutes an 'objective' or 'normative' perspective. (Langland and Gove, 1981, p. 3)

These words appeared in *A Feminist Perspective in the Academy: The Difference it Makes*, a book of essays about the impact of feminist ideas on a number of academic disciplines, including literature, drama, economics, sociology, history, political science, anthropology, psychology, and religious studies. The authors of these essays suggested that a feminist perspective has only just begun to "affect the shape of what is known—and knowable—in their respective disciplines" (p. 2). The authors also asserted that a feminist perspective "challenges deeply held, often sacred beliefs, beliefs that are rooted in emotions and expressed in primitive imagery." As well, it "challenges vested interests, and uproots perspectives which are familiar, and, because familiar, comfortable." In short, "feminist ideas are a challenge to the status quo" (p. 2–3).

Given these perceptions about the transforming impact of feminism on the world of ideas in general, it is curious that this collection did not include an essay about the impact of feminist ideas on law.[1] Moreover, what seems at first glance a mere oversight becomes on closer inspection a question of great significance: to what extent can feminist theory im-

---

Reprinted from *Wisconsin Women's Law Journal* (1987); and *Australian Journal of Law and Society* (1986).

pact, if at all, on the structure of legal inquiry? In the law's process of determining facts, choosing and applying principles, and reaching reasoned decisions, is there any scope for feminism's fundamental challenge to our "ways of knowing?"[2]

This question needs to be addressed in the context of the definition of feminism adopted by the editors of *A Feminist Perspective in the Academy*:

> All feminists . . . would agree that women are not automatically or necessarily inferior to men, that role models for females and males in the current Western societies are inadequate, that equal rights for women are necessary, that it is unclear what by nature either men or women are, that it is a matter for empirical investigation to ascertain what differences follow from the obvious physiological ones, that in these empirical investigations the hypotheses one employs are themselves open to question, revision, or replacement. (Barnes as quoted in Langland and Gove, 1981, p. 3)

The first part of this definition, especially its assertion that "equal rights for women are necessary" assumes the existence of inequality and the need for societal change; in this respect, it represents a clear challenge to the status quo.

Yet, it is the latter part of the definition which represents an even more fundamental challenge: feminism's quest for an understanding of the nature of men and women demands a reassessment of the structure of our inquiry and the ways in which we ask our questions. Not only are the answers subject to scrutiny, but also the ways in which we search for them. In challenging the validity of "facts," the possibility of "neutrality" and the equity of "conclusions" which result from such analysis, a feminist perspective directs attention to our "ways of knowing" about men and women as well as to our efforts to seek greater equality for women. Such a quest, moreover, may require new methods of inquiry; as Jill McCalla Vickers has suggested, women may "learn little of themselves useful for achieving change by employing the intellectual tools of their oppressors" (McCalla Vickers in Miles and Finn, 1982, p. 32).

Can a feminist agenda be accommodated within the legal system? Traditionally, legal method has operated within a highly structured framework which offers little opportunity for fundamental questioning about the *process* of defining issues, selecting relevant principles, and excluding irrelevant ideas. In this context, decision making takes place according to a form which usually "sees" present questions according to patterns established in the past, and in a context in which ongoing consistency in ideas may be valued more often than their future vitality.

In beginning to explore this relation between feminism and legal method, I decided to try to identify the features of legal method in practice, and to do so in the context of "women's rights" cases where the claims being asserted might be expected to reflect feminist ideas and objectives. In this case study of two early twentieth-century cases, the approaches used by judges in deciding claims concerning new roles for women in society are very well illustrated. With the benefit of our historical perspective, moreover, it is clear that the structure of the legal inquiry significantly affected both these decisions. This conclusion, moreover, provides the basis for beginning to assess the potential impact of feminism's "transforming perspective" in present-day challenges to achieve sex equality.

The Idea of Difference

Just a few years before the nineteenth century drew to a close, Clara Brett Martin was admitted to the practice of law in Ontario, the first woman to become a lawyer in the British Commonwealth.[3] Her petition for admission was initially denied by the Law Society on the basis that there were no precedents for the admission of women as lawyers. However, in 1892 a legislative amendment was passed permitting women to be admitted as solicitors; three years later, another legislative amendment similarly permitted women to be admitted as barristers.[4] Clara Brett Martin herself was finally admitted in February 1897 as a barrister and solicitor (Backhouse, 1985, p. 31).

Because of the admission arrangements in Ontario, it was the Law Society of Upper Canada, rather than a superior court, which reviewed the issue of Clara Brett Martin's entitlement to admission as a lawyer (Backhouse, 1985, p. 7–9). By contrast, there was a court challenge in the Province of New Brunswick when Mabel Penury French sought admission as a lawyer there in 1905 (*In re French* (1905), 37 N.B.R. 359). When her application was presented to the court, the judges decided unanimously that there were no precedents for the admission of women, and denied the application. In the next year, however, after the enactment of a legislative amendment, French was admitted as a lawyer in New Brunswick (6 Ed. VII c. 5 (1906)).[5] The same pattern (judicial denial of the application followed by legislative amendment) occurred again some years later when she applied for admission by transfer in British Columbia,[6] and in a number of the other Canadian provinces when women applied for admission as lawyers.[7]

In contrast to the cases where women sought to enter the legal profession and were denied admission by the courts, the celebrated Privy Council decision in the Persons case (*Reference re Meaning of the Word "Persons" in S. 24 of the B.N.A. Act*, [1928] S.C.R. 276; *Edwards v. A.G. for Canada*,

[1930] A.C. 124) determined that Canadian women were eligible to participate in public life. In the Persons case, five women[8] challenged the meaning of the word "persons" in section 24 of the British North America Act. Section 24 provided that the Governor General "shall . . . summon qualified Persons to the Senate," and there was no express requirement that Senators be male persons. Yet, even though the language of the section was gender-neutral, no woman in Canada had ever been summoned to become a member of the Senate.

The Supreme Court of Canada considered a reference[9] as to the meaning of the word "persons" in the B.N.A. Act in 1928, and concluded that women were not eligible to become Senators. On appeal to the Privy Council the next year, the decision was reversed. Ironically, it was in the Privy Council, and not in the indigenous courts of Canada, that the claim of "equal rights for women" to participate in public life was successful.

The decisions in these cases offer an interesting historical picture of legal process in the cultural milieu of the early twentieth century. In the cases about the admission of women to the legal profession, judges accepted the idea that there was a difference between men and women, a difference which "explained" and "justified" the exclusion of women from the legal profession. Yet, the Privy Council's decision in the Persons case completely discounted any such difference in relation to the participation of women in public life.

The issue is why there were these differing approaches: was it the nature of the claims, the courts in which they were presented, or the dates of the decisions? More significantly, what can we learn from the reasoning in these cases about the nature of legal method, especially in the context of challenges to "deeply-held beliefs, vested interests, and the status quo"? In other words, what do these cases suggest about the potential impact of feminism on legal method?

French's case in New Brunswick provides a good illustration of judicial decision making on the issue of women in law. Her case was presented to the court for direction as to the admissibility of women by the president of the Barristers' Society of New Brunswick (as amicus curiae), and the court decided that women were not eligible for admission. Indeed, Mr. Justice Tuck emphatically declared that he had no sympathy for women who wanted to compete with men; as he said: "Better let them attend to their own legitimate business" (pp. 361–62).

Mr. Justice Tuck did not expand on his views as to the nature of women's "legitimate business." However, it seems likely that he would have agreed with the views expressed by Mr. Justice Barker in the case. Relying on the decision of the United States Supreme Court in *Bradwell v. Illinois* in 1873 (83 U.S. (16 Wall) 130), Mr. Justice Barker adopted as his own the "separate spheres" doctrine enunciated there:

> . . . the civil law, as well as nature herself, has always recognized a wide difference in the respective spheres and destinies of man and woman. Man is, or should be, woman's protector and defender. The natural and proper timidity and delicacy which belongs to the female sex evidently unfits it for many of the occupations of civil life. The constitution of the family organization, which is founded in the divine ordinance as well as in the nature of things, indicates the domestic sphere as that which properly belongs to the domain and functions of womanhood. (p. 365)

The language of the *Bradwell* decision expressed very clearly an unqualified acceptance of the idea of difference between men and women, a difference which was social as well as biological. From the perspective of legal method, however, it is significant that no evidence was offered for his assertions about the "timidity and delicacy" of women in general; no authorities were cited for the existence of "divine law"; and no studies were referred to in support of the conclusion that the domestic sphere belonged "properly" to women (and vice versa). The court merely cited the existence of divine and natural law in general terms.

The legal reasoning used by Mr. Justice Barker does not seem consistent at all with the recognized principles of legal method: the reliance on relevant and persuasive evidence to determine facts, the use of legal precedents to provide a framework for analysis, and a rational conclusion supported by both evidence and legal principles. Yet, if Barker, J.'s ideas are not the product of legal method, what is their source?

The answer, of course, is that the ideas he expressed were those prevailing in the cultural and professional milieu in which he lived. The ideas of mainstream religion, for example, emphasized the differences between men and women.[10] Moreover, even where women and men were regarded as equal in the eyes of God (in the ideas of reformers such as Calvin, for example), women were still expected to be subordinate to men, their subordination reflecting "the divinely created social order" in which God "ordained" the subjugation of wives to their husbands (Reuther, 1983, p. 98).[11]

The idea of a divinely-created "social office" in the religious tradition, which required women and men to perform quite different social roles, was reinforced by secular ideas in philosophy in which the role of the family prescribed defined roles for women (Okin, 1979). Even John Stuart Mill, who was well-known for his progressive views about the rights of women, considered that equal rights to education, political life, and the professions could be granted only to single women without the responsibilities of family (p. 279). Moreover, even if Mr. Justice Barker had turned to scientific thought at the turn of the century, he would have found these views confirmed. Because scientific inquiry took place within an already-existing framework of knowledge, it was almost inevitable that scientists would find the answers to questions they asked rather than to others which they did not ask, and confirmation of differences rather than similarities between women and men.[12]

The ideas described from religion, philosophy, and science were those current in the mainstream of intellectual life at the turn of the century. There were, of course, other ideas also current at that time: ideas of religious equality among the Shakers, and also with liberals such as the Grimke sisters (Reuther, p. 26); ideas about sex equality, however flawed, in the work of philosophers like Mill (Okin, p. 28); and scientific ideas about the influence of environment on traits of men and women. Yet such ideas were less well accepted than those in the mainstream, those so warmly embraced in the court by Barker, J.

What is significant here is the court's uncritical acceptance of ideas from the mainstream of intellectual life, as if they were factual rather than conceptual. Moreover, in accepting these ideas and making them an essential part of his decision, Barker, J. provided an explicit and very significant reinforcement of the idea of gender-based difference. In this way, the particular decision denying French's claim to practice law had an impact well beyond the instant case. Thereafter, in the law, as well as in other intellectual traditions, there was a recognized and "legitimate" difference between women and men.

Two other points must also be mentioned. It is significant to an assessment of legal method that the ideas about the role of women, first expressed in the *Bradwell* case in 1873, were adopted without question over thirty years later in French's case in 1905. That the court apparently did not question the appropriateness of applying a precedent from an earlier generation, and from a foreign jurisdiction, seems remarkable. The possibility of distinguishing the earlier decision is clear; and the court's acceptance, without question, of the *Bradwell* decision as both relevant and apparently binding is initially perplexing.

As well, the *Bradwell* decision relied in part on the inability of married women to enter into contracts because of their common law disability, still in existence in 1873. Barker J. might have been expected to comment on the fact that married women's property legislation, both in Canada and in the United States, had erased most of these disabilities by 1905, thereby providing a further reason for distinguishing rather than following *Bradwell*. As such analysis demonstrates, the *Bradwell* precedent was not self-applying; there was a choice to be made by the court in *French*. The more difficult problem, therefore, is to explain the reasons for the judicial choice.

Even more fundamentally, the ideas accepted in *Bradwell* and restated in *French* were quite inconsistent, and probably known to be so by the judges, with the reality of women's work outside the home at the turn of the century. In Canada, as well as in Great Britain:

> Very few of the women whom the judges knew, whether they were litigants, or cleaners of the courtroom, or servants in the home, actually corresponded in any way to the judicial representation. At the time when the judges were speaking, more than a million unmarried women alone were employed in industry, while a further three quarters of a million were in domestic service. . . . For the great majority of Victorian women, as for the great majority of Victorian men, life was characterized by drudgery and poverty rather than by refinement and decorum. (Sachs and Hoff Wilson, 1978, p. 54)

Despite this reality, Mr. Justice Barker reiterated without criticism or qualification the authoritative statement from *Bradwell* that "the paramount destiny and mission of women" was that of wife and mother—because "this is the law of the Creator" (p. 366). The conflict which is apparent to us between the judicial description of all women, and the known conditions in which at least some of them lived at that time, suggests a further element of legal method: abstraction from the real lives of women. Indeed, what seems evident is a willingness to use the ideas of (male) theologians, philosophers, and scientists as the basis of "reality," in preference to the facts of life in the real lives of actual women.

The judicial approach evident in *French* changed significantly, however, by the time of the Persons case. There is little mention of the idea of gender-based difference in the analysis of either the Supreme Court of Canada or the Privy Council in that case. In the Supreme Court of Canada, Mr. Justice Mignault referred to the petitioners' claim only as a "grave constitutional change" (p. 303), and Mr. Justice Anglin restated the "apologia" from *Chorlton v. Lings* ((1868), L.R. 4 C.P. 374) that:

> . . . in this country in modern times, chiefly out of respect to women, and a sense of decorum, and not from their want of intellect, or their being for any other such reason unfit to take part in the government of the country, they have been excused from taking any share in this department of public affairs. (p. 283)

However, nothing in the judgments of the Supreme Court of Canada reflects the rhetoric and ideas expressed by Mr. Justice Barker in Mabel French's case. And, by contrast, Lord Sankey commenced his opinion in the Privy Council by stating:

> The exclusion of women from all public offices is a relic of days more barbarous than ours, but it must be remembered that the necessity of

> the times often forced on man customs which in later years were not necessary. (p. 128)

His words represented a clear signal that, although the treatment of women in the past may have been understandable in the context of those times, the world had changed.

In the Persons case, that is all there is about the difference between men and women. The contrast between the reliance on gender-based difference as incontrovertible fact in *French* at the turn of the century, and the virtual absence of such ideas in the Persons case in the late 1920s, seems highly significant. It seems, indeed, to offer an explanation for the differing outcomes in the two cases: when difference was emphasized in *French*, women were excluded from membership in the legal profession, while when it was discounted in the Persons case, women were included with men in opportunities to participate in public life.

This analytical approach, based as it is on the methodology actually observed in these two judicial decisions, suggests that the dictates of legal method were not strictly followed in the decision-making process. In addition to this approach, however, it is necessary to assess the legal method actually described by the judges in the cases. The contrast between what they said they were doing, and what they actually did, also offers some important insights into legal method. To this contrast we now turn.

The Principles of Legal Method

The stated reasons in these cases were consistent with well-established principles of legal method. The principles can be analyzed in terms of three aspects: (1) the characterization of the issues; (2) the choice of legal precedents to decide the validity of the women's claims; and (3) the process of statutory interpretation, especially in determining the effect of statutes to alter common law principles. Both the principles themselves and their application to these specific claims are important for an understanding of the potential impact of feminism on legal method.

Characterizing the Issue

In both *French* and the Persons case, the judges consistently characterized the issues as narrowly as possible, eschewing their "political" or "social" significance, and explaining that the court was interested only in the law.[13] For example, in the Persons case in the Canadian Supreme Court, Chief Justice Anglin stated pointedly:

> In considering this matter we are, of course, in no wise concerned with the desirability or the undesirability of the presence of women in the Senate, nor with any political aspect of the question submitted. Our whole duty is to construe, to the best of our ability, the relevant provisions of the B.N.A. Act, 1867, and upon that construction to base our answer. (p. 281–2)

Even the Privy Council which came to a distinctly different conclusion framed the scope of its inquiry as narrowly as possible (p. 137). Clearly evident in these judicial statements is a felt need to distance the court from the "political" or moral issue, and a desire to be guided only by neutral principles of interpretation in relation to abstract legal concepts. The judges' confidence in the principles of legal method as a means of deciding the issue, even confined so narrowly, is also evident. While their comments suggest an awareness of broader issues, there is a clear assertion of the court's limited role in resolving such disputes.

Equally clearly, the women claimants never intended to bring to the court a "neutral" legal issue for determination; they petitioned the court to achieve their goals, goals which were unabashedly political. In the face of such claims, however, the court maintained a view of its process as one of neutral interpretation. More significantly, the court's power to define the "real issues" carried with it an inherent absence of responsibility on the part of the (male) judges for any negative outcome. It was the law, rather than the (male) person interpreting it, which was responsible for the decision. The result of such a characterization process, therefore, is to reinforce the law's detachment and neutrality rather than its involvement and responsibility; and to extend these characteristics beyond law itself to judges and lawyers.

Yet, how can we accommodate this characterization of detachment and neutrality with the opinions expressed, especially in *French*, about the role of women? The ideas about gender-based difference expressed forcefully by Mr. Justice Barker in that case appear very close to an expression about the "desirability" of women as lawyers and not merely a dispassionate and neutral application of legal precedents. Thus, at least in *French*, there is inconsistency between the legal method declared by the judges to be appropriate, and the legal method actually adopted in making their decisions. In this context, the expressed idea of detachment and neutrality both masks and legitimates judicial views about women's "proper" sphere.

Using Precedents in the Common Law Tradition

The existence of women's common law disability was regularly cited in both these cases as the reason for denying their claims to be admitted to the legal profession and to take part in public life. The judges used numerous precedents for their conclusion. For example, Chief Justice Anglin cited as a "fact or circumstance of importance . . . that by the common law of England (as also, speaking generally, by the civil and the canon law . . .) women were under a legal incapacity to hold public office, . . ." (p. 283). At the end of the nineteenth century, of course, there were a number of respects in which women (especially married women) suffered disabilities at common law: married women were denied the right to hold interests in property until the married women's property statutes,[14] and all women were denied the right to vote until the twentieth century. As well, however, courts regularly asserted that, because of women's common law disabilities, there were no precedents for admitting women to the legal profession or to full participation in public life.

It has been suggested that the absence of such a common law precedent can be traced to Lord Coke who (apparently *without* the benefit of precedent) "had stated that women could not be attorneys" three hundred years previously (Sachs and Hoff Wilson, p. 32). What is clear, at least, is that the absence of precedents declaring women eligible to take part in public life and enter the legal profession created a significant handicap for those presenting arguments in favour of the women's claims. From a broader perspective, this difficulty epitomizes the negative effects of the doctrine of precedent on newly-emerging claims to legal rights. If a precedent is required to uphold a claim, it is only existing claims which will receive legal recognition; the doctrine of precedent thus becomes a powerful tool for maintaining the status quo and for rationalizing the denial of new claims. Seen in this light, the law itself is an essential means of protecting the status quo, notwithstanding the challenge of feminist ideas.

Yet, if this conclusion is correct, how can we explain the Privy Council decision, a decision in which the same conceptual framework of law was viewed very differently. After canvassing the precedents, Lord Sankey stated:

> The fact that no woman had served or has claimed to serve such an office is not of great weight when it is remembered that custom would have prevented the claim being made or the point being contested. Customs are apt to develop into traditions which are stronger than law and remain unchallenged long after the reason for them has disappeared. The appeal to history therefore in this particular matter is not conclusive. (p. 134)

Obviously, the Privy Council was less concerned with the absence of precedent in their decision making than the judges in *French*. Is this approach simply an early example of a court of highest jurisdiction deciding not to be bound by precedent in appropriate cases, or is there some other explanation?

One suggestion is that the decision of the Privy Council in 1929 simply reflected the spirit of the times in relation to the role of women. Much had indeed changed since Clara Brett Martin and Mabel Penury French had sought admission to the legal profession at the turn of the century. As was noted earlier, there had been legislation enabling married women to enter into contracts and to hold interests in property even before the end of the nineteenth century. In the early part of the twentieth century, moreover, women had participated successfully in World War I, and they had attained suffrage in many jurisdictions after the War and the benefit of the Sexual Disqualification Removal Act in England in 1919. It may, therefore, be quite accurate to conclude that the explanation is not one of "legal logic"; instead, it is evident that "what had changed was not . . . the modes of reasoning appropriate to lawyers, but the conception of women and women's position in public life held by the judges" (Sachs and Hoff Wilson, p. 41).

At the same time, if this explanation is accepted, it is difficult to account for the differences in perspective of the judges of the Supreme Court of Canada in 1928 from those in the Privy Council in 1929. It is true that Lord Sankey sat in the English Cabinet alongside Margaret Bondfield, the first woman to hold Cabinet office in Britain; and it is, therefore, possible that he had become accustomed to the idea of women holding public office as a result of this "precedent" (Sachs and Hoff Wilson, p. 42). This conclusion, of course, depends on the assumption that no similar role models existed in Canada. Yet such a conclusion denies the importance of the roles of the five women challengers in the Persons case: Henrietta Muir Edwards was the Alberta Vice-President of the National Council of Women for Canada, Nellie McClung and Louise McKinney had been members of the Legislative Assembly in Alberta, while Irene Parlby was then a member of the same Legislative Assembly and of its Executive Council; and Emily Murphy was the first woman police magistrate in Alberta. It is therefore difficult, if not impossible, not to accept these Canadian women as "precedents" equal to Margaret Bondfield. What, then, is the explanation for these differing perspectives and the different outcomes which resulted in the two courts?

In terms of the legal method described by the judges, of course, there is no answer to this question. Neither the judgments in the Supreme Court of Canada nor Lord Sankey's opinion in the Privy Council expressly consider the reality of women's experience at that time at all, and they specifically do not consider the reality of experience for the actual women claimants in the Persons case. Thus, even if the judges' perspectives on women's place were different in the two courts, there is virtually nothing in their judgments expressly reflecting them. For this reason, it is impossible to demonstrate that Lord Sankey's differing perspective was the reason for the different outcome in the Privy Council. At the same time, it is hard to find any other convincing explanation.

What does, of course, seem clear is the existence of judicial choice in the application of precedents. In the process of choosing earlier cases and deciding that they are binding precedents, judges make choices about which aspects of earlier cases are "relevant" and "similar," choices which are not neutral but normative. In suggesting that the earlier decisions (relied on by the Supreme Court of Canada as binding precedents) were not determinative, Lord Sankey was declaring that the earlier decisions should not be regarded as exactly the same as the situation before the court in the Persons case. In this way, Lord Sankey's decision demonstrates the availability of choice in the selection of facts, in the categorization of principles and in the determination of relevance. At the same time, his opinion completely obscures the process and standards which guided the choice he actually made. To the myth of "neutrality," therefore, Lord Sankey added the "mystery" of choice.

Interpreting Statutes and Parliament's Intent

The interpretation of the law relating to women's claims was complicated by the need for judges to construe statutes as well as take account of common law principles. In some earlier cases, for example, women had challenged their exclusion from rights in statutes where the statutory language referred to "men." Such claims were based on the 1850 legislation (Lord Brougham's Act, 1850 (Imp.) c. 21)[15] in England which provided that "words importing the masculine gender should be deemed and taken to include females, unless the contrary was clearly expressed." In *Chorlton v. Lings*, a case involving the right to be registered to vote under legislation which gave such a right to any "man," the court dismissed the women's claim on the basis that it could not have been the wish of Parliament to make so drastic a change; had Parliament wished to enable women to vote, it would not have used the word "man" in setting out the qualifications for voting in the statute.[16]

Even in the statutes which used gender-neutral language, however, there were problems of statutory interpretation in relation to these cases. The legislation reviewed in the Persons case, as well as that at issue in the admission of both Martin and French, used the word "person" in describing the qualifications for being appointed to the Senate and called to the bar respectively. In the Persons case in the Supreme Court of Canada, Chief Justice Anglin expressed his surprise that such a monumental change in the position of women could be conferred by Parliament's use of such insignificant means; as he stated rhetorically: "Such an extraordinary privilege is not conferred furtively" (p. 285). Not surprisingly, he concluded that the women's claim must be dismissed because there was no evident express intent on the part of Parliament to effect the change advocated by them; the use of the word "person" was not, by itself, sufficient.

A similar result occurred in French's challenge in the New Brunswick court. The legislation governing the admission of lawyers used the word "person"; indeed, the legislation in New Brunswick had used gender-neutral language for many years. Unfortunately, this latter fact reinforced the judges' conclusion that the statute could not have been intended to include women, since they had never been lawyers (p. 370–71). Mr. Justice Barker had no doubt at all as to the appropriate resolution of this problem of statutory interpretation, concluding that any suggestion that the word "person" encompassed females was a "radical change" indeed (p. 371).

Thus, Canadian judges uniformly interpreted the word "person" in a way which seemed most consistent with their time and experiences. For them, it was radical indeed to think of a woman in public office or in the legal profession, and their interpretation of the statutory language reflected their own understanding of what Parliament might have intended, had Parliament considered the matter explicitly. Presumably, the judges also felt confidence that members of Parliament, (male) people much like the judges themselves, would have agreed with their interpretation.

Once again, however, the opinion of the Privy Council is different. After reviewing at some length the legislative provisions of the B.N.A. Act, Lord Sankey stated conclusively:

> The word 'person' . . . may include members of both sexes, and to those who ask why the word should include females, the obvious answer is why should it not. In these circumstances the burden is upon those who deny that the word includes women to make out their case (p. 138).

Lord Sankey cited no precedent to support this presumption in favour of the most extensive meaning of the statutory language, even though it expressly contradicted the principles of statutory interpretation adopted by all the judges in the decision of the Supreme Court of Canada.

In the end, just as the Privy Council decision was puzzling in relation to the effect of legal precedents about women's common law disabilities, it is also difficult to reconcile Lord Sankey's conclusions about the interpretation of the statute to the principles and precedents accepted in the

Supreme Court of Canada. Clearly, the Privy Council departed from the Supreme Court's approach to legal method in reaching its conclusion to admit the women's claim. What remains unclear are Lord Sankey's reasons for doing so.

Feminism and Legal Method

In such a context, what conclusion is appropriate about feminism's potential for perspective transforming in the context of legal method?

The analysis of these cases illustrates clearly the structure of inquiry identified as legal method. First of all, legal method defines its own boundaries: questions which are inside the defined boundaries can be addressed, but those outside the boundaries are not "legal" issues, however important they may be for "politics" or "morals," etc. Thus, the question of women becoming lawyers or Senators was simply a matter of interpreting the law; it did not require any consideration of utility or benefit to the women themselves or to society in general. The purpose and the result of the boundary-defining exercise is to confer "neutrality" on the law and on its decision makers; in so doing, moreover, the process also relieves both the law and its decision makers of accountability for (unjust) decisions—("our whole duty is [only] to construe . . . the provisions of the [constitution]").

More serious is the potential for judicial attitudes to be expressed, and to be used in decision making (either explicitly or implicitly), when there is no "objective" evidence to support them; because of the myth of neutrality which surrounds the process, such attitudes may acquire legitimacy in a way which strengthens and reinforces ideas in "politics" and "morals" which were supposed to be outside the law's boundary. After the decision in *French*, for example, women were different as a matter of law, and not just in the minds of people like Mr. Justice Barker. Thus, the power to name the boundaries of the inquiry (and to change them, if necessary) makes legal method especially impervious to challenges from "the outside."[17]

Second, legal method defines "relevance" and accordingly excludes some ideas while admitting others. Some facts, such as inherent gender-based traits, were regarded as relevant in *French*, for example, while in both cases the actual conditions in which women lived their lives were not relevant at all. What was clearly relevant in both cases were earlier decisions about similar circumstances from which the judges could abstract principles of general application. That all of the earlier cases had been decided by men, who were interpreting legislation drafted when women had no voting rights, was completely irrelevant to the decision making in the cases analyzed; even though the cases represented direct and significant challenges to the continuation of gender-exclusive roles and the circumstances of the historical context may seem quite significant to women now. The irony of solemn judicial reliance on precedent in the context of significant efforts by women to change the course of legal history underlines the significant role of legal method in preserving the status quo.

Finally, the case analysis demonstrates the opportunity for choice in legal method: choice as to which precedents are relevant and which approach to statutory interpretation is preferred; and choice as to whether the ideas of the mainstream or those of the margins are appropriate. The existence of choice in legal method offered some possibility of positive outcomes in the women's rights cases, at the same time as legal method's definition of boundaries and concept of relevance ensured that positive outcomes would seldom occur. Lord Sankey's opinion in the Privy Council is an example of choice in legal method, however, which is as remarkable for its common sense as it is for its distinctiveness in legal method. Yet because Lord Sankey obscured the reasons for his choice, he also preserved the power and mystery of legal method even as he endowed women with the right to be summoned to the Senate. Thus, the opportunity for choice of outcome, positive as it appears, will not automatically lead to legal results which successfully challenge "vested interests" or the "status quo," especially in relation to the law itself.

The conclusion that legal method is structured in such a way which makes it impervious to a feminist perspective is a sobering one. Within the women's movement, it has concrete consequences for the design of strategies for achieving legal equality: it suggests, for example, the general futility of court action for achieving significant change in women's rights, even though such action may be useful to monitor interpretation by courts or to focus attention on legal problems. For a feminist who is also a lawyer, however, the effort of "double-think" may be both taxing and ultimately frustrating; the needs of clients require her to become highly proficient at legal method at the same time as her feminist commitment drives her to challenge the validity of its underlying rationale.

This dilemma also exists for feminist scholars. Feminist legal scholars are expected to think and write using the approaches of legal method: defining the issues, analyzing relevant precedents, and recommending conclusions according to defined and accepted standards of legal method. A feminist scholar who chooses instead to ask different questions or to conceptualize the problem in different ways risks a reputation for incompetence in her legal method as well as lack of recognition for her scholarly (feminist) accomplishment. Too often, it seems almost impossible to be both a good lawyer and a good feminist scholar (Lahey, 1985).

This dilemma is similarly acute for feminist law teachers and students.

With the advent of large numbers of women law students and increased numbers of women on law faculties (Mossman, 1988), many have concluded that there is now a feminist perspective in the law school. Such a conclusion ignores the power of legal method to resist structural change. For example, discussions about whether feminist law teachers should create separate courses with feminist approaches and content, or whether we should use such approaches and content in "malestream" courses, or whether we should do both at once, etc. clearly confirm the "reality" of the existing categories of legal knowledge, and reinforce the idea of the feminist perspective as "Other" (Mossman, 1985). While the separate course approach marginalizes the feminist perspective, the process of "tacking on" feminist approaches to malestream courses only serves to emphasize what is really important in contrast to what has been "tacked on." Even efforts to give equal time to the feminist perspective and to reveal the essential maleness of the "neutral" approach may underline that what is male is what really has significance. On this basis, adding women's experience to the law school curriculum cannot transform our perspective of law unless it also transforms legal method.[18]

Taking this conclusion seriously, as I think we must, leads to some significant conclusions for women who are feminists and who are lawyers, law teachers and law students. It is simply not enough just to introduce women's experience into the curriculum or to examine the feminist approach to legal issues, although both of these activities are important. Yet, especially because there is so much resistance in legal method itself to ideas which challenge the status quo, there is no solution for the feminist who is a law teacher except to confront the reality that gender and power are inextricably linked in the legal method we use in our work, our discourse, and our study. Honestly confronting the barriers of our conceptual framework may at least permit us to begin to ask more searching and important questions.[19]

Notes

1. A similar collection in Dale Spender, ed., *Men's Studies Modified: The Impact of Feminism on the Academic Disciplines* (Pergamon Press: 1981) does include an analysis of feminism in the context of law as an academic discipline. See Katherine O'Donovan, "Before and After: The Impact of Feminism on the Academic Discipline of Law" in Spender, p. 175.
2. The phrase is similar to that used by O'Donovan in *Sexual Divisions in Law, op. cit.*, p. 59, where she refers to a "way of seeing":

   > When a particular way of seeing is analysed, what was accepted as natural is made strange. Part of that strangeness is the realisation that beneath the accepted order of life lie hidden power relations.

Both phrases focus on the method of understanding ideas, but "ways of knowing" is more explicit about the cognitive process itself. See also Geraldine Finn, "On the Oppression of Women in Philosophy—Or, Whatever Happened to Objectivity?" in Angela Miles and Geraldine Finn, *Feminism in Canada: From Pressure to Politics* (Black Rose Books, Montreal: 1982) p. 145.

3. Martin was admitted to practice in 1897 as a barrister and solicitor. For an excellent account of her efforts to become a lawyer, see Constance Backhouse, " 'To Open the Way for Others of my Sex;' Clara Brett Martin's Career as Canada's First Woman Lawyer" (1985), 1 *Can. Journal of Women and the Law* 1.

4. The amendment to the Law Society Act which permitted Martin's entry to the legal profession was originally drafted in gender-specific language: "the admission of women"; it was only in 1970 that the Act was amended so as to refer to "the admission of persons." See 55 V. c.32, s.1 (1892) readmission of women as solicitors; 58 V. c.27, s.1 (1985) readmission as barristers-at-law; and S.O. 1970, c. 19 for the admission of persons. The original provisions permitted the Law Society to exercise discretion in relation to admission, but this power was removed by 2 Geo.V. c.26, s.43 (1927).

5. See Alfred Watts, Q.C., *History of the Legal Profession in British Columbia 1869–1984* (Law Society of B.C.:1984) at 133–35; he states that French was admitted in New Brunswick on April 21, 1906 (p. 133).

6. The Benchers in B.C. decided that " . . . they had no power . . . to admit ladies to the practice of law"; on an application for mandamus to the British Columbia Court of Appeal, the application was refused. See *In re French,* [1912] 1 D.L.R. 80. According to Watts "the Law Society rather ungallantly, and contrary to what had happened to (sic) New Brunswick, [collected] its costs" in the case. In February 1912, after concerted efforts on the part of a number of women activists, legislation was passed permitting women to become lawyers. Mabel Penury French was admitted on April 1, 1912; according to Watts, the Benchers' minutes of that date record the call of twenty gentlemen, including Ms. French!

7. See, for example, *Langstaff v. Bar of Quebec* (1915), 25 Que. K.B. 11. A full list of the women first admitted for each province in Canada is found in Cameron Harvey, "Women in Law in Canada" (1970–71), 4 Man. L. J. 9.

8. A petition was submitted by Henrietta Muir Edwards, Nellie L. McClung, Louise C. McKinney, Emily F. Murphy and Irene Parlby; as a result, a reference was submitted to the Supreme Court of Canada by the Minister of Justice for a determination of the question.

9. There is some evidence that the government of the day recognized the potential controversy of the matter, and that a conscious decision was made to refer it to the court to avoid having to deal with it in the political arena. See David Ricardo Williams, *Duff: A Life in the Law* (The Osgoode Society: 1984) p. 142–48; and James G. Snell and Frederick Vaughan, *The Supreme Court of Canada: History of the Institution* (The Osgoode Society: 1985) p. 141–43.

10. See Rosemary Radford Reuther, *Sexism and God-Talk: Toward a Feminist Theology* (Beacon Press, Boston: 1983) and M. Warner, *Alone of All Her Sex: The Myth and the Cult of the Virgin Mary* (Pan Books Ltd.: 1985); as well as the earlier work of Mary Daly.

11. The author also examines some "egalitarian theologies" which rejected the mainstream patriarchal ideas about the relation of men and women to God; *op. cit.*, pp. 99–109. See also Radford Reuther, "The Feminist Critique in Religious Studies" in Langland and Gove, *op. cit.*, pp. 52ff.

12. See also Hubbard, "The Emperor Doesn't Wear any Clothes: The Impact of Feminism on Biology" in Spender, p. 213.

13. The same approach occurred in relation to Clara Brett Martin's application to the Law Society in Ontario. The lawyer chairing the Committee responsible for looking into the matter reported to the Benchers that the issue was whether the Law Society was "permitted to allow a woman to be entered as a student of Laws" rather than whether it was "desirable" that they be so admitted. See Backhouse, p. 8; citing "Women as Students-at-Law" (1891), 2 *Western Law Times* 118–9.

14. There are several monographs analyzing the process of matrimonial property reform on both sides of the Atlantic in the latter half of the nineteenth century; for example, see L. Holcombe, *Wives and Property: Reform of the Married Women's Property Law in Nineteenth-Century England* (University of Toronto Press: 1983); N. Basch, *In the Eyes of the Law: Women, Marriage and Property in Nineteenth-Century New York* (Cornell University Press: 1982); and E. Griffith, *In Her Own Right: The Life of Elizabeth Cady Stanton* (Oxford University Press: 1984).

15. S.4 stated:

    That in all Acts words importing the masculine gender shall be deemed and taken to include females . . . unless the contrary as to gender . . . is expressly provided.

16. According to Sachs and Hoff Wilson, p. 23, John Stuart Mill had made some efforts, at the time of the enactment of the Second Reform Bill in 1867 (which extended the Parliamentary suffrage), to change the word "man" in the statute to "person"; his efforts were unsuccessful, but one of his opponents had suggested that the legislation of 1850 would nonetheless enfranchise women. The negative outcome of *Chorlton v. Lings*, of course, demonstrated that the 1850 legislation would also be interpreted in accordance with prevailing cultural values.

17. It is interesting that Cynthia Fuchs Epstein, in her study of women lawyers in the United States, referred to them as "outsiders"; see *Women in Law* (Basic Books, New York: 1982) p. 385.

18. For a challenging account of a different kind of inquiry and method of analysis, see Carol Gilligan, *In a Different Voice* (Harvard University Press: 1982). Gilligan's research focused on the ethical development of young children—boys and girls aged 11. She presented subjects with an ethical dilemma and measured the responses of Jake and Amy. According to her research, Jake's response placed him at an appropriate level of development on the Kohlberg scale, while Amy's response, according to the scale, make her ethical development seem deficient. Gilligan, however, claimed to have heard "a different voice" in Amy, one often heard in women, and less frequently in some men.

19. Christine Boyle has begun to do this, I think, in "Teaching Law as if Women Really Mattered, or, What About the Washrooms?" (1986), 2 *Can. J. Women and the Law* 96.

17

The Dialectics of Rights and Politics: Perspectives from the Women's Movement

Elizabeth M. Schneider

The Nature of legal rights has long been a subject of interest to legal scholars and activists. Recently, dialogue on the issue has intensified, provoked by numerous critiques of liberal rights, particularly by Critical Legal Studies (CLS) scholars. These recent critiques have tended to view rights claims and rights consciousness as distinct from and frequently opposed to politics, and as an obstacle to the political growth and development of social movement groups.

Recent critiques of rights have looked at rights and politics as static categories, and focused primarily on the way in which rights claims and rights consciousness mask and obscure important political choices and values. In this article I develop a dialectical perspective on rights. Central to this perspective is an understanding of the dynamic interrelationship of rights and politics, as well as the dual and contradictory potential of rights discourse to blunt and advance political development. Here I detail the rich, complex, and dynamic process through which political experience can shape the articulation of a right, and the way in which this articulation then shapes the development of the political process. I also explore the expressive aspect of rights claims and rights consciousness. I focus on the way in which the assertion or "experience" of rights can express political vision, affirm a group's humanity, contribute to an individual's development as a whole person, and assist in the collective political development of a social or political movement, particularly at its early stages. In addition, I examine the importance of context to rights assertion. The ability of a rights claim to constrain or assist a movement's political vision and struggle for change depends upon the particular movement that asserts the right and the particular time at which it does so. Thus, I turn to the recent women's movement's experience with rights

---

The complete version of this article appears in *New York University Law Review* (1986).

as an example of the complex dimensions of the dialectic of rights and politics.

My views emerge directly from my experience as a civil rights lawyer who has assisted groups in asserting rights, and as a law teacher who seeks to help students understand the role of law in social change. As lawyer and law teacher, I have sought to understand how, when, and under what circumstances the use of rights claims by social movement groups is useful. Further, my perspective has been shaped by social philosophy, feminist theory, and my experience as an activist in the women's movement. Here, I seek to integrate these diverse experiences as part of an effort to understand the relationship between theory and practice. Both the form and substance of this discussion reflect my view that it is important to explore theory and practice simultaneously and look closely at how they are interrelated.

The Debate on Rights

The idea that legal rights have some intrinsic value is widespread in our culture. A rights claim can make a statement of entitlement that is universal and categorical. This entitlement can be seen as negative because it protects against intrusion by the state (a right to privacy), or the same right can be seen as affirmative because it enables an individual to do something (a right to choose whether to bear a child). Thus, a rights claim can define the boundaries to state power and the entitlement to do something, and by extension, provide an affirmative vision of human society. Recently, however, legal scholars, in particular CLS and feminist scholars, have debated the meanings of rights claims and have questioned the significance of legal argumentation focused on rights.

CLS scholars question whether rights claims and rights discourse can facilitate social reconstruction. The CLS critique has several interrelated themes which flow from a more general critique of liberalism. CLS scholars argue that liberalism is premised on dichotomies, such as individual and community or self and other, that divide the world into two mutually exclusive spheres. Rights claims only perpetuate these dichotomies, limiting legal thinking and inhibiting necessary social change.

CLS scholars base their critique of rights on the inherently individualistic nature of rights under legal liberalism, the "reification" of rights generally, and the indeterminate nature of rights claims. CLS scholars argue that rights are "permeated by the possessive individualism of capitalist society" (Lynd, 1984, pp. 1417–18; Gabel 1984, p. 1577). Because rights "belong" to individuals—rights rhetoric portrays individuals as "separate owners of their respective bundles of rights" (Olsen 1984, p. 393)—they are necessarily individualistic. CLS also see rights discourse as taking on a "thing-like" quality—a fixed and external meaning—that "freezes and falsifies" rich and complex social experience (Gabel and Kennedy, 1984, pp.1, 3–6; Gabel, 1984, p. 1582; Tushnet, 1984, p. 1382). This reification of socially construced phenomena "is an essential aspect of alienated consciousness, leading people to accept existing social orders as the inevitable 'facts of life' " (Gabel and Harris, 1982–83, p. 369). Similarly, CLS scholars argue that the use of rights discourse by a social movement group and the consequent reliance on rights can keep people passive and dependent on the state because it is the state which grants them their rights. Legal strategies based on rights discourse tend to weaken the power of a popular movement by allowing the state to define the movement's goals. Further, it fosters social antagonisms by magnifying disagreement within and conflicts between groups over rights.

Some feminist critiques of rights see rights claims as formal and hierarchical—premised on a view of law as patriarchal. From this perspective, law generally, and rights particularly, reflect a male viewpoint characterized by objectivity, distance, and abstraction. As Catharine MacKinnon, a leading exponent of this position writes, "Abstract rights will authoritize the male experience of the world" (MacKinnon, 1983, pp. 644–45).

The CLS and feminist critiques of rights, though insightful, are incomplete. They do not take account of the complex, and I suggest dialectical, relationship between the assertion of rights and political struggle in social movement practice. They see only the limits of rights, and fail to appreciate the dual possibilities of rights discourse. Admittedly, rights discourse can reinforce alienation and individualism, and can constrict political vision and debate. But, at the same time, it can help to affirm human values, enhance political growth, and assist in the development of collective identity.

By failing to see that both possibilities exist simultaneously, these critiques have rigidified, rather than challenged, the classic dichotomies of liberal thought—law and politics, individual and community, and ultimately, rights and politics. Radical social theory must explore the dialectical dimensions of each dichotomy, not reinforce the sense that the dichotomies are frozen and static. Radical social theory must explain how these dichotomies can be transcended.

Dialectics and Praxis as Methodology: The Examples of Feminist Theory and Feminist Legal Practice

My perspective on rights is grounded in a view of the dialectical nature of consciousness and social change and a view that theory and practice must be understood as interrelated. The concept of dialectics has shaped much of contemporary social theory and has developed different meanings and uses. The dialectical approach that I use here explores the process which connects ideas that appear to be in opposition to one another. One "moment" in the process gives rise to its own negation, and "out of this negativity, emerges a 'moment' which at once negates, affirms, and transcends the 'moment' involved in the struggle" (Bernstein, 1971, p. xiii). Thus, an idea may contain the seeds of its own contradiction, and ideas that appear to be in opposition may really be the same or connected. The dialectical process is not a mechanical confrontation of an opposite from outside, but an organic emergence and development of opposition and change from within the "moment" or idea itself.[1]

The critiques of rights that I have described suffer from an analysis that divorces theory from practice. Rights are analyzed in the abstract, viewed as static—as a form of legal theory separate from social practice—and then criticized for being formal and abstract. My approach to rights views theory and practice as dialectically related, and I look to the philosophical concept of praxis to describe this process. The fundamental aspect of praxis is the active role of consciousness and subjectivity in shaping both theory and practice, and the dynamic interrelationship that results.[2]

Feminist Theory

Feminist theory is characterized by an emphasis on dialectical process and the interrelationship of theory and practice.[3] Feminist theory emphasizes the value of direct and personal experience as the place that theory should begin, as embodied in the phrase "the personal is political" (Eisenstein, 1984, p.11). This phrase reflects the view that the realm of personal experience, the "private" which has always been trivialized, is an appropriate and important subject of public inquiry, and that the "private" and "public" worlds are inextricably linked. The notion of consciousness-raising as feminist method flows from this insight. This method is a form of praxis because it transcends the theory and practice dichotomy. Consciousness-raising groups start with personal and concrete experience, integrate this experience into theory, and then, in effect, reshape theory based upon experience and experience based upon theory. Theory expresses and grows out of experience but it also relates back to that experience for further refinement, validation, or modification.

The fact that this process begins with the self, and then connects to the larger world of women, is important. For feminists, theory is not "out there," but rather is based on the concrete, daily, and "trivial" experiences of individuals, and so emerges from the shared experience of women talking. Because feminist theory grows out of direct experience and consciousness actively asserting itself, feminist theory emphasizes context and the importance of identifying experience and claiming it for one's own.

Feminist theory involves a particular methodology, but it also has a substantive viewpoint and political orientation. Recognizing the links between individual change and social change means understanding the importance of political *activity,* not just theory. Theory emerges from practice and practice then informs and reshapes theory. At the same time, because of its dialectical cast, feminist theory encompasses a notion of process that encourages a grounded and reflective appreciation of this interrelationship—its possibilities and limits, visions and defeats.

Feminist Legal Practice: Feminist Theory in Practice

While feminist theory has shaped my view of the relationship between theory and practice, much of my perspective on the use of rights has understandably been shaped by my own experience. As a college student in the 1960s, active in civil rights and other political work, and studying political science and social theory, I saw many instances of lawyers from the civil rights movement using the law to advance group political efforts. Yet I also observed that the law could be used to constrain political organizing and vision. For that reason, although strongly drawn to law school, I chose to do other work instead.

During this time I became actively involved in the women's movement, and my experience as an activist gave me the incentive and impetus to go to law school. It was 1970, and efforts to reshape the law to include women's experience were just beginning. There was a need for women with a feminist perspective to go to law school.

First as a law student and then as a lawyer, I was privileged to work at the Center for Constitutional Rights. Center Lawyers had a long history of using the law to affect social change and to change the law to reflect the experience of those previously excluded by the law. In the early 1970s, women lawyers on the Center's staff began to work on women's rights issues.

Of the many cases on which I worked at the Center, one, *State v. Wanrow*[4] stands out for me because it so clearly demonstrates that legal argumentation which is tied to and expresses the concerns of a social movement can assist in the political development of that movement. In *Wanrow,* a jury convicted Yvonne Wanrow, a Native American woman, of second-degree murder for shooting and killing a white man named William Wesler, whom she believed had tried to molest one of her children. Wesler had entered her babysitter's home uninvited when Wanrow and her children where there. Wanrow, who had a cast on her leg and was using crutches at the time, claimed that, based on her perceptions of the danger created by Wesler, she had acted in self-defense. The trial court, however, instructed the jury to consider only the circumstances "at or immediately before the killing" when evaluating the gravity of the danger the defendant faced, even though Wanrow claimed that she had information which led her to believe that Wesler had a history of child molestation and had previously tried to molest one of her children. The trial court also instructed the jury to apply the equal force standard, whereby the person claiming self-defense can only respond with force equal to that which the assailant uses. Wesler had not been carrying a gun.

Center lawyers became involved in the case on appeal to the Washington Supreme Court. Reading the trial manuscript, we realized that the judge's instructions prevented the jury from considering Yvonne Wanrow's state of mind, as shaped by her experiences and perspective as a Native American woman, when she confronted this man. The jury had not been presented with evidence concerning the lack of police protection generally in such situations, the pervasiveness of violence against women and children, the effect on Wanrow of her knowledge of Wesler as a child molester, and Wanrow's belief that she could only defend herself with a weapon. Moreover, the judge directed the jurors to apply the equal force standard and not to consider Wanrow's perspective when evaluating her claim of self-defense. Consequently, our decision to challenge the sex-bias in the law of self-defense—as reflected in these instructions—was formed from the insight that Yvonne Wanrow's perspective as a Native American woman had to be included in the courtroom.

We developed the legal argument for women's "equal right to trial," which challenged sex-bias in the law of self-defense, based upon our knowledge of the particular problems women who killed men faced in the criminal justice system: the prevalence of homicides committed by women in circumstances of male physical abuse or sexual assault; the different circumstances in which men and women killed; myths and misconceptions in the criminal justice system concerning women who kill as "crazy"; the problems of domestic violence, physical abuse and sexual abuse of women and children; the physical and psychological barriers that prevented women from feeling capable of defending themselves; and stereotypes of women as unreasonable. If the jury did not understand Yvonne Wanrow's experience and the way in which it shaped her conduct, it could not find her conduct to have been reasonable and therefore an appropriate act of self-defense. Since the jury would not be able to consider this defense plausible, Wanrow could not be treated fairly.

On appeal, Wanrow's conviction was reversed. A plurality of the court voted to reverse on the ground that the trial court's instructions violated Washington law in three ways. First, the instruction that limited the jury's consideration to the circumstances "at or immediately before the killing" misconstrued Washington law. Properly construed, state law allowed the jury to consider Wanrow's knowledge of the deceased's reputation, prior aggressive behavior, and all other prior circumstances, even if that knowledge were acquired long before the killing. Second, the instruction concerning equal force misstated state law and denied Wanrow equal protection:

> The impression created—that a 5′4″ woman with a cast on her leg and using a crutch must, under the law, somehow repel an assault by a 6′2″ intoxicated man without employing weapons in her defense, unless the jury finds her determination of the degree of danger to be objectively reasonable—constitutes a separate and distinct misstatement of the law and, in the context of this case, violates the respondent's right to equal protection of the law.[5]

Third, the trial court's instructions failed to direct the jury to consider the reasonableness of Wanrow's act *from Wanrow's perspective,* "seeing what [s]he sees and knowing what [s]he knows."[6] The Washington Supreme Court affirmed a standard of self-defense based on the individual defendant's perception, as required by Washington state law, and underscored the need for this standard by recognizing the existence of sex-bias in the law of self-defense generally.

Thus the political insights into sex-bias in self-defense that could help explain Yvonne Wanrow's situation arose out of legal formulation and argumentation. But the legal argument concerning the "equal right to trial" grew out of a political analysis of sex discrimination that the legal team shared, discussed, and applied to the particular case. The legal argumentation brought together diverse strands of feminist analysis and theory concerning sex-biased treatment of women in the criminal justice system.

This legal argumentation reflected a perspective which feminist activists and lawyers were beginning to express and share. Feminist writers were beginning to explore these issues as well. Further, aspects of this argument were asserted at the same time in other courts in different cases. The rights formulation reflected the political analysis and activity of women's groups concerned with violence against women, the treatment of women within the criminal justice system and the work of defense committees organizing around particular women defendants' cases. It was a formulation which made sense to many women on an experiential level.

In this sense, the legal formulation grew out of political analysis, but it also pushed the political analysis forward. The particular legal focus on sex-bias in the law of self-defense, and on the absence of a women's perspective in the courtroom, clarified feminist analysis of the problems facing women who kill. It explained why women defendants and lawyers representing them were more likely to claim insanity or impaired mental state rather than assert self-defense (Schneider, 1980, pp. 636–38; Schneider and Jordan, 1978, pp.159–60). The legal formulation thus moved the political work to a different level. It raised the political question of what a women's perspective might be and what equal treatment would look like. It focused further legal work on the disparate hurdles that limited women defendants' choice of defense—particularly the various ways in which women's experiences were excluded from the courtroom—and laid the foundation for political and legal strategies to remedy the problems created by this exclusion.

What has become known as women's self-defense work is now an established part of both feminist litigation and legal literature.[7] Many courts have now accepted the view that there is sex-bias in the law of self-defense.[8] Still, the ongoing legal work in this area teaches us new lessons. It demonstrates the difficulty courts have in hearing women's experiences and modifying the law to take them into account. Some courts which have applied the insight reflected in the equal trial argument have unwittingly recreated the very sex stereotypes of female incapacity that women's self-defense work was intended to overcome. But these new dilemmas of feminist theory can also help to clarify issues, sharpen debate, and deepen insight into these matters.

Towards a Dialectical Understanding of Rights and Politics

The dialectical methodology detailed in the previous section suggests that rights discourse and politics can be understood as interconnected, even though they may appear at times to be in opposition. The rights claim can emerge from a political vision and can itself be a form of political statement. Further, rights discourse can be a form of praxis—a form of legal practice that can define and reshape the articulation of theory.

As suggested earlier, recent rights critics have viewed the experience of rights discourse and rights assertion in a static and rigid way. They have accepted the opposition of rights and politics and the reification of rights generally. A dialectical perspective, however, sees rights and politics as part of a more dynamic, complex, and larger process characterized by the possibility the rights discourse can simultaneously advance and obscure political growth and vision. A dialectical view of rights develops the expressive, transformative, and problematic aspects of rights. Rights discourse can be an alienated and artificial language that constricts political debate, but it can also be a means to articulate new values and political vision. The way in which a social movement group uses the rights claim and places it in a broader context affects the ability of rights discourse to aid political struggle. Rights discourse and rights claims, when emerging from and organically linked to political struggle, can help to develop political consciousness which can play a useful role in the development of a social behavior.

Rights discourse can express human and communal values; it can be a way for individuals to develop a sense of self and for a group to develop a collective identity. Rights discourse can also have a dimension that emphasizes the interdependence of autonomy and community. It can play an important role in giving individuals a sense of self-definition, in connecting the individual to a larger group and community, and in defining the goals of a political struggle, particularly during the early development of a social movement.

Communal Rights

Although it has been argued that rights are inherently individualistic because individuals "posses" them, rights need not be perceived this way. Staughton Lynd, for example, has developed the idea of rights as "communal," infused with the values of community, compassion, and solidarity (Lynd, 1984). Although he focuses on some rights as particularly communal, he argues in favor of fighting for the communal content of as many rights as possible and challenging the zero-sum perspective on rights generally. He looks to the historical context in which a right develops as a primary force shaping the particular collective aspect of the right. For example, Lynd's view of the right to engage in collective bargaining activity under section 7 of the National Labor Relations Act as a paradigmatic communal right is based on his perception of this right as "derived from the actual character of working-class solidarity and accordingly a right that foreshadows a society in which group life and individual self-realization mutually reinforce each other" (Lynd 1984, p.1430).

Lynd's understanding of the collective aspect of rights has several dimensions. He maintains that a right developed in the context of a social movement struggle may have a collective cast to it. Further, the exercise of rights by an individual can expand the ability of the larger group to exercise their rights generally. Finally, Lynd suggests that the concept of the inalienability of rights—that an individual cannot give up a right because it belongs to the group—is premised on an underlying assumption based on the communal aspect of rights. Lynd's analysis, then, provides a framework to challenge the notion that rights claims must be articulated and perceived exclusively as the property of rights-bearing individuals.

Individual Selfhood and Collective Identity

Another aspect of a dialectical view of rights is the role that rights discourse can play for individual self-development and collective identity. Carol Gilligan's work in charting differences between male and female moral and psychological development provides a basis for exploring this issue (Gilligan, 1982). She suggests that these differences can shape the way that individuals experience rights.

Gilligan posits that the developmental challenges of maturity are different for men and women. Men, whose lives have emphasized separateness, must ultimately learn care and connection. Women, whose lives have emphasized connection to and caretaking for others, must ultimately learn to value and care for themselves. Mature moral and psychological development for both sexes would seek to synthesize moral perspectives based on both rights and responsibilities.

For this reason, Gilligan suggests that the assertion of rights can play a particularly important role in women's moral development. She suggests that women's articulation of rights challenges women's sense of self and transforms women's experience of selflessness, "allowing them to see themselves as stronger and to consider directly their own needs" (Gilligan, p.149).

Gilligan outlines a process of moral development for women that moves from an emphasis on selflessness and care for others, to a recognition of self and autonomy, and then to a self-reflective understanding of the way in which self and other are interconnected. She suggests that assertion of rights, particularly women's rights, can play a crucial role in the transformation of women's sense of self. Public assertion of women's legal rights reverberates in the consciousness of individual women. Furthermore, the assertion of women's rights can provide women with a sense of collective identity, a sense that self and other are connected.

Gilligan's suggestion that the psychological experience and social function of rights assertion may perform different developmental tasks for men and women may be overboard in its link to gender.[9] But the sense of self-definition and collective identification that Gilligan details is, nevertheless, an important aspect of rights claims.

Interdependent Rights

Gilligan implies that the gender-linked oppositions of rights and care-based morality can be transcended in a dialectical fashion in a third stage of development in which men and women see the importance and interconnection of rights and responsibilities. Gilligan imagines that this third stage of development will be based upon the synthesis of the voices of rights and responsibilities. The inclusion of both voices will transform the very nature of the conversation; the discourse is no longer either simply about justice or simply about caring; rather it is about bringing them together to transform the domain. Although feminist scholars have questioned whether this third stage is really transformative,[10] Gilligan's vision of rights articulated in this different voice has stimulated attempts by legal scholars to reimage rights and to conceive of them as "interdependent."

For example, in a number of recent articles Martha Minow has sought an understanding of rights that resolves the tension between autonomy and caretaking (Minow 1985a, 1985b, 1983). Minow attempts to redefine the substance of purportedly individualistic rights by positing a right to connection, by developing the interconnection of rights and responsibilities, and by suggesting that rights claims can focus on the social and economic preconditions for rights (Minow, 1986).

William Simon's 1985 article on welfare rights which contrasts the New Deal social work jurisprudence of welfare rights with the contemporary New Property conception of rights, suggests a similar perspective (Simon, 1985). Simon sees the New Property conception of rights as reincarnating classical legalist views of rights based on the protection of individual independence and self-sufficiency from the collective power of the state. In contrast, he suggests that rights in New Deal social work jurisprudence differed from the classical model because they challenged this distinction between the individual and the community and reflected a norm of interdependence. Rights were used as part of a dialectical process of political development, rights claims providing a means by which people on welfare came to understand and articulate their goals and a way for the individual claimant to get involved in political activity. Finally, Kenneth Karst's effort to reconstruct constitutional law as a "jurisprudence of interdependence" (Karst, 1984, p. 495) also rests on an attempt to infuse rights-talk with the morality of care.

Rights as Conversation

The theoretical efforts discussed above focused on the way that rights connected to political struggle can be part of an ongoing conversation and can have a character, content, and meaning that is more communal because they reflect the very political struggle from which they emerged. This political context might affect both the process by which rights are articulated as well as the content of the rights themselves: what the rights mean to individuals and members of the group who claim them at a particular time, and how they are understood and experienced at that time. However, even if rights discourse is understood as part of a process of political education and mobilization, how do we ensure that the articulation of rights claims will truly assist in that larger process? How can we be sure that if rights discourse starts the conversation of politics, the conversation will ever move beyond rights? We must take seriously Peter Gabel's caution that rights can substitute the illusion of community for a more authentic and genuine sense of community. (Gabel, p.1577) A preoccupation with or excessive focus on rights consciousness can reinforce alienation or powerlessness and weaken popular movements. In and of themselves, rights claims are not a basis for building a sustained political movement, nor can rights claims perform the task of social reconstruction. Still, their importance should not be underestimated. Articulation of political insight in rights terms *can* be an important vehicle for political growth, and can help develop a sense of collective identity.

Women's Rights and Feminist Struggle

Recent experience with claims of legal rights for women suggests the importance of understanding the relationship between rights and political struggle from a dialectical perspective. This experience demonstrates the richly textured process by which a social movement articulates political demands through a rights claim and the way in which that claim affects the development of the group. Most significantly, the experience of the women's rights movement simultaneously reveals the communal possibilities of rights and underscores the limits of political strategy focused on rights.

Over the last twenty years, claims for women's rights have increasingly been used to articulate political demand for equality and for change in gender roles. A claim of right can transmit a powerful message concerning "the kind of society we want to live in, the kind of relations among people we wish to foster, and the kind of behavior that is to be praised or blamed. [It] is a moral claim about how human beings should act toward one another" (Olsen, 1984, p. 391). As we have already seen, on an individual level, a claim of right can be an assertion of one's self-worth and an affirmation of one's moral value and entitlement.

The women's rights movement has had an important affirming and individuating effect on women's consciousness. The articulation of women's rights provides a sense of self and distinction for individual women, while at the same time giving women an important sense of collective identity. Through this articulation, women's voices and concerns are heard in a public forum and afforded a legal vehicle for expression.

But rights claims do not only define women's individual and collective experience, they also actively shape public discourse. Claims of equal rights and reproductive choice, for example, empowered women. Women as a class had not previously been included within the reach of the fourteenth amendment.[11] Women's concerns now rose to the level of constitutional (serious, grownup) concerns. By claiming rights, women asserted their intention to be taken seriously in society.

The history of the women's movement's advocacy of rights to equality and to reproductive choice, however, illustrates the limitations as well as advantages of rights strategies. The women's rights movement articulated women's right to equal treatment as a claim of equal protection under the fourteenth amendment, and women's right to procreative freedom as a claim of liberty and privacy under the due process clause of that amendment. They way in which equality and reproductive rights issues were formulated by women and distorted and limited by the courts raises serious questions about how rights claims affect social movements.

The issue of equal treatment poses the theoretical problem of sameness and difference. Equal protection of the law is guaranteed only to those who are similarly situated. Thus, the issue for equality theory is comparative—who is the same as whom. In deciding this issue of comparability, difficult questions must be considered concerning whose standards are the norm, what differences are real, and whether these differences, if they do exist, really matter.

The comparative equal rights approach has had limited political and doctrinal success in the courts and legislatures. The equal rights vision was substantially limited by the defeat of the federal equal rights amendment, which had been viewed by both the public and the courts as a litmus test of political support for the women's movement. Further, despite efforts by feminist litigators to formulate women's rights claims as if no differences existed between men and women, the Supreme Court has read in differences. Finally, the Supreme Court has viewed equality claims as distinct from reproductive choice claims. Despite the vigorous efforts of feminist litigators to argue that pregnancy discrimination violates equality principles the Supreme Court has held that since the capacity to become pregnant is "unique" to women, rules concerning pregnancy do not violate equal protection.[12] Thus, despite widespread acknowledgement by the women's movement of the centrality of pregnancy and reproductive choice to women's subordination, pregnancy and reproductive choice have not been seen by the Court as problems of equality.

The movement for reproductive choice played a critical role in the early development of the women's movement. In the early 1970s large groups of women organized to demonstrate against state laws that criminalized abortion and to challenge abortion laws in courts. Although feminists originally articulated this "women's right" as a right to liberty, the Supreme Court in *Roe v. Wade* decided the issue on privacy grounds.

Although the development of rights to equality and reproductive choice have had an important ideological effect on the women's movement, the doctrinal evolution of these rights, as the above example suggests, has muddied their ideological meaning. Feminist commentators widely believe that the Court's distinct theoretical articulation of reproductive control as a right to privacy separate from equality constrains political analysis on both a practical and ideological level and reinforces the ideological separation of deeply interrelated oppression.[13]

Furthermore, the very articulation of women's right to procreative freedom as a matter of privacy is problematic, because it reinforces and legitimizes the public and private dichotomy which historically has been damaging to women. For women, the domestic sphere and sexuality—primary areas of subordination—have been viewed as private and unregulated. Although the right has a powerful collective dimension which could be used to emphasize group values, as interpreted by the Court it is primarily individualistic in that it simply protects an individual's right to choose. Most significantly, analyzing the right to reproductive choice as a right of privacy emphasizes the process of decision making, which entails a balancing of interests throughout the pregnancy, rather than the importance of abortion itself, which concerns the control that a woman should have over her own body and life decisions.

The impact on social movements of a court's particular decision or doctrinal formulation cannot be easily measured. For example, how do we know what effect the doctrinal limitations which the Supreme Court has placed on the right to reproductive choice has had on the consciousness and politics of the women's movement? Winning the right to procreative choice certainly has helped many women regardless of the particular doctrinal formulation. Winning it as a right of privacy may have given some activists a false sense of security, but it has led others to greater insights into the mutable nature of the legal right to choose. The articulation of the right was necessary to allow new contradictions to unfold.

The early emphasis on equal rights in the women's movement provides another good example of this dialectical perspective, the way in which rights formulation have simultaneously expanded and limited our perspective on women's subordination. This emphasis, although historically understandable, arguably narrowed the movement's focus and constricted its vision of possible change. It certainly tended to cause women to analyze their experience from a comparative perspective and to stress political debate about equal treatment with men, rather than about empowerment, self-actualization or "women-centered" perspectives generally. This limitation on the scope of equality rights was also encouraged by the fact that many of the plaintiffs raising and benefitting from equal rights claims were men.[14] The factual context of much litigation that featured an individual plaintiff's attempt to "get" something from society, such as military dependents benefits,[15] increased social security,[16] property tax exemptions,[17] or admission to a sex-segregated nursing school,[18] appeared to narrow the focus of equality rights even further.

Moreover, because the women's movement articulated its equality concerns using a rights language that frequently becomes symbolic and reified, the movement's ability to account for the range of potential political strategies and to determine appropriate reforms in any area became more difficult. The equal rights perspective also made it easier for women to avoid the complex question of biological and social differences. Finally, some argue that the pervasiveness of an equality perspective contributed to an emphasis within the women's movement on the "symbolic" equality of rules that reflected formal, as opposed to substantive, fairness and justice.

Nevertheless, the struggle over equal rights was a necessary development for the women's movement. Through the beginning efforts to articulate equal rights, the women's movement acquired a broader and clearer understanding of what it wanted, what obstacles it faced, how deep the phenomenon of sexism went, and how hard it was to affect meaningful change. The movement also learned about the limitations and inadequacies of rights to perform the prerequisite economic and social reconstruction for meaningful change for women. The development of an equality perspective enabled women to understand the tenacity of "neutral" standards based on male experience and legitimized discussion of equality within public discourse.

Further, both the legal movements for equal rights and reproductive rights emerged organically out of the women's movement. At the grass roots level, the movement helped shape legal strategies, particularly for reproductive rights. The articulation of these rights expressed a collective project that began with a description of women's experience, translated that experience into legal formulation, and through that formulation asserted a demand for power. By providing a public vehicle for expressing what women want[19] the rights struggle clarified and heightened the debates within the movement itself[20] and then turned these insights back into theory.

The experience of rights in the women's movement supports the need for a perspective on rights and politics grounded in a dialectical sensibility, a view that allows us to acknowledge both the universal, affirming, expressive, and creative aspects of rights claims and at the same time, maintain a critical impulse toward rights. We must hold on to and not seek to deny the contradictions between the possibilities and the limits of rights claims and discourse. A struggle for rights can be both a vehicle of politics and an affirmation of who we are and what we seek. Rights can be what we make of them and how we use them. The experience of rights assertion in the women's movement can move us forward to a self-reflective recognition of the importance and the limitations of political and legal strategy that utilizes rights.

Notes

1. In *Praxis and Action,* Richard Bernstein describes the process of dialectics in the following way: "There has been a lot of loose talk about Hegel's dialectic being a movement from thesis to antithesis to synthesis. Not only do these concepts play an insignificant role in Hegel's philosophy, they are essentially static concepts and completely misrepresent what Hegel means by "dialectic." The dialectic of *Geist* is essentially a dynamic and organic process. One "moment" of a dialectical process, when it is fully developed or understood gives rise to its own negation; it is not mechanically confronted by an antithesis. The process here is more like that of a tragedy where the "fall" of the tragic hero emerges from the dynamics of the development of his own character. When *Geist* is dirempted, alienated from itself, a serious struggle takes place between the two "moments." Out of this conflict and struggle, out of this negativity, emerges a "moment" which at once negates, affirms, and transcends the "moments" involved in the struggle—these earlier moments are *aufgehoben.* In the course of *Geist* realizing itself, this process which involves a stage of self-alienation that is subsequently *aufgehoben* is a continuous, restless, infinite one. The logic of the development of *Geist* is dialectical where *Geist* struggles with what appears to be "other" than it—a limitation, or obstacle which must be overcome. *Geist* "returns to itself" when it overcomes the specific obstacle that it encounters, only to renew the dialectical process again. *Geist* finally "returns to itself" when all obstacles and determinations have been overcome, when everything that has appeared "other" than itself is fully appropriated and there by subjectivized. This is the final aim or goal of *Geist.* The negativity and activity of *Geist* comes into focus in this dialectical characterization (Bernstein, 1971, pp. 20–21). Kathleen Lahey observed that although I use the notion of dialectic as a means of transcending a dualistic or dichotomized formulation of rights and politics, the notion of dialectic is nonetheless premised on a dualistic framework. As I see it, however, the dialectical process has many dimensions and is not simply dualistic since, as Bernstein writes, it is a process of constant and organic change.

2. See Bernstein, 1971, pp. 42–43. Praxis describes "a unity of theory and action" (Sparer, 1984 p. 553) (footnote omitted). It is used in this essay as it was used in Sparer's "as a shorthand term for the theory-practice-social change relationship." Id. at 553 n.10. Klare, 1979, p. 124 n.5.

3. The notion of a dialectical process is a critical aspect of feminist theory. The term dialectical and the concept of dialectic are frequently used by feminist theorists in wide range of contexts. See, e.g., S. De Beauvoir, *The Second Sex* xvi-xxi (1952) (discussing dialectical relationship between one and other, master and slave); K. Ferguson, *The Feminist Case Against Bureaucracy,* 1984, p. 197 (writing that "[a] community that recognizes the dialectical need for connectedness within freedom and for diversity within solidarity would strive to nurture the capacity for reflexive redefinition of self"); C. Gilligan, *In a Different Voice,* 1982, p. 174 (discussing "the dialectic of human development"); A. Jaggar, *Feminist Politics and Human Nature,* p. 12 (1983) (discussing "the on-going and dialectical process of feminist theorizing"); *New French Feminisms: An Anthology* pp. xi-xii (E. Marks & I. de Courtivron ed. 1981) (writing that recent French feminists "take from . . . dialectics those modes of thinking that allow them to make the most connections between the oppression of women and other aspects of their culture"); "Feminist Discourse, Moral Value, and the Law—A Conversation," p. 34, *Buffalo L. Rev.* 11, (1985) p. 86 (comment by C. Menkel-Meadow) (discussing process of development within women's movement as "part of a much larger dialectical process where we begin with a reform, be it liberal, radical, or in some cases even conservative, and some of us unite behind it while others do not").

4. *State v. Wanrow,* 88 Wash. 2d 221, 559 P. 2d 548 (1a77). Nancy Stearns and I were co-counsel in *Wanrow* on appeal. For a fuller discussion of *Wanrow,* see Schneider, 1980; Schneider & Jordan, 1978; Schneider, 1986a; "Recent Developments," 54 *Wash. L. Rev.* p. 221 (1978); MacKinnon, "Book Review," 34 *Stan. L. Rev.* pp. 703, 725–34 (1982).

5. *Wanrow,* at 240, 559 P.2d at 558–59.

6. Id. at 238, 559 P.2d at 557 (citing *State v. Dunning,* 8 Wash. App. 340, 342, 506, P.2d 321, 322, (1973)).

7. There is an enormous legal literature on Women's self-defense issues. See, e.g., A. Jones, "Women Who Kill" (1980); Crocker, "The Meaning of Equality for Battered Women Who Kill Men in Self-Defense," (1985); Robinson, "Defense Strategies for Battered Women who Assault Their Mates: State v. Curry," (1981); Rosen, "The Excuse of Self-Defense: Correcting a Historical Accident on Behalf of Battered Women who Kill," (1986) and sources cited in footnote 4.

8. See, e.g.; *State v. Anaya,* 438 A.2d. 892 (Me. 1981) (holding trial court committed reversible error in excluding testimony concerning battered wife syndrome); *State v. Kelly,* 97 N.J. 178, 478 A.2d 364 (1984) (holding battered women's syndrome to be relevant to honesty and reasonableness of defendant's belief of imminent danger and exclusion of testimony concerning it required reversal and remand for new trial).

9. While Gilligan's work is powerful and rich, and her characterizations feel subjectively accurate in many ways, *In A Different Voice* is also troubling. See, "On In A Different Voice: An Interdisciplinary Forum," 11 *Signs: J. Women Culture & Soc'y,* p. 304 (1986). For example, Gilligan's work has been criticized for its insensitivity to race and class differences, and its disregard of historical context. See Nicholson, "Women, Morality and History," (1983); O'Loughlin, "Responsibility and Moral Maturity in the Control of Fertility—Or, a Woman's Place is in the Wrong," (1983); Travis, "Women and Men and Morality," (1982). It has also been criticized for a failure to analyze the social and

political context of the spheres in which women's care-based approach develops. See, e.g., Colby & Damon, "Listening to a Different Voice: A review of Gilligan's In A Different Voice," (1983); Walker, "In A Diffident Voice: Cryptoseparatist Analysis of Female Moral Development," (1983). Gilligan also fails to identify properly the problem of self-sacrifice when women emphasize caretaking for others without recognizing their own autonomy and needs.

10. Commentators have noted that the premise of Gilligan's third stage is that there can be a dialogue or conversation between the different voices. This premise may be unrealistic and overly romanticized if men cannot hear women's voices and tend to universalize based on their own particular experience. For example, Kathy Ferguson criticizes Gilligan's analysis of a different voice for its lack of political context. She also criticizes Gilligan's analysis of the third stage of development for its failure to emphasize the degree to which it rests on political struggle (Ferguson, 1984). Kathleen Lahey has told me that she questions whether this third stage involves a conversation in which there is genuine mutuality.

11. See *Hoyt v. Florida,* 368 U.S. 57 (1961); *Goesaert v. Cleary,* 335 U.S. 464 (1948); *Muller v. Oregon,* 208 U.S. 412 (1908); *Bradwell v. State,* 83 U.S. (16 Wall.) 130 (1872) (Bradley, J., concurring).

12. *Geduldig v. Aiello,* 417 U.S. 484, 492–97 (1974). See also Law, "Rethinking Sex and The Constitution," 132 *U. Pa. L. Rev.* 955, 985–86.

13. See, e.g., Colker, "Pornography and Privacy: Towards the Development of Group Based Theory for Sex Based Institutions of Privacy," 1983 at 232–37; Law, supra note 12, at 987–1002. Rhonda Copelon has helped me to understand this.

14. See Cole, "Strategies of Difference: Litigating for Women's Rights in a Man's World," (1984) (analyzing now equality doctrine has been shaped by claims of male plaintiffs).

15. *Frontiero v. Richardson,* 411 U.S. 677 (1973).

16. *Weinberger v. Wiesenfeld,* 420 U.S. 636 (1975).

17. *Kahn v. Shevin,* 416 U.S. 351 (1974).

18. *Mississippi Univ. for Women v. Hogan,* 458 U.S. 718 (1982).

19. Fran Olsen suggests that feminists should "stop trying to fit our goals into abstract rights arguments and instead call for what we really want" (Olsen, 1984, p. 430).

20. Olsen has also suggested that, in the context of the women's movement, rights formulations have an arguably negative impact on the development of social movements because they magnify disagreement. See id. at 430. Martha Fineman has raised a related question with me: is there a difference between a dialogue among ourselves on issues of disagreement and going to court (particularly since courts and judges have not been receptive to women's rights claims)? My response reflects the recent women's movement experience with the issue of pornography.

    The strategy of raising the issue of pornography as a violation of a woman's civil rights (through legislation, not merely claims of rights in court) has generated much controversy and disagreement within the women's movement. See MacKinnon, 1984 (pornography is a politics of male dominance, distinct from obscenity law, based on male morality, and therefore free speech arguments applied to obscenity should not bar efforts to stop pornography); Emerson, 1984 (governmental suppression of pornography is not proper method to increase power of women because it involves "dangerous evisceration of the first amendment"); Hoffman, 1985 (although antipornography laws have some value, feminists should be wary of male-dominated state and should according avoid endorsing state regulation of pornography). This disagreement has certainly been experienced by many women as unfortunate and painful, particularly when women's groups have argued opposing positions before courts. See, e.g., *American Booksellers Ass'n, Inc. v. Hudnut,* 771 F. 2d 323, 325 (7th Cir. 1985). Further, some feminists who proposed antipornography ordinances did not submit their strategy to wide critique before their implementation, nor were they receptive to critique after implementation, thereby creating friction within the movement. I found this friction particularly evident during a debate between Catharine MacKinnon and Nan Hunter at the Sixteenth National Conference on Women and the Law (New York, New York 1985). Any controversial strategy that goes "public" can magnify disagreements which many would rather debate internally within the women's movement. This problem may be exacerbated, of course, when we are arguing contrary positions in court.

18

Strategizing In Equality

Diana Majury

Feminist lawyers, legal scholars, and activists have for some time been engaged in a debate about the usefulness of framing legal arguments in terms of equality. For those who consider that equality is a concept that can be used to further women's interests, the debate is over what theory or model of equality can most effectively be presented and pursued in legal forums. Similar debates over the meaning and desirability of equality are taking place in most other disciplines and in feminist theory generally. Given the adisciplinary nature of feminism, the debates within feminist legal communities are both informed by and contribute to feminist debates taking place in other disciplines.

Although acknowledged to encompass a wide range of diverse issues, the legal equality debate in the United States has, to a large extent, centered around the question of maternity leave for women in the paid labor force. The maternity leave discussion has fostered important analysis and provided access to a fuller understanding of the complexity of the issues involved. However, because so much of the discussion has been in the form of a debate, the discussion has been both limited and limiting. The focus appears to have been more on justifying one's own position while exposing the shortcomings of the arguments of those "on the other side" than on the problem of the inadequacies of the protection of pregnant women in the paid labor force and what to do to redress that situation. The style and method of the discussion seems to impede the resolution of these very complex and difficult questions. Debating seems to me a very "male" style of discussion, directed more toward scoring points and defeating one's opponent than toward furthering knowledge on the subject under discussion. The prevalence of debates within femi-

---

A slightly more extensive version of this paper was first published in *Wisconsin Women's Law Journal* (1987).

nist discourse suggests that we need to bring our consciousness-raising skills to assist us in addressing the appropriateness of "debates" within feminist communities. Such a consciousness-raising process would not be intended to create some artificial "nice" agreement among feminists but to eliminate the combative and destructive aspects of our discussions.

The equality debate among feminist legal thinkers in the United States is polarized between those who describe themselves as equal treatment proponents and those who support some level of legal recognition of women's specificity. I refer here to women's specificity even though I think the term "specificities" is more appropriate. I use the singular rather than the plural here because most of the writers who wish to affirm at least some of women's "differences" from men seem to treat women as an undifferentiated group and to ignore differences among women. This assumption—that all women are the same—is one of my major concerns with this approach to equality.

I refer to the women who acknowledge, at least to a limited extent, women's specificity in their approach to equality, as women's difference advocates, rather than women's specificity advocates, because I think it is a more accurate characterization of their position. However, I have problems with the use of the term difference in the context of equality. Difference is used to refer to women's difference from men, with a clear, implicit acceptance of men as the norm and women as the deviators therefrom. While attempting to affirm and accommodate women's specific attributes, there is within the language of the theory a subtle devaluing of those attributes. The term "women's specificities" reflects an attempt to circumvent the acceptance of the male norm implicit in the term women's difference. It is an indication of the thoroughness of male domination of our language that we cannot find a term that avoids any implication of male as the norm.

The "equal treatment" model of equality requires absolute adherence to gender neutrality in the wording of rules and laws and, to a lesser extent, in their effect (Williams, 1982). Under an equal treatment analysis, any acknowledgement of women's specificity is characterized as "special treatment" and dismissed as practically dangerous and theoretically inconsistent.

On the other hand, women's difference advocates propose models of equality that affirmatively provide for at least some differences between women and men. Ann Scales (1981), for example, argues for what she describes as an "incorporationist approach." Pursuant to Scales's approach women are recognized as having rights different from men only with respect to those aspects of childbearing and childrearing which are completely unique to women, that is pregnancy and breastfeeding. Following a similar approach, Sylvia Law (1984) proposes an equality model which would distinguish between laws drawing explicit sex-based distinctions and those governing reproductive biology. According to Law, sex-based distinctions are based on culturally imposed stereotypes and are therefore appropriately dealt with through a comparative equal treatment analysis. Distinctions relating to reproduction, however, are based on "real differences" and therefore require an impact analysis. This distinction between a comparative equal treatment analysis and an impact analysis can be understood by looking at the issue of maternity leave. A refusal specifically to provide maternity leave would constitute equal treatment pursuant to a comparative equal treatment analysis—women and men are being treated in the same way and therefore equally. However, an impact analysis would characterize the refusal to provide maternity leave as discrimination against women because the impact of not providing maternity leave places women at a significant disadvantage in their participation in the paid labor force.

The maternity leave issue similarly provides a useful vehicle through which to examine the contrast between an equal treatment approach and a differences approach, as well as to highlight the limitations shared by both sides of the debate. The equal treatment model would require that maternity be dealt with in exactly the same manner as any other disability which renders a worker temporarily unable to work. On the other hand, difference advocates support some form of maternity leave, separate and distinct from any disability benefits which may be available to the woman worker.

Despite their apparent dissimilarity, the equal treatment model and the women's difference models share a common understanding of equality, an understanding that severely limits the ability of each to address the very real inequalities that women experience. For both sides of the debate, equality means treating people the same. Equal treatment advocates allow no deviation from identical treatment; women's difference advocates justify limited deviation in the name of "real" difference. Only when the same treatment is seen, for physiological reasons, as not possible for women and men do these feminists argue that we need to expand our understanding of equality to incorporate women's differences. Difference advocates presumably would not support, for example, women-only professional associations because such associations would not be seen to be reproductively or physiologically based.

Those who wish to "accommodate" women's difference are in search of a clear definition or principle according to which one would be able to determine the appropriate deviations from the norm of identical treatment. They seek an equality formula which can be applied to any situation with consistent and foreseeable results. A variety of different formulae have been proposed. For equal treatment advocates, the equality formula is self-evident—identical treatment in *all* circumstances. Any formulaic approach to equality, whether based on an equal treatment or a differences model, denies the complexity, variety, and compound nature of the problems of inequality that women experience. In the name of clarity, consistency and ease of application, an equality formula collapses women's inequalities into a male-defined standard and reduces those inequalities to biologically-based differences.

In this paper, I wish to add my voice to the equality debates. I recognize the apparent contradiction presented by my participation in the debate when I profess to reject debates as a mode of discussion. It is a contradiction which I am experiencing increasingly in my life; not wishing to "fight" other women on specific issues or strategies and yet feeling the need to act in a concrete and specific way because of strongly felt positions which I hold on specific issues. I recognize that simply raising concerns about debates as a means of discussing issues does not absolve me from responsibility for my participation in them. Nor do I in any way wish to absolve myself. But I hope that we can work toward a more feminist and productive way to talk, and to disagree, about difficult issues.

I wish to propose what, for a lack of a more adequately descriptive term, I describe as an inequality-based strategy. I find myself in somewhat of a terminological quandary in my attempts to describe my approach to equality. Although my approach has a methodology, it is not itself a methodology. My approach is a tool, but not just a tool. It is informed by a theory, but is not a theory . . . I have settled for the word strategy because it is an active, process-based word.

I refer to equality as a strategy rather than a goal because as a strategy equality can be used to address women's current inequalities (Lahey, 1987; MacKinnon, 1987; Sheppard, 1986). Equality as a goal is somewhat of an oxymoron—if women and men were treated "equally" then equality would have no meaning; there would be nothing or no-one with whom to be "equal." However, in the absence of an "equal" world, the dominant groups in a society will inevitably set the standards for "equality." Because men are the dominant sexual group, it is unavoidable that a focus on sexual equality will require a comparison of women to men and will seek to bring women to the male standard of treatment. Thus it is that women's specificities become "difference." I object to the notion of expanding the male standard to incorporate women whether this is done in gender neutral terms (as by the equal treatment advocates) or in terms which affirm women's biological difference (as by the women's difference advocates). Both of these approaches continue to accept the male standard as the standard of comparison.

I do not share the vision of equality as some abstract ideal that is to be imposed on society to solve the problems of women and other oppressed groups. To me, the focus and emphasis presently placed on equality is more effectively seen as a means that can be used to address the inequalities that women in our society experience. These inequalities to which I refer are the disadvantages, risks and deprivations which women suffer because we are women. The focus on inequality does not eliminate the problem of comparison, nor the use of "the male" as a basis for that comparison. It does however, shift the comparison to questions of power and powerlessness, advantage and disadvantage (MacKinnon, 1987). An inequality-based approach asks how to redress the power imbalance which inheres in a specific inequality rather than whether or not it is appropriate to treat women the same as men in specific circumstances. Equality focuses on men; inequality focuses on women. From this perspective, equality is given meaning and substance only by the inequalities which give rise to the need for a guarantee of equality. Equality does not define inequality; inequality defines equality.

Why Equality?

I see myself participating in very much the same project on equality that Alison Jaggar (1983) describes with respect to feminism:

> My goal is not the discovery of a Platonic ideal form of [equality] and exposure of rival theories as pretenders. Instead, I want to contribute to formulating a conception of [equality] that is more adequate [I would say more effective *at this time*] than previous conceptions in that it will help women to achieve the fullest possible liberation.
>
> [L]iberation is not some finally achievable situation; instead it is the process of eliminating forms of oppression as long as these continue to arise. (pp. 5–6)

There are a number of reasons why equality might be a useful strategy to employ in the process of "eliminating forms of oppression" against women. One of the major advantages of equality as a concept is that it allows for a focus on inequality, on the specific and concrete manifestations of women's oppression. This, of course, is not an attribute unique to "equality." Other words might similarly be used to direct attention to inequalities or are perhaps themselves more specifically focused on inequality. Ruth Colker (1987) suggests the use of an anti-subordination principle; Robin West (1987) discusses these issues in terms of women's pain. However, there is no reason to see these concepts as competing with each other, or as mutually exclusive. In its abstractness, equality may provide a useful platform upon which more precise inequality-based arguments can be raised. For example, Colker's anti-subordination principle and West's analysis of women's pain could be brought to bear with respect to a particular issue when an equality guarantee has opened the door enabling that issue to be addressed. Given the current "interest" in equality and the cooptability of any word we may try to tailor to address women's oppressions, it seems unproductive to put our energies into trying to create and promote the "perfect" word or concept instead of trying to make the current word work for women.

For some critics of equality the lack of precision and open-endedness of equality are its major shortcomings. For some, this indeterminacy is sufficient to render equality a useless concept (Westen, 1982). The attempt to develop some kind of equality formula is very much a response to this criticism of equality as meaningless. The intention underlying such a formula would be to delineate the meaning of equality and eradicate any uncertainty as to its application or effect. To me, the indeterminacy of equality offers greater promise and provides more fertile ground for exploration and argumentation than any equality formula. An open-ended approach allows "equality theory" to respond to the different circumstances and factors which combine to make a specific woman's situation unequal or to perpetuate women's inequalities more generally.

Equality is a useful tool because it enables women to speak in a language which is counter to domination and subordination. This does not mean that equality rhetoric cannot be, and is not, also used as a tool of legitimation to maintain the status quo and to reinforce and perpetuate the subjugation of women. Equality arguments are increasingly being used as a weapon against women and to further men's interests. However, at the same time, equality can be used to open up a discussion within which these injustices can be exposed and confronted.

Pragmatically, at least in Canada, women have no choice but to address equality-based arguments; at the very least, we have to be ready to respond to arguments framed in terms of equality. Equality is, at present, too much a part of the dominant discourse in Canada to be ignored. The prominence which equality has gained in the dominant (liberal) discourse in Canada is due, at least in part, to the efforts of the Canadian women who organized and lobbied for the inclusion of the equality rights provisions in the Charter of Rights and Freedoms. The fact that Canadian women were successful in their lobbying efforts for the inclusion of three equality provisions in the Charter (S.15(1), S.15(2) and S.28) may be an indication that formal equality has reached the limits of its utility for women and that it is time for us to develop a more woman-centered understanding of equality. It might be that we attain our victories only at the point when what we win will no longer be of use to us.

Be that as it may, the equality provisions are now firmly in place. The inclusion of equality rights in the Canadian Charter should put an end to, or perhaps more accurately, foreclose, any discussion of whether or not Canadian women should advocate or support an equality-based approach to issues. Although women in Canada could still reject equality and decide not to invoke or rely upon the charter equality provisions, this would seem to be a "high risk" strategy. Whether we like it or not, by virtue of its "entrenchment" in the Charter, equality has gained a level of prominence which makes it difficult for Canadian women simply to opt out of the equality discourse.

The Charter equality provisions are being used in a large number and variety of cases. In many cases, equality arguments have been employed directly against women, as for example, in the challenge to the Women's Teachers' Federation of Ontario as a women-only professional association. In others, equality arguments have been used to further men's interests at the expense of women's interests, as for example, in the consent to adoption by the unmarried father cases. In a number of cases where other Charter rights have been used against women, women have defended themselves by relying on the Charter equality provisions, as for example, in response to the Charter challenges to rape shield laws being brought by accused rapists. These situations demonstrate the need for women in Canada to focus on how best to use the equality provisions to address the inequalities which women suffer and how best to protect women against the use of the equality provisions to entrench and perpetuate existing inequalities. As feminist legal advocates, we need to prepare ourselves to be able to counter male-based equality arguments with women-centered equality arguments.

It is, of course, possible to argue that equality is inappropriate in the particular circumstances under review. Section I of the Charter would provide the constitutional basis for such an argument:

> 1. *The Canadian Charter of Rights and Freedoms* guarantees the rights and freedoms set out in it subject only to such reasonable limits prescribed by law as can be demonstrably justified in a free and democratic society.

However, given the current prominence and touting of equality, this might be a risky strategy. In relying upon a section 1 exemption, women would be arguing that it is desirable in the circumstances to treat women "unequally." We might then find ourselves in the "special treatment" trap of which feminists are so fearful. This is not to say that women will not be put in the position of having to rely upon section 1 in an attempt to avoid the harshness of a decision framed in terms of formal equality. However, it might be better for women in these situations to use section 1 as a safety valve of last resort rather than an initial response to an equality argument. It is only when the argument to have their position characterized as one of equality has been lost that women should defend that position as a demonstrably justified inequality under section 1. To concede the equality characterization from the outset would be to concede too much.

Trapped in Equality

It is only recently that I have begun to approach equality as a strategy and to appreciate the flexibility which the indeterminacy of equality offers. A few years ago, I was very much struggling to determine to which "side" of the equality debate I subscribed and how the different models of equality might apply to the specific issues I was anxious to address. I was, at that time, working on a project which was set up to review Ontario and Federal legislation and government policy to assess their compliance with the Charter equality provisions. In order to carry out this assessment, the project participants had to look at a great variety and range of women's issues.

I, and perhaps the same could be said by all of the project participants, felt completely overwhelmed by the task of fitting these diverse and varied problems into an existing equality analysis so that the Charter could be used to address them. I desperately needed a definition or theory of equality which could make sense of these issues when taken as a whole. I sought a unified and coherent understanding of equality which would enable lawyers and advocates to argue consistently and effectively for an equality which furthered women's interests.

None of the existing equality models seemed adequate to address all, or even most, of the situations of women's inequalities that we were examining. The range of issues included, for example, custody and support, pregnancy leave, boys only sports teams, social assistance, sexual assault, the testing and regulation of women's health products, housing and women only professional associations. Proponents of the various equality models seemed to agree (some explicitly, some implicitly) that one must adopt a single model of equality and use it exclusively. Within the common law legal system, consistency is considered to be of paramount importance. Given this reverence for consistency, it is generally considered unthinkable to go into court to argue that equality means one thing in one situation and something different (often inappropriately characterized as contradictory) in another. Thus, for example, it is generally seen as a contradiction (and therefore untenable) to argue against men only educational institutions and in favour of women-only educational institutions, both on the basis of "equality."

I was caught in the prototypical dilemma which characterizes the feminist equality debates. Any attempt to specify and respond to the many varied inequalities to which women are subjected elicits accusations that one is reproducing and perpetuating those inequalities. For example, Wendy Williams (1985) argues against "special" pregnancy legislation on the following basis:

> First, it makes women who are likely to become pregnant less desirable employees and thus increases the incentive to discriminate against women of the "vulnerable" age and marital status. Second, special treatment can shift attention from the fact that the employer has a generally inadequate sick leave policy to the fact that some employees have special privileges. Energies which might constructively be directed toward improved working conditions are diverted into hostility toward fellow workers, specifically women who become pregnant and have children. Last and certainly not least, the legislation perpetuates an outmoded ideology—women as unique and separate, with a special reproductive role in which the state has sufficient interest to single her out for special treatment. That is the precise principle on which the state has historically singled out women for special "protection," a "protection" that has operated in almost all cases, to women's detriment. (p. 371; footnotes omitted)

The criticism that "protective" legislation is used to women's detriment is a valid one. However, there is a similar and equally valid critique of the ways in which formal equality and gender neutral legislation have been used to women's detriment.

Conversely, to premise legislation on the understanding that women and men can, or should, or will be, treated equitably under a gender neutral, "androgynous" approach is to be accused of ignoring the very real conditions of inequality under which most women live. For example, including pregnancy under general disability leave or promoting the "nurturing leave" advocated by Nadine Taub (1984–5) among others, denies the substantial extra burdens which pregnancy, child-bearing and child care place on women in this society—burdens which are in no way shared "equally" by men. There are debates about what an "ideal" world might look like with respect to child care, but there is little disagreement that, at present, the vast majority of child care is done by women.

I took, and still do take, these criticisms of the different feminist equality models very seriously. The criticisms raise very real concerns that need to be considered in any equality strategy. But taking all of the criticisms seriously leaves one without a theory of equality. Accepting the need for a single, comprehensive approach to equality, while at the same time noting the inadequacy of any one approach to address all of women's inequalities, and the potential for any formula to be used against women, there seemed no way out of the equality/inequality box in which I saw women trapped. This may be seen as an argument for abandoning equality altogether. However, equality debates merely reflect the problems; they do not cause them. Changing the rhetoric will not change the issues; the contradictions and dilemmas will remain, regardless of how they are characterized.

This was a profoundly depressing realization. Yet, as is often the case, as I was reaching the depths of despair with equality, I was developing an analysis which would assist me to work my way out of this paralyzing pessimism. The recognition that there is no perfect equality formula was very liberating. I no longer felt so restrained and hesitant in my approach to the issues on which I wanted to work.

I realized that the pursuit of an equality formula was itself the trap. I saw that I had allowed myself to be constrained and silenced by the abstract concept of equality. I had felt that we had to get the application of the Charter equality provisions "right" and that, if somehow we couldn't or didn't, we would have failed. There is a large amount of women-blaming involved in the characterization of unsuccessful attempts to get a law to benefit women as failures on the part of women. Women should not be held responsible for the shortcomings of the law, either in terms of wording or interpretation. How can women ever get it "right" in a system in which women are, almost by definition considered "wrong"? This "fear of failure," meant that I had accepted that the potential offered by the Charter equality provisions could never be brought to fruition until the inconsistencies and contradictions were eliminated from the feminist analysis of equality. I feared that, without a "model of equality," feminist advocates could easily be dismissed as muddle-headed and inconsistent. I feared we would be plagued by the chronic criticism that "women don't really know what they want."

In my pursuit of an equality formula, I had not ignored the existence of liberal and other models of equality. I had understood that no feminist approach would be adopted immediately as "the" meaning of equality, displacing the dominant liberal concept. However, it was my expectation that, once developed, the feminist model of equality would compete with these other models, and hopefully, eventually gain acceptance as the prevailing approach to equality. Thus articulated, the unrealistic optimism of my expectations is painfully clear. Even were it possible to develop "the" feminist equality theory, or even a feminist equality model, the expectation that a feminist theory could gain ascendancy, either on its own "merits" or through feminist advocacy, seems naive, at the very least. To argue in terms of competing theories and "merits" ignores the power dynamics and vested interests, the psychological and cultural systems, and the social institutions through which women's oppression is maintained and reinforced. In ignoring these factors, I myself fell victim to the liberal equality myth, the "anymore can make it" American dream.

Further, "the" feminist equality theory project is not only impractical on political grounds, it is also impossible on practical grounds. No feminist theory of equality capable of application within the existing legal system could, in operation, retain its integrity and function effectively to eliminate women's subordination. The recurring feminist experience is that once any "theory" developed to assist women in the legal arena starts to become effective in that arena, that is it starts to be adopted in some form by decision makers, the theory is reformulated and redirected by those decision makers so as to limit its potential and contain women's self-determination. While some improvements for women are made, such gains are usually limited and are almost always accompanied by a countervailing loss. Phyllis L. Crocker in her article, "The Meaning of Equality for Battered Women Who Kill Men In Self-Defense" (1983), provides a good illustration of this point in her discussion of the "battered wife syndrome." Evidence of this "syndrome" was originally introduced into court to support women's claims to self-defense. This syndrome has since become a new stereotype used against any battered woman who does not conform to it. By the time that feminist advocates have refined an approach or a strategy into a "theory," it has generally reached its maximum utility for women. At that point, the theory is very likely to be coopted into liberal service and used to limit women's options or to impede their progress.

The equality strategy in which I see myself engaged is substantially different from the feminist sexual equality model that I initially pursued with such desperate intensity. I no longer seek in equality a concept capable of generating a theory which can provide answers and direction to the difficult legal questions which face women. In fact, many of the legal questions facing women are made more difficult and complicated by the perceived need for a theory of equality and the desire to comply with some predetermined understanding of equality. The notion that it is possible to develop an equality theory which, when applied, would always benefit women without ever operating to our detriment, places far too great a burden on equality as well as on feminists working in the legal equality field. Because of sexism, stereotypes and myths, and the varied, multiple and compound inequalities to which women are subject, no single model of equality could possibly work exclusively in women's interests. In an unequal society, equality will always be a double-edged instrument: a tool which can be used to assist women in some circumstances, or some women, or a woman; but also a weapon which can be used to restrict women, to punish them for failure to conform to the male standard, or to take away women's "advantages."

The recognition that the best we could do was to try to use the equality guarantees to make some limited improvements for some women in some circumstances enabled me to start looking for ways to apply the Charter to do just that. Instead of looking for an external solution, called "equality," that could be imposed on a situation to rectify an existing inequality, I realized that the solution had to be developed from the problem itself and that "equality," as a concept, had nothing to contribute to this process.

Equality as Strategy

To pursue equality as a strategy, I have had to turn away from definitions of equality, legal models, and frameworks. Instead I have begun to look at the specific needs and problems that women experience and the inequalities that women suffer in order to develop ways of addressing these issues in an equality context. The strategy is to argue from the particularized inequality as the means to get it recognized as such—heard, seen and felt as inequality. In this undertaking, none of the existing equality models are of any help. As abstract constructs, these models do not and cannot address the realities of women's lives. An equality framework does not assist one in identifying problems nor in figuring out how to respond to them. In fact, the imposition of an equality model can tend to obscure or distort the realities of women's lives and the inequalities as they are experienced by women. It seems to me, for example, a distortion to characterize the problem of women losing their jobs because of pregnancy as a problem with disability benefits. This is not to downplay the seriousness of inadequate disability benefits nor to say that the solution to the absence of maternity benefits might not be improved disability benefits. But the problem is not the rules regarding disability benefits, it is an unwillingness to accommodate pregnancy within the paid labor force. Once the problem is identified and the desired solution determined, an equality-based approach might be helpful as a tool to work toward the desired result. However, an "equality" analysis, as such, provides no insight into the problem.

My concern when a lot of time and energy are spent talking and theorizing about equality is that "equality" becomes vested with a life and meaning of its own, divorced from the particularized experiences of inequality it is intended to address. Equality then becomes a formulaic solution to be imposed on situations of inequality with little or no consideration for the particularities of that situation. In this process, people tend to become wedded to their own equality formula, thereby losing their ability to respond to changing circumstances. The "equality debates" flow from these rigidly-held positions. Given the ability of our male-dominated systems (legal, political and social) to coopt, appropriate, mis-interpret and subvert feminist challenges, it is dangerous for feminists to become too attached to any particular approach or strategy. We then lose our ability to recognize a strategy's limitations in a male-dominated system and we are unwilling to change course when our strategy has been overtaken or subverted.

An equality strategy involves two very separate undertakings. First, one has to isolate the problem, the specific inequality to be addressed and determine the desired solution. Second, one has to devise an appropriate way to achieve that solution. Many equality theorists seem to have collapsed these two undertakings into one and in so doing have lost sight of the original problem. Isolating the problem is usually a fairly clear task, although the problem itself is often complex. Determining the desired solution is usually more difficult. The various equality models really do not assist in developing solutions; the answers must necessarily flow from the specifics of the situation itself.

The second undertaking in the equality as strategy approach is to identify the method(s) that can be employed toward the desired solution. The legal process is, of course, only one possible method: it can be rejected as inappropriate in the circumstances; it can be adopted as the exclusive strategy or as the strategy of first instance; or it can be used in conjunction with other methods. Having decided to use the legal system, reliance upon an equality guarantee is only one of a number of possible legal approaches. In making the choice for or against using an equality guarantee, it is inappropriate to allow pre-existing equality formulae to foreclose or constrain one's decision. It is, however, important, in assessing equality as a strategy, to consider the prominence of such equality formulae and their acceptance by decision makers. One must be prepared to argue against the application of an equality formula where such a formula would operate to women's detriment. It would be a mistake, however, to reject equality arguments altogether. Given the current ambiguity about the legal meaning of equality, it would be short sighted, at this time, to concede equality to the equal treatment proponents or to those who argue for a limited acknowledgement of women's difference. These approaches are too easily turned against women.

In this undertaking, it is critically important that feminists not evaluate strategies and desired results in terms of their impact on a particular model of equality. This is not to say that the potential effect of a particular strategy should not be part of the evaluation process. The rigidity and inflexibility inherent in a formulaic approach to equality are probably more harsh and limiting for the most vulnerable groups in our society; women of color, women with disabilities, lesbians. We need to retain a flexible approach to equality in order to be able to respond to multiple inequalities. An assessment of the anticipated "costs" of a particular strategy, and upon whom the burden of those costs might principally fall, is a critical part of the evaluation of any strategy (Fineman, 1983). Strategies and results need to be evaluated in terms of their effect upon women and other disadvantaged groups, not in relation to some abstract theory of equality. Solutions should not be adjusted to fit a narrow concept of equality. Reliance upon an equality guarantee should not be rejected as a strategy simply because the desired solution does not seem to fit into an accepted model of equality.

Feminist equality discussions would be better focused on specific issues rather than on the abstract polar notions of "equal treatment" and so-called "special treatment." I have had numerous conversations with feminist equality litigators in which their response to a proposed solution or strategy has been "Oh no, we can't argue that, it conflicts with our approach to equality" or "that's special treatment, not equality" or "we have to argue X because that's what is 'equal'." These attitudes reflect an inappropriate privileging of equality over the very real needs of the women who are suffering the very real inequality. In contrast, equality strategy seeks to expand the meanings and understandings of equality to address the inequalities to which women are subjected. Given the prominence and lip-service currently paid to equality discourse in Canadian legal forums, women would be foolish to abandon "equality" to those who seek to use it against women. Rather, we should use the indeterminacy of equality to argue on women's behalf in a variety of different circumstances.

The equality project, as I have outlined it, requires that the identification of the problem and the determination of the solution be seen as distinct and separate from implementation. Notions of "equality" should not dictate the solution. The role of legal advocates should be to create and develop implementation strategies, that is, to determine how to pursue the desired solution most effectively.

An Equality Process

I became involved in equality strategizing in Canada through my work with the statute audit project, a review of Federal and Ontario legislation and policy conducted in order to document non-compliance with the sex equality guarantees of the Charter (CREF, 1985). The statute audit project was sponsored by the Charter of Rights Education Fund (CREF). CREF is an organization, established by a group of women who were active in lobbying for the equality provisions in the Charter. CREF was set up to pursue Charter implementation issues on behalf of women. CREF's goal is to make Charter equality work for Canadian women. The founders of CREF recognized, only too clearly, that the enactment of the equality sections was only the beginning of a lot of hard work. Because of the three-year delay in the implementation of section 15 required by section 32(2) of the Charter, CREF started to compile and analyze a list of the inequalities to which women are subject and which might be capable of redress through the Charter. Although the provincial and federal governments were supposed to be engaged in these tasks during the three-year moratorium, CREF members did not trust government commitment to the equality project. Nor did we think that they had sufficient understanding of the issues to enable them to do anything more than a superficial review based on a formal equality approach. CREF wanted to be prepared by the implementation date for section 15 (April 17, 1985) with background research and analysis upon which to base a litigation and lobbying strategy which relied on sections 15 and 28. Because the charter's jurisdiction is limited to government under section 32(1), the statute audit project focused on legislation and government policy.

The statute audit project was an important learning process for me and, I think, for all those involved in the project, which included almost 100 lawyers, community workers, students, academics and feminist activists. We conducted the project in the absence of a specific model of equality to inform or direct us. We did this, not based on any preference for an unstructured, open-ended approach, but because we were unable, as a group, to choose or develop a model of equality. Ironically, in retrospect I think we approached "equality" in the most appropriate and productive manner. We started from what we knew—the inequalities as women experience them—and strove to present those inequalities in an equality context. We sought either to direct our analysis toward a particular solution, or, if we did not yet have a specific solution to propose, to present the analysis so that women's inequalities would be recognized as such. Without an equality model to impose on the problems we were addressing, we were able to be more responsive and creative. In the absence of a commitment to a particular meaning of equality, we were open to any equality-based argument which might assist in redressing the specific problem under review. Rather than allowing the law to define the issues for us, we started with women's experiences of inequality and worked from there.

The statute audit participants were divided into seven groups: criminal, education, employment, family, health, immigration, and poverty. Each group was to ascertain the problems women experience in that area and to develop an analysis of those problems as equality issues. We desperately wanted to have a theory or model of equality that would provide us with the analysis of the issues and lead us to the appropriate solution. But we had not developed such a theory and we were unable to find one with which we were all comfortable. At the time, I attributed our inability to agree upon a theory of equality to the time constraints under which we were operating and to our lack of familiarity with the equality discourse. I now see that the inability to agree upon a theory did not stem from the shortcomings of the audit participants but from the equality theories themselves.

In the absence of an equality formula, each group was asked to generate its own model, based upon its analysis of the issues. We hoped that at the end an appropriate model of equality would emerge fully formed from the collective thinking of all the participants. Of course, no such phantom emerged and we remained without an equality formula. In contrast to my earlier feelings of anxiety and incompleteness, I now feel relieved and challenged by the absence of such a formula.

I learned a number of important things from the statute audit project. First, through my work with the statute audit project, I came to see equality and equality work as a process and not as an end in itself. The project reaffirmed for me the importance, not only of what we do, but of how we do it. In the ways in which the participants worked together, in our approach to the issues, in our reliance upon and belief in our own and other women's experiences, in all of these ways, we were trying to "do equality." We struggled to promote equality not only through our work product but through the work itself and the process of working together. Of course, it was an inadequate "doing of equality." There were tensions and disputes among participants and uneven divisions of labor. Although there were women of color, women with disabilities and lesbians participating in the project, their numbers were disproportionately small; the issues of multiple oppressions and of the inequalities experienced by other disadvantaged groups were not adequately addressed. All of the issues were filtered through the participants, all of whom would be considered "professionals," which gave a definite class bias to the project.

The second lesson I learned from the project is how difficult it is to articulate women's experience within an equality context, despite the fact that women know and experience a multitude of issues as inequalities. Women's narratives generally do not speak in terms of equality. We clearly impose something upon those narratives when we try to put them into a legal equality framework. We need to be sure that we do not lose the meaning and power of the narrative, of the experience, in the equality process.

Finally, I came to recognize that it was not an accident that no model of equality emerged from our analysis. No consistent and precise model of equality can be applied to the inconsistencies and contradictions which make up women's inequalities. Attempts to squeeze and cajole women's experiences into some predetermined equality model deny the complexity and depth of the inequalities which women suffer, and fail to respond to the realities of women's lives. In our overwhelming desire to see and have "equality," we have tended to ignore the inequalities.

Conclusion

Instead of a theory of equality which can be applied in the legal process to further women's dreams of equality, feminists need to develop some equality-based tools which might assist feminist advocates in their work on specific issues. This is the limited use to which I think equality discourse can be put for women within the existing legal system.

Equality's primary value to women is the forum it provides for the raising of issues and presenting of arguments on behalf of women. I now see equality as the packaging through which one attempts to sell a particular end result with respect to a particular issue, rather than itself the end result. The choice of equality as the package is, to a large extent, pragmatic. It is not exclusively pragmatic; it is also historically determined. Although equality has long been perceived as one of the fundamental principles of feminism, women's claims have not always been framed in terms of equality. The current acceptance of equality within the dominant discourse is in large part due to feminist advocacy and struggle. In the discourse which currently dominates legal and political forums in Canada, equality is, for the moment, highly marketable.

At least on the abstract level, current support of sexual equality is motivated in part by the perceived need for logical consistency. Logical consistency has not always been seen to require the inclusion of women within the liberal ideal of equality. The fact that women's equality has only recently been seen as necessarily included in the liberal equality package is testament to the extent of the indeterminacy of equality. This ideological commitment, in conjunction with the perception that women (and other oppressed groups) are increasingly powerful political forces, make equality arguments something to which liberal decision makers are forced to listen and respond. Because of the prominence which equality has played within feminist discourse, this, in and of itself, is a significant victory for women.

The current debate is taking place almost exclusively on the terrain of the meaning of equality. In this context, I argue that it is in women's interest to refuse to subscribe to, or commit themselves to, any single meaning of equality. Feminist advocates need to learn to use the equality discourse on behalf of women in as many and in as diverse situations as the term can bear. The needs and experiences of women will dictate the meaning of equality in each particular context. It is these needs and experiences which should be brought into the open and promoted, not some reified ideal of equality.

I have proposed a strategy for using Canada's new equality provisions on behalf of women, a strategy which I regard as particularly well suited to the legal process and which will take advantage of the prominence which equality discourse has gained within that forum. However, similar to the problems which inhere in advocating a single meaning for equality, reliance upon a single strategy is dangerously limited. Feminists have tended to accept the revolution versus reform dichotomy and the rigid and mutually exclusive choices that such dichotomized thinking requires. This is the same mode of thinking, frequently described as "male," which posits a dichotomy between "special treatment" and "equality." Women who accept this dichotomy are forced into the box of choosing between the two. In contrast, the strategy which I have outlined cannot stand alone. Its effectiveness is, in large measure, dependent upon the simultaneous pursuit of other more "revolutionary" and other more "reform" strategies.

It is vital that women continue to theorize about the meaning of equality and question equality as a goal for women; that women continue to expose and denounce their oppression; that feminists continue to question women's participation in the legal process and raise the specter of cooptation; that women continue to struggle to be heard within the male discourse and struggle to create a women's discourse. Far from being seen as mutually exclusive these strategies must be recognized as mutually supportive. Possibly in this way, through feminist process and methodology, women will be able to operationalize equality. We will not be merely defining equality through legal analysis and theory making; we will be trying to improve women's lived realities.

References: Books and Articles

Abel, R. 1982. "Torts." In *The Politics of Law: A Progressive Critique,* edited by D. Kairys. New York: Pantheon.

Abramovitz, M. 1988. *Regulating the Lives of Women: Social Welfare Policy from Colonial Times to the Present.* Boston: South End Press.

Adams, Carolyn Teich and Kathryn Teich. 1980. *Mothers at Work: Public Policies in the United States, Sweden, and China.* New York: Longman.

Ahrons, Constance. 1980. "Joint Custody Arrangements in the Postdivorce Family." *The Journal of Divorce* 3:189–205.

Aiken, J. H. 1984. "Differentiating Sex from Sex: The Male Irresistible Impulse. *New York University Review of Law and Social Change* 12:357–413.

Alcoff, Linda. 1988. "Cultural Feminism Versus Post-Structuralism: The Identity Crisis in Feminist Theory." *Signs* 13:405–36.

Althusser, Louis. 1971. "Ideology and Ideological State Apparatuses (Notes towards an Investigation)." In *Lenin and Philosophy and Other Essays.* London: New Left Review Editions.

Anderson, Mary. 1951. *Women at Work: The Autobiography of Mary Anderson as Told to Mary N. Winslow.* Minneapolis: University of Minnesota Press.

Appelbaum, Eileen. 1987. "Restructuring Work: Temporary, Part-Time and At Home Employment." In *Computer Chips and Paper Clips: Technology and Women's Employment,* edited by Heidi Hartmann. Washington, DC: National Academy Press.

Aristotle. 1925. *Nicomachean Ethics,* translated by W. D. Ross. Oxford: Clarendon Press.

Arnold, T. 1962. *The Symbols of Government.* New York: Harcourt.

Ashe, M. 1987. "Mind's Opportunity: Birthing a Poststructuralist Feminist Jurisprudence." *Syracuse Law Review* 38:1129–53.

Backhouse, Constance. 1985. " 'To Open the Way for Others of My Sex'; Clara Brett Martin's Career as Canada's First Woman Lawyer." *Canadian Journal of Women and the Law* 1.

Baer, Judith. 1978. *The Chains of Protection: The Judicial Response to Women's Labor Legislation.* Westport, CT: Greenwood Press.

Baker, Paula. 1984. "The Domestication of Politics: Women and American Political Society, 1780–1920." *American Historical Review* 89(3): 620–47.

Banner, Lois. 1983. *American Beauty*. New York: Knopf.

Barnes, A. 1977. "Female Criticism: A Prologue." In *The Authority of Experience: Essays in Feminist Criticism,* edited by A. Diamond and L. Edwards. Amherst: University of Massachusetts Press.

Barron, J. 1987a. "Polar Bears Kill a Child at Prospect Park Zoo." *New York Times*. (May 20). sec. A.

———. 1987b. "Officials Weigh Tighter Security at Zoos in Parks." *New York Times*. (May 22). sec. B.

Bartky, S. L. 1982. "Narcissism, Femininity and Alienation." *Social Theory and Practice* 8:127–43.

Basch, Norma. 1982. *In the Eyes of the Law: Women, Marriage and Property in Nineteenth-Century New York*. Ithaca: Cornell University Press.

Baudrillard, J. 1988. "Simulacra and Simulations." Pp. 166–84 in *Jean Baudrillard: Selected Writings,* edited by M. Poster. Cambridge: Polity Press.

Becker, Susan. 1981. *The Origins of the Equal Rights Amendment: American Feminism between the Wars*. Westport, CT: Greenwood Press.

Belenky, M. F. et al. 1986. *Women's Ways of Knowing: The Development of Self, Voice, and Mind*. New York: Basic Books.

Bell, W. 1965. *Aid to Dependent Children*.

Benhabib, S. 1987. "The Generalized and the Concrete Other: The Kohlberg-Gilligan Controversy and Feminist Theory." Pp. 77–95 in *Feminism as Critique,* edited by S. Benhabib and D. Cornell. Cambridge: Polity Press.

Benjamin, Walter. 1969. "The Storyteller." In *Illuminations,* edited by Hannah Arendt. New York: Schocken.

Berman, M. 1982. *All That is Solid Melts into Air*. New York: Simon and Schuster

Bernhard, J. 1971. *Women and the Public Interest*. Chicago: Aldine.

Bernstein, Richard. 1971. *Praxis and Action*. Philadelphia: University of Pennsylvania Press.

Blassingame, J. 1977. *Slave Testimony: Two Centuries of Letters, Speeches, Interviews and Autobiographies*. Baton Rouge: Louisiana State Univ. Press.

Borchard, Edwin. February 22, 1922. "Edwin Borchard to Ruth Dadaunian." In *Papers of the National Consumers' League,* Reel 51, Library of Congress, Manuscripts Division. Washington, DC.

Boris, Eileen, 1985. "Regulating Industrial Homework: The Triumph of 'Sacred Motherhood.'" *Journal of American History* 71(March).

———. 1986a. "The Quest for Labor Standards in the Era of Eleanor Roosevelt: The Case of Industrial Homework." *Wisconsin Women's Law Journal* 2(June).

———. 1986b. "A Woman's Place?" *The Nation* 243 (October 18):365–66.

———. 1987. "Looking at Women's Historians Looking at Difference." *Wisconsin Women's Law Journal* 3.

———. 1988. "Homework in the Past, Its Meaning for the Future." In *The New Era of Home-Based Work,* edited by K. Christensen. Boulder: Westview Press.

———. 1989. "Regulating Industrial Homework: An Update." *Proceedings of the First Annual*

Conference on Women's Policy research. Washington, DC: Institute for Women's Policy Research.

Boris, Eileen and Cynthia R. Daniels. 1989. *Homework: Historical and Contemporary Perspectives on Paid Labor at Home.* Urbana: University of Illinois Press.

Bottomley, A. K. 1979. *Criminology in Focus: Past Trends and Future Prospects.* London: Martin Robinson.

Bottoms, A. E. 1977. "Reflections on the Renaissance of Dangerousness." *The Howard Journal of Penology and Crime Prevention* 16(2):70–96.

Bourdieu, Pierre. 1987. "The Force of Law: Toward a Sociology of the Juridical Field." *The Hastings Law Journal* 38:805–53.

Boyle, Christine. 1985. "Sexual Assault and the Feminist Judge." *Canadian Journal of Women and the Law* 1(1):93–107.

———. 1986. "Teaching Law As If Women Really Mattered, or, What about the Washrooms?" *Canadian Journal of Women and the Law* 2:96.

Boyle, J. 1985. "The Politics of Reason: Critical Legal Theory and Local Social Thought." *University of Pennsylvania Law Review* 133:685.

Brants, C. and E. Kok. 1986. "Penal Sanctions as a Feminist Strategy: A Contradiction in Terms?" *International Journal of the Sociology of Law* 14(3/4):269–86.

Bromley, Dorothy. 1927. "Breach of Promise—Why?" *The Woman Citizen* 12.

Brooke, J. 1988. "New Surge of AIDS in Congo May Be an Omen for Africa." *New York Times.* (January 22):sec. A.

Brophy, J. and C. Smart. 1985. *Women in Law: Explorations in Law, Family and Sexuality.* London: Routledge & Kegan Paul.

Brown, Robert. 1929. "Breach of Promise Suits." *University of Pennsylvania Law Review* 77:474–97.

Brown, Robert. 1978. "The New Criminology." *Law and Society,* edited by E. Kamenka and Tay Erh-Soon. London: Edward Arnold.

Buffalo Symposium. 1985. "Feminist Discourse, Moral Values, and the Law—A Conversation." *Buffalo Law Review* 34:11–87.

Bumiller, Kristin, 1987. "Victims in the Shadow of the Law: A Critique of the Model of Legal Protection." *Signs* 12:421–39.

Burstyn, V., ed. 1985. *Women Against Censorship.* Vancouver: Douglas & McIntyre.

Butler, J. 1986a. "Variations on Sex and Gender: Beauvoir, Wittig and Foucault." *Praxis International* 5:505.

———. 1986b. "Sex and Gender in Simone de Beauvoir's *Second Sex.*" *Yale French Studies* 72:35–49.

Calamari, J. and J. Perillo. 1987. *Contracts,* 3d ed. St. Paul: West Publishing.

Califia, P. 1988. *Saphistry: The Book of Lesbian Sexuality.* Tallahasee, FL: Naiad Press.

Card, Claudia. 1979. "Love, Friendship, and Eroticism: An Essay on Carnal Knowledge." Presented to the Society of Women in Philosophy, East Lansing Michigan.

———. 1984. "The Symbolic Significance of Sex and the Institution of Sexuality." Presented to the Society for the Philosophy of Sex and Love at the Eastern APA, New York City.

Cassirer, E. 1985. *Symbol, Myth, and Culture: Essays and Lectures of Ernst Cassirer*, edited by D. P. Verne. New Haven: Yale University Press.

Chambers, David. 1979. *Making Fathers Pay: The Enforcement of Child Support*. Chicago: University of Chicago Press.

Chodorow, Nancy. 1979. *The Reproduction of Mothering*.

Clarke, D. H. 1978. "Marxism, Justice and the Justice Model." *Contemporary Crises* 2:27–62.

Cleveland Plain Dealer. 1935. (March 21):1.

———. 1935. (May 9):1.

Colby and Damon. 1983. "Listening to a Different Voice: A Review of Gilligan's *In a Different Voice*." *Merrill-Palmer Quarterly* 29:473–481.

Cole, D. 1984. "Strategies of Difference: Litigating for Women's Rights in a Man's World." *Law and Inequality: Journal of Theory and Practice* 2:33–96.

Coles, Robert. 1987a. *Dorothy Day: A Radical Devotion*. Reading, MA: Addison-Wesley Pub. Co.

———. 1987b. *Simone Weil: A Modern Pilgrimage*. Reading, MA: Addison-Wesley Pub. Co.

Colker, Ruth. 1983. "Pornography and Privacy: Towards the Development of Group Based Theory for Sex Based Institutions of Privacy." *Law and Inequality: Journal of Theory and Practice* 1:191–237.

———. 1987. "The Anti-Subordination Principle: Applications." *Wisconsin Women's Law Journal* 3:59.

———. 1988. "Feminism, Sexuality and Self: A Preliminary Inquiry into the Politics of Authenticity." Boston University Law Review 68:217–64. Included in modified form in this volume as Chapter 8.

Commager, H. 1958. *Documents of American History*. New York: Appleton-Century Crofts.

Committee on Education and Labor, House of Representatives. 1982. "The Reemergence of Sweatshops and the Enforcement of Wage and Hour Standards." 97th Cong., 1st and 2nd sess. Washington, DC: U.S. Government Printing Office.

Conference Editorial Collective. 1986. "Special Issue: Feminist Perspectives on Law." *International Journal of the Sociology of Law* 14(3/4):233–37.

Coombe, Rosemary. 1988. " 'The Most Disgusting, Disgraceful, and Inequitous Proceeding in our Law': The Action for Breach of Promise of Marriage in Nineteenth Century Ontario." *University of Toronto Law Journal* 38:64–108.

Coombs, Mary. 1990. "Agency and Partnership." *Yale Journal of Law and Feminism* 2:1–23.

Corea, Gena. 1985. *The Mother Machine: Reproductive Technologies from Artificial Insemination to Artificial Wombs*. New York: Harper and Row.

Cott, Nancy. 1978. "Passionlessness: An Interpretation of Victorian Sexual Ideology, 1790–1850." *Signs* 4:219–36.

———. 1987. *The Grounding of Modern Feminism*. New Haven: Yale University Press.

Coward, R. and J. Ellis. 1977. *Language and Materialism: Developments in Semiology and the Theory of the Subject*. London: Routledge & Kegan Paul.

CREF. 1985. *Report on the Statute Audit Project*. Toronto: Charter of Rights Education Fund.

Crocker, Phyllis L. 1983. "The Meaning of Equality for Battered Women Who Kill Men in Self-Defense." *Harvard Women's Law Journal* 8:121–53.

Crocker, Phyllis L. and A. E. Simon. 1981. "Sexual Harassment in Education." *Capital University Law Review* 10:541–84.

Daggett, Harriet. 1935. "The Action for Breach of Marriage Promise." In *Legal Essays on Family Law.* Baton Rouge: Louisiana State University Press.

Dahl, T. S. 1986. "Taking Women as a Starting Point: Building Women's Law." *International Journal of the Sociology of Law* 14(3/4):239–48.

Dahl, T. S. and A. Snare. 1978. "The Coercion of Privacy: A Feminist Perspective." In *Women, Sexuality and Social Control,* edited by C. Smart and B. Smart. London: Routledge & Kegan Paul.

Daly, Mary. 1979. *Gyn/Ecology: The Metaethics of Radical Feminism.* Boston: Beacon.

Daniel, Annie S. 1905. "The Wreck of the Home: How Wearing Apparel Is Fashioned in the Tenements." *Charities* 14 (April 1).

Davis, A. 1941. *Deep South: A Social Anthropological Study of Caste and Class.* Chicago: Univ. of Chicago Press.

Davis. 1981. "Reflection on the Black Woman's Role in the Community of Slaves." *Black Scholar* Nov.–Dec. 1981.

Day, Dorothy. 1963. *Loaves and Fishes.* San Francisco: Harper & Row.

de Beauvoir, S. 1973. *The Second Sex.* New York: Vintage Books.

De Cecco, John P. and Michael G. Shively. 1985. "From Sexual Identity to Sexual Relationships: A Contextual Shift." In *Origins of Sexuality and Homosexuality,* edited by J. P. De Cecco and M. G. Shively. New York: Harrington Park.

Degler, Carl. 1980. *At Odds: Women and the Family in America from the Revolution to the Present.* New York: Oxford University Press.

Delacoste, Frederique and Priscilla Alexander, eds. 1987. *Sex Work: Writings by Women in the Sex Industry.* Pittsburgh: Cleis.

de Lauretis, T. 1984. *Alice Doesn't: Feminism, Semiotics, Cinema.* Bloomington: Indiana University Press.

Delagado, Richard. 1987. "The Ethereal Scholar: Does Critical Legal Studies Have What Minorities Want?" *Harvard Civil Rights and Civil Liberties Law Review* 22:301–22.

Derrida, J. 1976. *Of Grammatology,* translated by G. C. Spivak. Baltimore: Johns Hopkins Univ. Press.

———. 1981. *Dissemination,* translated by Barbara Johnson. Chicago: Chicago University Press.

Diamond, Arlyn and Lee Edwards, eds. 1977. *The Authority of Experience: Essays in Feminist Criticism.* Amherst: University of Massachusetts Press.

Diamond, I. and L. Quinby, eds. 1988. *Feminism and Foucault: Reflections on Resistance.* Boston: Northeastern University Press.

Dickens, Charles. 1937. The Posthumous Papers of the Pickwick Club. London: Chapman and Hall.

Didion, Joan. 1974. "Self-Respect." Pp. 121–25 in *Slouching Toward Bethlehem.* New York: Penguin.

Dinnerstein, D. 1976. *The Mermaid and the Minotaur.* New York: Harper & Row.

District of Columbia Minimum Wage Board. 1920. *A Study of Wages of Women Employed as Cleaners, Maids, and Elevator Operators in Office Buildings, Banks and Theatres and as Car Cleaners in the District of Columbia.* Washington, DC: The Board.

Dollard, J. 1937. *Caste and Class in a Southern Town.* London: Oxford Univ. Press.

DuBois, Ellen. 1978. *Feminism and Suffrage: The Emergence of an Independent Women's Movement in America, 1848–1869.* Ithaca and London: Cornell University Press.

———. 1981. *Elizabeth Cady Stanton, Susan B. Anthony: Correspondence, Writings, Speeches.* New York: Schocken Books.

DuBois, Ellen, M. Dunlap, Carol Gilligan, Catharine MacKinnon, and Carrie Menkel-Meadow. 1985. See Buffalo Symposium.

DuBois, Ellen and Linda Gordon. 1984. "Seeking Ecstasy on the Battlefield: Danger and Pleasure in Nineteenth Century Feminist Sexual Thought." in *Pleasure and Danger: Exploring Female Sexuality,* edited by Carole Vance. Boston: Routledge & Kegan Paul.

Duncan, M. L. 1982. "The Future of Affirmative Action: A Jurisprudential Legal Critique." *Harvard Civil Rights-Civil Liberties Law Review* 17:503–53.

Duncanson, I. W. 1978. "Balloonists, Bill of Rights and Dinosaurs.' *Public Law* 391.

———. 1982. "Jurisprudence and Politics." *Northern Ireland Legal Quarterly* 33:1–19.

———. 1984. "Moral Outrage and Technical Questions: Civil Liberties, Law and Politics." *Northern Ireland Legal Quarterly* 35:153–79.

———. 1988. "Law, Democracy and the Individual." *Legal Studies* 8:303–16.

———. 1989a. "The Politics of Common Law in Theory and History." *Osgoode Hall Law Journal* 27:1–21.

———. 1989b. "Power, Rights and Ronald Dworkin." *University of Tasmania Law Review* 9:278–301.

Dunlap, M. C. et al. 1985. See Buffalo Symposium.

Duras, Marguerite. 1985. *The Lover.* New York: Harper & Row.

Dworkin, Andrea. 1981. *Pornography: Men Possessing Women.* New York: Perigee Books.

———. 1983. *Right-Wing Women: The Politics of Domesticated Females.* New York: Perigee Books.

Dworkin, Ronald. 1985. "How Law Is Like Literature." Pp. 146–66 in *A Matter of Principle.* Cambridge: Harvard University Press.

———. 1986. *Law's Empire.* London: Fontane.

Dye, Nancy Schrom. 1980. *As Equals and As Sisters: Feminism, the Labor Movement, and the Women's Trade Union League of New York.* Columbia: University of Missouri Press.

Edelman, Murray. 1977. *Political Language: Words That Succeed and Policies That Fail.* New York: Academic Press.

———. 1988. *Constructing the Political Spectacle.* Chicago: University of Chicago Press.

Edgeworth, B. 1984. Review Article. *Australian Journal of Law and Society* 2:144–59.

Ehrenreich, Barbara. 1984. *The Hearts of Men: American Dreams and the Flight from Commitment.* Garden City, NY: Anchor Press/Doubleday.

Eisenstein, H. and A. Jardine, eds. 1984. *The Future of Difference.* Boston: G. K. Hall.

Eisenstein, Zillah. 1984. *Feminism and Sexual Equality: Crisis in Liberal America.* New York: Monthly Review Press.

Elkins, Stanley. 1963. *Slavery.* New York: Grosset & Dunlap.

Ellis, Challen R. and Joseph W. Folk. 1920 *A Reply to the Brief of Mr. Felix Frankfurter, The*

Children's Hospital v. Adkins, et al., Willie A. Lyons v. Adkins, et al. Court of Appeals, District of Columbia, October Term 1920. Washington, DC.

Ellis, R. 1984–85. "Victim-Specific Remedies: A Myopic Approach to Discrimination." *New York University Review of Law and Social Change* 13:519–74.

Ely, Richard T. 1920. *Outlines of Economics.* New York: Macmillan.

Emerson, Thomas I. 1984. "Pornography and the First Amendment: A Reply to Professor MacKinnon." *Yale Law and Policy Review* 3:130–143.

Enzensberger, H. M. 1974. *The Consciousness Industry: On Literature, Politics and the Media.* New York: Seabury Press.

Epstein, Cynthia Fuchs. 1982. *Women in Law.* New York: Basic Books.

Erickson, Nancy. 1982. "Historical Background of 'Protective' Labor Legislation: *Muller v. Oregon.*" In *Women and the Law: The Social-Historical Perspective,* edited by D. Kelley Weisberg. Cambridge: Scheckman.

Eser, A. 1965–66. "The Principle of 'Harm' in the Concept of Crime." *Duquesne University Law Review* 4:345–417.

Estrich, Susan. 1987. *Real Rape.* Cambridge: Harvard University Press.

Evans, S. 1979. *Personal Politics: The Roots of Women's Liberation in the Civil Rights Movement and the New Left.* New York: Knopf.

Fee, Elizabeth. 1983. "Women's Nature and Scientific Objectivity." In *Woman's Nature: Rationalizations of Inequality,* edited by M. Lowe and R. Hubbard. New York: Pergamon.

Feinsinger, Nathan. 1935. "Legislative Attack of 'Heart Balm.'" *Michigan Law Review* 33:979–1009.

Felstiner, W. L. F., R. L. Abel, and A. Sarat. 1980–81. "The Emergence and Transformation of Disputes: Naming, Blaming, Claiming . . ." *Law and Society* 15:631–54.

Ferguson, K. 1984. *The Feminist Case Against Bureaucracy.* Philadelphia: Temple Univ. Press.

Fineman, Martha L. 1983. "Implementing Equality: Ideology, Contradiction and Social Change: A Study of Rhetoric and Results in the Regulation of the Consequences of Divorce." *Wisconsin Law Review* 1983:789–886.

———. 1986. "Illusive Equality." *American Bar Foundation Journal* 781.

———. 1988. "Dominant Discourse, Professional Language, and Legal Change in Child Custody Decisionmaking." *Harvard Law Review* 101:727–74.

———. 1989. "Societal Factors Affecting the Creation of Legal Rules for Distribution of Property at Divorce." *Family Law Quarterly* 23(2):279–99. Included in this volume as Chapter 15.

———. 1991. *The Illusion of Equality: The Rhetoric and Reality of Divorce Reform.* Chicago: University of Chicago Press.

Fineman, Martha and Ann Opie. 1987. "The Uses of Social Science Data in Legal Policymaking: Custody Determinations at Divorce." *Wisconsin Law Review* 1987:107–158.

Finley, Lucinda M. 1986. "Transcending Equality Theory: A Way Out of the Maternity and the Workplace Debate." *Columbia Law Review* 86:1118–82.

Finn, Geraldine. 1982. "On the Oppression of Women in Philosophy—Or, Whatever Happened to Objectivity?" In *Feminism in Canada: From Pressure to Politics,* edited by A. R. Miles and G. Finn. Montreal: Black Rose Books.

Firestone, Shulamith. 1970. *The Dialectic of Sex: The Case for Feminist Revolution.* New York: Morrow.

Fiss, Owen M. 1976. "Groups and the Equal Protection Clause." *Philosophy and Public Affairs* 5:107–177.

Folbre, Nancy. 1988. "Whither Families? Toward a Socialist-Feminist Family Policy." *Socialist Review* 18:57–75.

Foley, M. 1983. "The Revolution in Law—Towards a Jurisprudence of Social Justice." *Australian Journal of Law and Society* 1:60–79.

Foucault, Michel. 1972. *The Archaelogy of Knowledge,* translated by A. M. Sheridan. London: Tavistock.

———. 1973. *The Birth of the Clinic,* translated by A. M. Sheridan. London: Tavistock.

———. 1977. *Discipline and Punish: The Birth of the Prison.* New York: Vintage Books.

———. 1979. *The History of Sexuality, Volume I: An Introduction,* translated by Robert Hurley. New York: Random House. London: Allen Lane.

———. 1980a. *Herculine Barbin, Being the Recently Discovered Memoirs of a Nineteenth-Century French Hermaphrodite,* translated by R. McDougall. New York: Pantheon.

———. 1980b. "What Is an Author?" Pp. 113–38 in *Language, Counter-Memory, Practice,* edited by D. F. Bouchard. Ithaca: Cornell University Press.

———. 1980c. *Power/Knowledge: Selected Interviews and Other Writings, 1972–1977,* edited by C. Gordon. New York: Pantheon.

———. 1982. "The Subject and Power." Pp. 208–26 in *Michel Foucault: Beyond Structuralism and Hermeneutics,* edited by H. L. Dreyfus and P. Rabinow. Brighton: Hamestor Press.

———. 1984. "The Order of Discourse." In *Language and Politics,* edited by M. Shapiro. Oxford: Blackwell.

———. 1986a. *The Use of Pleasure,* translated by R. Hurley. New York: Vintage Books.

———. 1986b. *The Care of the Self,* translated by R. Hurley. New York: Pantheon.

Frank, J. 1949. *Courts on Trial.* Princeton: Princeton University Press.

Frankfurter, Felix. c. 1922. "Lawyers' Opinions." In *National Consumers' League Collection,* Reel 51, Library of Congress, Manuscripts Division. Washington, DC.

———. 1924. "The Equal Rights Amendment." *New Republic* (November 26).

Frankfurter, Felix and Mary Dewson. 1923. *District of Columbia Minimum Wage Cases, Brief for Appellants,* Supreme Court of the United States, October Term, 1922. New York: Steinberg Press.

Fraser, N. 1987. "Social Movements vs. Disciplinary Bureaucracies: The Discourses of Social Needs." Center for Humanistic Studies, University of Minnesota Occasional papers, No. 8.

———. 1989. "Talking About Needs: Interpretive Contests as Political Conflicts in Welfare-State Societies." *Ethics* 99:291.

Frazier, E. 1939. *Negro Family in the United States.* Chicago: University of Chicago Press.

Freedman, A. E. 1983. "Sex Equality, Sex Differences, and the Supreme Court." *Yale Law Journal* 92:913–67.

Freeman, A. D. 1978. "Legitimizing Racial Discrimination through Anti-Discrimination

Law: A Critical Review of Supreme Court Doctrine." *Minnesota Law Review* 62:1049–119.

———. 1982. "Anti-Discrimination Law: A Critical Review." In *The Politics of Law: A Progressive Critique,* edited by D. Kairys. New York: Pantheon.

Freeman, 1983. "Antifeminists' and Women's Liberation: A Case Study of a Paradox." *Women and Politics* 3(1).

Freud, Sigmund. 1965. *Three Essays on the Theory of Sexuality,* translated by J. Strachey. New York: Basic Books.

Friedman, L. M. and J. Ladinsky. 1967. "Social Change and the Law of Industrial Accidents." *Columbia Law Review* 67:50–82.

Frug, Gerald E. 1984. "The Ideology of Bureaucracy in American Law." *Harvard Law Review* 97:1276.

Frye, Marilyn. 1983. "To See and Be Seen: The Politics of Reality." In *The Politics of Reality: Essays in Feminist Theory.* Trumansburg, NY: The Crossing Press.

Gabel, Peter. 1984. "The Phenomenology of Rights-Consciousness and the Pact of the Withdrawn Selves." *Texas Law Review* 62:1563–99.

Gabel, Peter and Paul Harris. 1982–83. "Building Power and Breaking Images: Critical Legal Theory and the Practice of Law." *New York University Review of Law and Social Change* 11:369–411.

Gabel, Peter and Duncan Kennedy. 1984. "Roll Over Beethoven." *Stanford Law Review* 36:1–55.

Garfield, James R. February 6, 1922. "James R. Garfield to Mrs. Gifford Pinchot." In *League of Women Voters Collection,* Series 2, Box 102, Library of Congress, Manuscripts Division. Washington, DC.

Gay, Peter. 1984. *Education of the Senses.* New York: Oxford University Press.

Gaze, B. 1986. "Pornography and Free Speech." *Legal Service Bulletin* 11(3):123–27.

Gelpi, Barbara, Nancy Hartsock, Clare Novak, and Myra Strober, eds. 1986. *Women and Poverty.* Chicago: University of Chicago Press.

Germanis, Peter. 1984. "Why Not Let Americans Work at Home." *Heritage Foundation Backgrounder* 325 (January 30).

Gilbert, William S. and Arthur Sullivan. 1911. *Trial by Jury.* London: Chappel.

Gilligan, Carol. 1982. *In a Different Voice: Psychological Theory and Women's Development.* Cambridge: Harvard University Press.

Gillis. 1983. "Servants, Sexual Relations and the Risk of Illegitimacy in London 1801–1900." in *Sex and Class in Women's History,* edited by J. Newton, M. Ryan, and J. Walkowitz. Boston: Routledge & Kegan Paul.

Gilman, Charlotte Perkins. 1898. *Women and Economics.* Boston: Small, Maynard.

———. 1911. *Man-Made World: or, Our Androcentric Culture.* New York: Charlton.

Gilmore, Grant. 1974. *The Death of Contract.* Columbus: Ohio State University Press.

Gilson, Mary. 1923. "What Women Workers Mean to Industry." Proceedings of the Women's Industrial Conference, U.S. Department of Labor Bulletin, No. 33. Washington, DC: U.S. Government Printing Office.

Glendon, M. 1981. *The New Family and the New Property.* Toronto: Butterworths.

Goldman, Alan. 1977. "Plain Sex." *Philosophy and Public Affairs* 6(3):267–87.

Gordon, Felice. 1986. *After Winning: The Legacy of the New Jersey Suffragists, 1920–1947*. New Brunswick: Rutgers University Press.

Gordon, Linda. 1986. "Family Violence, Feminism, and Social Control." *Feminist Studies* 12:453–78.

———. 1988a. *Heroes of Their Own Lives: The Politics and History of Family Violence, Boston, 1880–1960*. New York: Viking.

———. 1988b. "What Does Welfare Regulate?" *Social Research* 55:609–630.

Grayear, R. 1986. "Yes, Virginia, There Is Feminist Legal Literature: A Survey of Some Recent Publications." *Australian Journal of Law and Society* 3:105–35.

Gregory, J. 1979. "Sex Discrimination, Work and the Law." In *Capitalism and the Rule of Law,* edited by B. Fine et al. London: Hutchinson.

Griffin, S. 1986. *Rape: The Politics of Consciousness*. New York: Harper & Row.

Griffith, Elizabeth. 1984. *In Her Own Right: The Life of Elizabeth Cady Stanton*. Oxford: Oxford University Press.

Grimes, Barbara N. 1924. "Protective Legislation for Women and the Twentieth Amendment." *Bulletin of the California Civic League of Women Voters* 1(3).

Griswold, Robert. 1982. *Family and Divorce in California 1850–1890: Victorian Illusions and Everyday Realities*. Albany: State University of New York Press.

Grossberg, Michael. 1985. *Governing the Hearth: Law and the Family in Nineteenth Century America*. Chapel Hill: University of North Carolina Press.

Gutman, H. 1976. *The Black Family in Slavery and Freedom, 1750–1925*. New York: Vintage Books.

Gwaltney, John. 1981. *Drylongso*. New York: Random House.

Habermas, J. 1983. *The Theory of Communicative Action,* translated by T. McCarthy. Boston: Beacon Press.

———. 1985. "Law as Medium and Law as Institution." In *Dilemmas of Law in the Welfare State,* edited by G. Teubner. New York: W de Gruyter.

Hamilton, Edith and Huntington Cairnes, eds. 1961. *Plato: The Collected Dialogues*. New York: Pantheon.

Harding, S. and M. B. Hintikka. 1983. *Discovering Reality: Feminist Perspectives on Epistemology, Metaphysics, Methodology, and Philosophy of Science*. London: D. Ridel.

Hartog, Hendrick. 1987. "The Constitution of Aspiration and 'The Rights That Belong to Us All.' " *The Journal of American History* 74(3).

Harvey, Cameron. 1970–71. "Women in Law in Canada." *Manitoba Law Journal* 4:9.

Hatch, Orrin. 1983. "Women's Initiative." *Congressional Record—Senate*. 98th Cong, 1st sess. November 18.

Hawkes, Terence. 1977. *Structuralism and Semiotics*. Berkeley: University of California Press.

Hayden, Dolores. 1984. *Redesigning the American Home: The Future of Housing, Work, and Family Life*. New York: Norton.

Heller, Joseph. 1961. *Catch-22*. New York: Simon and Schuster.

Hewitt, Nancy. 1984. *Women's Activism and Social Change: Rochester, New York, 1822–1872*. Ithaca: Cornell Univ. Press.

Hicks, Julia Margaret. 1927. "Special Legislation for Women in Industry." National League of Women Voters Committee on the Legal Status of Women. Papers of National

Woman's Party, Box 260, Library of Congress, Manuscripts Division. Washington, DC.

Higginbotham, Jr. A. L. 1978. *In the Matter of Color: Race and the American Legal Process.* New York: Oxford University Press.

Hill, Ann Corinne. 1979. "Protection of Women Workers and the Courts: A Legal Case History." *Feminist Studies* 5:247–73.

Hillesum, Etty. 1983. *An Interrupted Life,* translated by A. Pomerans. New York: Pantheon Books.

Hoagland, Mercia. 1923. "Labor Legislation for Women." Proceedings of the Women's Industrial Conference, U.S. Department of Labor Bulletin, No. 33. Washington, DC: U.S. Government Printing Office.

Hoagland, Sarah. 1988. *Lesbian Ethics.* Palo Alto: Institute for Lesbian Studies.

Hoffman, Eric. 1985. "Feminism, Pornography and Law." *University of Pennsylvania Law Review* 133:497–534.

Hohfeld, Wesley Newcomb. 1919. *Fundamental Legal Conceptions.* New Haven, CT: Yale University Press.

Holcombe, Lee. 1983. *Wives and Property: Reform of the Married Women's Property Law in Nineteenth-Century England.* Toronto: University of Toronto Press.

Holly, Marcia. 1976. "Joint Custody: The New Haven Plan." *Ms.* (September):70–71.

Holmes, O. W. 1953. "Holmes to Harold Laski, 14 April 1923." In *Holmes-Laski Letters, 1916–1935: The Correspondence of Mr. Justice Holmes and Harold J. Laski,* edited by Mark De Wolfe Howe. Cambridge: Harvard University Press.

Hosmer, William. 1969; originally published 1852. *The Higher Law in Its Relation to Civil Government.* New York: Negro Universities Press.

Howe, Adrian. 1987a. "The Problem of Privatized Injuries: Feminist Strategies for Litigation." Paper presented at the Feminism and Legal Theory Conference, Madison, WI. Included in abridged form in this volume as Chapter 9.

———. 1987b. " 'Social Injury' Revisited; Towards a Feminist Theory of Social Justice." *International Journal of the Sociology of Law* 15:423–38.

———. 1988. "Toward Critical Criminology and Beyond." *Law in Context* 6(2):97–111.

Hubbard, Ruth. 1981. "The Emperor Doesn't Wear Any Clothes: The Impact of Feminism on Biology." In *Men's Studies Modified: The Impact of Feminism on the Academic Disciplines,* edited by D. Spender. New York: Pergamon.

Hunter, Nan and Sylvia Law. 1985. Amicus Brief on behalf of the Feminist Anti-Censorship Taskforce. In *American Booksellers Association v. William Hudnut* (7th Cir.), No. 84–3147.

Hurlbut, Elisha P. 1845. *Essays on Human Rights and Their Political Guarantees.* New York.

Husson, C. A. Desan. 1986. "Expanding the Legal Vocabulary: The Challenge Posed by the Deconstruction and Defense of Law." *Yale Law Journal* 95:969–91.

Indianapolis News. 1935. (February 1):1.

Interrante and Lasser. 1979. "Victims of the Very Songs They Sing: A Critique of Recent Work on Patriarchal Culture and the Social Construction of Gender." *Radical History Review* 20:25–40.

Jaggar, Alison. 1983. *Feminist Politics and Human Nature.* Totowa, NJ: Rowman and Allanheld.

Jardine, Alice. 1985. *Gynesis: Configurations of Women and Modernity.* Ithaca: Cornell University Press.

Jeffreys, Sheila. 1985. *The Spinster and Her Enemies: Feminism and Sexuality 1880–1930.* London: Pandora Press.

Johnson, Barbara. 1981. "Translator's Introduction." P. xlv in *Dissemination.* Chicago: University of Chicago Press.

———. 1987. "Is Writerliness Conservative?" in *A World of Difference.* Baltimore: Johns Hopkins Univ. Press.

Johnson, Ethel. 1924. Editorial. *Woman Citizen* (August 9):17.

Jones, A. 1980. *Women Who Kill.* New York: Fawcett Columbine.

Jordan, Winthrop. 1968. *White over Black.* Baltimore: Penguin.

Kane, Francis Fisher. January 12, 1922. "Francis Fisher Kane to Ethel Smith." In *League of Women Voters Collection,* Box 102, Library of Congress, Manuscripts Division. Washington, DC.

Kane, Frederick. 1936. "Heart Balm and Public Policy." *Fordham Law Review* 5:63–72.

Karst, Kenneth L. 1984. "Woman's Constitution." *Duke Law Journal* 1984:447–508.

Kelley, Florence. 1924. "The Equal Rights Amendment." *New York Evening Sun* (March 11).

———. 1925. "Speech of Florence Kelley." In *National Consumers' League Collection,* Reel 100, Library of Congress, Manuscripts Division. Washington, DC.

Kelman, Mark. 1982. "Criminal Law: The Originals of Crime and Criminal Violence." In *The Politics of Law: A Progressive Critique,* edited by D. Kairys. New York: Pantheon.

Keohane, N., M. Rosaldo, and B. Gelpi. 1982. *Feminist Theory, A Critique of Ideology.* Chicago: Univ. of Chicago Press.

Kessler-Harris, Alice. 1982. *Out to Work: A History of Wage-Earning Women in the United States.* New York and Oxford: Oxford University Press.

———. 1985. "The Debate over Equality for Women in the Workplace: Recognizing Difference." In *Women and Work: An Annual Review,* vol. 1, edited by L. Larwood, A. Stronberg, and B. Gutek. Beverly Hills: Sage.

King, Gertrude Besse. November 8, 1922. "Gertrude Besse King to Wenona Osborne Pinkham." In *National Consumers' League Collection,* Reel 53, Library of Congress, Manuscripts Division. Washington, DC.

Kingdom, E. 1980. "Women in Law." *m/f* 71–88.

———. 1985. "Legal Recogntiion of a Woman's Right to Choose." In *Women in Law: Explorations in Law, Family and Sexuality,* edited by J. Brophy and C. Smart. London: Routledge & Kegan Paul.

Kirchheimer, O. 1961. *Political Justice: The Use of Legal Procedure for Political Ends.* Princeton: Princeton University Press.

Kirkby, D. 1982. Review Article. *Law in Context* 3:151–53.

Klare, Karl. 1979. "Law-Making as Praxis." *Telos* 40:123–135.

Koertge, Noretta, ed. 1985. *Philosophy and Homosexuality.* New York: Harrington Park.

Kolko, Gabriel, 1963. *The Triumph of Conservatism.* New York: The Free Press.

Kraditor, Aileen, 1965. *The Ideas of the Woman Suffrage Movement, 1890–1920.* Garden City, NY: Doubleday.

Kurzweil, E. 1986. "Michel Foucault's *History of Sexuality* as Interpreted by Feminists and Marxists." *Social Research* 53:647–63.

Lahey, Kathleen A. 1985. "Until Women Themselves Have Told All That They Have to Tell . . ." *Osgoode Hall Law Journal* 23:519–41.

———. 1987. "Feminist Theories of (In)Equality:." *Wisconsin Women's Law Journal* 3:5–28.

Lambert, B. 1988. "Study Finds Antibodies for AIDS in 1 in 61 Babies in New York City." *New York Times.* (January 13):sec. A.

Langland, Elizabeth and Walter Gove, eds. 1981. *A Feminist Perspective in the Academy: The Difference It Makes.* Chicago: University of Chicago Press.

Laqueur, T. 1987. "Orgasm, Generation and the Politics of Reproductive Biology. pp. 1–41 in *The Making of the Modern Body,* edited by C. Gallagher and L. Laqueur. Berkeley: University of California Press.

Law, Sylvia. 1984. "Rethinking Sex and the Constitution." *University of Pennsylvania Law Review* 132:955.

Lawyer, George. 1894. "Are Actions for Breach of the Marriage Contract Immoral?" *Central Law Journal* 38:272–75.

Lazere, D., ed. 1987. *American Media and Mass Culture: Left Perspectives.* Berkeley: University of California Press.

Leach, William. 1980. *True Love and Perfect Union.* New York: Basic Books.

League of Women Voters. No date. "Definition of Position of National Woman's Party and National League of Women Voters on Special Legislation." In *League of Women Voters Collection,* Series 2, Box 98, Library of Congress, Manuscripts Division.

———. 1924. *Specific Bills for Specific Ills.*

Lederer, Laura, ed. 1980. *Take Back the Night: Women on Pornography.* New York: Morrow.

Lemons, Stanley. 1973. *The Woman Citizen: Social Feminism in the 1920s.* Urbana: Univ. of Illinois Press.

Levins, Richard and Richard Lewontin. 1985. *The Dialectical Biologist.* Cambridge: Harvard University Press.

Levinson, Sanford. 1982. "Law as Literature: Do Legal Texts Have Authoritative Interpretations?" *Texas Law Review* 60:373.

Lewis, William Draper. December 5, 1922. "William Draper Lewis to Mildred S. Gordon." In *League of Women Voters Collection,* Series 2, Box 102, Library of Congress, Manuscripts Division. Washington, DC.

Lindsey, Benjamin and Wainwright Evans. 1927. *The Companionate Marriage.* New York: Boni & Liveright.

Lipsky, Michael. 1984. "Bureaucratic Disentitlement in Social Welfare Programs." *Social Service Review* 58:3–27.

Littleton, Christine. 1981. "Note, Toward a Redefinition of Sexual Equality." *Harvard Law Review* 95:487–508.

———. 1987. "Equality Across Difference: A Place for Rights Discourse?" *Wisconsin Women's Law Journal* 3.

Loos, Anita. 1963. *Gentlemen Prefer Blondes: The Illuminating Diary of a Professional Lady.* New York: Liveright.

Lorde, Audre. 1983. "The Master's Tools Will Never Dismantle the Master's House." in

This Bridge Called My Back: Writings by Radical Women of Color, 2nd ed., edited by C. Moraga and G. Anzaldua. New York: Kitchen Table, Women of Color Press.

———. 1984a. "Poetry is not a Luxury." In *Sister Outsider, Essays and Speeches by Audre Lorde.* Trumansbury, NY: Crossing Press.

———. 1984b. "Uses of the Erotic: The Erotic as Power." In *Sister Outsider,* Essays and Speeches by Audre Lorde. Trumansbury, NY: Crossing Press.

Lovelace, Linda and McGrady, Mike. 1980. *Ordeal.* Secaucus, NJ: Citadel. Cited by C. MacKinnon, pp. 10–14 in *Feminism Unmodified.* Cambridge, MA: Harvard University Press.

Lowe, Marian and Ruth Hubbard, eds. 1983. *Woman's Nature: Rationalizations of Inequality.* New York: Pergamon.

Lubove, Roy. 1968. *The Struggle for Social Security, 1900–1935* Cambridge: Harvard Univ. Press.

Luker, Kristen. 1984. *Abortion and the Politics of Motherhood.* Berkeley: University of California Press.

Lustig, R. Jeffrey. 1982. *Corporate Liberalism: The Origins of Modern American Political Theory, 1890–1920.* Berkeley and Los Angeles: Harvard University Press.

Lynd, Staughton. 1984. "Communal Rights." *Texas Law Review* 62:1417–1441.

MacKinnon, Catharine. 1979. *Sexual Harassment of Working Women: A Case of Sex Discrimination.* New Haven: Yale University Press.

———. 1981. "Introduction." *Capital University Law Review* 10(3):i–viii.

———. 1982. "Feminism, Marxism, Method and the State: An Agenda for Theory." *Signs* 7:227–256.

———. 1983. "Feminism, Marxism, Method and the State: Toward Feminist Jurisprudence." *Signs* 8:635–58.

———. 1984b. "Not a Moral Issue." *Yale Law and Policy Review* 2:321–45.

———. 1985. "Pornography, Civil Rights, and Speech." *Harvard Civil Rights—Civil Liberties Law Review* 20:1–70.

———. 1987. *Feminism Unmodified: Discourses on Life and Law.* Cambridge and London: Harvard University Press.

Mander, C. 1985. *Emily Murphy, Crusader.* Toronto: Simon and Pierre.

Marcus, Isabel. 1987. "Reflections on the Significance of the Sex/Gender System: Divorce Law Reform in New York." *University of Miami Law Review* 42:55–73.

Marcus, Isabel and Paul Spiegelman. 1985. See Buffalo Symposium.

Marks, Elaine and Isabelle de Courtivron, eds. 1981. *New French Feminisms: An Anthology.* New York: Schocken.

Martin, Biddy, 1982. "Feminism, Criticism, and Foucault." *New German Critique* 27:3–30.

Marx, Karl. 1848. 1983. *The Communist Manifesto.*

———. 1983. "Eighteenth Brumaire of Louis Bonaparte." P. 287 in *The Portable Karl Marx,* edited by E. Komenka. New York: Penguin. Cited by Interrante and Lasser, "Victims of the Very Songs They Sing: A Critique of Recent Work on Patriarchal Culture and the Social Construction of Gender." *Radical History Review* 20:25.

Masters, William H. and Virginia E. Johnson. 1966. *Human Sexual Response.* Boston: Little, Brown.

May, Elaine Tyler. 1980. *Great Expectations: Marriage and Divorce in Post-Victorian America.* Chicago: University of Chicago Press.

Mazur, Jay. 1986. "Back to the Sweatshop." *New York Times* (September 6):sec. A.

McBarnett, D. 1984. "Victim in the Witness Box—Confronting Victimology's Stereotype." In *Criminal Law in Action,* 2nd ed., edited by W. Chambliss. New York: Wiley.

McCloud, S. G. 1986. "Feminism's Idealist Error." *New York University Review of Law and Social Change* 14:277–321.

Mead, George Herbert. 1934. *Mind, Self and Society from the Standpoint of a Social Behaviorist.* Chicago: University of Chicago.

Menkel-Meadow, Carrie. 1985. "Portia in a Different Voice." *Berkeley Women's Law Journal* 1:39–63.

———. 1987. "Excluded Voices: New Voices in the Legal Profession Making New Voices in the Law." *University of Miami Law Review* 42:29–53.

"Mendel v. Gimbel." 1936. *Newsweek.* (April 18):22–27.

Merleau-Ponty, M. 1962. *Phenomenology of Perception,* translated by C. Smith. London: Routledge & Kegan Paul.

———. 1963. *The Structure of Behaviour,* translated by A. Fisher. Boston: Beacon Press.

———. 1964. *Signs.* Evanston: Northwestern UniversMerton, Robert. 1967. *On Theoretical Sociology.* New York: The Free Press.

Miles, Angela. 1985. "Feminism, Equality and Liberation." *Canadian Journal of Women and the Law* 1:42–68.

Miles, Angela and Geraldine Finn. 1982. *Feminism in Canada: From Pressure to Politics.* Montreal: Black Rose Books.

Miller, Nancy K. 1986. "Changing the Subject: Authorship, Writing and the Reader." Pp. 102–20 in *Feminist Studies/Critical Studies,* edited by T. de Lauretis. Bloomington: Indiana University Press.

Minow, Martha. 1983. "Book Review." *Harvard Education Review* 53.

———. 1985a. "Book Review." *Harvard Law Review* 98:1084–1108.

———. 1985b. "Book Review." *Reviews in American History* 13.

———. 1986. "Rights for the Next Generation: A Feminist Approach to Children's Rights." *Harvard Women's Law Journal* 9:1–24.

"Miss Wing Raps Equality Bill." 1924. *Ohio Press* (April 22).

Mitchell, J. 1984. "Women and Equality." In *Women: The Longest Revolution: Essays in Feminism, Literature and Psychoanalysis.* London: Virago.

Mnookin and Kornhauser. 1979. "Bargaining in the Shadow of the Law: The Case of Divorce." *Yale Law Journal* 88:950–997.

Moi, Toril. 1985. *Sexual/Textual Politics.* London: Methuen.

Mossman, M. J. 1985. " 'Otherness' and the Law School: A Comment on Teaching Gender Equality." *Canadian Journal of Women and the Law* 1:213.

———. 1988. "Portia's Progress: Women as Lawyers—Reflections on Past and Future." *Windsor Yearbook Access to Justice* 8:252.

Murray, Charles. 1984. *Losing Ground: American Social Policy 1950–1980.* New York: Basic Books.

Nagel, Thomas. 1969. "Sexual Perversion." *The Journal of Philosophy.* 66:5–17.

———. 1979. "Moral Luck." In *Mortal Questions*. Cambridge, England. New York: Cambridge Univ. Press.

Nash, G. 1974. *Red, White, and Black: The Peoples of Early America*. Englewood Cliffs, NJ: Prentice Hall.

National Consumers' League. No date. "The Case for Special Legislation for Women Workers." In *Women's Bureau Records*, Record Group 86 National Archives. Washington, DC.

———. May 1922. *Why It Should Not Pass: The Blanket Equality Bill Proposed by the National Woman's Party for State Legislatures*. New York: National Consumers' League.

National Women's Trade Union League. 1922. "Declaration Adopted by the Conference of Trade Union Women at the Call of the National Women's Trade Union League." 26 February, Reel 51. *National Consumers' League Collection*. Library of Congress, Manuscript Division. Washington, D.C.

New York Civil Rights Law. 1987. New York: McKinney. 61–a.

New York Post. 1987. (May 22):1.

New York State Department of Labor. 1981. Public Hearing on Industrial Homework, April 2.

New York Times. 1914. (April 22):7.

———. 1933. (January 4):1.

———. 1935. (April 3):25.

———. 1936. (November 26):24.

———. 1937. (April 28):16.

———. 1988. "Study Traces AIDS in African Children." (January 22):sec. A.

Nicholson, Linda J. 1983. "Women, Morality and History." *Social Research* 50:514–536.

Nietzsche, Friedrich. 1969. *On the Genealogy of Morals*, translated by W. Kaufmann and R. J. Hollingdale. New York: Vintage Books.

Noddings, Nell. 1984. *Caring: A Feminine Approach to Ethics and Moral Education*. Berkeley: University of California Press.

Norris, C. 1985. *The Contest of Faculties: Philosophy and Theory After Deconstruction*. London: Methuen.

Note. 1986. "To Have and to Hold: The Marital Rape Exemption." *Harvard Law Review* 99:1255–73.

O'Donovan, Katherine. 1981. "Before and After: The Impact of Feminism on the Academic Discipline of Law." In *Men's Studies Modified: The Impact of Feminism on the Academic Disciplines*, edited by D. Spender. New York: Pergamon.

———. 1984. "Protection and Paternalism." In *The State, the Law and the Family*, edited by M. D. A. Freeman. London: Tavistock.

———. 1985. *Sexual Divisions in Law*. London: Weidenfeld and Nicholson.

Okin, Susan Moller. 1979. *Women in Western Political Thought*. Princeton: Princeton University Press.

O'Loughlin. 1983. "Responsibility and Moral Maturity in the Control of Fertility—Or, a Woman's Place is in the Wrong." *Social Research* 50:556.

Olsen, Frances. 1983. "The Family and the Market: A Study of Ideology and Legal Reform." *Harvard Law Review* 96:1497–578.

———. 1984. "Statutory Rape: A Feminist Critique of Rights Analysis.' *University of Texas Law Review* 63:387–422.

———. Forthcoming. "The Sex of Law." *Telos.*

"On *In a Different Voice:* An Interdisciplinary Forum." 1986. *Signs* 11:304–333.

O'Neill, William. 1967. *Divorce in the Progressive Era.* New Haven: Yale University Press.

———. 1969. *Everyone Was Brave.* Chicago: Quadrangle Books.

O'Reilly, Mary. 1895. "Sweat-Shop Life in Pennsylvania." *International Association of Factory Inspectors of North America, Ninth Annual Convention.* Cleveland: Forest City Printing House.

Panichas, G., ed. 1977. *The Simone Weil Reader.* New York: McKay.

Patterson, Orlando. 1982. *Slavery and Social Death, A Comparative Study.* Cambridge, MA: Harvard Univ. Press.

Payne, Elizabeth Anne. 1988. *Reform, Labor and Feminism: Margaret Dreier Robins and the Women's Trade Union League.* Urbana: University of Illinois Press.

Pear. 1983. "Anecdotes and the Impact They Have Had on Policy." *New York Times* (December 27):sec. B, p. 6, col. 3.

Pearce. 1986. "The Feminization of Poverty: Women, Work, and Welfare." Pp. 29–46 in *For Crying Out Loud, Women and Poverty in the United States,* edited by R. Lefkowitz and A. Withorn. New York: Pilgrim Press.

Pepinsky, H. E. 1974. "From White Collar Crime to Exploitation: Redefinition of a Field." *Journal of Criminal Law and Criminology* 65:225–33.

———. 1976. "Constraints on the American Administrator: the Law Imposes Social Bias." In Pepinsky, *Crime and Conflict: A Study of Law and Society.* New York: Academic Press.

Perry, Lewis. 1973. *Radical Abolitionism: Anarchy and the Government of God in Anti-Slavery Thought.* Ithaca: Cornell Univ. Press.

Petchesky, Rosalind P. 1984. *Abortion and Woman's Choice: The State, Sexuality, and Reproductive Freedom.* New York: Longman.

Petrement, Simone. 1976. *Simone Weil: A Life.* New York: Pantheon Books.

Physicians' Task Force on Hunger in America. 1986. *Increasing Hunger and Declining Help: Study of Barriers to Participation in the Food Stamp Program.* Harvard School of Public Health.

Piercy, Marge. 1976. *Woman on the Edge of Time.* New York: Fawcett Crest.

Pitch, T. 1985. "Critical Criminology, the Construction of Social Problems, and the Question of Rape." *International Journal of the Sociology of Law* 13:35–46.

Pivar, David. 1973. *Purity Crusade: Sexual Morality and Social Control, 1868–1900.* Westport, CT: Greenwood.

Piven, Frances Fox and Richard Cloward. 1971. *Regulating the Poor: The Functions of Public Welfare.* New York: Random House.

Polan. 1982. "Toward a Theory of Law and Patriarchy." in *The Politics of Law: A Progressive Critique,* edited by D. Kairys. New York: Pantheon.

Pollack, Andrew. 1986. "Home-based Works Stirs Suit." *New York Times.* (May 26). Pp. 27–28.

Popenoe. 1934. "Betrothal." *Journal of Social Hygiene* 20:442.

Pound, Roscoe. No date. "Excerpt of Pound's letter to Alice Paul." In Margaret Dreier

Robins Papers, *Papers of the National Women's Trade Union League and Its Principal Leaders,* Reel 16. Gainesville: University of Florida.

———. February 3, 1922. "Roscoe Pound to Felix Frankfurter." In *League of Women Voters Collection,* Series 2, Box 102, Library of Congress. Washington, DC.

Powers, Kathy L. 1979. "Sex Segregation and the Ambivalent Direction of Sex Discrimination Law." *Wisconsin Law Review* 55:56–124.

Prisoners Action Group. 1980. "Submission to the Royal Commission into N. S. W. Prisons." *Alternative Criminology Journal* 3(4).

"Protective Legislation vs. 'Equal Rights.' " 1923. *The Nation* (August 8). Reprinted in *The Catholic World.* Found in *Papers of Felix Frankfurter,* Reel 97, Library of Congress, Manuscripts Division. Washington, DC.

"Providing Effective Representation in Welfare Fraud Cases." 1981. *Clearinghouse Review* 15:53.

Rae, D. 1981. *Equalities.* Cambridge, MA: Harvard Univ. Press.

Rawls, John. 1955. "Two Concepts of Rules." *The Philosophical Review.* 64:3–32.

Reich, Charles. 1970. *The Greening of America.* New York: Random House.

Reuther, Rosemary Radford. 1981. "The Feminist Critique in Religious Studies." In *A Feminist Perspective in the Academy: The Difference It Makes,* edited by E. Langland and W. Gove. Chicago: University of Chicago Press.

———. 1983. *Sexism and God-Talk: Toward a Feminist Theology.* Boston: Beacon.

Rhode, D. L. 1986. "Feminist Perspectives on Legal Ideology." In *What is Feminism: A Reexamination,* edited by J. Mitchell and A. Oakley. New York: Pantheon.

Rich, Adrienne. 1979a. "Power and Danger: The Works of a Common Woman." In *On Lies, Secrets and Silence.* New York: Norton.

———. 1979b. "Toward a Woman-Centered University." In *On Lies, Secrets and Silence.* New York: Norton.

Rifkin, J. "Toward a Theory of Law and Patriarchy." *Harvard Women's Law Journal* 3:83–95.

Robinson. 1981. "Defense Strategies for Battered Women who Assault Their Mates: *State v. Curry.*" *Harvard Women's Law Journal* 4:161–175.

Rodgers, Daniel T. 1987. *Contested Truths: Keywords in American Politics Since Independence.* New York: Basic Books.

Rorty, Richard. 1980. *Philosophy and the Mirror of Nature.* Oxford: Blackwell.

Rosen, Cathryn J. 1986. "The Excuse of Self-Defense: Correcting a Historical Accident on Behalf of Battered Women who Kill." *American University Law Review* 36:11–56.

Rosen, Ruth. 1982. *The Lost Sisterhood: Prostitution in America, 1900–1918.* Baltimore: Johns Hopkins University Press.

Rosenberg, Charles E. 1973. "Sexuality, Class, and Role in Nineteenth-Century America." *American Quarterly* 25(2):131–53.

Ross, Dorothy. 1977–78. "Socialism and American Liberalism: Academic Social Thought in the 1880s." *Perspectives in American History* 11.

Rothman, Ellen. 1987. *Hands and Hearts: A History of Courtship in America.* Cambridge: Harvard University Press.

Rubin, Gayle. February 1978. "Sexual Politics, the New Right and the Sexual Fringe." *Leaping Lesbian* 2.

Ruth, Sheila. 1981. "Methodocracy, Misogyny and Bad Faith: The Response of Philosophy." In *Men's Studies Modified: The Impact of Feminism on the Academic Disciplines,* edited by D. Spender. New York: Pergamon.

Sachs, Albie and Joan Hoff Wilson. 1978. *Sexism and the Law.* London: Martin Robertson.

Santos, B. 1982. "Law and Revolution in Portugal: The Experiences of Popular Justice after the 25th of April 1974." In *The Politics of Informal Justice,* vol. 2, edited by R. Abel. New York: Academic Press.

Scales, Ann. 1981. "Towards a Feminist Jurisprudence." *Indiana Law Journal* 56:375–444.

———. 1986. "The Emergence of Feminist Jurisprudence: An Essay." *Yale Law Journal* 95:1373–1403.

Schamberg, Sidney. 1984. "The Rape Trial." *New York Times.* March 27.

Schiebinger, L. 1987. "Skeletons in the Closet: The First Illustrations of the Female Skeleton in Eighteenth Century Anatomy. Pp. 42–82 in *The Making of the Modern Body,* edited by Gallagher and Laqueur. Berkeley: University of California Press.

Schneider, Elizabeth M. 1980. "Equal Rights to Trial for Women: Sex Bias in the Law of Self-Defense." *Harvard Civil Rights-Civil Liberties Law Review* 15:623–647.

———. 1986a. "Describing and Changing: Women's Self-Defense Work and the Problem of Expert Testimony on Battering." *Women's Rights Law Reporter* 9:195–222.

———. 1986b. "The Dialectic of Rights and Politics: Perspectives from the Women's Movement." *New York University Law Review* 61:589–652.

Schneider, Elizabeth M. and Jordan. 1978. "Representation of Women Who Defend Themselves in Response to Physical or Sexual Assault." *Women's Rights Law Reporter* 4:149–164.

Schopenhauer, Arthur. 1966. *The World as Will and Representation,* vols. 1 and 2, translated by E. F. J. Payne. New York: Dover.

Schouler, James. 1921. *A Treatise on the Law of Marriage, Divorce, Separation and Domestic Relations.* 3 vols. 6th ed. Albany: M. Bender.

Schur, Edwin. 1971. *Labeling Deviant Behavior: Its Sociological Implications.* New York: Harper & Row.

Schwendinger, H. and J. 1970. "Defenders of Order or Guardians of Human Rights?" *Issues in Criminology* 5:123–57.

Sekyi, Kobina. 1970 (originally published 1934). "Extracts from 'The Anglo-Fanti.' " Pp. 442–47 in *Negro: An Anthology,* edited by Nancy Cunard (abridged ed. Hugh Ford). New York: Frederick Ungar.

Seligman, E. R. A. 1921. *Principles of Economics.* New York: Longmans, Green and Co.

Sennett, R. and J. Cobb. 1973. *The Hidden Injuries of Class.* New York: Knopf.

Shabecoff, Philip. 1981. "Dispute Rises on Working at Home for Pay." *New York Times.* (March 10):sec. A.

Shallcross, Ruth. 1939. *Industrial Homework: An Analysis of Homework Regulation Here and Abroad.* New York: Industrial Affairs Publishing Co.

Sheppard, Colleen. 1986. "Equality, Ideology and Oppression: Women and the Canadian Charter of Rights and Freedoms." *Dalhousie Law Journal* 10:195.

Shrager, L. S. and J. F. Short, Jr. 1977. "Toward a Sociology of Organisational Crime." *Social Problems* 25:407–19.

Simon, William. 1985. "The Invention and Reinvention of Welfare Rights." *Maryland Law Review* 44:1–37.

Sinclair, M. B. W. 1988. "Seduction and the Myth of the Ideal Woman." *Law and Inequality* 5:33–103.

Singer, Jana and W. L. Reynolds. 1988. "A Dissent on Joint Custody." *Maryland Law Review* 47:497–523.

Skinner, Mary. 1938. "Prohibition of Industrial Home Work in Selected Industries under the National Recovery Administration." Children's Bureau Publication, no. 244. Washington, DC: U.S. Government Printing Office.

Smart, Carol. 1982. "Law and the Control of Women's Sexuality: The Case of the 1950s." In *Controlling Women,* edited by B. Hutter and G. Williams. London.

———. 1984. *The Ties that Bind: Law, Marriage and the Reproduction of Patriarchal Relations.* London: Routledge & Kegan Paul.

———. 1985. "Legal Subjects and Sexual Objects: Ideology, Law and Female Sexuality." In *Women in Law: Explorations in Law, Family and Sexuality,* edited by J. Brophy and C. Smart. London: Routledge & Kegan Paul.

———. 1986. "Feminism and the Law: Some Problems of Analysis and Strategy." *International Journal of the Sociology of Law* 14(1):109.

———. 1989. *Feminism and the Power of Law.* London: Routledge.

Smart, Carol and B. Smart. 1978. "Accounting for Rape: Reality and Myth in Press Reporting." In *Women, Sexuality, and Social Control,* edited by C. Smart and B. Smart. London: Routledge & Kegan Paul.

Smith, . 1973. "Family Limitation, Sexual Control and Domestic Feminism in Victorian America." *Feminist Studies* 1(3-4):40.

Smith, Dorothy. 1974. "The Social Construction of Documentary Reality." *Social Inquiry* 44:257–68.

———. 1979. "A Sociology for Women." In *The Prism of Sex: Essays in the Sociology of Knowledge,* edited by J. A. Sherman and E. T. Beck. Madison: Univ. of Wisconsin Press.

Smith, Elizabeth Oakes. 1974; originally published 1851. *Woman and Her Needs.* New York: Gordon Press.

Smith, T. V. 1927. *The American Philosophy of Equality.* Chicago: Univ. of Chicago Press.

Smith-Rosenberg, Carroll. 1985. *Disorderly Conduct: Visions of Gender in Victorian America.* New York: Knopf.

Snell, James G. and Frederick Vaughan. 1985. *The Supreme Court of Canada: History of the Institution.* The Osgoode Society.

Snitow, A., C. Stansell, and S. Thompson, eds. 1983. *Powers of Desire: The Politics of Sexuality.* New York: Monthly Review Press.

Soble, Alan, ed. 1980. *Philosophy and Sex.* Littlefield, Adams.

Sparer. 1984. "Fundamental Human Rights, Legal Entitlements, and the Social Struggle: A Friendly Critique of the Critical Legal Studies Movement." *Stanford Law Review* 36.

Spender, Dale, ed. 1981. *Men's Studies Modified: The Impact of Feminism on the Academic Disciplines.* New York: Pergamon.

Spitzer, S. 1980. "Left-Wing Criminology—An Infantile Disorder?" In *Radical Criminology: The Coming Crisis,* edited by J. A. Inciardi. London: Sage.

Spivak, Gayatri C. 1987. *In Other Worlds: Essays in Cultural Politics.* London: Methuen.

Stacey. 1983. "The New Conservative Feminism." *Feminist Studies* 9.

Stack, Carol. 1974. *All Our Kin: Strategies for Survival in a Black Community.* New York: Harper & Row.

Stampp, Kenneth. 1956. *The Peculiar Institution.* New York: Vintage Books.

Stanworth, Michelle, ed. 1987. *Reproductive Technologies: Gender, Motherhood and Medicine.* Minneapolis: University of Minnesota Press.

"State Cost of Living Measures and AFDC Payments." 1987. *Clearinghouse Review* 20:1202.

Steakley, James D. 1975. *The Homosexual Emancipation Movement in Germany.* New York: Arno.

Stewart, I. 1981. "Sociology in Jurisprudence: The Problem of 'Law' as Object of Knowledge." In *Law, State and Society,* edited by B. Fryer et al. London: Croom Helm.

Sutherland, E. 1940. "White-Collar Criminality." *American Sociological review* 5:1–12.

Szasz, Thomas. 1970. *The Manufacture of Madness.* New York: Harper & Row.

Szold, Robert. January 4, 1922. "Robert Szold to Florence Kelley." In *National Consumers' League Collection,* Reel 51, Library of Congress, Manuscripts Division. Washington, DC.

Tappan, P. 1947. "Who Is the Criminal?" *American Sociological Review* 12:96–102.

Taub, Nadine. 1980. Review. *Columbia Law Review* 80:1686–95.

———. 1984–85. "From Parental Leaves to Nurturing Leaves.' *New York University Review of Law & Social Change* 13:381.

———. 1986. "Nurturing Leaves: A Public Policy of Private Caring." *The Nation* 242 (May 31):756–58.

Taub, Nadine and Elizabeth M. Schneider. 1982. "Perspectives on Women's Subordination and the Role of Law." In *The Politics of Law: A Progressive Critique,* edited by D. Kairys. New York: Pantheon.

Taylor, Barbara. 1983. *Eve and the New Jerusalem: Socialism and Feminism in the Nineteenth Century.* New York: Pantheon.

Taylor, C. 1985a. *Human Agency and Language.* London: Cambridge University Press.

———. 1985b. "Language and Human Nature." In *Human Agency and Language: Philosophical Paper 1.*

———. 1987. "Overcoming Epistemology." Pp. 464–88 in *After Philosophy: End or Transformation?,* edited by K. Baynes, J. Bohman, and T. McCarthy. Cambridge: MIT Press.

Thomas, Keith. 1959. "The Double Standard." *Journal of the History of Ideas* 20:195–216.

Thornton, M. 1985a. "Affirmative Action and Higher Education." In *Program for Change: Affirmative Action in Australia,* edited by M. Sawer. Sydney: Allen & Unwin.

———. 1985b. "Affirmative Action, Merit and the Liberal State." *Australian Journal of Law and Society* 2:28–40.

———. 1986. "Feminist Jurisprudence: Illusion or Reality?" *Australian Journal of Law and Society* 3:5–29.

Time. 1935. (February 18):16.

Travis. 1982. "Women and Men and Morality." *New York Times* (May 2):32, sec. 7.

Trebilcot, Joyce. 1984. "Taking Responsibility for Sexuality." In *Philosophy and Sex*, 2d ed., edited by R. Baker and F. Elliston. Buffalo: Prometheus.

Trofimenkoff, Susan Mann and Alyson Prentice. 1977. *The Neglected Majority*. Toronto: McClelland and Stewart.

Trubek, David. 1977. "Complexity and Contradiction in the Legal Order: Balbus and the Challenge of Critical Social Thought about Law." *Law and Society Review* 11:529–69.

———. 1980–81. "The Construction and Deconstruction of a Disputes-Focused Approach: An Afterword." *Law and Society* 15:727–48.

Turano, Anthony. 1934. "Breach of Promise: Still a Racket." *American Mercury* 32:40–47.

Tushnet, Mark. 1981. *The American Law of Slavery*. Princeton: Princeton University Press.

———. 1984. "An Essay on Rights." *Texas Law Review* 62:1363–1403.

U.S. Department of Labor, Women's Bureau. 1926. "For release to afternoon papers." January 20 press release in *Papers of National Woman's Party*, Box 234, Library of Congress, Manuscripts Division. Washington, DC.

U.S. Department of Labor. 1981a. Official Report of Proceedings before the Office of Administrative Law Judges, docket no. FLSA, "In the Matter of: A Public Hearing to Commence Labor Department Review of 'Homeworker Rules.' " Burlington, VT, January 13.

———. 1981b. Official Report of Proceedings before the Office of Administrative Law Judges, docket no. FLSA, "In the Matter of: A Public Hearing to Commence Labor Department Review of 'Homeworker Rules.' " Washington, DC, February 17.

U.S. Senate, 98th Cong., 2nd sess. 1984. Hearing before the Subcommittee on Labor of the Committee on Labor and Human Resources, "Amending the Fair Labor Standards Act to Include Industrial Homework." Washington, DC: U.S. Government Printing Office.

U.S. Women's Bureau. 1935. *The Commercialization of the Home through Industrial Home Work*. Washington, DC: U.S. Government Printing Office.

Vance, C., ed. 1984. *Pleasure and Danger: Exploring Female Sexuality*. Boston: Routledge & Kegan Paul.

Vernier, Chester. 1931–38. *American Family Laws: A Comparative Study of the Family Laws of the Forty-Eight American States, Alaska, the District of Columbia, and Hawaii*. 5 vols. Stanford: Stanford University Press.

Vickers, Jill McCalla. 1982. "Memoirs of an Ontological Exile: The Methodological Rebellions of Feminist Research." Pp. 27–46 in *Feminism in Canada: From Pressure to Politics*, edited by A. Miles and G. Finn. Montreal: Black Rose Books.

Walker. 1983. "In a Diffident Voice: Cryptoseparatist Analysis of Female Moral Development." *Social Research* 50:665–695.

Walkowitz, Judith. 1980. *Prostitution and Victorian Society: Women, Class and the State*. New York: Cambridge University Press.

Wallace, M. 1985a. "Regulating the Rat-Race: Notes Towards a Critique of Anti-Discrimination Law." Paper presented at the 3rd Australian Law and Society Conference, Canberra, December.

———. 1985b. "The Legal Approach to Sex Discrimination." In *Program for Change: Affirmative Action in Australia*, edited by M. Sawer. Sydney: Allen & Unwin.

Wallerstein and Blakeslee. 1989. *Second Chances: Men, Women and Children, a Decade after Divorce*. New York: Ticknor & Fields.

Wandersee, Winfred. 1981. *Women's Work and Family Values, 1920–1940*. Cambridge, MA: Harvard Univ. Press.

Ware, Susan. 1987. *Partner and I: Molly Dewson, Feminism, and New Deal Politics*. New Haven: Yale University Press.

Warner, Mary. 1976. *Alone of All Her Sex: The Myth and the Cult of the Virgin Mary*. New York: Random House.

Watt v. Regional Municipality of Niagara and Alex Wales. 1984. *Canadian Human Rights Reporter* 2453.

Watts, Q. C., Alfred. 1984. *History of the Legal Profession in British Columbia 1869–1984*. Law Society of British Columbia.

Weedon, Chris. 1987. *Feminist Practice and Poststructuralist Theory*. Oxford: Basil Blackwell.

Weeks, Jeffrey. 1977. *Coming Out: Homosexual Politics in Britain, from the Nineteenth Century to the Present*. London: Quartet.

Weinstein, James. 1968. *The Corporate Ideal in the Liberal State, 1900–1918*. Boston: Beacon Press.

Weitzman, Lenore. 1985. *The Divorce Revolution: The Unexpected Social and Economic Consequences for Women and Children*. New York: Free Press; London: Collier MacMillan.

Wellman, Judith. 1980. "Women and Radical Reform in Upstate New York: A Profile of Grassroots Female Abolitionists." In *Clio Was a Woman: Studies in the History of American Women*, edited by M. E. Deutrich and V. C. Purdy. Washington, DC: Howard University Press.

West, Helen. 1934. "Florida Laws Concerning Women." *The Women Lawyer's Journal* 21(2):22–5.

West, Robin. 1986. "The Difference in Women's Hedonic Lives: A Phenomenological Critique of Feminist Legal Theory." Paper presented at the Feminism and Legal Theory Conference, Madison, WI.

———. 1987. "The Difference in Women's Hedonic Lives: A Phenomenological Critique of Feminist Legal Theory." *Wisconsin Women's Law Journal* 3:81–145. A shorter version is included in this volume as Chapter 7.

Westen, Peter. 1982. "The Empty Idea of Equality." *Harvard Law Review* 95:537.

White, Lucie. 1990. "Subordination, Rhetorical Survival Skills, and Sunday Shoes: Notes on the Hearing of Mrs. G." Included in this volume as Chapter 3.

Wickes. 1985. "The 1984 Comparison of AFDC Payments and Poverty Income Levels.' *Clearinghouse Review* 18:967.

Williams, Bernard. 1981. "Moral Luck." In *Moral Luck: Philosophical Essays 1973–1980*. Cambridge, England Cambridge University Press.

Williams, David Ricardo. 1984. *Duff: A Life in the Law*. The Osgoode Society.

Williams, Patricia. 1986. "Grandmother Sophie." *Harvard Blackletter* 3:79.

———. 1987a. "Alchemical Notes: Reconstructing Ideals from Deconstructed Rights." *Harvard Civil Rights-Civil Liberties Law Review* 22:401–33.

———. 1987b. "The Meaning of Rights." Address to the Annual Meeting of the Law and Society Association, Washington, DC, June 6.

———. 1988. "On Being the Object of Property." *Signs* 14:5–24. Also included in this volume as Chapter 2.

Williams, Wendy. 1982. "The Equality Crisis: Some Reflections on Culture, Courts, and Feminism." *Women's Rights Law Reporter* 7.

———. 1985. "Equality's Riddle: Pregnancy and the Equal Treatment/Special Treatment Debate." *New York University Review of Law & Social Change* 13.

Wilson, P. R. and J. Braithwaite, eds. 1979. *Two Faces of Deviance: Crimes of the Powerless and Powerful.* Brisbane: University of Queensland Press.

Woolgar, S. 1988. *Science: The Very Idea.* Chichester: Ellis Harwood Ltd.

Wortman, M. Stein. 1985. *Women in American Law.* New York: Holmes and Meier.

Wright. 1924. "Action for the Breach of a Marriage Promise." *Virginia Law Review* 10:361–383.

Wright, Benjamin. 1931. *American Interpretations of Natural Law.* Cambridge, MA: Harvard University Press.

Yaeger, Patricia. 1988. *Honey Mad Woman.* New York: Columbia Univ. Press.

Young, I. M. 1986. "The Ideal of Community and the Politics of Difference." *Social Theory and Practice* 12:1–26.

Cases

Adkins v. Children's Hospital 1923. 261 U.S. 525.

Aid to Families with Dependent Children. 42 U.S.C. 601 *et seq.*

American Booksellers Ass'n. v. Hudnut. 1985. 771 F.2d 323 (7th Cir.)

American Steel Foundaries v. Tri-City Central Trades Council. 1921. 257 U.S. 184.

Blickstein v. Blickstein. 472 N.Y.S. 2d 110. (N.Y. App. Div. 1984).

Bradwell v. Illinois. 1873. 83 U.S. (16 Wall) 130.

Children's Hospital v. Adkins, et. al. 1922. 284 Fed 613.

Chorlton v. Lings. 1868. L.R. 4 C.P. 374.

Commonwealth v. Rapozo, Cordeiro, Silva, and Viera. (Mass. Super. Ct., March 17, 1984).

D'Arc v. D'Arc. 395 A.2d 1270. (N.J. Super Ct. Ch. Div. 1978) aff'd, 421 A.2d 602 (N.J. Super Ct. App. Div. 1980).

Edwards v. A.G. for Canada. [1930] A.C. 124. (The Persons Case).

Frontiero v. Richardson. 1973. 411 U.S. 677.

Geduldig v. Aillo. 1974. 417 U.S. 484.

Gemsco v. Walling. 1945. 365 U.S. 244.

Goesaert v. Cleary. 1948. 335 U.S. 464.

Goldberg v. Kelly. 1970. 397 U.S. 254.

Hoyt v. Florida. 1961. 368 U.S. 57.

In the Matter of Baby "M," A Pseudonym for an Actual Person. Superior Court of New Jersey, Chancery Division. Docket no. FM-25314-86E. (March 31, 1987).

In re French. 1905. 37 N.B.R. 359.

Jefferson v. Hackey. 1972. 406 U.S. 535.

Kahn v. Shevin. 1974. 416 U.S. 351.

Langstaff v. Bar of Quebec. 1915. 25 Que. K.B. 11.

Madrigal v. Quilligan. October 1979. U.S. Court of Appeals, 9th Circuit. Docket no. 78-3187.

Missippi Univ. for Women v. Hogan. 1982. 458 U.S. 718.

Muller v. Oregon. 1908. 108 U.S. 412.

Painter v. Painter. 320 A.2d 484. (N.J. 1984).

Ralevski v. Dimovski. 1968. N.S.W.L.R. 487.

Reference re Meaning of Word "Persons" in S. 24 of the B.N.A. Act. [1928] S.C.R. 276. (The Persons Case).

Roe v. Wade. 1973. 410 U.S. 113.

State v. Anaya. 438 A.2d 892. (Me. 1981).

State v. Dunning. 8 Wash. App. 340. (1973).

State v. Kelly. 97 N.J. 178, 478 A.2d 364. (1984).

State v. Wanrow. 88 Wash. 2.d 221, 559 P.2d 548 (la77).

Stover v. Stover. 696 S.W.2d 750. (Ark. 1985).

Thornburg v. Gingles. 1986. 478 U.S. 30, 106 S. Ct. 2752.

Truax v. Corrigan. 1921. 257 U.S. 312.

Watt v. Regional Municipality of Niagara and Alex Wales. 1984. *Canadian Human Rights Reporter* 2453.

Weinberger v. Wiesenfeld. 1975. 420 U.S. 636.

Notes on Contributors

Eileen Boris, Associate Professor of History, Howard University, is the author of *Art and Labor: Ruskin, Morris, and the Craftsman Ideal in America* (Temple University Press, 1986) and coeditor with Cynthia Daniels of *Homework: Historical and Contemporary Perspectives on Paid Labor at Home* (University of Illinois Press, 1989). In 1988–89 she was a fellow at the Woodrow Wilson International Center for Scholars, working on a book length study, *In Defense of Motherhood: The Politics of Industrial Homework in the U.S.* In 1989 she also attended an international conference on home-based labor in Ahmedahad, India. A mother, she works at home under conditions of relative privilege as a salaried professional.

Kristin Bumiller is a member of the Departments of Women's and Gender Studies and Political Science at Amherst College and the Board of Trustees of the Law and Society Association. Her current research focus is on the structure of beliefs about law as reflected in symbolic criminal trials.

Claudia Card is Professor in the Department of Philosophy at the University of Wisconsin-Madison, where she is also a member of The Women's Studies Program and the Institute for Environmental Studies. She has published articles in ethics, feminist theory, and lesbian culture in *The Philosophical Review, The American Philosophical Quarterly, Ethics, The Canadian Journal of Philosophy, Hypatia: A Journal of Feminist Philosophy, The Journal of Social Philosophy* and *Women's Studies International Forum.* She is presently at work on a book, *Character and Moral Luck,* for which she has the research support of a two-year Vilas Associate Award.

Elizabeth B. Clark has a J.D. from the University of Michigan and a Ph.D. in history from Princeton University. Her article "Matrimonial Bonds: Slavery, Contract, and the Law of Divorce in Nineteenth-Century

America" is forthcoming in the Law and History Review. She is on the faculty at the University of Pennsylvania Law School, currently on leave on a fellowship at the Harvard Divinity School.

Ruth Colker is Professor of Law at Tulane University, teaching in the areas of Constitutional Law, federal jurisdiction, and feminist theory. She is a member of the ACLU AIDS Task Force and an active cooperating attorney for the Louisiana Affiliate of the American Civil Liberties Union. She has recently helped found a new journal entitled *Law and Sexuality: A Review of Lesbian and Gay Legal Issues.*

Mary Coombs is Professor of Law at the University of Miami. She teaches criminal law and procedure, family law and feminism and law. She has written on rape, search and seizure law, and new reproductive technologies. She is also engaged as an advocate for women in academia.

Martha Albertson Fineman is a Professor of Law at the University of Wisconsin. She is a 1975 graduate of the University of Chicago Law School. She organized the Feminism and Legal Theory Conference in the summer of 1985.

Judith Grbich is a Senior Lecturer in the Department of Legal Studies in the School of Social Sciences at La Trobe University in Melbourne, Australia. She is an Executive Member of the National Centre for Socio-Legal Studies in Melbourne. Her research and teaching interests lie in feminist legal theory, women's studies in law, and feminist scholarship in revenue law and practice.

Adrian Howe is Lecturer in Criminology in the Legal Studies Department at La Trobe University, Melbourne, Australia. She has published in the fields of colonial American history, feminist legal theory, criminology, women's prisons and Australian feminist politics. She is currently writing a book titled *Beyond Penology* for a new book series called: "Sociology of Law and Crime: Feminist and Socialist Perspectives," edited by Carol Smart and Maureen Cain.

Sybil Lipschultz studied American History in the Department of American Civilization at the University of Pennsylvania, where she earned her M.A. and Ph.D. Currently Assistant Professor of History and Women's Studies at the University of Miami, she recently completed a year in residence at the Library of Congress as the J. Franklin Jameson Fellow. She is completing a book on women's labor laws, American feminism, and the Supreme Court.

Kathleen A. Lahey teaches feminism and law at Queen's University in Kingston, Ontario. She has participated in the development of an alternative feminist approach to legal scholarship, working on topics that include child abuse, constitutional law, lesbian jurisprudence, criminal law, taxation, and liberal economic theory. She is one of the founders of the *Canadian Journal of Women and Law* and has consulted in lesbian and feminist litigation.

Diana Majury has been actively involved as a feminist advocate, organizer, lobbyist, consultant, writer and teacher, in the struggle for women's equality in Canada. She is Assistant Professor at the Faculty of Law, University of Western Ontario, London, Ontario.

Mary Jane Mossman is Professor of Law at Osgoode Hall Law School of York University in Toronto, Canada. She has taught law both in Canada and in Australia, and has published widely on topics of Feminism and the Law, Family Law, Property Law and Access to Justice. For a number of years, she worked in the Community Legal Services movement in Ontario and has remained actively involved in community organizations focussing on issues of women and access to justice.

Barbara Omolade is a founding staff member and instructor at the City College of New York's Center for Worker Education and also conducts faculty development seminars on balancing the curriculum for race, gender, class and ethnicity. She is known nationally for her writings and lectures on feminism, racism, education and the family. Her most recent publications include: "Black Men, Black Women and Tawana Brawley: The Shared Condition" (*Harvard Women's Law Journal,* Spring 1989); "We Speak for the Planet" in *Rocking the Ship of State: Towards a Feminist Peace Politics* edited by Adrienne Harris and Ynestra King; "The Silence and the Song" in *Wild Women in the Whirlwind.* She is working on a book on Black Single Mothers.

Elizabeth M. Schneider is Professor of Law at Brooklyn Law School. She graduated from Bryn Mawr College in 1968, received an M.Sc. degree in Political Sociology in 1969 from The London School of Economics and Political Science where she was a Leverhulme Fellow, and graduated from New York University Law School, where she was an Arthur Garfield Hays Civil Liberties Fellow in 1973. Professor Schneider clerked for United States District Judge Constance Baker Motley of the Southern District of New York in 1973 and was staff Attorney at the Center for Constitutional Rights in New York City from 1973–80. From 1980–83 she was Staff Attorney and Administrative Director of the Constitutional Litigation Clinic at Rutgers Law School-Newark and has taught at Brooklyn Law School since 1983. She was Chair of the Association of American Law Schools' (AALS) Section on Women in Legal Education in 1988, and is active in many organizations focusing on women's issues and law reform. She has been a long-time feminist activist and lawyer in the women's rights movement, and has written widely in the fields of women's and civil rights.

Robin West is Professor of Law at University of Maryland Law School, and Research Fellow of the Institute for Philosophy and Public Policy at College Park Maryland. She is presently Visiting Professor of Law at the University of Chicago Law School. Professor West has written widely on various aspects of feminist legal theory, including its ambiguous relation to nonfeminist political theory and jurisprudential movements. She has also written extensively on liberal legal thought, and contributed to the Law and Literature movement.

Lucie White is Acting Professor of Law at the University of California at Los Angeles. Prior to teaching law, she studied comparative literature at Yale and worked as a legal aid lawyer in a rural community in North Carolina. She teaches in the areas of civil procedure, civil litigation, and poverty law.

Patricia Williams is Professor of Law and of Women's Studies at the University of Wisconsin-Madison. A lawyer, poet, and critic, she writes widely on issues of race, gender, and class.